AGE OF SECRETS

The Conspiracy that Toppled Richard Nixon and the Hidden Death of Howard Hughes

Gerald Bellett

MEIER PUBLISHING

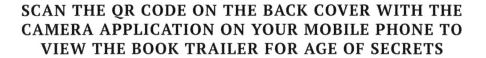

SCAN THE QR CODE ON THE BACK COVER WITH THE CAMERA APPLICATION ON YOUR MOBILE PHONE TO VIEW THE BOOK TRAILER FOR AGE OF SECRETS

The Major Motion Picture in development 'Meiergate' is
about the life story of John Meier with details at:
meiercitypictures.com

The Age of Secrets Website is at:
ageofsecrets.com

Information on John Meier is available at:
johnmeier.com

All inquiries should be sent to: info@meierpublishing.co

Hardcover ISBN: 978-1-7782874-2-8

Paperback ISBN: 978-1-7782874-1-1

Ebook ISBN: 978-1-7782874-0-4

Audiobook ISBN: 978-1-7782874-3-5

Dedicated to John Herbert Meier
"The Living Legend"
September 28, 1933 – June 23, 2023

In memory of Nancy
And for Gillian
"fairer than the evening air"

CONTENTS

CRITICAL COMMENTS

"John Meier's story is really interesting and, I believe, important. I've spent a number of years studying the American cryptocracy and there is no question in my mind that Meier is dead-right when he says that the CIA was running the Hughes empire. So, too, with Intertel. I was the first journalist to write about the firm (in Harper's), and it's apparent to me, as it is to Meier, that its business plan was drawn up in Langley.

That said, this is complicated stuff. The way I see it, American politics from 1954-74 is a continuum defined by the struggle between the Richard Nixon apparat and the Kennedy machine, with the Howard Hughes empire serving as a fulcrum in what amounted to a secret war for the country's soul. CIA spooks, mobsters on three coasts and a coven of Texas oligarchs built the 'magic box'. *

John Meier's story is a fungible one in the sense that it could serve as the basis for a rock-'em-sock-'em tv series, motion picture or documentary about the Deep State. By that, I mean the cryptocracy that has evolved since the Cold War along a political continuum defined by assassination, surveillance and cover-up.

The Howard Hughes organization, with its ties to Texas oil, Las Vegas gambling, Hollywood and the CIA was the secret fulcrum of that continuum, mediating a political struggle that, by turns, saw the Kennedy's devastated by murder and the Nixon camp destroyed by what looks, increasingly, like a soft coup d'etat. In this, John Meier was a Zelig-like figure, at once a witness and a participant, so well-connected - and so deeply involved - that it could only have ended in exile or a grave.

The focal point of that tale, from which everything else proceeds, is obviously the secret war for the Hughes empire.

If it were a film, it would be as exciting as The Bourne Identity, and I think it would pull in the same audience (and for many of the same reasons) that both The Bourne Identity and JFK did."

-NEW YORK TIMES BESTSELLING AUTHOR JIM HOUGAN

Editor's note:*In international political terms, a MAGIC BOX is a "cover" organization used by a nation's spy apparatus. A MAGIC BOX allows its inhabitants to hide anything they possess or do, regardless of the importance of what is being done or hidden. The Hughes Organization supplied the CIA with a very special MAGIC BOX. It is from within this MAGIC BOX that the CIA and its corporate and political friends operate. When John Meier opted out of the MAGIC BOX, he became an impediment to its continued existence.

PREFACE

Under a government which imprisons any unjustly the true place for a just man is also a prison.

— HENRY DAVID THOREAU

The Watergate burglary can only be understood if one knows the actual target being sought by that group of CIA mercenaries captured inside the offices of the Democratic National Committee. Without this information the unprecedented fall of a presidency would simply appear as a scandal caused by a petty act of breaking and entering.

Identifying the prize worth risking the ruin of America's highest official would undoubtedly settle the greatest unresolved issue: did Nixon know of and approve the operation? Did he act as a political mastermind, dispatching a gang of thieves into the night while sitting in the Oval Office awaiting the haul?

No single event in American political history has prompted such scrutiny as the Watergate burglary. It has inspired books by the score, articles and newspaper stories by the thousands. The televised inquisition of its cast of characters held a nation spellbound. One by one the guilty went to prison, leaving behind a host of riddles and no satisfactory answer to one of the greatest whodunits in modern politics. It was a symphony with no finale. It has remained so since 1973.

In Cold War days, while the Soviet Empire still existed, Western democracies perpetuated the image of communist bloc governments as sufficiently hostile to human freedom to pit the apparatus of the State against dissenting individuals. Heroes have been made out of Solzhenitsyn and Sakharov for their fortitude in resisting.

Ironically, in the United States of America — for many a symbol of freedom — the government marshalled equally sweeping forces to crush dissent.

Where openly repressive regimes silenced their dissidents through committal to psychiatric wards and banishment, the American way led to more subtle forms of harassment by government agencies and ruin through the courts. If one method was cruder, it was only because it operated in a climate in which there was no need to maintain an illusion of freedom while punishing enemies of the state. John Herbert Meier's story is the shocking account of what happened to one American dissenter.

Meier was no trivial opponent of Nixon's, as were most of those on the infamous *Enemies List;* he was not crushed because of petty acts against the presidency — the effects of his actions were monumental. From 1966 to 1970 he was Howard Hughes' most trusted courtier, a paladin who undertook strange and marvelous missions, many into Nixon's camp. From this ease of entry would arise the means to subvert Richard Nixon, the 37th President of the United States. Meier led Nixon into the folly of Watergate, destroyed his second term and was responsible for his downfall. Even before Nixon fell — disgraced, with his aides and advisors jailed almost en masse — Meier was singled out for punishment. Nixon's resignation brought no relief, as the tailings of his supporters were still powerfully placed in government. Also seeking vengeance were the CIA and the enigmatic Howard Hughes organization.

Watergate was a set-up, a classic ploy as old as espionage itself. In its favor it had simplicity of execution, an irresistible bait and a spy on the inside. It was flawless. So completely were the anti-Nixon conspirators in control, that they knew an intrusion into the Democratic Party's national headquarters was being plotted yet did nothing to prevent it. Indeed, the odor of entrapment was so strong in the aftermath of the arrests that most of those who went to jail did so feeling betrayed. As for the burglary's masterminds, they melted away, sharing with their enemies an unwillingness to disclose their part in the affair.

Because of this silence, gaps remain in the record of Watergate. Not only is the target of the burglary mysteriously obscured but also absent is one crucial participant in the drama. Watergate had a cast of hundreds, but only three stars — Richard Nixon, Howard Hughes and John Meier. Since Watergate, John Meier has been the missing man.

Meier's name has cropped up in many books written about Hughes or the Watergate affair: *Empire, The Life, Legend and Madness of Howard Hughes; Citizen Hughes; Spooks; Hoax; Howard Hughes in Las Vegas; High Stakes; Confessions of a Secret Agent; Secret Agenda; The Haldeman Diaries; The Hughes Papers* and *Howard Hughes — The Secret Life*. Almost a chapter is devoted to him in John Ehrlichman's autobiography, *Witness To Power* — his name is found in dozens of pages of transcripts that record the Senate Watergate Committee deliberations. In April 1992, Robert Maheu's autobiography *Next To Hughes* was published with unflattering references to his arch-rival.

Yet none of it describes the part Meier played in Nixon's downfall. It was Meier who poured the poison into Nixon's ear which led to Watergate. Meier's escapades did not stop there. He would, in time, penetrate the heart of one of the greatest secrets that Hughes' mysterious CIA-infested empire possessed.

Although Meier fled the United States to escape his enemies' wrath, their retribution followed. He was a gifted entrepreneur who owned a film company, thoroughbreds, a shopping center, an environmental foundation, a computer software company, a food manufacturing business and an electronics company. He had world-wide business interests which were stripped from him piece by piece. In the years since 1972, he was chased out of England, Japan, Australia and Tonga by the CIA — his escapes facilitated by such diverse entities as the British and Cuban intelligence services. He is the only person to be distinguished by two extraditions from Canada. He has been falsely charged with income tax evasion, fraud, obstruction of justice, forgery and murder. His life has been threatened and his family stalked for kidnapping.

Due to its complexity, Meier's remarkable story could never have been told had it not been for his habit of keeping careful diaries, upon which much of this book is based. His diaries tell what he did but do not record the effects of his actions. Only years later, when the absolute paroxysm of Watergate forced certain documents out of the CIA, the White House and the Hughes organization, and compelled people like Ehrlichman to write their memoirs, could the results be seen. His detractors, and they are legion, have had their turn. In numerous books, newspaper articles and magazines he has been written off as a criminal, a fraud, an historical nonentity who somehow — like the stranger who appears in the wedding photographs — has pushed his way in where he wasn't invited.

This is his story.

AGE OF SECRETS

1

BEGINNINGS OF INTRIGUE

Perhaps it was the urgency in the voices that woke him as he lay asleep that June night. Unfamiliar German voices pulled him from his slumber and he became aware, while only half awake, that there were strangers in the apartment. He crept from his bedroom and pushed open the kitchen door to find his mother and father talking with two men. The Meiers were a German family who lived quietly in the middle class New York suburb of Astoria on Long Island. It was 1942 and their adopted country was at war with Germany. The reality of that conflict was about to be presented to a confused eight-year-old.

All conversation ceased as he entered the room. His father and mother were wearing dressing gowns; clearly these visitors had arrived unannounced. They looked worried and their son sensed some of the unease. Seeing the boy's concern, his father beckoned him to the kitchen table.

"This is John," said his father. "Now don't be scared, son, but these two gentlemen are here from Germany."

Germany and America were at war. How could people from Germany come to Long Island? The war itself and the turmoil it created within the family had already caused him to seek solace in his parents' explanations and their soothing reassurances that it was not for children to worry over. He should continue his schooling, enjoy his sports and try to ignore the children who called him a Nazi. The meaning of this unexpected visit was beyond him, but he did understand the calm and familiar tone of his father's voice.

"I don't want you to worry about it, son. They will just be here for a few days. You haven't got to mention it to anyone. Do you understand?"

With that he took the boy's hand and led him back to the bedroom he shared with his sister, Mildred. She was still asleep. Both children were put to bed in their parents' room while their beds were made up for the visitors.

Within weeks these two strangers would be dead, executed in the electric chair. Their arrests and quick execution would be headline news in the weeks to come as all America — except for those sympathetic to the German cause — were clamoring for blood and vengeance.

For Herbert Meier and his wife Hedwig, the time following their visitors' arrests would be fraught with terror. Hourly, they expected the FBI to arrive. Already the Bureau had picked up sympathizers within the German community who were known to have helped the men. The penalty for treason was death.

HERBERT FELIX MEIER was born July 6, 1901 in Friedland, Breslau, a part of Germany given to Poland following the Second World War and renamed Wroclaw. His family were food merchants. As a boy he showed a flair for languages and was fluent in French, English, Spanish and Italian as well as his native German. During the First World War he served as an infantryman. In 1924, he became engaged to Hedwig Agnes Wiemer, a dental assistant, born April 14, 1902 in Kotzman in the county of Luben.

Following the First World War, the German economy was ruined by postwar reparation payments and the German citizenry demoralized by the provisions of the Treaty of Versailles. Unable to find work, and not wanting to marry without a job, Herbert emigrated to the United States. He would send for his fiancee as soon as he had established himself. When he arrived in New York he tried for a job in the airplane industry but his military background made him a security risk. To make ends meet he took a job in a kitchen and soon established himself as a master chef. Ironically enough, by September 1924 he was working in the Hotel Astor preparing a banquet in honor of General John Pershing, who had led American armies in the liberation of France.

In 1929, Herbert sent for Hedwig and she arrived in April aboard the German liner S.S. *Columbus*. The couple were married in St. Raphael's Chapel, a Roman Catholic church on 23rd Street. In 1930, they moved into a two bedroom apartment on 33rd Street, in Astoria, Long Island, which has been in the family ever since. The Meiers' first child, John Herbert, was born September 28, 1933. His sister Mildred was born February 20, 1935.

They mixed mostly with other German emigrés who had escaped the drudgery and turmoil of post-war Germany to come and live on the fringes of the most rambunctious American city. Unlike many of those German-Americans, Herbert would never be assimilated. A German first and foremost, he was a man who did not let his surroundings change him.

Sometime in the early 1930s Herbert became an agent of the German Foreign office. For many Germans living in America it was nothing less than a miracle to see their country removing the sackcloth and ashes it had been wearing since the humiliation of Versailles. Under Hitler, Germany had been revitalized, and with it, a new and menacing nationalism.

In early 1934, Herbert was called into the German Embassy in Washington. At the time it was German policy to be conciliatory towards the United States. Americans were natural isolationists and it was in Germany's best interests to encourage them to stay that way. As a chef, whose services were much in demand, Herbert was exposed to many of the wealthy and influential in New York. The embassy felt his contacts were useful enough to retain his services and he became a part of the lobby compiled to promote Germany's position to Americans. This was the year Herbert began making a series of trips to Germany at an expense which should have been far beyond what a chef could afford. He never spoke to his family of their purpose. Perhaps these trips were a quiet way of passing on intelligence; they ceased in 1941 when the Japanese attack on Pearl Harbor ended the United States stance of non-involvement and the Americans joined the war against Germany.

In 1940, Hitler's armies were achieving overwhelming victories in Europe. Where the Kaiser's army twenty-five years earlier had been fought to a standstill by the British and French, these old foes were being blown away like smoke. While German-Americans basked in the reflected glory of these victories, there was a disquieting respect shown by many Americans towards the British, who now stood alone tensed for invasion.

For the Meiers, and for many like them, this was a twilight time; as they watched American sympathy for the British grow, they dreaded the day that inevitably their adopted country would be dragged into the conflict. When America entered the war, those emigrés who had shown Nazi sympathies were interned. Many Germans had returned home in anticipation of that event but the Meier family seemed resolved to live out the war peacefully in the United States.

Whatever torment of loyalties the Meiers suffered when America entered the war, they paled into insignificance the night Heinrich Heinck and Richard Quirin tapped lightly on their door.

A few days earlier on the night of June 12, 1942, the German submarine U202 surfaced just off the Long Island resort of Amagansett. Fog covered the beach, enabling a seaman and four men dressed in German Navy fatigues to paddle ashore. These four had all lived in America before the war. They brought with them four cases of high explosives to attack railway and light industrial targets, especially factories manufacturing alloys for the airplane and armaments industries. Four nights later, a second U-boat put another team ashore near Jacksonville, Florida. The eight saboteurs planned to rendezvous in Chicago before commencing operations. Operation Pastorius, as this ill-fated scheme was named, was one of the most short-lived and unsuccessful operations in the annals of covert activity. Hardly was the Long Island group ashore when it was detected by a U.S. Coast Guardsman patrolling the beach and the alarm was raised. The group escaped but their weapons and explosives were found the next day where they had hastily buried them on the beach.

The group's leader, George Dasch and his companion Ernest Burger, realizing the hopelessness of their situation, decided to turn traitor and handed over the others to the FBI. Dasch apparently expected lavish rewards from J. Edgar Hoover. The Meiers were fortunate that it was Heinck and Quirin who sought them out, as Dasch and Burger would have betrayed them as willingly as they had sold out their compatriots. As it was, Heinck and Quirin, once captured, kept retribution from the family by misleading FBI interrogators as to their whereabouts since coming ashore.

Some time after the two strangers had departed, John came home to find his father sitting at the kitchen table weeping. Spread on the table was a newspaper whose front page was covered with the account of the sabotage team's execution. Dasch and Burger saved their lives through treachery. Their six companions went to the electric chair, the executions starting at noon August 8. By 1:20 p.m. it was over and the evening papers made the most of it.

An eight-year-old boy has little understanding of treason. The Meiers were a close family and John loved and obeyed his father. His life and his family were threatened by a conflict far beyond his understanding; but even at such a young age the fear in the house seeped into him.

The remainder of the war years passed uneventfully for the Meiers. John, always big for his age, played baseball, football, basketball and competed in track and field. He was a star baseball player in New York while attending William Cullen Bryant High School and was picked for one of the New York All Star baseball teams.

Following graduation in 1951, John went to work for the New York Life Insurance Company. The insurance industry was among the first to use computers and Meier wanted to learn all he could about them. However, his curiosity would have to wait until after he completed his military service. In 1952 he was inducted into the army.

He was 18, athletic, a lean six-foot-two. After basic training at Camp Kilmer, New Jersey and a stint at Fort Belvoir, Virginia, he joined the U.S. Army Corps of Engineers, received parachute training, and then was posted overseas to Korea. One morning Meier found himself in a foxhole on the crest of a hill, while in the valley below thousands of Chinese troops were massing. It would be a typical Korean battle. The outnumbered United Nations troops sat on the top of a ridge while hordes of Chinese tried brute force to dislodge them. The defenders' superior firepower, artillery and air strikes evened out the odds. Meier, like the rest of the company, was both frightened and fascinated as the bugles and screams of the enemy heralded the onslaught. The artillery lieutenant in a forward observation post began calling out coordinates. Within seconds, the distinctive whooump of distant howitzers and the whine of incoming shells were obliterated as the rounds exploded among shocked U.N. troops, who had been expecting to see their awful orange plumes blossom amid the enemy.

Before the lieutenant could shift the barrage off his position, a number of soldiers were dead and scores injured, among them Meier. Like the others killed or wounded, he had still been peering over the top of the foxhole when the first salvo plunged among them. One shell landed within yards of his trench, sending pieces of shrapnel into the corner of his eye and ear. He was evacuated by helicopter to a M.A.S.H. unit and then flown to Japan.

A few weeks later while Meier lay in Tokyo Army Hospital, a sergeant came through the wards asking the wounded what jobs they had held in civilian life. Meier said he was a computer analyst but the sergeant didn't know what that was.

He was looking for a fireman. The next day when another sergeant arrived asking the same question, Meier said he had worked for a fire department. If the army wanted someone to work in a fire department this would be preferable to being bombarded by friendly fire in Korea.

Two weeks later, Meier was told to put his kit in the jeep and a sergeant drove him to a large hall in downtown Tokyo filled with Japanese firemen. In the center was a podium. Meier was directed towards it and climbed the steps, followed by the sergeant. The Japanese brought food and saki. The saki had an immediate effect on Meier, a teetotaler. Every once in a while the assembled Japanese jumped up, shouted *"Banzai!"* and knocked back more saki. Etiquette demanded Meier and the sergeant follow suit.

Mystified by the proceedings, Meier turned to the NCO. "Sergeant, this is nice, but what does it all mean?"

"They're doing it to honor you."

"Why would they want to do that?"

"Because you're the new military fire chief of Washington Heights."

"I'm the what?"

"The military fire chief."

Meier felt weak. The hundred or so firemen drinking his health would be working for him. Washington Heights in downtown Tokyo with its diplomatic and military establishments was one of the poshest areas of the city. It was like being made fire chief of Lower Manhattan.

With a final *Banzai* the party broke up and Meier was taken to the fire station. On the way he pondered the mixed blessing of possessing a glib tongue. When he arrived it was to find every piece of equipment — from pumper to axhead — gleaming. The firemen, equipped in their American-style helmets and turnout suits, stood in rows before their trucks. Still a little drunk, Meier took himself off to a corner and fell asleep.

He had been down for about an hour when he felt his interpreter Shiego Shigeta shaking his shoulder. He struggled to his feet and was aware of the alarm bells pealing. Someone clapped a helmet on his head, shoved him in the chief's white jeep and off they went.

It was a major fire. When he arrived, the Japanese municipal firemen were running around but Meier's military crew stood waiting beside the trucks. They hadn't even uncoiled a hose.

"What are they waiting for?" Meier asked Shigeta.

"Orders."

How could he possibly give them orders? He turned to Shigeta and said: "Just look straight ahead and don't say anything, but I don't know a thing about fighting fires. I don't know a hose from a nozzle."

"This must be a joke," said Shigeta, staring at him expectantly.

Meier gave him a weak smile. The interpreter muttered some Japanese oaths under his breath.

"Do you know anything about fires?" Meier asked.

Shigeta nodded.

"Well, why don't you just give the orders?"

The interpreter sprang forward and within minutes the crews were in action. Meier, meanwhile, walked about waving his arms as if he knew what was going on while Shigeta organized not only his crew but the municipal firemen as well. Before long, the fire was extinguished.

Hours later, with a smoke-blackened face and an awful hangover, Meier collapsed on his firehall bunk — only to be frightened out of his wits minutes later by a terrific scream of *Banzai,* from the firemen who had silently gathered around his bunk. One man spoke on behalf of the crew who were impressed by Meier's honorable efforts. Surprisingly, Shigeta managed to keep a straight face during the translation.

After they had gone, Meier asked an unimpressed Shigeta to train him. Shigeta taught him the rudiments of firefighting and gave him a crash course on the Japanese psyche. This became a necessity on the day they were called to a fire in a whorehouse. They arrived to find the building in flames and the female employees in various states of indecency running up and down the street screaming and shouting. Amidst all the confusion a drunken customer was discovered trapped on the second floor bellowing for help. When the firemen didn't move, Meier asked Shigeta why they weren't unloading the ladders, which could easily reach the window where the unfortunate customer stood trapped.

"No. They are honoring you," said Shigeta. "As the new chief you must be given the opportunity to rescue him. It is for you to go and bring him out."

Meier thought it was a joke but Shigeta wasn't smiling.

"Are you kidding? I'm not going in there — the place is on fire."

"But you must — we will be behind spraying water on you."

Shigeta took him by the arm and dragged him to the doorway while the other firemen formed up behind with a hose. Before he knew it, he was shoved inside and stumbling up the flame-engulfed stairs while the gang behind doused him with water. He reached the second floor and saw the victim through the smoke — and then fainted.

Some hours later he regained consciousness in hospital. Shigeta was sitting on the end of the bed, all smiles.

"You brought us great honor."

"I did?"

Shigeta flourished a newspaper with a front page picture of Meier, an arm around the drunk, coming through the front doors of the whorehouse — both men wedged between Shigeta and a crowd of happy firemen.

In 1954, Meier's military service ended and he was ordered to report to Tokyo military headquarters. Meier ignored the order as he had become strongly attached to Japan and to his fire crew. When news of his disobedience reached headquarters, a jeep filled with MPs retrieved Meier without ceremony. He was honorably discharged from the army and he returned to his position at New York Life.

He met Jennie Cravotta in the actuarial department. She didn't appear impressed by his flashy clothes or cocky self-assurance but he persisted in asking her for a date and finally she accepted. They were married a year later. Their first child, John Jr., was born on November 16, 1956.

2

DIALOGUES WITH THE GREAT ENIGMA

Howard Robard Hughes Junior was born on Christmas Eve, 1905, in Houston, Texas. His birth wasn't registered. His father's passions were the mining and the oil business and he would, three years after his son's birth, strike it rich — not by finding some fabulous motherlode or sinking a well into a river of oil but by buying the rights to a new rotary drill bit capable of cutting through the hard rock which was impervious to the bits then in use by the oil industry. So revolutionary was it, that it became the foundation of the Hughes Tool Company, the source of family wealth upon which the younger Hughes would build a $2 billion fortune.

In 1924, when Hughes was in his nineteenth year, his father died and the company passed into his hands. Rather than stay in Texas managing the family firm, Hughes set off for California where he used his wealth to finance movies. He hired Noah Dietrich to handle his business affairs while he produced movies such as *Hell's Angels* — an enormous extravaganza in which squadrons of First World War fighters and bombers were assembled to recreate the aerial battles fought over France. But movies were not his biggest passion — flying was. In the age when flying records were being established Hughes sought to place his name alongside Lindbergh's and Earhart's. In July 1938, he succeeded, when he broke the record for flying around the globe and received a hero's welcome upon his return to New York.

He formed Hughes Aircraft to build his own racing aircraft. After the outbreak of the Second World War, the company moved to a new plant in Culver City, California and was awarded government contracts to build a series of experimental aircraft, none of which would go into production. While designing and test flying aircraft Hughes had two spectacular crashes. In 1943 he crashed into Lake Mead in Nevada. In July 1946 he was critically injured when his plane crashed through the roof of a house in Los Angeles. His notorious dependency on codeine probably began during his recovery in hospital.

In 1948 he bought a controlling interest in RKO Pictures, which would produce over 50 movies before he sold out in 1955. He purchased two small regional airlines to create Trans World Airlines, which was eventually taken from him by the courts because of financial mismanagement.

Hughes ignored the modern corporate model in running his business empire. Instead of shareholders, boards of directors and stock options for key executives, Hughes resorted to a sort of industrial feudalism. Nothing stood between him and the managers he appointed to look after his holdings. All of Hughes' activities were coordinated through a stucco warehouse in Los Angeles that he had bought during his early Hollywood days. Bill Gay was in charge of these headquarters on Romaine Street which began as a storehouse for Hughes' films, company documents and personal effects. It evolved into a clearing house for messages between Hughes and his executives.

In the 1940s and '50s, Hughes experienced a number of mental breakdowns from overwork during which he developed the bizarre and obsessive behavior that created the legends of his being a paranoid hermit with a pathological fear of infection. He devised elaborate written protocols to protect himself from contamination by his environment. For example, everything his aides handled for his use was to be picked up with several thicknesses of paper tissue. Aides were to wash their hands without letting their fingers touch the side of the bowl and were required to set the soap down with great care so that their clean fingers would not touch any part of the sink. In his mind, anything that entered Hughes' presence from the outside world represented a potential threat.

By the mid-1950s, Hughes was rich almost beyond imagination. In the years to come, government contracts would pile even more wealth upon him as the space race began in earnest and the war in Vietnam pushed along the development of electronic hardware and missiles for which his aircraft company successfully bid.

Hughes was one of America's great eccentrics — inventor, aviator, industrialist and a playboy with a penchant for Hollywood starlets.

It was in the summer of 1956 that John Meier met Hughes who, always on the lookout for bright young men, had noticed Meier and dispatched Dietrich to invite him to a meeting in a New York hotel room. Meier knew something of Howard Hughes. His father had prepared the celebratory banquet that welcomed Hughes back to New York on his return from his flight around the world in 1938.

In 1956 Hughes was still given to meeting mortals in hotel rooms. Meier found him to be a tall, thin man with the frank and engaging manners of a Texas aristocrat, whose face bore the scars of his spectacular airplane crashes. He wanted to discuss computers and asked Meier to brief him on how they were being used in the insurance business. They talked for hours and it was late in the evening when Meier finally left.

Meier was in bed when the phone rang. It was Dietrich. He said Hughes wanted to give him a job in California at Hughes Aircraft. Meier, though flattered, was not interested in uprooting his family from New York and turned him down. He stayed a couple of years in New York, then joined Chrysler's computer division in Detroit. His second child, Jeannie, was born in February 1958. One evening in 1959 Hughes called again, and this time Meier impulsively agreed to join him in California.

Packing Jennie and the two children into a Plymouth, Meier drove from Detroit to Los Angeles and took an apartment in Inglewood, close to Hughes Aircraft. From his new management position in the computer division he had an opportunity to observe the workings of the aerospace industry. Occasionally, Hughes would call him at home — usually at night — and direct him to a meeting in his bungalow at the Beverly Hills Hotel, or more frequently, to a quiet part of Mulholland Boulevard overlooking the city. Hughes used him to confirm information he had received from other sources and most of these early conversations dealt with the plant.

Meier stayed with Hughes Aircraft for two years before moving to Remington Rand Univac as manager of technical sales. Within two years Bill Gay lured him to Hughes Dynamics, a company which was developing automation and computer equipment capable of transforming the operations of the U.S. postal service, or so Meier was told when he was given

an office in the Kirkley Center on Wilshire Boulevard. He had not spoken
with Hughes for more than a year and was surprised when he was called out
to the old rendezvous on Mulholland.

"What the hell's going on in the Kirkley Center?" Hughes shouted.
Meier, taken aback, didn't understand. "What's Hughes Dynamics all
about?"

Hughes raved about being deceived and Meier realized that he didn't
know anything about the company which bore his name. Hughes insisted
on knowing how Meier had come to be there and what he was doing. Gay,
he said, was a Mormon and that was at the root of it. "They set this thing up
for the Mormon Church so they can computerize their genealogical
research. Well, I'm damn well going to close it down." And he did.

With the demise of Hughes Dynamics, Meier started a consulting
company with Hughes Aircraft as one of his clients. Hughes Aircraft was a
major manufacturer of weapons and electronic equipment and had
pioneered the development of guided missile systems and the electronic gear
necessary to give the United States its first all-weather fighter. Later his
company designed the world's first communications satellite and *Surveyor,*
the first vehicle to soft land on the moon.

Hughes Aircraft was fueling the arms race with its high-tech successes
and their military applications. Meier felt misgivings about working with it,
especially during the Cuban Missile Crisis of 1962. This crisis caused Meier,
and millions of others, to contemplate the unthinkable. He was horrified by
the apparent ease with which the world had trundled to the brink of nuclear
war. He wasn't alone. Hughes had also been profoundly shaken by the
experience, as Meier discovered during meetings the pair had on Mulholland
that year.

Hughes was inquisitive about Meier's political leanings and his attitude
toward nuclear weapons. Meier told him he was a proponent of nuclear
disarmament and was surprised to hear Hughes express similar sympathies,
particularly after the Kennedy-Khrushchev confrontation over Cuba.
Hughes spoke at length about what a nuclear attack would do to Los
Angeles; the prospect clearly terrified him.

Previously, Meier was approached by someone from Fund For Survival,
a small group of anti-nuclear activists from the Los Angeles area which had
attracted a number of celebrities such as comedian Steve Allen and actor
Robert Ryan. Meier thought of joining the group and Hughes encouraged

him. Hughes later made a modest donation to the fund. The fund was the brainchild of U.S. Mitchell, who gave up his equipment leasing business in order to crusade for the elimination of nuclear weapons. At the height of the Cold War, Mitchell was visiting Germany, Czechoslovakia and the Soviet Union where his campaigning was reported in such Communist state periodicals as Moscow's *Literary Gazette.*

The group's mandate was simple: to mobilize a peace movement within the United States. Its money would fund advertisements to offset the propaganda of the military and the Atomic Energy Commission. Meier's hope was that this campaign would arouse such protest from ordinary Americans that the legislators would be forced to negotiate a disarmament treaty with the Soviet Union. The fund did not advocate unilateral disarmament but rather a controlled dismantling of nuclear umbrellas by the United Nations, followed by a conversion of the world's economies from weapons production to peaceful enterprises.

Given the paranoia of the time it took courage to belong to the fund. It was treated as a radical organization by the government and came under the scrutiny of domestic intelligence organizations. Peace groups were traditionally viewed with suspicion by western intelligence agencies who judged their membership to be infiltrated by Communists. And while many activists were as anticommunist as they were anti-nuclear, the perception of the peace movement in general was that it was made up of well-meaning dupes directed by Moscow.

Howard Hughes was in many ways eccentric, even irrational, but to imagine him a "Red" sympathizer would be ludicrous. Yet here he was encouraging Meier to join the struggle, an indication that Hughes' fear of the bomb outweighed his reluctance to embrace this activity of the political left.

Meier joined the fund and was named a director. His involvement seemed innocuous enough at the time, but to government agencies interested in monitoring the disarmament movement, the presence of someone with Meier's connections in Fund For Survival would be of more than passing interest. Before long, government agents began surveillance of those quiet meetings at dusk on Mulholland.

In August 1965, Hughes again sought Meier's company. August was the month of the Watts riots and Hughes was numbed by the violence that came pouring out of the black ghettos of Los Angeles. Thirty-four people were killed, over 1,000 injured and nearly 4,000 arrested as rioters hooting "get Whitey" and chanting "burn, baby, burn" firebombed and looted, exchanged gunfire with police and sniped at firemen.

The riots disturbed Hughes and fueled his racist paranoia. In a meeting with Meier he inveighed against black militants attempting to burn down the city — an exaggeration, as most of the damage was inflicted inside Watts. Meier, a proponent of civil rights, blamed discrimination and poverty for the violence.

Their conflicting beliefs about race relations resurfaced three years later when Meier, who was by then representing Hughes' Nevada Operations, promised African-Americans equal employment opportunities in Nevada during a speech he made in Tulsa, Oklahoma. Hughes was not impressed with Meier's comments reported in the Las Vegas press. When the assassination of Martin Luther King provoked nation-wide riots, out came the canary yellow pad Hughes always used in order to fire off a missive to Robert Maheu, the head of the Nevada Operations. In it Hughes equally deplores the violence and the pressure on casino owners to "adopt a more liberal attitude towards... negroes." He continued:

> Now, Bob, I have never made my views known on this subject. And I certainly would not say these things in public. However, I can summarize my attitude about employing more negroes very simply — I think it is a wonderful idea for somebody else, somewhere else... I know this is a hot potato, and I'm not asking you to form another chapter of the K.K.K. Just let's try to do what you can without too many people getting upset about it. I don't want to become known as a negro-hater or anything like that. But I am not running for election and therefore we don't have to curry favor with the NAACP either. I thought I'd better get this to you before somebody — probably John Meier — commits you to head up some pro-negro committee.

3

THE ATOMIC ENERGY COMMISSION

In July of 1966, Howard Hughes left California to escape state income tax. Hughes — though he had lived there many years — had claimed he was a Texan and a resident of Houston. However, when he left Los Angeles, he didn't return to Texas but went to Boston.

What Hughes wanted was a haven for his wealth, safe from tax collectors. He had considered Montreal or the Bahamas, but his xenophobia turned his attention to Nevada. Even this state did not provide a perfect sanctuary, for while there were no taxes, the Atomic Energy Commission routinely tested large nuclear weapons in the desert north of Las Vegas. Hughes' concern over this possible risk to his health and corporate holdings would grow into an obsession.

While in Boston he dispatched Meier to Nevada to investigate reports that the AEC's testing program was not as safe as the agency wanted people to believe.

Meier heard rumors in Las Vegas that radiation had been vented into the atmosphere from underground tests but the AEC resolutely denied any emissions had escaped. Though inclined to believe something was amiss, Hughes nevertheless said he intended to move to Las Vegas and would contact Meier once he arrived.

Legalized gambling had come to Nevada in 1931 as a means to raise state revenue during the Depression. Las Vegas was the town the mob built. It provided organized crime with a place where it could flourish, practicing a way of life denied elsewhere. It was founded by Benjamin (Bugsy) Siegel — gunman, gangster, gambler and visionary — the mobster who built the Flamingo hotel-casino and, in so doing, gave root to the most garish place on earth. While large casinos had been built in northern Nevada, in and around Reno, Siegel wanted no competition. He picked a patch of sand on Las Vegas Boulevard South, now known as the Strip — and planted a seed which has since blossomed into a jungle, kept thriving on neon and kilowatts, that flowers day and night and knows no season. One piece of Las Vegas folklore says that Siegel once became so incensed with an employee, Abe Schiller, that in front of a poolside full of horrified guests, he pulled a .38 from his cummerbund and took aim at Schiller's head. He forced him down on all fours and made him crawl around the pool, while aiming shots over his head which splashed in the water. When Siegel died as violently as he had lived, his casino passed into the hands of like-minded entrepreneurs. Organized crime has had a proprietary interest in Las Vegas ever since.

Here the Sicilian crime bosses, the *capi mafiosi,* set up a society in their own image pandering to every human weakness and exploiting human folly on a scale never before imagined. They derived profits from gambling, prostitution and narcotics, and their natural by-products — extortion and blackmail.

Nevada has tolerated the presence of the most depraved and infamous of mobsters; as a result, local and state government became the most corrupt in the nation. *Green Felt Jungle,* written by Ed Reid and Ovid Demaris in 1964, lifted up the rock from Las Vegas and showed what was crawling beneath.

The arrival of Howard Hughes was greeted with almost messianic enthusiasm by those Las Vegans desperately waiting to be redeemed from the stigma of Siegel and his heirs. *Las Vegas Sun* publisher Herman (Hank) Greenspun's joy spilled all over his front page in praise of Hughes — and all his money stood for. Greenspun, perhaps more than anyone else in town, had earned the right to welcome Hughes. Although Greenspun had once worked for Siegel, toiling as a flack for the gangster at his Fabulous Flamingo, he had been a thorn in the mob's side for years.

Hughes represented wealth devoid of violence. His was legitimate money, in contrast to the illicit fortunes which everyone knew lay behind the glitter of those luxury casinos, the "carpet joints" of local idiom. The greatest of American eccentrics had arrived in this most eccentric state.

The Atomic Energy Commission had been operating there since 1951 and for the first eleven years had been blithely exploding nuclear devices above ground while reassuring the public that there was no danger. It is impossible to know how many deaths were caused or how many people were contaminated by fallout. The practice was revoked by international treaty in 1963 when the Soviet Union and the United States finally admitted it to be dangerous. Consequently, all tests went underground. Were they safe? The AEC, naturally, said they were — but the AEC had said that about atmospheric testing.

Ordinary people would have to accept the AEC's word; Howard Hughes had the resources to find out for himself. He had barely settled into the Desert Inn when the AEC set off an atomic device codenamed Project Greeley beneath the Pahute Mesa. The explosion rocked buildings in Las Vegas, including Hughes' penthouse suite, for more than a minute. As usual, the AEC announced there had been no radiation leaks but a month later, in January, there was yet another nuclear explosion which cracked open the desert floor leaving a 4,000-foot long trench. People were justified in wondering how radiation could be prevented from escaping when the earth was being ruptured.

Hughes panicked and called Meier in Los Angeles. Like many people, Hughes had an inadequate understanding of radiation. The fatal effects of radiation hardly seemed important if — as many expected — they would be vaporized during a nuclear attack. Hughes wanted to know the insidious and invisible effects created by the detonation of a thermonuclear device and the physical consequences of being exposed to radiation. Meier abandoned all other projects as Hughes impatiently demanded the information. Meier gathered whatever information he could get from his friends in Fund For Survival and scientific journals at the University of California.

On February 2, 1967, he handed the report to Bob Maheu, who would soon become the head of Hughes' Nevada operations. It was Meier's first meeting with Maheu. These men — destined to become enemies — would perform varied clandestine tasks for Hughes until the moment of Hughes' mysterious disappearance from Las Vegas in 1970.

Meier's report, with its references to mutations, leukemia, cancer, the effects of exposure on cells and body tissues — how German girls employed in factories painting radium dials on watches died horrible deaths from cancer of the mouth — scared Hughes witless. A week later, Meier was summoned to the Desert Inn where he was paged to pick up the house phone.

"John, this is really shocking," said Hughes of his report. "I just never imagined that radiation affected the body this way. We've got to do something to stop these underground tests. What we need is information to show they're unsafe. If we get this we can put pressure on the AEC to stop. I'd like you to work on it."

The AEC was a powerful government entity intimately tied to the military and defense interests of the nation. How could anyone — even Howard Hughes — think he could hustle the AEC out of Nevada? Many Americans regarded the AEC's very existence as the country's main deterrent to Communist aggression and its secrets were considered among the nation's most valued possessions. Meier argued that such a campaign would consume all his time and that he had his other businesses to consider. "I've got to eat too," he protested.

"Well, you can come and work for me. I'd like you to be my scientific advisor," said Hughes.

There could be no more stalling. Hughes proposed to have Meier placed on Maheu's payroll. When he demurred, Hughes hastily added that he would prefer this arrangement as his campaign against the AEC might provoke a violent reaction from the government. He wished to shield his companies, especially Hughes Aircraft, from official retribution.

"Frankly, John, I want to be able to deny you if things get too hot. Better if you appear to be with Bob."

After accepting Hughes' commission, Meier returned to Los Angeles and began dismantling his business affairs. He returned to Las Vegas on weekends posing as an out-of-state businessman who was considering a move to the state but worried about radioactive contamination.

He needed information showing the AEC's testing program was flawed. He visited newsrooms, the AEC and other government offices.

The press was skeptical about the AEC's routine assurances and a number of reporters said they were convinced something was wrong. Workers at the test site had given them information of leaks but no proof was available. The AEC's Las Vegas office gave him leaflets and tolerant smiles and told him that his fears, while natural, were groundless.

Meier travelled to the small towns ringing the test site. He visited all the settlements which housed AEC personnel: Beatty, Indian Springs and Parump.

Meier stalked his quarry in bars. There he would sit nursing a coke, lying in wait for AEC workers with a story to tell. He would engage them in small talk, buy them drinks, joke and try to tease from them anything that smacked of a cover-up. Finally, his perseverance was rewarded.

Earlier, Meier had met two AEC workers in the Exchange Club in Beatty. They chatted and drank but neither was ready to volunteer information about radiation leaks. When he arrived this time, they were sitting in the saloon with a companion; Meier was welcomed with all the bonhomie that comes from booze and dim lights, loud music and commotion — the euphoria that rises on the vapors of happy hour. Keeping up a steady flow of liquor to the table, Meier was soon deep in conversation with the third party.

The man was an AEC engineer but was quitting the test site because he was terrified by the unsafe conditions. The AEC, he said, was protecting neither its employees nor the public from radiation leaks. There had been serious venting of radioactive gases into the atmosphere and contamination of subterranean water systems in the desert. The engineer took out a pencil to draw diagrams on a table napkin showing how radiation was being spread through ground water. He said the AEC knew the water table was being contaminated but counted on it taking hundreds of years to work its way to Las Vegas, by which time those responsible would have the grave between them and retribution. When he had queried the amounts of radioactivity being vented into the atmosphere, he was told not to concern himself — the wind was blowing it over to Europe and the Soviet Union.

Meier was on the brink of discovering perhaps the most perfidious display of government callousness to the rights and health of a free people in the modern era. Although the AEC never officially admitted it, some underground nuclear tests in Nevada are known to have vented enormous quantities of radiation into the atmosphere. The AEC dissembled and deceived, swearing mighty oaths that its program caused no harmful effects. As a consequence, clouds hot with radiation passed over the heads of an unsuspecting and unprotected populace.

Meier's report triggered an immediate and enduring state of hostility between Hughes and the AEC. For the next three years, the AEC would find itself engaged in a battle royal. It was a contest without precedent. This was not a political movement mobilized against a government agency by the usual bunch of ragtag protesters and dissidents; this was a single, wealthy man up against an enormously powerful bureaucracy which had the unchecked support of the entire federal government. Hughes would eventually disrupt the AEC's program and at times force the agency into a strategic retreat.

Hughes told Meier he was not only convinced that nuclear testing placed the population at risk but also that it was responsible for causing earthquakes which had undermined buildings in Las Vegas and might conceivably threaten the stability of the Hoover Dam. This dam, located between Nevada and Arizona, is 1,244 feet long, 726 feet high and holds 10 trillion gallons of water in its 247 square miles of reservoir. He constantly reminded Meier of the 1928 disaster at Santa Paula, California when the St. Francis Dam collapsed killing 450 people.

By 1967, the tests were becoming bigger and bigger: Hughes' apprehension rose with the megatonnage. In late March, shortly after Hughes bought the Desert Inn, Meier was introduced to the press as Hughes' scientific advisor.

Within weeks of being coaxed by Hughes into the mad scheme of forcing the AEC from its Nevada testing grounds, Meier made the disturbing discovery that his services were not to be confined to the physical world. Meier was expected to deal with the occult.

Legend portrays Hughes in his glory days as an ice-cold entrepreneur fearlessly hacking his way through the industrial jungle guided by an infallible inner compass. In reality, Hughes was not loath to seeking assistance from the supernatural. To his bemusement, Meier soon found himself carrying sealed packages between Hughes' penthouse and his psychic, Peter Hurkos.

Hurkos described himself as a psychometrist — one who could make psychic pronouncements after handling an object belonging to the person seeking his advice. Once Meier escorted him up the back stairs to the Desert Inn penthouse through the guards and into Hughes' suite. Hughes was waiting behind a one-way glass which permitted him to see Hurkos without being visible himself. Hughes' intensified use of the psychic when considering major business decisions showed his mental and emotional deterioration. Meier was not privy to Hughes' discussions with the psychic but on occasion he did have to listen in respectful silence to Hughes' ramblings on life and death.

Hughes was at this time 61 years old, in failing health, and obsessed with his mortality. One night, he speculated about the possibility of cheating death by using an experimental procedure called cryonics, the process of freezing the newly deceased until science would be advanced enough to resuscitate the frozen body and prolong life. Meier was reduced to shocked silence. It was the beginning of the most esoteric assignment he ever undertook for Hughes.

Howard Hughes did not want to molder in the grave. He was one of the richest men living. In death he would have nothing, his power would be extinguished and his wealth surrendered to governments and distant relatives he cared nothing for. Hughes demanded that Meier gather whatever literature was available on cryonics and send it to the penthouse.

For the next two years Meier diligently searched libraries and clipped periodicals and newspapers. He obtained two copies of Robert C.W. Ettinger's *The Prospect of Immortality* in which the author enthusiastically promised the frozen dead would be brought back to life, although he couldn't promise when.

Ettinger's fanciful theory was based on little more than a belief that sooner or later science would be able to accomplish anything. According to Ettinger, the procedure was to drain the blood from a body, replace it with glycerol and then store it in liquid nitrogen at temperatures hundreds of degrees below zero. At these temperatures the corpse was supposed to remain viable until Ettinger's future supermen were technically able to perform their miracles, perhaps in 1,000, 2,000, or 30,000 years. If the "resuscitees" didn't like the era in which they'd been revived, they could hop into the deep-freeze and wait a thousand more years until a more genial age arrived. Ettinger visualized a lot of hopping in and out — a sort of time travel in a freezer. Here is the prophet Ettinger speaking through his book to Hughes, setting the scene for immortality:

> The tired old man then, will close his eyes and he can think of his impending temporary death as another period under anaesthesia in the hospital. Centuries may pass, but to him there will be only a moment of sleep without dreams. After awakening, he may be already young again and virile, having

been rejuvenated while unconscious; or he may be gradually renovated through treatment after awakening. In any case he will have the physique of a Charles Atlas if he wants it, and his weary and faded wife, if she chooses, may rival Miss Universe. Much more important, they will be gradually improved in mentality and personality. They will not find themselves idiot strangers in a lonely and baffling world... you and I, the frozen resuscitees, will not merely be revived and cured, but enlarged and improved, made fit to work, play and perhaps fight, on a grand scale and in a grand style...

To the cynics and gamblers he addressed the following:

Clearly the freezer is more attractive than the grave, even if one has doubts about the future capabilities of science. With bad luck, frozen people will simply remain dead, as they would have in the grave. But with good luck, the manifest destiny of science will be realized, and the resuscitees will drink the wine of centuries unborn. The likely prize is so enormous that even slender odds would be worth embracing.

Hughes agreed. He demanded lists of doctors who had expertise in cryonics or were involved in cryogenic research. He wanted Meier to find out what machines were being manufactured to keep bodies permanently frozen. And most significantly, he made a will seeking to keep his treasure on earth intact so that when he returned, it would all be waiting for him. His assets were to go into the Howard Hughes Medical Institute, of which he was the only trustee. This will was placed in a Texas bank. Meier found the best equipment was being designed in Germany and he placed an order for Hughes' high-tech coffin to be purchased with funds from Hughes' Swiss bank account.

Hughes' phobia of disease has been regarded as the root of his refusal to see anybody but his body servants and on rare occasions, a few intimates such as Meier. He lived in the Desert Inn penthouse, attended by "nursemaids" who were solicitous to his every whim. Legends have been made of his many idiosyncrasies and phobias; his fear of germs and human contact; his deranged insistence on controlling everything within his immediate environment and the absurd lengths his nursemaids would go to satisfy him.

To that part of the Hughes mythology, Meier can add little. However, between 1966 and 1970 he saw no sign of demented behavior or the long fingernails, flowing hair and beard of popular imagination.

Because Hughes was so inaccessible, civic and state officials had to direct whatever warmth they would have lavished upon him to his lieutenants. Meier quickly found himself a celebrity. He was besieged with requests to join service clubs, give speeches and take up charitable causes. In 1966, he was named Aerospace Man of the Year and while in Las Vegas he became a trustee for the Nevada Essential Development Surveys Foundation; became a member of the Child Welfare Advisory Committee; sat on the Impact Priority Committee; joined the Governor's Gaming Task Force and was an advisor to the Inter-Agency Water Pollution Control committee. In setting Meier the task of forcing the AEC out of Nevada, Hughes chose a lieutenant whose scientific credentials were nonexistent. Rather, Meier had a rough and ready education in business and his acumen soon forced the AEC to take notice. He possessed a tidy and precise mind, was a fast learner, articulate, and displayed a flair for deviousness which Hughes — a master of that himself — put to good use.

Meier's first move was to investigate whether the engineer at the Exchange Club was correct: that the ground water near the test sites was contaminated. He decided it would be necessary to set up a monitoring system to check for traces of tritium (radioactive water) in the water table and hired George Roth, a man of eclectic taste and education, as his assistant. Roth engaged a number of scientists. At the same time, Meier began a public relations blitz to dispute the AEC's repeated assurances that all was safe. For the first time, the AEC had to defend itself, not against leftists and long-haired environmentalists who could be summarily dismissed as un-American, but against a true blue capitalist, Howard Hughes, one of the bulwarks of the American way.

Hughes' interest could hardly have arisen at a more inauspicious time for the government. With the civil rights and the anti-war movements, civil disobedience in America was at its height. Now Hughes was threatening to incite the anti-nuclear lobby. While Hughes would hardly have regarded himself as having anything in common with the great demagogues who were stirring up Americans against the evils of war and racism, he would later threaten to lead the anti-nuclear campaign. In a memo sent in April of 1968 he tells Maheu to let the AEC know that after the "fears and curiosity of the public has (sic) been aroused the entire situation, not only in Nevada but throughout the nation, is going to prove highly explosive. It will only require a leader. I could easily be that leader...”[1]

As the pressure on the AEC increased, the commission singled out its most troublesome critic for a crude display of its secret resources. Meier was invited to visit the AEC's headquarters in Las Vegas, ostensibly for a meeting with Robert Miller, the director of the AEC's Nevada program.

When he entered Miller's office he found the director seated at a desk flanked by two men who stared at him with focused hostility. Stuffed as they were into black suits, they evoked the presence of government muscle.

The director quickly cut Meier's questions short. Miller intimated that the Hughes organization was inflicting damage on national interests. He demanded that Meier put a stop to it. When Meier refused, the interview deteriorated into a nasty row, with Meier claiming the AEC was covering up radiation leaks. Miller finally blurted what was uppermost on his mind — it wasn't Hughes who wanted the testing stopped, it was John Meier.

The accusation caught Meier by surprise. "Yes, it's true I'm opposed to nuclear arms testing," he said finally. "But so is Mr. Hughes and you're mistaken if you think he's indifferent."

"Bullshit!" growled one of the men behind Miller. He slammed down a brown concertina file on the desk so hard that a pile of photographs flew out.

Meier was astounded to see pictures of himself and Mitchell and, most startling, photographs of his meetings with Hughes on Mulholland. Meier stood up and began collecting his papers. One of the men shouted "Forget the whole goddamned thing. It's national security and you don't know what you're meddling with. Just back off."

Meier phoned Hughes and reported the gist of the AEC's theory about who was really behind the campaign. At first Hughes merely snorted, but the realization that his elaborate rituals to escape attention during the meetings on Mulholland had been in vain made him almost apoplectic.

"I'll spend every dime I have to stop those bastards," he ranted. "Every dime I have." He authorized Meier to hire anyone he wished to fight the AEC, including Washington lobbyists to foment trouble for the agency on Capitol Hill. Meier chose Joseph Napolitan and Associates, a firm close to the Democratic Party whose executives, such as Larry O'Brien, exercised high political influence within party ranks.

In April 1968, the AEC announced it would detonate its largest underground nuclear device to date. This bomb, called Boxcar, exploded with the force of a million tons of TNT. Buildings shook in Las Vegas as Boxcar's shockwave caused the ground to heave for 250 miles around. An immense cloud of dust rose hundreds of feet over the firing point. Although the bomb had been buried almost 4,000 feet below the surface, the desert floor leapt 20 feet in the air. Seismic instruments recorded the explosion in New York and Alaska.

Hughes had pleaded with the AEC for a ninety day postponement of Boxcar until an independent panel of scientists could study its effects. He made the same request of President Lyndon Johnson. Both requests were ignored. As the chandeliers in the gaming parlors swayed to the rhythm of the shockwaves rippling Las Vegas' foundations, Hughes examined all his options.

This was a tumultuous and confusing time in America. The country was divided into those eager to save the military's honor in Vietnam by any means and those demanding an armistice. President Johnson had grown weary of the turmoil. Senator Eugene McCarthy was preparing to oppose him for the presidential nomination in the Chicago convention. Robert Kennedy entered the race in the middle of March. Two weeks later, Johnson announced his political retirement, leaving Vice President Hubert Humphrey free to announce his candidacy.

Meier had first met Humphrey through Milton Polland, a canny political advisor with whom he was in business. Meier met the Vice President on many occasions, both socially and while conducting Hughes' business. Hughes ordered cash overtures to be made to both Johnson and Humphrey to stop the AEC's operations in Nevada. Much has been written about these incidents and Humphrey went to the grave bearing the stigma of a bought man. According to John Meier, Humphrey was unjustly maligned.

Hughes hoped to persuade Johnson to stop the AEC before the end of his administration. He sent Maheu to offer Johnson "$1 million after he left the office of the presidency if he would stop the atomic testing before he left." Maheu met with Johnson at the LBJ Ranch but denied ever delivering the offer. He instead talked obliquely of Hughes' interest in the President's future and how he would like to help him once he left office. Johnson is said to have replied that he would be happy if Hughes would make a donation to the Johnson Library which was to be built in Austin.

The Humphrey matter was entirely different. Immediately upon hearing of his decision to seek the presidency, Hughes moved to buy him and instructed Maheu to tell Humphrey that he could have the campaign money necessary to win the White House if he would dismantle the AEC once President.

Maheu has testified that on May 10, 1968, he met Humphrey at the Denver Hilton. There Humphrey promised to scuttle the AEC for a $100,000 campaign contribution. The first installment of $50,000 was allegedly delivered to him that July in Los Angeles.

Meier's account is different. Maheu, who did not know Humphrey, asked Meier to arrange a meeting with the Vice President in order to receive Humphrey's undertaking that, if elected, he would stop underground testing in Nevada. Meier argued that it was unnecessary. "Humphrey's behind us one hundred percent on this. I don't see why we need to meet him."

Finally at Maheu's insistence, Meier flew with him to Denver. After listening to Humphrey's campaign speech in the Denver Hilton, Meier introduced Maheu to Humphrey, who suggested they come to his room.

When they entered, they found Humphrey relaxing in his shirt sleeves, his necktie loosened and his shoes off. He was sitting on a sofa in front of a small table. He beckoned them to take the chairs opposite. Maheu placed his briefcase on the table.

"Okay, what is it you boys want to talk about?" asked Humphrey, his mobile features arranged into that patented smile. Before Meier could say anything, Maheu reached over and unclipped the catches of his briefcase with all the adroitness of a brush salesman. Stacked neatly inside was a considerable sum of money. Meier almost choked as the famous grin froze on the Vice President's face. Maheu, unabashed, said the money was Humphrey's in return for promising to stop the AEC in Nevada.

Humphrey looked venomously at Meier, who was shaking his head to signal his innocence — then he reached over and grabbed Maheu by the lapels. Humphrey was not a small man and in his fury he almost pulled Maheu right over the table. "What kind of a son-of-a-bitch do you think I am?" he yelled, as Maheu hung halfway across the table being jerked this way and that.

Maheu pulled himself free, grabbed his briefcase and cleared out.

Meier stayed to apologize. He had had no inkling of what Maheu was planning and begged Humphrey not to let it influence him against Hughes' position. Humphrey quickly cooled down, but allowed that the only reason he didn't "kill the son-of-a-bitch" was because Meier had brought him.

A week later Meier and Roth met a group of scientists from MIT and Harvard who agreed to assess the environmental data their consultants had collected which challenged the AEC's perennial assertion that its nuclear testing was perfectly harmless.

Hughes, a notorious insomniac, phoned to wake Meier at three in the morning for a briefing. Meier reported that a scientific panel was examining their data and was confident Johnson would commission an independent study, as Humphrey was solidly behind the initiative and would urge him on. The mention of the Vice President's name provided the opening Hughes sought.

"Well, the reason I'm calling, John, is to check what Bob has been telling me about the progress we're making."

Meier said he had no idea what Maheu was reporting.

"Well, at least we've got the Vice President in our hip pocket," said Hughes.

Not quite sure what that meant, Meier said that Humphrey — like Hughes himself — believed the AEC was covering up the risks involved in testing.

"No, John," said Hughes testily, "I mean once a man takes a bribe we've got him."

"What bribe?" asked Meier.

"What do you mean? You were there when Bob took care of him."

"Mr. Hughes — there was no bribe."

"But you saw Humphrey take the money," Hughes persisted.

"No, he didn't take any money. In fact it was a very embarrassing meeting."

Hughes fell silent for a moment. "Well, I guess I must have been mistaken. Bob probably meant he did it privately with the Vice President."

But for once Meier refused to let Hughes have the last word.

"Mr. Hughes, I was there the whole time. He didn't see him alone."

It was a conversation of considerable importance for Meier, since Hughes came to believe his version of events. When the time came again for Hughes to offer a bribe — this time an enormous one — it would be Meier, not Maheu, who was assigned to monitor the transaction.

Although a personal friend of Humphrey's, and at the time a Republican, Meier nonetheless supported Robert Kennedy from the moment he entered the race for the Democratic nomination. Unlike Meier's employer, who was making enormous profits from the Vietnam War, Meier was opposed to it and saw in Kennedy a President who would stop it.

On June 4, Meier phoned Kennedy and arranged to meet him in Los Angeles two days later to discuss ending the underground nuclear testing program. Kennedy then gave the phone to Paul Schrade. Schrade, a highly influential official of the United Auto Workers union, and a close friend of Meier's, said the California primary was in the bag and that they were all on their way to the White House.

On the night of June 5, Kennedy, as predicted, swept the primary in California. In what would be his final speech, Kennedy thanked Schrade for his help in delivering the labor vote. After that, Schrade followed Kennedy and his entourage into the kitchen of the Ambassador Hotel where Sirhan Sirhan waited with a .22 calibre pistol. Schrade remembers a burst of gunfire, stars filling his eyes and his body trembling violently.

Kennedy, who was shot in the head, fell to the ground. His appalled entourage heard him whisper: "Is Paul all right?"

Meier cut himself while shaving in preparation for his meeting with Kennedy the next morning when the news of the shooting came over the radio. He was unable to reach any of his friends in the Kennedy entourage for details. He phoned a Los Angeles radio station and a reporter told him Kennedy was not expected to live and that Schrade's chances were equally bleak.

Later Hughes called to say they should do whatever they could for Schrade. "He helped us, John, and I'm grateful." Hughes was remembering Schrade's assistance in organizing the auto workers, whose union had tried to interfere with the firing of the Boxcar test earlier that year. He said if Schrade survived he would fly him to Nevada for recuperation at Spring Mountain Ranch.

Meier was devastated by the shooting. Kennedy had held such great promise for liberal America and the assassination left his supporters completely demoralized. What made Meier's loss even more bitter was that instead of meeting with Kennedy on June 6, he was now meeting with Don Nixon, brother of Richard whose political star was now in the ascendant, as Hughes was quick to point out.

While common decency should have kept even Kennedy's most virulent political foes from gloating over such a tragedy, it did not constrain Don Nixon, who was literally rubbing his hands with delight when he met Meier. The brothers Nixon didn't care about Hubert Humphrey but feared Kennedy.

Nixon's glee, insufferable as it was, had to be borne by Meier without outward signs of distress. Kennedy died in the early morning of June 7 and the assassination violently threw the scales against the Democrats' chances of remaining in power. For Meier, it was a nightmare. After Kennedy's death, Meier quietly switched allegiance to Humphrey, as did most of Kennedy's supporters.

While his political loyalty was with Humphrey, he nevertheless met Don and Edward Nixon and Bebe Rebozo, Richard Nixon's confidant, in New York on July 8. By then, it was obvious that Nixon would win the Republican nomination in Miami. Hughes had instructed Meier to make his position clear to Nixon's camp concerning the AEC. Meier was assured Hughes' position would be conveyed to Nixon.

Meier was under orders to hire Thomas E. Murray Jr. to join what was becoming a sort of mercenary army — Hughes' Legion — marshalled against the AEC. Hughes remembered Thomas E. Murray Sr. as a former director of the AEC during the Truman administration. The senior Murray was in an airforce observation plane near Eniwetok Atoll on November 16, 1952 when the world's first hydrogen bomb was exploded.

Hughes hoped that with Murray Jr., who had all the right contacts in Washington, he might be able to get to the AEC from within. Hughes hoped to gain access to weak spots in the commission which had so far displayed an unexpected resistance to his money and influence.

Fresh from his meeting with the Nixons, Meier met Murray and explained how Hughes wanted to use his expertise in Washington. He didn't want a lobbyist — they had to be registered, and Hughes characteristically didn't want it known that Murray was working for him. He was to keep Hughes informed and use his influence to advance Hughes' opposition to the AEC — but quietly.

When they met the next day Murray was still undecided and asked for a little more time. Just as Meier was leaving Murray playfully asked if Hughes would like to buy an airline. It was a question Meier could not ignore as he knew Hughes was passionate about the airline industry. Murray told him that Air West was for sale and that David Grace, the airline's executive chairman and second largest shareholder, was his friend.

Air West was having trouble with the Civil Aeronautics Board. Although cash poor with aging equipment, it had good routes.

In 1966 the courts had dispossessed Hughes of Trans World Airlines due to financial mismanagement and ordered him to sell the company for $546 million — money he was now busily spending in Nevada. Meier knew Hughes would seize any opportunity to get back into the airline business if for no other reason than to prove the banks, the courts and the airline industry wrong.

When Meier informed him about Air West, Hughes was elated at the prospect of picking up another airline and promised Murray a finder's fee of ten percent. Given the price paid for Air West, Murray's fee should have been $800,000. Murray, however, would never see a penny. The job of handling Murray and of negotiating with Grace for Air West was given to Maheu.

Three weeks later, on July 29, Meier accompanied Maheu to Los Angeles where Maheu introduced him to a number of men he thought should be employed by Hughes Aircraft. Maheu needed Meier's help in getting these men hired, as the rancor that existed between himself and those running Hughes Aircraft precluded his making any such request, and Meier had friends in the company from years past. What Maheu failed to tell Meier was that they were all CIA operatives looking to use the company as a cover for activities abroad. Meier ensured that the men were found jobs.

What else did or didn't happen that day — July 29 — in Los Angeles is critical to the good name and reputation of Hubert Humphrey. Maheu would say that on that day, he delivered a $50,000 bribe to Humphrey after climbing into the back of the Vice President's limousine as it drove away from a Los Angeles hotel. Humphrey, the conscience of American liberal politics, was according to Maheu, apparently bought and paid for in the back of a black limo.

Meier is certain Humphrey wasn't, for he was with Maheu all that day. They were discussing the Air West situation and Maheu was on his way east to meet with Grace. There was no contact with Humphrey's party.

Humphrey, too, would deny ever accepting a bribe from Maheu or seeing Maheu in his limousine. Further, if the object of the bribe was to assure Humphrey's assistance against the AEC, it would have been money wasted. Without any bribery Humphrey had already convinced Johnson to commission a presidential panel to study Meier's data.

The President had rejected the scientists recommended by Meier because they were regarded as being too anti-AEC. Instead, a more hawkish group was assembled to consider Meier and Roth's data. It didn't take them long to reach a conclusion. When Meier heard that the President had received their report he went to Washington to obtain a copy. He was in the Vice President's White House office when Humphrey called Johnson and asked to see the report. Meier listened to the exchange over a speaker phone.

"No, you can't have a copy, Hubert," he heard Johnson say.

"But Lyndon, I'm the Vice President."

"I don't give a goddamn who you are. It's national security and you're not getting it. You'd only give it to Meier and he'll give it to Hughes."

Johnson's hawks had done the unexpected. Instead of clearing the AEC, they had found something disturbing. Humphrey and Meier wondered just how bad it could be if Johnson was so adamantly opposed to their seeing it.

4

THE CIA TAKES NOTICE

As his glee at Robert Kennedy's Assassination showed, Don Nixon was a ruthless supporter of his brother. He knew Meier's political leanings were incompatible with his own but was dazzled by the prospect of using Meier's position with Hughes for his own purposes. He could not afford to let political differences sour their relationship. Meier's motives for working with Nixon were equally calculated. Hughes wanted Don Nixon kept happy and it was Meier's duty to oblige.

Don Nixon regarded himself as one of his brother's greatest assets as John Ehrlichman, Richard Nixon's domestic affairs advisor, noted in his autobiography *Witness to Power*. Ehrlichman admitted that Nixon's professional campaigners showed little enthusiasm for Don's help. Don Nixon was convinced that Meier was his precious pipeline into the highest echelons of the Democratic Party through which he could keep his brother informed on his political enemy's plans, a singular service which Ehrlichman and all the rest could never match. Even though the polls suggested Nixon enjoyed an insurmountable lead over the Vice President, Don Nixon began quizzing Meier about Humphrey within days of the Democratic Party leadership convention in Chicago. Don meant his partisan interest in Humphrey to appear innocuous but he was far from discreet and before long Meier told the Vice President about his probing.

Humphrey saw this as a unique opportunity to feed disinformation to

Richard Nixon. Meier's opportunity arrived when Don began questioning him about Humphrey's thoughts concerning national issues — the war, civil unrest — and what he might do if elected. It was an obvious attempt to discover Humphrey's agenda through gossip. Meier said he didn't know but sometimes he received advance copies of Humphrey's proposed speeches and that it probably wouldn't do any harm if he let Don have them, provided he didn't tell anyone. Nixon swore he wouldn't. With Humphrey's approval, Meier turned over a number of speeches which Humphrey delivered verbatim some days later.

Emboldened by these little triumphs, Don began asking if Meier had any information from Humphrey's pollsters. Meier grew evasive. All he knew was that his friend Napolitan had conducted a poll but it was being closely guarded by Humphrey's campaign team, led by Larry O'Brien.

It was through George Clifford, a journalist, that Meier and Humphrey found a way to subvert Richard Nixon. Meier first met Clifford through Bill Haddad, a backroom political power broker he had enlisted against the AEC. One of columnist Jack Anderson's confederates, Clifford had a career as rich in intrigue as Meier's. He infiltrated radical organizations such as the Nazi Party and was one of the first American reporters to interview Fidel Castro in the mountains. Clifford loathed Richard Nixon with an intensity surpassing even Meier's.

Meier told Clifford of Don Nixon's barefaced enquiries and of Humphrey's plan to let him trawl in a couple of mines along with the catch. Clifford pounced on the opportunity. He said that Meier should convince Humphrey to let him have a copy of the poll and he would produce a counterfeit that could be fed to the Nixons. If they fell for it, this might influence their strategy to their own disadvantage. Humphrey was amused by the notion.

"Sure," he said when Meier told him of Clifford's plan. "What harm can it do. I'm so far behind in the polls anyway, what does it matter?"

Humphrey had a copy delivered to Clifford in Washington, who went to work on it immediately. The finished article was brought to Meier in Las Vegas.

The poll given to Clifford was the most extensive sampling of public opinion undertaken by the Democrats in the campaign and truly top secret. It contained an exhaustive study of both Humphrey's and Nixon's strengths and weaknesses, state by state, and issue by issue. It recommended how the

Democrats should structure their resources and campaign funds, which states were safe, which hung in the balance, which to abandon and which to fight for.

Clifford's brushwork was exquisite. Not only did he create a dreamscape of how the Democrats visualized the country — gilding the dreary and darkening the hopeful — but also he pastelled new portraits of Humphrey and Nixon, creating subtlety of character and psychology that existed in his fertile imagination only, but which were purported to be a synthesis of the country's feelings towards the candidates.

Within a few days of the document's arrival in Meier's office in the Frontier Hotel, Don Nixon entered to find twelve bound copies of the poll spread across the desk. Large letters on the outside plainly marked them as private polling results for Hubert Humphrey. Meier was liberally plastering "Confidential" over the covers. Nixon's eyes almost popped from his head.

"Er, John," he said. "What's that?"

"Oh, just some private information my friends compiled for Hubert Humphrey. We're doing him a favor and Xeroxing it. He wants about a hundred copies sent to party organizers."

"Gee, John, could I take a look?"

"I don't think so, Don. It's pretty private. I'm sorry you had to see it."

Don stood there with his eyes glued to the papers when the phone rang. Meier listened, then told Don he would have to hurry off — would he like to have lunch? Don nodded, but when Meier returned there was no sign of Don and one of the copies was missing.

Don's exuberance almost undid the plot. Later that afternoon Gene Bowen, the public relations agent at the International Hotel, asked Meier, "John, I'm a friend of yours and Don's — but are you missing any documents?"

"Not that I know of. Why?"

"Well, it's just that Don came rushing in here waving around a folder and hollering that it was the Democrats' blueprint for the election and he had to get it to his brother right away."

While Nixon had been chortling over his good fortune, Bowen asked where he obtained the document and was told that the Hughes organization was running off copies. His schoolboyish glee had so alarmed Bowen that he wondered if Don had taken something that perhaps he shouldn't have. It was essential that the story not proceed any further or suspicions might be aroused — Meier said nothing had been taken. Bowen looked doubtful but Meier assured him it was just Don being Don.

Another visitor to his office gave Meier more to ponder than Don Nixon's delight in purloining George Clifford's little book of tricks. Mike Merhige was one of Maheu's friends whom Meier had helped find a job in Hughes Aircraft. Meier had arranged for Merhige to be sent to Ecuador after putting him in touch with government officials there. After the usual courtesies Merhige became reflective and said the Company wanted to thank him for all his help. Meier couldn't imagine how his visitor could be speaking on behalf of a company he had only recently joined or why Hughes Aircraft would be so grateful.

Merhige added that Meier's help was especially important in the Company's fight against subversion. Meier stared at him in bewilderment. The euphemisms then disappeared as Merhige announced that if it weren't for "us in the CIA" the world would be overrun by Communists. Meier tried to hide his amazement. Maheu had never mentioned who these men were.

Never having met a self-confessed CIA agent, Meier attempted to satisfy his curiosity about how they worked and before long Merhige had showed him his identification and was expanding on the topic of the Cold War, which would assuredly be lost, he said, without the agency's efforts and the help of its numerous friends among whom Meier was now numbered. Merhige had adroitly maneuvered the conversation to its climax. "The agency," he said, "is concerned about the election this year and wants to see our friends elected."

He made no mention of the presidency but spoke of lesser lights, of Senators and Congressmen. "Howard Hughes has a number of companies as well as his medical foundation and the agency would be most appreciative if he would support the campaigns of our friends," Merhige said.

Specifically, he was asking for money and Meier did his best not to appear stunned by the realization that the CIA was asking Hughes to finance an unspecified number of political campaigns. Meier knew enough about the CIA to know that it was forbidden by charter from operating within the United States. But here was a CIA agent brazenly announcing a scheme to sprinkle the Senate and Congress with politicians it favored.

Meier promised to bring it up with Hughes, who then requested a list of eligible politicians. A single sheet of paper containing thirty-one names arrived on September 2, satisfying Meier's curiosity about which candidates the CIA found politically acceptable. In hindsight, the most intriguing name among them was that of Gerald Ford, then an obscure congressman from Michigan. Meier passed it up to Hughes' suite.

It didn't take Meier long to deduce that Robert A. Maheu and Associates[1] was little more than a CIA front in the very heart of Hughes' empire. In retrospect, Hughes' decision to place him on Maheu's payroll so he could conduct guerrilla warfare against the AEC — one of the institutions the CIA would protect at all costs — was an example of how preposterous Hughes could be.

Merhige went off to Ecuador under cover of selling a Hughes Aircraft satellite communications system. He blundered about so badly that he was spotted as a phony and Meier later received some awkward letters from his contacts wondering what Merhige was doing and why Meier had recommended him. He was too embarrassed to be truthful.

When Nixon's victory was announced, Meier was sitting at home feeling depressed and wretched. A year of such promise had been laid waste. Kennedy was dead, King was dead, Humphrey had been denied the White House by the slimmest of margins, and the despised Richard Nixon was President-elect. His depressing reflections were interrupted by the sound of his telephone ringing. Hubert Humphrey's controlled stammer was on the other end.

"John, John, I — I heard from my boy Bob that you're feeling down. Well, John don't worry. We fought a good fight and we nearly pulled it off. If we'd had another week we'd have done it for sure. Now about Nixon, John, don't feel bitter for his beating us because that's just the way of politics."

Soon Democrats, particularly Humphrey and Meier, would be so disgusted by Nixon that by 1972 such magnanimity would give way to plotting vengeance. Their success was made possible by Nixon's inability to refrain from playing the moth to Hughes' candle.

On January 20, 1969, Richard Nixon was inaugurated. A grand ball was held in the White House to mark his accession and among the thousands of guests at the ceremonies were John and Jennie Meier.

Nixon had gained the reputation of a bought man during the 1960 presidential campaign, following the disclosure of a $205,000 payment from Hughes four years earlier. Surely now that his feet were planted firmly inside the White House, all the taint of scandal was behind him. It mattered little that he had enjoyed an enormous lead over Hubert Humphrey at the beginning of the race and had almost lost it at the end when the contest turned into one of the closest of the century.

At the Inaugural ball Don pulled Meier aside. The President's brother was tasting bliss. Here under the roof of the White House the cream of American society was paying homage to a Nixon. Don was as derisive and partisan as ever in mocking Humphrey, whom he knew to be Meier's friend. His theory of how Humphrey had almost stolen the race back made Meier think wistfully of the faked dossier and what might have happened had the campaign gone on longer.

"I just can't believe how dumb those Democrats were," Don began. "We heard through the grapevine" — he managed this without a blush — "that they were going to give up certain states and work like hell in others. But it just shows you how disorganized they were." He shook his head and rolled his eyes in disbelief. "Their local people just didn't follow orders. In the states they were ordered to abandon they worked like hell and it just about cost us the election."

At another time, in another place, Meier probably would have fallen down laughing. But the defeat was still bitter and all he could manage was a wan smile.

It would take Richard Milhous Nixon precisely forty-eight days from this inauguration to renew his surreptitious relationship with Hughes — this time it would cost him everything. As for John Meier, it was his tragic misfortune to witness what passed between them.

The stage for Nixon's downfall was set the moment Hughes' emissaries arrived in Washington, at the height of the celebrations, determined that Hughes would have Air West. Meier had already spoken to Don about the need for political goodwill and Don was busy convincing his contacts in the Senate not to get in Hughes' way. The job of getting the Civil Aeronautics Board to approve Hughes' takeover was handled by Maheu and Chester Davis, Hughes' New York lawyer.

That spring while Maheu and company worked in Washington, Meier was off in Puerto Rico meeting with the Governor. On March 5, Hughes reached Meier in San Juan and ordered him to Miami. He was to see Ken Wright, the head of the Howard Hughes Medical Institute three days later.

"John, I'm arranging to give some financing to Mr. Nixon from the

Institute," Hughes told him. "You go over there and get in touch with Wright."

Hughes did not disclose what he expected of him or why he wanted to give Nixon money only two months after his inauguration. Obviously, it could not be a campaign contribution, but Meier had long since learned not to ask unnecessary questions. He left San Juan and arrived in Miami as instructed on March 8. He stayed at the Airport Hotel, contacted Wright and was invited to dinner.

In the afternoon a blustering Don Nixon called from Washington.

"John, I've heard through the grapevine that Howard Hughes is going to give a sizable contribution to my brother today. Is that right?"

Not knowing what Hughes had in mind, Meier said nothing. Don complained that the contribution should be made through him.

"I've done a lot of work for Howard Hughes on the Air West deal. You know I have. I should be the one handling any contributions to my brother."

Meier took refuge in ignorance. He said he wasn't sure what was going on. Nixon kept complaining until Meier hung up. That night Meier noticed unusual activity around the hotel. The comings and goings of various parties of men had the trappings of a security sweep. He spotted them active in the lobby, near the elevators, in and around the dining room.

In the dining room he met Wright, who was accompanied by his wife and two other men he said were members of the CIA. By now, there was nothing unusual in Meier running into CIA agents while conducting Hughes' business, but it was odd that these two agents would be involved with the Medical Institute. It was, after all, a public charity.[2]

During dinner Wright asked Meier if he would do him a favor.

"Could you keep this until tomorrow?" he asked, offering Meier a large, locked briefcase. Meier took it.

"I'm having a meeting in the morning with Bebe Rebozo, so leave this in your room and I'll come by for it."

Wright gave Meier Rebozo's phone number at Key Biscayne and then the party broke up. With the briefcase under his arm, Meier went back to his room and slept.

He was awakened by Wright at 7 a.m. Wright had barely stepped inside when he asked for the briefcase. Meier pulled it from under the bed.

"My God, John, thanks a lot," said Wright. He tossed it on the bed and worked the combination locks until the lid popped open. Meier held his breath at the sight. The bills were stacked in two rows — each about 18 inches long —on opposite sides of the briefcase. Wright fussed with the blocks of money, nervously straightening them out as if so much cash demanded the dignity of an orderly presentation. Meier remained transfixed until he recovered enough of his composure to ask "What the hell's that?"

"What the hell's it look like?" Wright shot back. "It's a million dollars." The rows were made up of $100 bills. They weren't lying flat but stacked neatly on edge — two rows, five thousand bills in each.

"A million dollars? For what?" demanded Meier. But he knew for what. Wright was about to open his mouth when the phone rang.

"Hi, Bebe," Meier heard him say. "Come right up." He gave the caller Meier's room number. Meier found he couldn't take his eyes off the money. There was a knock on the door and while Wright went to open it, Meier walked into the bathroom and closed the door. He wanted no part of this. Hughes was giving Nixon $1 million from the Medical Institute, ostensibly a public charity but in reality a tax haven. The magnitude of the deal caused Meier to sweat. He panicked at the thought of being involved, no matter how innocently.

Beyond the door he heard Rebozo and Wright talking and the shuffling hiss of banknotes being dealt into new piles. He wiped the moisture from his brow and gave a short nervous cough before joining them, feeling he had been trapped into witnessing an obscenity.

In his heart Meier now knew why Hughes had placed him there. Political payoffs were not his forte — they were Maheu's — but the discrepancy in stories over the supposed Humphrey payoff, trivial compared to this, had obviously been resolved in his favor. His discreet cough caused Rebozo to leap from the bed in fright.

"What the fuck's Meier doing here?" he shouted in alarm.

"It's all right," said Wright. "Mr. Hughes knows all about it."

"Well, I don't know all about it," snarled Rebozo, unable to restrain his shock and anger at Meier's sudden appearance. Grabbing at the money strewn over the bed, he began furiously stuffing it into the briefcase. He slammed the case shut and ran from the room.

Still sweating, Meier asked Wright for an explanation. Wright, bewildered by Rebozo's abrupt departure, didn't offer much.

"Didn't Mr. Hughes tell you?"

"No," said Meier. "It was a just a vague call to come and see you about some contribution being made to Nixon. Nothing about this."

Wright just shrugged. "All I know is it's for the President. Mr. Hughes arranged it. The President wanted Bebe to handle it, not his brother Don."

One casual phone call from Hughes had thus implicated Meier in the event which would haunt Richard Nixon for the remainder of his presidency. It is certain that Rebozo would have reported his consternation at Meier's presence to the President, thus fixating Nixon's attention on John Meier.

Hughes' and Nixon's parts in the affair are obvious but the CIA's role is mysterious. The agency was riding shotgun on the delivery of an immense bribe destined for the highest public official in the land. The CIA's presence at the dinner table when Meier innocently accepted charge of the money showed this. As for the activity around the Airport Hotel prior to the arrival of the briefcase, undoubtedly this was to ensure the safety of its contents.

What bargain had been struck between Hughes and Nixon, Meier was never sure. Pacts such as theirs are never committed to paper. Still, while Meier understood the money was for Air West, he could not ignore the possibility that Hughes thought he was also buying a halt to AEC tests.

Four months later, Hughes got his way with Air West. The Civil Aeronautics Board fast-tracked its approval and shortly afterwards Nixon gave the deal his blessing.

Richard Nixon and Howard Hughes were not the only ones with good reasons for not wanting their business known; the CIA would be nervous too. The secret transaction linked three powerful entities — the presidency, the CIA and the Hughes empire — whose vital interests would be imperilled by any disclosure of what had happened in that room in the Airport Hotel. Meier was safe with his secret as long as he was one of Hughes' trusted lieutenants.

Barely a month after being party to a scandal involving a Nixon, Meier was privy to one involving a Kennedy. The affair in Miami was stamped with the familiar Nixon greed; the Kennedy affair in Las Vegas bore that family's hallmark — sordid sexuality. The CIA was also present, though this time its agents were not merely watchers. They were pulling all the strings.

In the spring of 1969, Senator Edward Kennedy was the great hope of the Democrats to beat Richard Nixon in the 1972 election. A handsome, tragic figure, the latent sympathy for him attracted thousands of well-wishers and supporters whenever he appeared in public. The fates of his brothers created a desire among many to see a Kennedy in the White House — as if this could provide national absolution. Nixon, who had narrowly scraped by Humphrey, was being measured for his political coffin.

On April 25, 1969, Kennedy came to Las Vegas. He met with Meier and discussed the anti-ballistic missile program that would involve a new range of nuclear tests in Nevada. As well, he came to pay a political debt to Nevada Senator Howard Cannon who had helped him become Senate Whip.

He arrived like visiting royalty. Crowds jammed the airport and later that night two thousand people came to hear him speak. However, travelling ahead of the Senator was a CIA dirty tricks team which had arranged with a hotel employee to hire a woman to seduce the Senator. One of the team members was a Cuban-American with the *nom de guerre* Virgino Gonzales. A showgirl was admitted to Kennedy's room while Gonzales and his team took pictures and recorded the details.

Two days later, Meier was at the Washington Hilton attending the annual meeting of the Chamber of Commerce of the United States when one of Attorney General John Mitchell's staff approached and asked if Meier would step into an adjoining room for a chat with Mitchell. Meier found him in high spirits.

"John, tell me all about the situation in Las Vegas," Mitchell said in a suggestive tone.

"What situation?"

"The situation with Teddy Kennedy."

"What situation is that?"

"The one with him in the hotel room with a woman. We have information on it and we're looking into it."

He was almost snickering. Meier said he knew nothing of it, which seemed to disappoint Mitchell.

The CIA had a vested interest in never seeing another Kennedy elected President. The poisonous relationship which existed between the brothers and the agency dated back to John F. Kennedy's presidency. The White House would want Ted Kennedy ruined because of the man's popularity.

Within the hour, Meier called Napolitan, a close friend of Kennedy, to warn him. Then he called Moe Dalitz, owner of the Sands Hotel, where the affair had taken place. Dalitz promised retribution against any of his employees who were involved. Meier wrote a report to Hughes who accepted it without comment.

On the night of July 18, Kennedy's car rolled into the Chappaquiddick, a small Massachusetts river. His passenger, Mary Jo Kopechne, drowned. Kennedy escaped with only minor physical injuries but he was suspected of drunk driving and negligence in escaping without rescuing his passenger. There wasn't a newspaper in the world which didn't seize the story.

At the height of all this salacious speculation, when Kennedy's handlers were hardest pressed, Meier received a tip from a reporter that the two Las Vegas dailies were compiling a story of Kennedy's indiscretion with the showgirl. This would surely be the *coup de grace.* He called Kennedy's brother-in-law Steve Smith, who was appalled. "Good God, we can't have this coming out. It would be a disaster," said Smith.[3]

For the next couple of weeks Kennedy's aides did all they could to dissuade reporters from running the story. Smith told Meier they had called in all their markers with the press, pleading that Kennedy had been set up and deserved their sympathy. It worked on everyone except one reporter in Las Vegas, Cohn McKinlay. He published a periodical called the *Nevada Report,* a sort of *Private Eye* whose masthead promised to deliver "The Story Behind the News."

On August 23, Meier called Larry O'Brien and Napolitan and asked them to warn Smith that McKinlay's story would be out September first and nothing he could do would prevent it. Smith called and asked Meier to plead with McKinlay once more but nothing Meier said could alter McKinlay's determination. The story appeared as promised but remarkably went no further than the *Nevada Report's* limited circulation — testimony to the effectiveness of the smothering operation undertaken by Smith, Napolitan and O'Brien.

Meier met a rueful Kennedy in his Washington office on September 12.

"I was foolish enough to put myself in that position," Kennedy said, "and that's the last time that's going to happen."

Meier did not know it but the CIA was fully aware of his warning to the Democrats and his campaign to thwart their attempt to make full use of the sex trap. Later, Gonzales complained of the operation being ruined by Meier and noted ominously that "Meier annoyed the Company."

Just as portentous was the sudden hostility toward Meier emanating from the White House. His association with the President's two brothers,

Don and Edward Nixon, had recently been encouraged by Richard himself. Now he was being treated as an enemy. Ehrlichman documents this situation in *Witness to Power*, a chapter of which is devoted to the relationship between Meier and Don Nixon. Ehrlichman argues Richard Nixon feared his family's naivete might lead them into embarrassing business or personal relationships. For this reason Richard wanted Don Nixon separated from John Meier.

In advancing this idea, however, Ehrlichman is affecting ignorance of Richard Nixon's use of his family for dealing with the likes of Howard Hughes or grand embezzler Robert Vesco. Don was his surrogate in dealings with Hughes; it was his nephew Donald Jr. — Don's son — in dealings with Vesco. Richard Nixon's supposed fear of his family being associated with undesirables has little credibility since Nixon saw fit to send his nephew to work for Vesco, who looted hundreds of millions of dollars of investors' monies before fleeing the country.

Ehrlichman's account of the relationship between Meier and Don Nixon, whether through ignorance or malice, is misleading. It is, however, valuable as the personal memoir of an intimate collaborator in the Nixon intrigues — not only a witness to power, but to its systematic abuse at Nixon's hands.

Ehrlichman was a member of a clique that did not hesitate to engage all the massive gears of government to crush its enemies. He provides the only insight into the discussions of the Meier problem at the presidential level and his is the only story which hints at the anxiety which Nixon and Rebozo experienced after Meier unwittingly walked into a million dollar payoff. He writes:

> Don did not seem to understand the potential peril of his appearing once again to do business with Hughes. We could not convince him that the slightest hint of a contemporary connection between Hughes and Nixon would resurrect all the old innuendo surrounding Hannah's (the Nixons' mother) loan.

Nixon's great fear of a Hughes connection appeared at about the time of the business in Miami. Meier's witnessing of that transaction must have caused panic, as his ties to Humphrey and the Kennedys were well-known. It would seem that Ehrlichman had no direct knowledge of the bribe.

Obviously, the basis of the President's fear must have been that Meier might disclose details of the payoff, not the unlikely possibility that Don Nixon would somehow make himself Hughes' business partner. The fear was not of "old innuendo" being resurrected, but of a contemporary and hitherto unpublicized scandal which would make the old one appear trivial.

In November, immediately following his election, Nixon apparently was not worried about old innuendo when he sent Don off to Las Vegas with a letter to Meier seeking suggestions as to how the government could employ Edward Nixon. Hughes quickly spotted a double opportunity. For some time, Meier had been buying up mining properties in the southwestern states on Hughes' behalf and Hughes wanted federal subsidies to reopen many of the old mines. Meier coupled a recommendation for Edward Nixon's employment in environmental research to a proposal seeking federal money for Hughes' mining interests.

Here is Ehrlichman's account of the Meier-Don Nixon business:

> By the spring of 1969 I was hearing all kinds of stories of Don's dealings with John Meier, his solicitation of business from international airlines and other potential problems for the President; if I were going to discharge my responsibility to the President, I had to know at first hand what Don was doing. So I asked him to come East to review all his "activities" with me.
>
> When Don came to the White House, I asked him about his connection to the Hughes organization and John Meier. I knew something was going on because Bebe Rebozo had reports from some of the Hughes people he knew. Interestingly, the Hughes executives were as concerned as we were. They didn't want to be accused of attempting to influence the Administration through Don. (That was, perhaps, more a measure of their low opinion of Don Nixon than a testament to Hughes' reluctance to influence government.) Don denied any connection whatever with Meier or Hughes. His denial to me was so loud and red-faced that I felt intuitively he was lying...

Nixon wasn't lying, if Ehrlichman was accusing him of having business connections with Meier. Notwithstanding Ehrlichman's beliefs to the contrary, John Meier and Don Nixon were never in business together.

After delving into Don's hypothetical jealousy of Richard, the arch-achiever of the family, Ehrlichman says he didn't attempt to psychoanalyze the President's brother: "I just gave him the sermon: he was to get off the gravy train at once, leave John Meier alone and lead a life of quiet rectitude."

Ehrlichman implies he was the one who was concerned about the relationship, but when his words are sifted, the inescapable conclusion is that he is referring to reports from either Bebe Rebozo or Richard Nixon. They had transmitted their anxiety to Ehrlichman and Bob Haldeman, the White House chief of staff. This apprehension was manifested in the remarkable series of events which occurred shortly after his lecture to Don.

"Within a few days," writes Ehrlichman, "the President, Bob Haldeman and I again talked about Don's connection with Howard Hughes. I described Don's voluble but unconvincing denial of his frequent contacts with John Meier of Hughes. Don had given his brother the same denials when he met with him..."

How could Don Nixon possibly deny such a connection in speaking to his brother? The Nixons, Meier and Hughes were all aware of the liaison and its purpose. If the President feigned ignorance of this backstairs access to his office it was only to hide its existence from his aides. Nixon knew that it was how Hughes chose to do business with him and, as much as he wanted to break the Meier-Don Nixon pipeline, he was afraid of offending Hughes.

It didn't take the President long to call in the CIA. In the spring of 1969, John Meier was marked for special attention by a group of people who had the full apparatus of government at their command.

One must remember that ostensibly what was bothering Nixon was the potential for political fallout and whether his brother was still in contact with Meier. It seems odd that he required the services of the CIA to accomplish this. Ehrlichman is specific on the point that it had nothing to do with him — it was Nixon himself who casually mentioned the need for surveillance. More properly, Nixon could have gone to the FBI, which at least would have been operating within its jurisdiction, but he wasn't about to let J. Edgar Hoover know too much about his brother, says Ehrlichman. Just as likely, Nixon didn't want Hoover knowing too much about his recent enrichment.

"(Nixon) could not add Don to the Kissinger surveillance list if the FBI was going to do the work. On the other hand, having Don monitored by someone was clearly a good idea; we ought to know what sort of problems he was creating for us," writes Ehrlichman. "So Nixon instructed me to have the CIA put a 'full cover' on Don, reporting to the President through me. The agency could be counted on to keep a confidence, if J. Edgar Hoover could not."

Ehrlichman took the request to the CIA's deputy director, Robert Cushman, who declined the assignment, arguing piously that "the law specifically forbade the CIA to engage in such domestic surveillance activities and that the agency was afraid to undertake such a project."

It is ironic to hear such reticence from the CIA, considering what it had just done to Edward Kennedy. However, there is another explanation for the CIA's refusal. There was no need to carry out Ehrlichman's request. The agency had already begun surveillance of Meier in 1968 after finding he was involved in the campaign to set up a legal defense fund for Daniel Ellsberg, the Pentagon official who was indicted for his theft of the Pentagon Papers. The agency would already know everything about Meier's relationship with Don Nixon. Faced with this rebuff — if Ehrlichman is telling the whole story — Nixon again refused to call the FBI and turned to the Secret Service for help.

For six weeks, from May 27 until July 8, 1969, writes Ehrlichman, the Secret Service trailed Don Nixon around Southern California, New York, New Orleans and Las Vegas, sending in reports every three or four days. Between them, the CIA and the Secret Service had full cover on Meier and Don Nixon. Their sharing of surveillance data clearly showed it was a joint operation.[4]

The Secret Service received the President's approval to tap Don's phones. Ehrlichman said the results confirmed "our worst concerns." Despite the denials, "it was clear that he (Don) was up to his ears in the kinds of 'really big deals' with John Meier and others that might eventually embarrass his brother."

The agents followed the pair and their families to Disneyland where they watched Nixon and Meier in "heavy conversation" on a number of occasions.

Ehrlichman eventually reached the heart of the affair — the fabled finder's fee Hughes was paying for services rendered in his acquisition of Air West.

With the Secret Service eavesdropping, Don Nixon is heard talking about his part in helping Hughes acquire Air West. He is also overheard speaking of his claim to a "multimillion dollar finder's fee for his alleged part in the merger." No date is given for this phone call, but it seems to have occurred sometime in early June based on the order of other calls logged by the Secret Service.

At this point in his narrative, Ehrlichman says that Don's claims for the finder's fee were not taken seriously and that another item was "added to his litany of grievances." By the end of June, Don appears to realize his claim had been extinguished. "His callers were hearing Don blame me for his loss of the finder's fee for the Air West acquisition by Hughes. He felt I was interfering in his 'legitimate' business deals..."

By dismissing Nixon's complaints as little more than the ramblings of a crackpot, Ehrlichman gives the impression that he knows little of the background. Had he known the efforts made by the President and Rebozo to prevent Don Nixon getting between them and the finder's fee, and Don's subsequent outrage at being cut out, he might not have been so flippant.

On July 6, Don Nixon — apparently bowing to the pressure from Ehrlichman to distance himself from Meier — travelled to Las Vegas for the opening of the International Hotel and called Meier to say they could no longer meet publicly. The President's aide doesn't say how this piece of information was obtained. Either Nixon's hotel room phone in Las Vegas or Meier's home phone was bugged.

Ehrlichman then says the pair agreed to meet secretly on July 8 in California near Don's home in Orange County. Meier, using an assumed name, flew to Santa Ana Airport where the pair were photographed. In reality, Meier, as owner of Meier Thoroughbreds, had come to meet actor Dale Robertson who also owned horses. By coincidence Don Nixon was also in the airport. The pair met unexpectedly and had lunch. Meier invited Nixon to look at Robertson's horses and at 5:00 p.m. flew back to Las Vegas. Later, Secret Service agents visited Robertson and demanded to know what they had been discussing.

The intelligence gathered during this six-week surveillance of Don Nixon, comprising written reports and photographs of Nixon and Meier, was given to the President through Ehrlichman. Without elaborating, he says he also received oral reports of subjects "too sensitive" to be committed to paper, including information about Don's eldest son Donny. Only Ehrlichman knows the scope of those other subjects, but Meier knew Donny Nixon and had received a number of letters from him. Possibly the reason no one wanted to commit details about Donny to paper was that he, under orders from the President, was in the Bahamas working for the infamous Robert Vesco.

In July, the President and his advisors met again to discuss his brother and Meier. Nixon told Ehrlichman to confront Don with proof that he "had lied to us about Meier" but Ehrlichman warned him that Don, a compulsive talker, might get angry and "generate vast press attention." Nixon decided to summon Don to the White House.

"I later learned that the President had enlisted Bebe Rebozo to help. Rebozo knew Robert Maheu and Richard Danner, both of whom worked for Howard Hughes. They would be asked to order John Meier to stay away from Don," wrote Ehrlichman.

Again the President took the indirect route. Instead of telling Hughes he didn't want Meier to act as a go-between any longer, Nixon enlisted the help of those he imagined could pull rank on Meier within the organization. This approach indicates that he and Ehrlichman had an imperfect understanding of Meier's relationship with Hughes. Meier worked directly for Hughes, not Maheu. At this time in 1969, Meier was under orders from Hughes to find a way to have Maheu ousted and the Nevada Operations liquidated. Maheu had tried for a number of years to get Meier fired but Hughes would never allow it.

Finally, on August 31 the Nixon brothers met, wrote Ehrlichman, and Don handed Richard a list of his gripes. Nowhere in this list, or in the subsequent discussion, is John Meier mentioned. Considering the surveillance, the photographs, the phone taps and the subjects too sensitive for the written word, this might seem strange if the Nixons' understanding of Meier's role wasn't taken for granted. It was Ehrlichman and Rebozo who wanted Don to distance himself from the Hughes organization, not his brother. Rebozo had transacted the payoff without him and Ehrlichman had been levering him away from Meier by threats and intimidation ever since. Don Nixon, if nothing else, was truly loyal to Richard. It is inconceivable that he would have disobeyed a direct order, had the President ordered him to stop seeing Meier.

All this activity recorded by Ehrlichman — the requests for CIA assistance, the Secret Service surveillance, the meetings, the time and effort expended — can never be explained or justified on the basis of a White House fear that Don Nixon would draw attention to an old family indiscretion with Howard Hughes. What if someone did take notice of

Don's relationship with Meier? His attempts to capitalize on his brother's name had been extensively reported twelve years earlier. Only fear of the Miami payoff being made public could account for the hysteria gripping the Oval Office in the spring of 1969 and Meier's sudden unpopularity.

Ehrlichman writes of further escapades of Don Nixon and John Meier in the Dominican Republic leaving the impression that it was all a romp in the sun with Meier and Nixon hoping to enrich themselves at the expense of the Dominicans.

> The U.N. Ambassador of the Dominican Republic, Dr. Luis Gonzalez Torrado, was the host of a four-day junket for Meier and his party, which included Alaska Senator Mike Gravel; a political consultant to the Democrats, Joe Napolitan; one Anthony Hatsis, listed as a "geologist" and, of course, Don Nixon.

Meier was a frequent visitor to the Republic. He had business interests on the island and had met with President Joaquin Balaguer several times. Balaguer was fighting for a better deal from the U.S. government and the multinational corporations that controlled the prices paid for sugar and ore exported to the United States. Meier supported Balaguer's efforts and spoke out against the sugar quotas imposed by the Nixon administration. He also compiled reports on the possible treatment of pollution problems affecting the island.

Because of Meier's support, Balaguer invested him as a Knight Commander of the Order of Christopher Columbus, the highest honor the country could bestow on a foreigner. To mark the occasion, Balaguer declared October 23 John Meier Day. U.S. Ambassador Francis Meloy attended the ceremony.

According to Ehrlichman, the ambassador warned the White House that Don Nixon "might be heading the President into serious embarrassment in that warm pastoral island" when Meloy discovered Don was part of Meier's party. Meloy reports that Don Nixon and Meier had private meetings with the country's National Development Commission during which the commission was told a group of investors were interested in putting $200 million into mining ventures there. The story was leaked to the local press. Meloy also reports on the investiture, the party and receptions, and the cruise by Meier and his friends aboard a frigate as guests of the Dominican Republic's Navy.

When they left the island on October 26, several newspapers carried a contradictory statement from Nixon stressing the visit was unofficial and denying any interest in investing in the country.

"That statement," wrote Ehrlichman, "was, of course, the product of close collaboration between Meloy and me in our many telephone calls during Don's visit." He added that the ambassador did an effective job of explaining to the President's brother how his wheeling and dealing looked down there.

"The Dominicans wanted more U.S. aid. If they could gain favor with the Nixon family by granting mineral concessions... they'd be glad to trade."

Ehrlichman ends his account of the Dominican Republic caper on a note of mystery: "And finally, in June of 1971, for no apparent reason, President Joaquin Balaguer of the Dominican Republic wrote me a three line note, thanking me for my 'help and genuine sympathy for the problems' of his country. I don't know why he wrote me, but I like to think it's because Frank Meloy and I derailed Don Nixon before he could work out one of his big deals for the Dominicans."

More likely Balaguer was thanking him for his life, as there was more to Meier and Nixon's trip than Ehrlichman is letting on. The day following Meier's investiture, Torrado pulled Meier aside and asked if he could arrange for Don Nixon to meet secretly with President Balaguer on an urgent matter. The President, it seemed, had just received some startling information. Meier agreed to bring Nixon to the Presidential Palace. After slipping away from their companions they were picked up in a limousine and driven to the palace where they were received by Balaguer and Torrado in the President's private apartment. Torrado placed armed guards outside in the corridor and locked the door behind them. Meier felt the tension. Nixon appeared oblivious. Both Balaguer and Torrado were nervous and fidgety. Torrado paced back and forth until finally he said — "Gentlemen, we'd like to get some information directly through to the President of the United States."

Torrado said that they had an agent inside the American embassy who had discovered plans to have Balaguer overthrown, if not assassinated. The U.S. was unhappy with Balaguer's perceived threats to American interests in the Dominican Republic.

Meier protested that his government would never do such a thing. But Torrado reached into the desk and produced a tape recorder.

"Please, listen to this, if you doubt us," he said. Meier and Nixon could hear a recording of two men talking over the phone.

"I know that voice," said Don, "it's Francis Meloy, the ambassador."

Torrado said he was right, but they didn't know who the other was. The ambassador and his caller were discussing how troublesome Balaguer had become with his demands for a better sugar quota and other complaints, and how something would have to be done if he didn't stay in line. Meloy said he would have to be replaced and the other quite casually replied, "all we have to do is have him hit — we can set it up the right away and make it look like the Communists did it..."

At that point Balaguer leaned over and stopped the tape. "Mr. Nixon, all I'm interested in is seeing my country prosper. If you could get to your brother privately and tell him what has happened I would greatly appreciate it. I would just like him to know what was said. I am asking for no favors."

The President left and Meier and Nixon sat looking at Torrado who said the Dominicans had proof Meloy was a member of the CIA. (He did not disclose what exactly the proof was but later when Meloy was assassinated in Lebanon, Meier wondered if the word had been out on him.)

Torrado asked Don to consider taking Balaguer's plea to his brother. The next day, as planned, Meier's party went aboard a frigate for a jaunt up the coast. Then Meier and Nixon were again separated from the others and taken to Balaguer's beach house. When Nixon met Balaguer, he promised to go directly to his brother, much to Balaguer's relief. Nixon said he would not send a note or phone him but would meet him face to face.

Some weeks later Meier asked if he had talked to his brother.

"I did but geez, John, that's the last time I interfere in anything like that. I'll never do it again, not for Balaguer, not for anyone," huffed Nixon.

Don thought he was making a confidential report to his brother but found instead he had stirred up the CIA. Shortly after his report of plans to assassinate Balaguer, the agency sent agents to California to interrogate him. They forced him to write a report on what he had been told, who had been present at his meetings with Balaguer, what he had remembered of the tape recording and all the inconsequential details of his trip to the Dominican Republic.

It seems likely that once the President heard what was happening in the

Dominican Republic, he told Ehrlichman. Ehrlichman likely told the CIA and the CIA rounded up Don for an explanation.

Balaguer obviously felt the Nixon Administration had saved his life and so he thanked Ehrlichman. Meanwhile, Ehrlichman's account of the Secret Service surveillance of Meier and Richard Nixon's brother provides this curious observation:

> As the reports came in I took them to the President, sometimes summarizing their contents for him orally, sometimes simply handing them to him for reading. He spent a long time looking at the photographs of Don and John Meier walking together.

It is a vivid image of a worried man mesmerized by those pictures. Nixon's thoughts can almost be read even at this distance.

5

HUGHES CLEANS HOUSE

Upon his return from the Dominican Republic, Meier resumed the battle with the AEC. As the testing season got underway he presented the agency with a list of questions — more demands than inquiries — which were designed to infuriate them:

Would the commission provide university scientists in Nevada and Utah instruments capable of monitoring fallout and x-ray emissions? Would it provide them with seismic equipment to measure and determine the epicenter of the blasts? Would it allow deep wells to be drilled on the range to determine if contaminants were escaping into the water systems? What was the total megatonnage proposed to be exploded in 1969, including those firings for the defense department? What had been exploded last year? Was the Benham firing in 1968 a repeat of Boxcar because President Johnson's scientific committee found that the AEC had failed in monitoring the radioactive, hydrological and seismic effects of Boxcar? And more ominously still: Was the AEC using the "volcanic tuft" found in the Pahute Mesa region of the site to hide the megatonnage of its defense department explosions? (Meier pointed out that this type of stratum would absorb three times the megatonnage, thereby misleading seismograph readings.)

Meier addressed his questions to Miller, who passed them on to Glen Seaborg, the chairman of the AEC. Seaborg in turn ignored Meier and sent his reply to Hughes. He refused to answer most of the questions, claiming that some had already been answered and others could not be for reasons of national security. Seaborg acknowledged the effect Hughes' political and media campaign was having and complained that it created an atmosphere of "harassment in our national security operations." His reply clearly harbors the suspicion — first expressed to Meier during his confrontation with Miller — that Howard Hughes was not controlling his side of the battlefield: "We have difficulty believing that the tone of the questions and the tactics of distributing them through a public relations company almost simultaneously with their transmission to the AEC, really reflects your personal approval."

Then Seaborg added: "Since much of the information requested... in your name has previously been furnished to members of your organization, the commission is not disposed to generate further communications without assurance from you that these additional questions transmitted in your name reflected your considered need for information not previously furnished... I would be pleased to discuss these matters with you directly and personally at any mutually convenient time."

Many people had had the same desire. But Hughes saw few people and Seaborg was never to be among them.

In April, a month after his million dollar transaction with Nixon, Hughes was outraged when Herb Klein, Nixon's press aide, gave a speech in Las Vegas promoting the Antiballistic Missile program and expressing the need for more underground tests.

Hughes drafted an imperious letter to the President, arguing against the deployment of an ABM system, on the grounds that it would lead to a similar system being developed by the enemy and would require a nuclear war to demonstrate its effectiveness. Nixon treated the letter as though it had been delivered in a diplomatic pouch from the Kremlin.

Two weeks later, Nixon told his national security advisor, Henry Kissinger, to go to Las Vegas and brief Hughes on the necessity of developing the ABM. Thankfully for Kissinger, Hughes' phobia wouldn't allow a meeting.

When the AEC announced that it was moving its heavy nuclear tests to Amchitka Alaska and that the Nevada range would be used only for smaller tests, it looked like a compromise to keep Hughes happy. If so, it was an arrangement Hughes rejected, as Nixon discovered when the AEC announced it planned to detonate an allegedly sub-megaton device in September.

When the bomb went off as planned on the morning of September 16 — despite hysterical appeals from Hughes to the White House to delay it — Hughes told Meier to let Nixon know through his brother that he was planning to leave Nevada but wouldn't go quietly.

In time, Hughes and Meier were proven right. The conspiracy of silence which maintained the fiction of a safe underground testing program would evaporate once scientists and others inside the AEC began doubting the program's safety. Among the first to speak out were Dr. John Gofman and Dr. Arthur Tamplin of the AEC's radiation health program.

Gofman had been a disciple and former graduate student of Seaborg.[1] He had been an active member of the commission's "Truth Squad," which toured the country during the 1950s, arguing with scientists like Nobel prize winner Linus Pauling who were demanding an end to nuclear testing. Gofman was then appointed to head the AEC's radiation health program.

Tamplin was a distinguished nuclear weaponry researcher who joined Gofman's program. Both were brilliant. Gofman's work led to isolating the world's first milligram of plutonium.

In their book, *Population Control,* they said that by 1967 they were convinced the AEC was wrong and projects such as Operation Plowshare, promoting the peaceful use of nuclear energy, would irreversibly pollute the earth and should be abandoned. In October 1969, Gofman said that levels of radiation emissions from a commercial nuclear reactor, considered acceptable by the government, would kill thousands of people each year.

Another proselyte was Colonel Raymond E. Brim, the U.S. Air Force officer responsible for monitoring nuclear fallout which drifted from the Nevada test site. He assumed his duties in 1966, the year Meier first took on the AEC. Using aircraft specially equipped to monitor radiation, his group routinely tracked the course of radioactive clouds. Brim later told a Congressional House Subcommittee probing nuclear fallout that there was indisputable evidence that people — not just those living in Utah or Nevada, but also in Canada and the Eastern U.S. — were being showered with radioactive debris from the firings.

He particularly mentioned the Schooner blast on December 8, 1968 as one which sent up a storm of radioactivity. The radioactive cloud emitted by this 30-kiloton explosion was tracked to Canada, at which point the airforce planes turned back. In a 1980 magazine article Brim argued that Americans had been exposed to dangerous levels of radiation from supposedly "safe" underground tests in the 1960s and '70s and were still in danger, as the tests continued.

"Just as the risk of fallout continues so does the conscious government effort to cover up," Brim said. The most damning and self-accusatory statements came from Gofman[2] who said that there was no way he could justify his failure to sound the alarm in the 1950s when testing was in the atmosphere.

"I feel that several hundred scientists trained in the biomedical aspect of atomic energy — myself included — are candidates for Nuremberg-type trials for crimes against humanity through our gross negligence and irresponsibility." He argued that exposing unsuspecting people to radioactivity was to use them as involuntary guinea pigs. "Now that we know the hazard of low dose radiation the crime is not experimentation — it's murder."

All this soul searching was wasted on the AEC. Wrapping themselves in the flag and invoking national security, officials resolutely continued the Nevada program. As a consequence, a legacy of suffering has been inherited by the inhabitants of towns in Nevada, Utah and Arizona.

To give this needless suffering just one human face, there is the story of Preston Truman, born in the small Utah town of Enterprise in 1951, the year the AEC began testing in Nevada. By the time he was 28 years old, eight of his boyhood friends were dead, victims of cancer. He was diagnosed as having lymphoma, a form of cancer, while in high school. After $100,000 worth of medical treatment the cancer went into remission. Meier's battles against the AEC made him a hero to Truman and those like him. Years later, long after Hughes was dead, former Alaska Senator Mike Gravel — an ardent foe of the nuclear industry — credited Meier's campaign against the AEC with preventing the spread of nuclear power within the United States. Gravel's contention is that the doubts raised about the safety of underground testing created a wariness among the public at a time when the nuclear industry was proposing the United States follow the Soviet Union and rely on nuclear power as a major source of electrical energy.

If Gravel is correct and the United States was deterred from reliance on nuclear energy by the furor raised by Hughes, then Meier's battle, so futile at first glance, would seem in retrospect to have been a handsome victory.

For three years the fight against the AEC had absorbed most of Meier's energies. That changed abruptly in 1969 when Hughes could no longer tolerate the serious financial losses he was suffering in his casinos. He suspected he was the victim of skimming and asked Meier to devise an electronic accounting system to track the cash obviously flowing into, and somehow mysteriously out of, his casinos.

Hughes' turning to Meier indicates he felt the responsibility for his financial embarrassment lay with Maheu's stewardship of his affairs. Maheu, after all, was the generalissimo in Las Vegas, the boss of the Nevada Operations. He lived like a prince on the half million dollars a year he drew in salary; the casinos and millions of dollars worth of real estate and mining properties were under his control.

His role as Hughes' alter ego would be exposed in a celebrated series of memos written between them which surfaced after Maheu's dethronement in 1970. There is no hint in any of these memos that Maheu's days were numbered. In the early summer of 1969, Maheu was luxuriating in the fullness of his powers and prestige. Hughes was careful not to show his hand until the moment he vanished. Although they never met, Hughes and Maheu compiled a remarkable correspondence which at times resembled the diaries of a separated couple making their way through an uncertain life. Between the "Bobs" and the "Dear Howards" were compressed aspirations and disappointments, worries, successes, misunderstandings, and jealousies. At times they rejoiced, indulged in unashamed flattery, protested undying devotion; on other occasions they fought, vented harsh thoughts, expressed estrangement, suffered remorse and sought forgiveness.

What makes their letters even more fascinating is that the correspondents were not thousands of miles apart but merely separated by hundreds of feet — the distance between Maheu's sumptuous home at the edge of the Desert Inn golf course and Hughes' spartan penthouse hideaway. However, the distance was unimportant; what made the separation complete was Hughes' desire never to allow Maheu into his presence.

Meier, on the other hand, did see Hughes. He had clearance to pass unhindered through his guards and servants, which made Maheu intensely jealous as well as apprehensive. Graced as Maheu was with all the trappings of power, he was never asked to ascend the back stairway.

Maheu made no secret of his desire to be rid of Meier and took every opportunity to petition Hughes for permission to fire him. Hughes always stayed his hand. This protection has baffled observers trying to read between the lines of the Hughes-Maheu memos of the spring of 1968 when the millionaire began acquiring gold and silver mines in California and Nevada.

At the time, the world's monetary systems were in chaos and pressure on the U.S. dollar and the price of gold was intense. Meier gave a widely reported speech, authored by Hughes, in Las Vegas arguing that the U.S. could solve its monetary problems by reopening old gold and silver mines which held known reserves of precious metals. The idea came during one of Hughes' nocturnal phone calls to Meier in which he discussed the problems of the deteriorating dollar.

The speech called for the government to end restraints on the price of gold kept at the artificially low price of $35 an ounce. Hughes predicted the U.S. would go off the gold standard. Once it did, the price of gold would soar and many previously unprofitable mines would be re-opened. Around the time Meier gave that speech he was acting on Hughes' behalf surreptitiously buying up old mines in Nevada, California and Utah, and with them gold reserves. Once he had them, Hughes began lobbying for government subsidies to pay for their reopening.

When Maheu read Meier's comments in the newspapers, he denounced him as treacherous and again appealed for his dismissal. His memo has never surfaced but Hughes' reply makes clear what it must have contained.

> Bob: You ask my advice as a friend. The only substantial loss involved here is to tie up some of these properties for our benefit. However, this may not be lost. We may perhaps be able to obtain an option on these properties if we work quickly enough tonight.

Then Hughes quickly descended into deviousness. At this time Hughes was trying to buy the Stardust Casino from Maheu's friend Dalitz and saw in Maheu's request for Meier's head an opportunity to take advantage of Dalitz.

> Why don't you see Moe (Dalitz) and tell him everything this bastard Meier has done to us and how terribly upset you are about it. Sometimes a friend will do something out of sympathy he will not do for any other reason... You may be surprised Bob but many times a man like Moe will make concessions on a business deal like this for a friend's personal benefit —

when he would never make the same concession because he is driven to it by bargaining... You see if I try to bargain Moe into a deal his pride asserts itself and he says "Never" whereas, as a favor and gesture of personal friendship to you when you are depressed by the treachery of a trusted employee who betrayed your trust, Moe might easily do what he would not do for me. Anyway please try, Howard.

Then came the postscript carrying the bad news.

I urge you not to fire Meier until we discuss him just a little more. Let's please dispose of Moe and then I will give my full attention to Meier. I simply have a one-channel mind, please forgive me.

The memo was clearly intended to reassure Maheu by badmouthing Meier — and removed the possibility of Maheu's interfering with the plans Meier was executing on Hughes' behalf.

A year after promising to give his full attention to Meier, Hughes was instead moving to strip Maheu of his powers. Maheu, the desert prince, was to be purged along with all his followers and Meier was to organize the liquidation. Maheu's staff consisted of former IRS, CIA and FBI agents. His second in command was Edward H. Nigro, who quit the United States Air Force at the rank of major general to join Maheu. Nigro said he came to Nevada to serve his country, a *non sequitur* unless the general felt helping Howard Hughes make even more money was an act of patriotism. Meier realized that none of Maheu's staff had expertise in business or managing casinos.

Maheu enjoyed cordial relations with John Rosselli, an old time mobster. Rosselli was the overseer of the Chicago mob's Las Vegas interests who with Sam Giancana and Maheu had plotted Castro's demise.

In 1981 a book written by Ovid Demaris, *The Last Mafioso: The Treacherous World of Jimmy Fratianno,* contained what was alleged to be Rosselli's assessment of Hughes and Maheu. Jimmy (the Weasel) Fratianno, formerly the mob's most accomplished killer on the West Coast, fled to the Justice Department after his employers marked him for death. He brought with him an encyclopedic knowledge of the mob's activities. Fratianno said Rosselli claimed that Hughes had been threatened with eviction from his penthouse suite in the Desert Inn as a lever to get him to buy the casino.

"We roped Hughes into buying the D.I.," Rosselli told Fratianno. "Now it looks like he wants to buy the whole town, if we let him. He's just what we need, especially with Maheu running the show."

Obviously, Hughes' arrival and the prospect of easy money had caused a feeding frenzy among those whose professional code was never to give a sucker an even break. He spent almost $100 million in Nevada, mostly on casinos. Meier looked at the flow of money through the casinos. It was apparent that the old way of counting the money — by two people locked in a windowless room — had to stop. It was an invitation to skimming.

When Meier went to the counting room of the Desert Inn, he could never arrive unannounced, and the two Dalitz men always made a great show of taking off their coats, rolling up their sleeves and carefully counting out the bills before rolling them up into little cylinders held fast by rubber bands. If money had to be counted like this, Meier told Hughes, it should be done in a room with windows so the process could be watched from the outside. Otherwise, cameras should be installed in the counting room.

Eventually, Hughes' financial losses were so serious that he would even come to consider what for him had been the unthinkable — acquiring a partner. The possibility arose when Meier, visiting Humphrey in Washington, was introduced to George Allen, who knew Howard Hughes from years before and had asked to be remembered to him. George Allen had been a confidant to Presidents Roosevelt, Truman and Eisenhower and by his own admission was the clown prince of the White House during their administrations. A reading of his autobiography, outrageously entitled *Presidents Who Have Known Me,* shows the honor was well earned.

Meier carried Allen's regards to Hughes, who did remember him. Meier said Allen owned an oil company of which J. Edgar Hoover was a director; apparently the only directorship the FBI chief ever accepted. He added that Allen was a close friend of D. K. Ludwig, a name that meant nothing to Hughes. Considering the American billionaire's club was not that big, it is surprising that Hughes would not know of Daniel Keith Ludwig, although it likely says more for Ludwig's passion for anonymity than for Hughes' ignorance.

Compared to Ludwig, Hughes was a press agent's dream. Unlike Hughes, whose every movement was front page news, Ludwig moved through the world unnoticed. If anything, he was even richer than Hughes.

He may well have been the world's richest man, yet he was as mysterious as Hughes was reclusive.

Ludwig made his money in shipping and the oil tanker trade but eventually presided over a world-wide conglomerate that included financial services, real estate, hotels, casinos, agriculture, mining, manufacturing, oil refining and oil exploration. Meier told Hughes something of Ludwig's background and Hughes asked Meier to meet him. Meier said Allen would likely arrange it.

"Then do it, John, and see if you can line him up behind us against the AEC."

In the months that followed, Meier met Allen often. He was particularly interested in studying the subtleties of Ludwig's organization, which made Hughes' operation appear leaden footed. Meier became convinced Hughes needed Ludwig's expertise in Las Vegas. With some trepidation he asked Hughes if he would ever consider a merger with someone like Ludwig. Hughes reacted calmly and asked for a written summary of his discussions.

Meanwhile, Allen arranged for Meier to be appointed to the board of the prestigious International Eye Foundation, replacing Allen's old friend, President Eisenhower. The Ludwig meeting was set for August 2, at the International Hotel in Las Vegas.

Ludwig was 72 years old when Meier met him, a sparse, slim man who rationed his smiles. Meier found some warmth behind the austerity. He began by outlining Hughes' problems in Las Vegas, the poor returns from the casinos and the inability of Hughes' organization to provide prudent management. Ludwig inquired into the organizational structure — who did what and who reported to whom. He was interested in the relationships among various parts of Hughes' empire and Meier explained how Hughes ensured his companies remained separate and distinct entities, each one controlled by his hands only. Meier admitted there were great jealousies and intrigues among factions of the empire and that for years Hughes had hidden himself from all his top executives, refusing to see any of them.

This bizarre corporate structure amazed Ludwig, who had a completely opposite management style. He ran his empire from an office in Burlington House, a New York skyscraper he had built in mid-Manhattan. He walked to work from an apartment overlooking Central Park and was totally accessible to his senior employees. That his top executives could be brawling like Norman barons would have been beyond his comprehension; Ludwig expected nothing less than nautical discipline from them.

Meier left convinced that Ludwig could be Hughes' salvation in Las Vegas. Apart from his managerial philosophy he had expertise in the gaming business, having developed three hotels and a casino in Freeport on Grand Bahama Island. On August 7, Meier submitted the following report to Hughes:

> In regard to your memo of August 1, 1969, I would like to make the following recommendation: I think it very wise that you consider a joint venture with Mr. D. K. Ludwig as a way to reorganize our hotel and natural resource ventures. As you know, in my prior memos to you, I think very highly of George Allen who has been assisting me in Washington. Through him I met with Mr. Ludwig at the International Hotel on August 2 and was very impressed with Mr. Ludwig's evaluation of the international scene in regard to investments outside of this country. Mr. Ludwig's reputation as a businessman is that he is a cautious man on all ventures that he gets into, but is extremely honorable on any business venture that he involves himself with. He has a knack of picking out the best businessmen that he can lay hands on; in addition to top-notch lawyers and accountants. I was very impressed with his straightforwardness and would be willing to stake my reputation with you on associating with Mr. Ludwig. I did not mention this possibility to either Mr. Ludwig or Mr. Allen and will not until I hear from you; but let me stress that I consider our situation out here very critical and my one and only recommendation to you is the above.

Shortly after receiving the memo, Hughes confided that he was interested in having Ludwig involved in all his undertakings. Hughes was convinced he needed better management of all his companies, not just the Nevada Operations but also the Tool Company, Hughes Aircraft — everything he had. However, he instructed Meier that on no account was he to disclose this to Ludwig.

"Tell Ludwig that you feel you should recommend to Mr. Hughes that he should tie the Hughes organization to his and see the reaction," he told Meier.

In Hughes' mind, as Meier knew instinctively, it would never be a merger in which Hughes would take a subordinate role. He wanted to use Ludwig's organization without losing any control of his interests.

But there was more. Hughes said he was planning to bring the Howard Hughes Medical Institute from Miami to Las Vegas and promised Meier the management of its affairs. Had this come about, Meier would have become the most powerful of Hughes' lieutenants. Hughes planned to place all his wealth within this foundation, because of his will and the extraordinary plans he had made for himself after death.

Meier knew nothing of the financial state of Hughes' companies, with the exception of the Nevada Operations which were obviously in trouble, but Hughes was insistent that talks with Ludwig include all aspects of his holdings. On August 19, Meier again met with Allen and Ludwig, but this time he asked if Ludwig would consider involving himself in Hughes' many industrial endeavors. Ludwig was equally frank. "From what we've seen in Nevada his operations are totally mismanaged and the hotels are going to go down," he said.

Ludwig also wondered why Hughes employed so many former FBI agents. However, he showed no interest in getting involved in Hughes Aircraft or Hughes Tool Company. He would be prepared to help Hughes with Las Vegas and that was all. George Allen, because of his oil company, was interested in making a deal with the Tool Company for access to the famous oil-drilling bits.

Meier reported all this to Hughes, who quizzed him before instructing him to send the following memo. It was a typical Hughes maneuver. Meier would use his own words and write it from his own perspective but the sentiments would be all Hughes'. Sent August 20, it read:

Included is all the information that I could obtain on Mr. D. K. Ludwig per your request. My recommendations step by step are as follows:

(1) You personally contact J. Edgar Hoover and check on Mr. George Allen and Mr. D. K. Ludwig and at the same time for your own benefit, make an inquiry as to Mr. Hoover's evaluation of the half-dozen FBI people that you have hired over the past three years. As far as I am concerned anybody who would leave the FBI for outside business ventures is disloyal and untrustworthy.

(2) Consider taking all your hotel acquisitions and going public within the next year.

(3) Take your public company and try to interest D. K. Ludwig in a joint venture where you would each have a 50-50 arrangement and he and his people would be responsible for the management and direction of these operations. This would put you in a position where you could nicely eliminate the individuals around us that are causing you your present problems; as soon as the public corporation would be responsible for the hiring and firing of these people.

(4) The joint venture with Mr. Ludwig would also put you in a position where your monies could leave the United States with no problem, since Mr. Ludwig has many international ventures and is established throughout the world. I would like to pursue the above recommendations as soon as possible on any terms you give me. If at any time you feel that I was wrong in my evaluation of this program I will gladly terminate my business with you and part as friends.

The significance of this memo cannot be overstated. While not all of its provisions would be carried out, it was an astonishing outline of the wholesale changes which would sweep away Maheu and cause the total reorganization of Hughes' operations within a year.

Hughes' other executives, Gay in Los Angeles and Raymond Holliday who was running Hughes Tool Company, must have watched Hughes frittering away his fortune in Las Vegas casinos with despair. The enmity that existed between them and Maheu is proverbial. Here was the opportunity for which they and Chester Davis must have prayed: a scheme to depose Maheu. Just as significantly, it wedded Hughes to Ludwig. After he left Nevada in November 1970, Hughes would spend the rest of his life within Ludwig's orbit and under his control.

As a stratagem the memo shows Hughes at his most artful. It was he who wanted wholesale changes in Nevada, wanted Maheu and his crew out, yet had Meier put the fatal recommendations in writing; Hughes could feign innocence if anything went wrong.

It was only a question of time before Meier's memo — and the one previous — landed on Maheu's desk. When they did, Maheu had Meier brought to his house. He was in a towering rage. He hurled accusations at Meier, warning him never to go near Hoover.

"You're just a kid," he shouted, "and you don't know what you're getting into. Just keep the hell away from Hoover."

Maheu demanded he retract the memos and send Hughes another saying he had made a mistake. Meier refused.

"I'll have you kicked out of Nevada and you'll never get back, Hughes or no Hughes." With those memos in Maheu's hands, Meier could not remain on his payroll. On October 31 he resigned from Maheu's company. The *Las Vegas Sun* noted that Meier had left the company to form an ecological research foundation. Maheu would later testify that Hughes told him to rehire Meier.

"I explained to Mr. Hughes that I would not do that, that under no circumstances would Mr. Meier ever again be on the payroll of Robert A. Maheu and Associates."

The White House was relieved by Meier's departure. In Ehrlichman's autobiography he records that he received a letter from Rebozo with yet more information about Meier and Don Nixon which had come from Rebozo's contacts in the Hughes organization.

"John Meier had been fired by Hughes," writes Ehrlichman, in error. "He had violated 'special instructions' to stay away from Don Nixon. But as Rebozo wrote me, Meier and Don Nixon each still found the other irresistible."

He quotes Rebozo's letter as follows:

It appears that JM and DN may be working as a team. One supposedly with the land development and exploration contacts; the other is assumed to be an intimate advisor to the White House with access to administrative agencies of the government.

At one time, they made a very determined effort to place coin machines in various Hughes plants in Southern California. They put considerable pressure on management to replace machines that were already in there; however, they were not successful.

It appears that the reward (whatever it may be) must be substantial. Otherwise, why would JM continue to violate special instructions about his association with DN? In other words, he deliberately jeopardized and finally lost a dignified and well paying position apparently because he could not afford to give up his deals with DN.

The fellow appears to be an opportunistic intellectual who, because of his contacts, has been able to feather his nest substantially. He obviously has a phobia for recognition and has managed to get on innumerable committees etc.

For quite some time he has exaggerated his position in the Hughes organization in a continuing quest for recognition. This has, on occasion, proved embarrassing to his employers...

After more digs at Meier's showboating, Rebozo closes with this observation:

In summation, it is obvious that the problem basically is that these two individuals are both self-serving promoters to the point that truth and integrity are completely disregarded. One is trying to cash in on a family relationship, and the other on a vastly over-stated business relationship. This totally irresponsible alliance can only lead to trouble sooner or later. Now you have the problem, and you can solve it. Let me remind you however that assassination is illegal.

What does he mean by reminding Ehrlichman that "assassination is illegal"? There is no trace of levity in any other part of the letter; it is unlikely to be a joke. Rebozo knows Ehrlichman doesn't need telling that political killings are proscribed, although they happen. His comment to Ehrlichman that "now you have the problem, and you can solve it" clearly shows that even after Meier officially left Hughes, an act which effectively removed the potential for Don Nixon's association with Meier to hurt the President through "innuendo" — their problem remained.

The problem is not innuendo, it is John Meier — the carrier of dangerous secrets.

6

THE JENNIFER PROJECT

Meier stood in the lobby of the Desert Inn. Upstairs in the penthouse, he presumed, one of Hughes' body servants was counting the money. At the appointed time, a messenger appeared and handed over a briefcase. Meier waited until he was in the relative privacy of his car, locked the doors, carefully looked around, then unclipped the briefcase. Inside was a thick wad of $100 bills — $50,000. If Maheu or Ehrlichman imagined they had separated Meier from Hughes, they were mistaken.

Hughes' money was now financing the Nevada Environmental Foundation which Meier, at Hughes' urging, had created within weeks of leaving Maheu. Hughes' instructions were to continue working against the AEC while maintaining his relations with Don Nixon.

In late 1969 Meier was visited by two CIA agents who arrived unannounced at the foundation's office. They said Meier was aware that the government was involved with the Hughes Tool Company on a project which had been personally approved by Hughes. Meier nodded, but he had no idea what they were talking about. There were so many CIA interests in Hughes' companies that Meier had no idea which project they were discussing. They wanted to know if Meier's foundation would perform some consulting work on the project. Meier said he would ask Hughes.

This was Meier's official introduction to the ultra-secret Jennifer Project

— one of the most successful pieces of technological espionage undertaken in that century. The project's purpose was to build an enormous high-tech vessel capable of salvaging sunken submarines. It was inspired by the sinking of a Soviet Golf-class submarine about 750 miles to the northwest of Hawaii in the spring of 1968. The diesel powered submarine was armed with Serb-class missiles capable of carrying a one megaton warhead 700 miles.

The U.S. Navy detected and tracked the submarine using a web-like system of electronic detection gear which stretches through thousands of square miles of ocean protecting the approaches to the North American mainland and Hawaii. The Soviets were unable to locate where the submarine had gone down.

Although it was resting at a depth of 17,500 feet, beyond any known means of salvage, the submarine contained code books which would allow the United States to decode previously intercepted Soviet naval signals. This would provide extremely valuable military intelligence while recovery of its missiles, firing systems and nuclear-tipped torpedoes would give the United States information about Soviet weaponry.

Naval Intelligence convinced the administration that a vessel could be built to recover the submarine. The CIA received Howard Hughes' permission to use his tool company as a front. The vessel, eventually named the Hughes Glomar Explorer, would ostensibly be designed and built for undersea mining operations. If anyone thought it eccentric or implausible, the Hughes name gave the program legitimacy. No venture could be too ambitious for him.

Meier's involvement with the Jennifer Project began when Hughes asked if he was still involved with Goodwin Knight, the former Governor of California.

"Weren't you in business together? Didn't you tell me about a project you had going with Litton Industries on nuclear submarines?"

Knight had the contacts at Litton and he had handled all the negotiations, said Meier. Hughes asked for Knight's private number.

Later, Meier received a call from Knight. "I've just had the shock of my life. I answered the phone to find someone claiming to be Howard Hughes on the other end and I want to know if the whole thing's a joke."

"No," said Meier. "I gave Hughes your number because of your Litton contacts."

Knight said Hughes had asked for his contact's name but he wasn't sure it was Hughes and declined to supply the name until he had spoken with Meier. Hughes urged him to be quick. He was considering a business venture involving submarines. The following day Hughes phoned Meier before Knight did.

"Tell Goodie to cooperate on a project proposed to Mr. Hughes by the U.S. government," instructed Hughes, lapsing as usual into the third person when speaking of himself.

Hughes made no mention of the nature of this government business, but a week later he asked Meier to assess a three page memorandum the government had sent him. The document had gone to the Hughes Tool Company in Houston about a month earlier. The opening paragraphs proposed mining minerals from the ocean and outlined the economic possibilities of the venture. Then, it referred to a very sensitive proposal which could not be put in writing but would be discussed privately with Hughes. Mystified, Meier called Hughes and asked what it was he wanted. Hughes asked if he thought it were possible to engage in deep sea mining and Meier said perhaps in the future once the equipment had been developed. As for the mysterious second part of the document, he didn't understand any of it. Hughes did not explain.

Knight finally revealed that Hughes had been asked by the government to join the CIA in building a ship whose function would be to obtain data from a sunken Soviet submarine.

"Part of the deal was that, in exchange for Hughes' help, the ship would be made available to him for ocean mining," said Knight. In retrospect, Hughes had committed a glaring indiscretion by disclosing the military part of the operation. Perhaps Hughes felt he had to level with Knight in order to gain his help, but how would his CIA partners react if they knew Hughes was blabbing it all into the telephone? Despite his wealth and name he would have to be regarded as a grave security risk. By sending the memo to Meier, Hughes was again risking disclosure. The memo clearly showed Hughes was linked to some clandestine activity proposed by the government involving the use of a deep sea dredge. Any hint of government collusion in building the Hughes Glomar Explorer would have removed the possibility that the scheme could be shrugged off as the exotic ravings of the eccentric Howard Hughes. That the secret remained watertight to the very end — despite a few scares — was a measure of the CIA's vigilance.

The CIA's request for Meier's participation in the Jennifer Project made him uneasy. He was not happy with the prospect of fronting for the CIA and was so opposed to the agency's use of Hughes' companies that Hughes forbade Meier ever to discuss the topic again. Consequently, he was relieved when Hughes would have nothing to do with the idea.

"No, it's best to keep the foundation away from that. It might jeopardize what we are trying to do," said Hughes, who then admitted to being involved in intelligence work with the government concerning the ocean mining project which he didn't want to discuss further. Hughes never did give Meier details of the venture but the CIA believed Meier to be fully aware of them and had unsuccessfully attempted to recruit him into providing the agency with yet another front.

If he had relied solely upon Hughes for information, Meier would only have known of a mysterious government connection with ocean mining. But thanks to Knight, he knew enough vague details to collapse the whole effort if they were leaked to the press or to the Soviets, as the CIA was the first to realize.

The CIA's attempt to put Meier under contract was obviously designed more to gain control over him — and what he could do with what he knew — than to secure any other benefit to the CIA. Hughes' reluctance to have the foundation involved with the CIA might have been prompted by fear it would take Meier away from his prime task of forcing the AEC out of Nevada.

Had the AEC tests stopped, Hughes might never have left Nevada, but by early 1970 his obsession with beating the AEC was entering its finale. He wanted it known that he had no intention of sharing the state with the AEC and would leave if the underground program wasn't halted. When another bomb was exploded during Easter Week, 1970, it signaled the end of Hughes' stay in the state.

WHEN IT BECAME clear that domestic political pressure had failed to force the AEC out of Nevada, Hughes decided an international crusade might succeed. He ordered Meier to go abroad and foment trouble by developing an anti-nuclear coalition within countries allied to the United States.

Hughes was clearly meddling in matters of high state. The mission could not be easily discounted, given the palpable anti-American feeling found in many once friendly countries who lived under the shield of American nuclear weapons. Protests against the presence of U.S. air bases and installations were frequent and America's public image abroad had never been lower. Flag burnings and demonstrations against the Vietnam conflict had become routine. Even traditional allies were openly critical and demanding that the U.S. get out of Southeast Asia. Who could say what Hughes' money and influence could stir up in Greece or Australia, Britain or West Germany? At home, his money had caused problems for the AEC. Meier's campaign had come close to derailing the nuclear testing program, although the AEC would never admit it.

Meier was summoned to the penthouse to discuss his international itinerary. Hughes was lucid, painfully thin and dressed in slacks and a cotton shirt. He told Meier to take his family on the trip to distract the prying eyes of the White House which had been focused on Meier ever since his unexpected appearance in that Miami hotel room more than a year ago. Hughes asked him to visit Switzerland and make final arrangements for delivery of the German-made cryonic chamber.

For the first time, Meier allowed himself to ponder Hughes' mental state. He wondered if the drugs the CIA were supplying were affecting his faculties. He had discovered Hughes' dependence on the CIA for drugs while sharing a company plane with an agent who was on his way to Los Angeles. Meier knew the man made frequent trips between Las Vegas and Los Angeles and asked why.

"To get the old man some stuff he needs."

"What kind of stuff?"

The agent just laughed and said he was getting Hughes' medication. Meier asked why he didn't get it in Las Vegas. His companion winked and said it wasn't prescription drugs he was after.

In July, Meier, Jennie and the children caught a flight to London. After stopping in London the family went to Switzerland where Meier met Dr. Alfred Buhler, whom Hughes had described as his financial agent in Europe. What Meier didn't know was that Dr. Buhler was the CIA's paymaster in Europe, involved in such clandestine activities as illegal arms deals, stocks and tax fraud and kidnapping. Meier met Buhler and purchased the cryonics equipment and arranged for it to be shipped to the Hughes Medical Institute in Miami.

In August, at about the time his immortality chamber was heading across the Atlantic, Hughes discovered the Nixon administration was planning to dump surplus nerve gas canisters into the same ocean about 150 miles from Paradise Island where Hughes was considering moving. Hughes immediately mobilized. Maheu tried to prevent the dumping by appealing to the President through the Danner-Rebozo pipeline. Davis and Gay, hiding behind some hastily formed environmental groups, tried to get the courts to halt the shipment. Meier, then in Greece, was told to phone Don Nixon and tell him to convey Hughes' displeasure directly to his brother. Hughes also ordered Meier to call Tom Pappas, head of Pappas Oil and one of President Nixon's friends, to ask him to use his influence.

Originally the military had planned to incinerate the warheads in a nuclear explosion in Nevada but Nixon had vetoed this, knowing how Hughes would react. By the time Hughes attempted to stop the dumping it was too late. The warheads aboard a military train rumbled into the navy yards in North Carolina from depots in Kentucky and Alabama, and were loaded into an old Liberty ship. She was sailed to the prescribed spot and scuttled as planned.

For the past two years Hughes had been showing signs of mental deterioration. There was loss of concentration and a tendency to ramble and drift into monologues with sudden bursts of bad temper. Sometimes when his plans were thwarted, he would dumbfound Meier by screaming into the phone. His conversations grew stranger by the day. For example, after his conversation with Pappas, Meier was ordered to Australia because Hughes had heard there were silver properties available. He had Meier bring out a mining engineer, Bert Westman, to evaluate them. When Meier arrived in Sydney he called Hughes, who said: "What the hell are you doing in Australia?"

"You sent me here and Westman too."

"Oh, did I?" Hughes asked, then gave him the name of someone in Australia who might help organize the anti-AEC campaign. After considerable effort, Meier finally traced the man, only to find he had died 20 years earlier.

During one of his calls Hughes lambasted Meier for his hostility towards the CIA presence in his companies. Meier had complained to others in the company that the CIA was undermining Hughes' businesses; its agents were so numerous he was afraid Hughes was being taken over without realizing it.

He kept the information on the drugs supplied to Hughes to himself but his criticism had somehow found its way back to Hughes, who was furious.

"Meier, you're still opening your mouth about the CIA. I want you to stay out of it — it's nothing to do with you, it's political."

He then ordered Meier to bring Don Nixon to Australia to give him one last ultimatum for his brother.

7

FLIGHT

In October, 1970, there was no reason to suppose that Hughes wanted to leave the United States for good. He was desperate to stay in Nevada but would no longer tolerate the AEC. Hughes agreed with Meier that it would be easier to meet Don Nixon in Honolulu than Australia. On October 29 in the Kahala Hilton, Meier delivered the ultimatum. "Mr. Hughes is deadly serious about this. He wants you to tell your brother directly that if he doesn't help him on the AEC he's going to leave the U.S. and he's not only going to continue the fight abroad but he'll take on your brother and destroy him."

The plain speaking caused Nixon to wince. Did he understand the seriousness of Hughes' position? Nixon assured him he did. When Meier said that he had been abroad all summer laying the groundwork for an international movement against the ABM program, Nixon became even more agitated. He agreed to deliver the message and to meet Meier in California with an answer.

Meier's next three weeks were a blur of flights. He had just said goodbye to Don Nixon when the unexpected happened in Nevada. Mike O'Callaghan, a Democrat, beat Republican Ed Fike for the Governor's seat. Fike had been heavily backed by Hughes' people in Nevada. Meier, however, had put money into O'Callaghan's campaign. Meier had just arrived in Vancouver, British Columbia, to evaluate the city as a possible site for

Hughes and his entourage when he was ordered to return to Nevada and use his influence with O'Callaghan to patch up relations between Hughes and the Governor-elect. He met O'Callaghan in Reno, briefed him about Hughes' intentions and arranged to meet him in Hawaii a few days later for discussions on Hughes' plans for the state and what he wanted in return.

By now, a weary Meier had been travelling continuously since July. From Reno he dragged himself off to Los Angeles for a November 10 meeting with Don Nixon to hear the President's reaction to Hughes' barefaced threat.

The President, said his brother, was just as alarmed as Hughes about the state of affairs in Nevada. He, too, was worried the AEC might not be telling the truth about radiation leaks and had ordered an independent inquiry into the testing program. Meier knew this wasn't what Hughes wanted. There had been studies and nothing had come of them: The solution was to terminate all tests.

During his subsequent meeting in Honolulu with O'Callaghan, he explained that Hughes was unwell and his departure likely. Meier stressed that Hughes was serious about bringing the Medical Institute and its wealth to the state and of wanting to reopen the old mines and develop his vast holdings. The AEC had to go or he would leave and take everything with him. O'Callaghan was perturbed but said he had just won the election and needed time to assume control of the government. Meier reported back to the penthouse but Hughes had little to say. It was the middle of November. Meier returned home to Las Vegas, dead tired.

On November 26, 1970, Thanksgiving Day, Meier called the Desert Inn from California. There was no answer at the penthouse. There was nothing unusual in this. Hughes often slept for days at a time. Meier called the next day and the next, and the next. Still silence.

Finally, a strange voice answered and Meier asked to speak to Hughes.

"He's not available," was the reply and the phone was put down. He phoned repeatedly but it rang unanswered. Fearful that something had happened to Hughes, Meier flew to Las Vegas. When he arrived, the *Las Vegas Sun* had the story plastered all over page one — "Howard Hughes Vanishes."

While Meier had been away that summer the forces seeking to oust Maheu had been maneuvering. The alliance of Holliday, Gay and Davis carried out the reorganization of Hughes' Nevada Operations. Apparently in league with people from Ludwig's organization, Hughes had been spirited out of the Desert Inn under the very noses of Maheu and his men.

Whatever made Hughes leave Nevada must have occurred later than November 12 when Meier began his three days of meetings with O'Callaghan in Hawaii, for at that time Hughes had been determined to find a way to remain in the state.

However, on November 14 Howard Hughes — two days after the meetings began and after receiving a lukewarm report on their chances of succeeding — took the most momentous business decision of his life and signed away control of his vast Nevada holdings to Gay, Davis and Holliday. It could not be without significance that the day before he did this, Holliday — not Hughes — had signed an agreement with the CIA to build the Glomar Explorer.

To let others control his assets was an anathema to Hughes, who had a lifelong distaste for partners and shareholders. He had given up hope of forcing the AEC out of Nevada and was willing to abandon care of his affairs there to others. Beyond this, it showed that mentally and emotionally Hughes was now a mere husk of the man around whom the legends had grown. He finally had been maneuvered into relinquishing the authority he had resolutely guarded since inheriting his father's tool company.

Upon learning Hughes had been taken to Paradise Island in the Bahamas, Maheu claimed he had been kidnapped and launched an abortive rescue mission, but Hughes was now living under Ludwig's protection. His new guardians captured his self-appointed rescuers in a room under Hughes' at the Britannia Beach Hotel. The guard was captained by James Golden, formerly one of Richard Nixon's Secret Service bodyguards and the man who appears responsible for removing Hughes from Nevada.

Maheu, gathering his war party at the Frontier Hotel, evoked the name of his missing master as license to continue overseeing Hughes' Nevada Operations. On December 4, auditors escorted by agents from the security firm International Intelligence Inc. (Intertel) — a company unknown in Las Vegas but associated with the Ludwig organization — rushed the cashier's cages and began stuffing money and IOUs into bags. Caught by surprise, Maheu's security force couldn't prevent the invasion of some eleven cages before Maheu, supported by the Clark County Sheriff's Office, managed to evict them.

Maheu's counterattack was short-lived. Within days, the triumvirate convinced the authorities that Hughes had sacked Maheu and wanted his organization disbanded. On December 7, Intertel agents burst down the doors of Maheu's command post in the Frontier and routed his staff who fled out the back.

Meier, like the rest of Las Vegas, watched these events with fascination. Also watching were two people into whose hands Howard Hughes had committed himself, James Crosby and his partner Jack Davis. They were the major stockholders of Resorts International, the company which owned Hughes' new hideout, the Britannia Beach Hotel. Intertel, a subsidiary of Resorts International, was charged with maintaining security in the hotel's casino and was now also guarding Hughes on the hotel's ninth floor.

In his biography of Ludwig, *The Invisible Billionaire,* author Jerry Shields probes the complex financial world of the Bahamas and the hidden interests of those controlling the island's various casinos. He postulates that Crosby and Davis were front men for Ludwig and had cooperated with Ludwig in bringing Hughes to the islands. From now until the end of his life Hughes would be transported and maintained by Ludwig's organization.

For Richard Nixon, nothing could have worked better. Hughes was out of Nevada and under the care and protection of the President's friends in the Bahamas. His secrets were now offshore and safe from disclosure. How quickly it all came together once Hughes signed the proxy. He vanished from Nevada, went to the Bahamas, cut all ties with Meier, stopped plotting against the AEC, and uttered no more threats against Nixon. What might have happened had he resisted signing is anyone's guess.

There was never a coup without its liquidation list and this one was no exception. At the time Meier, Maheu, and Maheu's crowd in Las Vegas were being eliminated, so too were lobbyist Larry O'Brien, who had provided sterling service to Hughes in Washington, and Tom Murray, Hughes' secret lobbyist ensconced in the Watergate Hotel. As if to emphasize a new order had been created, Richard Danner, a Maheu executive who was also a friend of Nixon and Rebozo, was the sole survivor of the purge.

Howard Hughes, for what was left of his life, was a captive of his addictions, his paranoia, and the eccentricities that, in sealing him off from the world, had created a ready-made asylum into which he could be committed by his keepers without need or regard for due process. With his mental faculties failing, his health deteriorating and euphoria just an injection away, would Hughes know, or really care, that those around him had subtly altered his environment? To make Hughes a prisoner it was not necessary to deprive him of freedom of movement, for in truth he had none.

Howard Hughes could be imprisoned simply by isolating him from people through whom he could act independently. He would thus be deterred from making problems for the White House and the CIA. Certain of his being prevented from contacting Hughes, Meier vowed to find a way to reach him.

BY THE SPRING of 1971 Meier had been under government surveillance for three years. The agents had been efficient and carried out their duties without giving the slightest hint of their presence. However, on March 30, perhaps routine gave way to complacency and the shadows became material.

At dusk, Meier was driving through Beverly Hills to pick up Mike Gravel at Los Angeles International Airport when his car was hit from behind. Traffic was heavy and the collision shot his car forward into the one ahead.

Stepping out of his car, Meier was met by the driver he had rammed, who was screaming about being someone's agent and how she had whiplash and it was going to cost some son-of-a-bitch millions. To Meier's surprise, the passenger of the car was actress Sally Struthers, of *All In The Family*. He asked if she would wait in the hotel across the street while they sorted out the mess. The driver of the car that rear-ended Meier's apologized and said he had sneezed and accidentally hit the gas pedal instead of the brake. After exchanging the necessary particulars Meier went back to the hotel to talk to Struthers, who despite the hysterics of her agent assured him she wasn't hurt.

As Meier stepped back into the street he could see a policeman talking to the other drivers. Glancing at his own vehicle he saw two men going through it. One had the glove compartment open while the other was trying to force the trunk. Meier rushed over and asked the man inside the car what he was doing. The stranger hurriedly climbed out, mumbling about being with security.

"What security?" asked Meier. "We're in the middle of the damn street."

The confrontation attracted the attention of the policeman.

"You know this guy?" he asked

Meier said he didn't. The man looked ready to flee but the policeman pushed him across the curb to a wall. Meier turned to see what had become of his accomplice, and spotted him vanishing around a corner.

Meanwhile, the policeman was frisking his captive, who was attempting to take something from his inside pocket.

Meier watched as the policeman knocked his hands away and reached inside his coat for the man's wallet which he opened and examined. They spoke quietly before the policeman handed back the wallet and the man walked rapidly away.

The policeman was clearly perplexed.

"Those two are with the U.S. government. They were going through your car, any idea why?"

Meier had no idea and asked what they had been discussing. The policeman shook his head. "I can't say any more. It's bigger than I am, just forget it."

8

THE BAIT

The incident at the accident scene was evidence of a covert campaign against John Meier. The overt campaign began only a few months later when agents from the Internal Revenue Service arrived and searched his office in Los Angeles, where he was a partner in a film production company. The investigation, though unwelcome, came as no surprise. Don Nixon had warned him that Ehrlichman had set the IRS on him and Meier would be next.

Ehrlichman admits displaying an active interest in the IRS investigation of Meier. During the Watergate hearings he was shown to have routinely received IRS reports on Meier to which he had no legal right. This suggests that he did not know of the $1 million Miami payoff. Had he known, how could he have risked the strong possibility that Meier might disclose this payoff during badgering from investigators?

If Ehrlichman couldn't perceive the danger, others were aware of it. Meier began receiving inquiries from Richard Nixon's accountant, Arthur Blech, and Don Nixon who were anxious to know what he was saying to the IRS. Meier had become thoroughly fed up with the whole affair and would have delighted in turning Richard Nixon in.

By this time, Meier was receiving warnings from friends that government agents were asking questions about him. He and his friends were being followed and photographed and Don Nixon had become almost hysterical in his demands that he meet Blech. He even called Meier in the hospital while Jennie was giving birth to their fourth child, Jimmy. Meier refused to meet Blech but with an election year fast approaching, Don Nixon, who was still doggedly pursuing his role as the Republican's master spy, was not about to alienate him. Toward the end of 1971, Don returned to the trough from which he had been fed by Meier and Clifford in 1968. What he would be fed this time would poison the Nixon presidency.

Louis Russell was a private detective whom Meier first encountered on October 29 at Clifford's home in Maryland. Before Russell arrived, Clifford warned Meier to be careful about what he said in front of him. Although Meier had never heard of him, Russell displayed a disturbing familiarity with Meier's credentials. Russell was curious about what had happened to Hughes, why he left Nevada and Meier's relationship with the Nixons. Would Richard Nixon win the next election? Meier said it would be impossible — the Democrats had too much dirt on him. Russell naturally wanted to know what that could be, but Meier hesitated to answer. Russell assured him there was no need to worry — weren't they all Democrats? — whereupon Clifford stepped in and steered the conversation to shallower waters.

Meier, Clifford and Humphrey had debated many times how best to use the knowledge of Hughes' bribe. There was no doubt in their minds that once the story broke Nixon would be finished. Meier could hardly call a press conference and announce it; neither could Humphrey. Ironically, Don Nixon's insistence on gathering political intelligence for his brother's cause provided the opportunity.

When Hughes left Nevada, Meier moved his family to Newport Beach, California, only two miles from Don Nixon's home. On November 5 Don met him at Los Angeles Airport and they drove to a nearby restaurant. As they dawdled over dessert Don asked if Hughes had an office in the Watergate complex. Meier said it had been closed. Did he know that Larry O'Brien (now chair of the Democratic National Committee) had an office there? Meier nodded.

"Is he still working for Hughes?" asked Don.

"O'Brien? I have no idea."

"Well, what do you think's going on back there right now with O'Brien?"

"I don't know but the Democrats are confident they'll win the election."

"Why do you say that?"

"Because they've got a lot of information on your brother and Hughes that's never come out," replied Meier.

Don sat bolt upright. "What information?"

"Look, I can't say too much. I've been asked to run as a Democrat for the Senate. I don't want to get involved."

Don's mouth fell open. "But you can't run as a Democrat," he spluttered.

"Don, I think we're going to have a very awkward relationship on this. My friend Paul Schrade has offered to help me if I decide to go with the Democrats and I owe it to him to tell him everything that went on with Hughes."

The mention of Schrade, who was thick with the Kennedys and O'Brien, made Nixon turn white. "God. You can't do this to my brother," he gasped.

"I'm not doing anything to your brother. This is politics and that's the way it's done." They parted in silence.

The next day, Meier called Haddad and Clifford and reported his conversation with Don. Then he called Humphrey. The canny Humphrey cut Meier short, saying he didn't want to discuss it over the phone but would meet him in San Francisco at the Fairmont Hotel on November 8. There, he listened while Meier described Nixon's interest in O'Brien and the alarm that had greeted his comment that the Democrats possessed damaging information on his brother. Meier spoke of the Nixons' dread that the IRS would discover the $1 million payment and how he was being pressured by Blech and Don not to discuss it. Humphrey spoke of Richard Nixon's tendency to panic.

"We've got to push him into committing an irrational act, something that will cost him the election. If they are worried about Hughes — good. Let's put the pressure on and see what happens."

Watergate was that simple. Neither Meier nor Humphrey imagined Nixon's irrationality would lead to a burglary of Larry O'Brien's office.

In the meantime, the combination of the IRS investigation and the implications of Meier's declaration for the Democrats was unsettling Rebozo. In December Meier received a call from the President's friend asking him to go to the Newporter Inn. Rebozo gave no reason but said it was urgent.

When he entered the lobby, Meier was approached by two men who flashed Secret Service badges and asked him to step outside. Meier was nervous and hesitated but they coaxed him out. They escorted him to a large black car, motioned him inside, slammed the doors and frisked him. Meier asked what they were doing. "We're checking for microphones," said one.

He was driven to the beach where the car halted at a pay phone. One of the agents got out, dialed and waved Meier over. Rebozo was on the line. He was friendly and said he knew the IRS was looking into a lot of things and the White House would like Meier to keep him informed on his discussions with the IRS.

Meier replied he had no intention of telling him anything. "I've got two lawyers handling this for me in Los Angeles."

Rebozo's tone changed. "Look, quit screwing with us. We want to know everything they say and if they want to speak to you directly, no way you go near them, understand?"

"I've nothing to hide so why shouldn't I?"

"John, you make sure you contact us on anything the IRS wants to talk about. Now go and tell Don everything we've discussed and tell him to speak to no one or he'll be in a heap of trouble."

Meier insisted he had nothing to hide from the IRS.

"You are going to get everyone in trouble, including Howard Hughes."

"Bebe, I haven't spoken to Howard Hughes in over a year and I don't even know if he's alive or dead."

"Don't forget we are your friends. Remember President Nixon is in the White House and can help you. Will you go and speak to Blech?"

Meier said he had his own attorneys handling the IRS investigation and didn't need any advice from Blech. With that, Rebozo asked to speak to one of the agents. After they finished talking, Meier was dropped off at the hotel where the pair offered to buy him dinner. Meier fully understood the seriousness of what Rebozo had done and the reasons for his elaborate efforts to ensure the privacy of the call. Rebozo, on behalf of the President, had dispatched Secret Service agents like a couple of cheap gumshoes to frisk Meier and deliver him to a safe phone so he could ask him to break the law and avoid meeting the IRS.

Meier didn't have the opportunity to carry Rebozo's threat to Don Nixon until December 28 when he was invited to Don's home for lunch. He mentioned Rebozo's call but Don paid little attention. He appeared too preoccupied. He meandered in ever decreasing circles until finally he came to his point — almost. Don was concerned about the next election.

"John, what's that fellow's name we were talking about last time, er, let me see, Paul somebody or other. Paul, er?"

It was a game Meier always played along with. "Paul? What Paul?"

"Y'know he works for that union."

"Union?"

"Y'know the one that makes cars?"

"Cars?"

"The auto workers."

"Oh, a Paul from the autoworkers? I don't know."

"You do. Now it's not Paul Smith, it's Paul er, Paul Sch... Let me see Paul Schrrrade. That's right — Paul Schrade."

"Oh, Paul Schrade. What about him?"

"Well, John, we were talking about Paul last time, and y'know there's nothing to it politically, that Hughes stuff. People make up stories all the time. It'd be good if we could have a clean election — stay with the issues."

"That's right but as a friend, Don, I have to tell you that maybe the Democrats have a lot of questions about things that aren't true and I'm sure your brother can answer them, but O'Brien's got everything together on the Hughes situation and I'm sorry but — "

Don interrupted: "You don't mean he collected stories and lies about my brother and Howard Hughes?"

"He's just doing his job, Don. Sure, he's got papers and documents."

"You mean he's going to make us go through all that again like we did in 1960?"

"I'm sure your brother will be able to answer all the allegations the way he did then."

Don appeared catatonic. Meier excused himself and went to the bathroom. On the way back, he heard Don talking on the phone in his usual booming voice. Meier stopped instinctively. He realized Don was talking to the President.

"Dick, I've just found out Meier's given all his Hughes information to the Democrats. O'Brien has it..."

Meier backed up and returned to the bathroom. The deed was done. Within minutes of the ghastly news being presented to Don Nixon, it had been transmitted to the President. The conspirators could now only wonder how badly it would shake him. If he kept his head and did nothing, he had a slim chance of survival, for if Nixon failed to react, then the Democrats' presidential candidate would have to smear him. But mudslinging has its risks and it would take some nerve. The Democrats possessed no internal Hughes memos offering proof of the deal; no financial documents showing the transfer of cash from the Howard Hughes Medical Institute to Bebe Rebozo during March 1969; no paper trail following the money to Rebozo's bank and then to the Bahamas or wherever it disappeared. There was not even an affidavit from Meier affirming that one night in a Miami hotel room he had inadvertently kept guard over a million dollars destined for Richard Nixon. Larry O'Brien's safe contained nothing potent. But Nixon could not know this. His enemies were banking on guilt to make him think the worst, and that his celebrated tendency to panic would lead him into committing a great folly.

Even if common sense told him that Hughes would hardly incriminate himself by describing his part in grand bribery and corruption, there would be doubt. Hughes' eccentricity, if not madness, might manifest itself in many ways. Had he not left the country in an absolute fit, threatening to destroy Nixon? These doubts must have rung in Nixon's head until it ached.

The initial concern of Don Nixon and Bebe Rebozo, that Meier might disclose details to the IRS about the Hughes-Nixon relationship, must now have seemed trivial. Information given the IRS was one thing; however incendiary, it could be extinguished by damage control parties dispatched from the Oval Office. In the hands of the Democrats, such material would burn beyond reach.

9

HOAX

Meier abandoned what was left of his innocence and entered politics. On January 11, 1972, he announced he was seeking the Democratic Party's nomination for U.S. Senator from New Mexico. It was an announcement not likely to make headlines even in that humble state, let alone the larger world. However, within weeks, Meier's candidacy would be extensively reported by the nation's press, his picture splashed across the most influential magazines of the country. He would be interviewed on national television and local radio.

The seat he was seeking was held for the Democrats by Senator Clinton Anderson, whose term ended in November. The Senator had lapsed into senility and there were moves to have him resign in the fall of 1971 which would have allowed the Governor of New Mexico to appoint a caretaker to serve the remainder of his term. Humphrey promised to arrange for Meier to be appointed to give him the advantage of incumbency in the election.

Meier arranged residency in Albuquerque in September of 1971 expecting at any time to receive a call from the Governor. It never came. Anderson seemed oblivious to pressure for his resignation. Meier was in Washington with Anderson the day Humphrey tried talking him into resigning. They were in the Senate when Humphrey arrived. Anderson looked at Humphrey and asked: "Have we met before?"

"Goshsakes, Cliff, I'm Hubert — Hubert Humphrey." But the blank

look remained. Later, Humphrey decided against inducing the resignation.
It just wouldn't look right. Meier would have to contest the nomination
without shortcuts. His candidacy was an oddity. For all his liberal opinions
he was a registered Republican in Nevada. Now he was being parachuted
into another state over the heads of local Democrats with political
aspirations of their own.

George Roth handled the office duties while Schrade sent over Harry
Evans, an organizer with the United Auto Workers, as campaign manager.
Meier sought the liberal vote and his campaign was principally directed to
the workers, the poor and the underprivileged, many of whom in that
state were Mexican-Americans. He ran ads in the *AFL-CIO Labor News*
and spoke against "Right to Work" legislation (an unpopular position
during a time when organized labor was being blamed for rampant
inflation), Nixon's wage restraint policies and, of course, the Vietnam
War.

In announcing his candidacy he told skeptical reporters he would win.
However, his campaign ended the minute he was pitchforked into the
infamous Clifford Irving affair, the most celebrated event of 1972 until
Watergate all but erased it from the national consciousness. His involvement
in this piece of literary chicanery was plotted by Chester Davis in collusion
with the CIA.[1]

Irving achieved both fame and infamy within a month. His rise began
on December 7, 1971, when McGraw-Hill announced the publishing coup
of the decade. It had paid $650,000 for the rights to Howard Hughes'
biography, allegedly compiled by Irving during clandestine interviews with
Hughes in the United States, Mexico and Puerto Rico. *Life* magazine
announced it would serialize the book and Irving floated overnight from
literary obscurity to international recognition. The Hughes organization
denounced the work as a hoax. McGraw-Hill denounced the Hughes
organization as dissemblers.

By the end of 1971 the dispute concerned the following issues: whether
Hughes had bared his soul to Irving only to change his mind later; whether
the Hughes organization was trying to stop a biography Hughes had
engineered behind his executives' backs; or whether Irving was no more than
a clever liar.

What initially sustained McGraw-Hill and Time-Life was the apparent
authenticity of the work. Senior editors claimed they could feel Hughes

talking through it and, as far as anyone could gather, the manuscript's details for the most part were historically correct.

To explain how so obscure a literary personality had stumbled upon so rare a gem, Irving said he had sent Hughes a copy of his latest book, *Fake* — the biography of an adroit forger with whom he was acquainted — and that Hughes had been so impressed with the work as to offer himself as the author's next subject. Irving said he was aided and abetted by Hughes' intermediary, a person he identified as George Gordon Holmes. Holmes quickly became almost as intriguing a persona as Irving or Hughes. Holmes, Irving said, provided details of Hughes' life and was present at his meetings with Hughes. He would apply blindfolds to cover Irving's eyes at various moments when he was brought into Hughes' presence. It was Holmes who handled Hughes' share of the publisher's advance, and so on. Irving created a labyrinth of tales into which he bolted hoping to lose his pursuers whose questions relentlessly chased behind.

Irving's monumental fraud caused Hughes to convene his famous last press conference. He spoke from the Britannia Beach Hotel in Nassau via a radio link with seven handpicked reporters collected in a Los Angeles hotel room on January 7, 1972. Hughes denied knowing Irving. Irving huffily dismissed the voice as a fake. By January 18, Irving's story was coming apart. McGraw-Hill discovered that the H. R. Hughes who had cashed the company's check in a Swiss bank was Helga R. Hughes.

While Irving's story was evaporating, one lie stubbornly remained — his mythical George Gordon Holmes. It was commonly accepted that McGraw-Hill could not have been so completely hoodwinked by Irving without inside help and that Holmes therefore must be a real person, someone with exclusive information on Hughes, likely a former employee. The authorities and the press were determined to uncover Holmes' true identity. Time-Life's New York bureau chief Frank McCulloch was the first to sniff out John Meier.

McCulloch appeared to be a favorite with the Hughes organization.

Nine days after McGraw-Hill's announced coup, Chester Davis who, as the organization's senior attorney, was leading the effort against Irving, arranged for McCulloch to receive a telephone call from Hughes in which Hughes told him the autobiography was a fake. It was the first time Hughes had spoken to a reporter since 1958 and McCulloch was the reporter who had last interviewed him 14 years before.

On January 27, he and another reporter visited Irving in New York ready to extract an admission from Irving that Meier was the missing link, the mysterious George Gordon Holmes. McCulloch came prepared with a picture of Meier contained in a sheaf of photographs of others known to be associated with Hughes. He planned to present them to Irving, confident that he would pick out Meier. There are conflicting accounts of their meeting. According to the authors of *Hoax,* a book written with the cooperation of McCulloch, the reporters were shown into the home of Irving's lawyer, Marty Ackerman, but Irving, afraid to see them, hid in the basement. McCulloch, frustrated at Irving's failure to come out of the basement is supposed to have said to Mrs. Ackerman: "Tell Cliff we know all about Meier." She dutifully took the message downstairs where it is said to have sandbagged Irving, as Irving's secret source of the Hughes material was in fact a Meyer — Stanley Meyer, not John Meier.

Tricked by phonetics Irving left the house and went to the district attorney's office to make a clean breast of it, or so the *Hoax* scenario goes. When he returned, McCulloch was still there with his photo gallery and Irving humored him by looking through it. When he came to Meier's picture he shook his head and said he didn't know him.

Irving, in his book *What Really Happened,* tells a different tale. He was aware McCulloch felt he knew the identity of Holmes and had arrived with pictures for him to examine. He admits avoiding him. But he mentions nothing of a Meier message being delivered or that it caused him to panic and seek out the district attorney. Instead, he visited the district attorney because his lawyer had arranged the meeting earlier in the day. He admitted to the district attorney that his wife was Helga, as the authorities were on the verge of discovering; but he still insisted he was acting for Hughes. Upon returning to Ackerman's house he played out the charade with McCulloch, looked at the pictures, but picked none out. McCulloch drew Meier's from the pile and insisted he look at it carefully, asking if he were certain it was not Holmes. Irving said he was positive it wasn't. McCulloch swore in frustration.

Meier, in faraway New Mexico, was oblivious to the fact that his name and photograph were being bandied about in a New York melodrama. Three days after McCulloch confronted Irving, Meier received a call from Chester Davis at his home in Albuquerque. Davis sounded cheerful.

"What is it you want?" Meier asked.

"Oh, nothing much, John. But I'd like to call you back in about an hour. Will you be in?"

Meier said he would be home all evening. Half an hour later he was startled by heavy banging on the door. He found two agents from the United States Postal Inspection Service bearing a subpoena demanding his presence before a Federal Grand Jury in New York.

Meier looked at them in confusion. The subpoena ordered him to be present in New York in two days. He told them he couldn't possibly be there as he had important business in Albuquerque. The agents threatened to arrest him.

"I'm running for the U.S. Senate," Meier protested. "Why didn't you call me instead of coming around here like this?"

One of the agents apologized and said that less than an hour before, they had received a call from Davis telling them where to find Meier and to hurry so he couldn't escape service.

Watching these agents deliver the subpoena was CIA agent Virgino Gonzales, who had taken over surveillance of Meier from other agents at the beginning of January and was now part of the effort to sabotage Meier's political ambitions. Once the subpoena was served, Gonzales phoned local newspapers to make sure they knew of Meier's involvement.

Meier's attorney, Bob Wyshak, managed to get his appearance postponed for a few days, but by then Meier had displaced Irving on the evening news.

NBC interviewed him February 1, followed by a parade of reporters asking the same questions — did he supply Irving with his material? Was he Holmes? His denials were routinely noted, but in McCulloch's *Time* magazine they were treated with contempt.

Meier appeared before the grand jury on February 4 to deny ever knowing Irving, his wife, or anyone connected with preparing the purported biography of his former boss. The denials failed to stop the harmful publicity.

In the February 11 edition of *Life* magazine, Meier's name never once surfaced in the story but there appeared a large picture of him speaking with New Mexico Governor Bruce King under which the cutlines read: "Meier... denied that he was the George Gordon Holmes who Irving said was his liaison with Hughes" — a cute juxtaposition of words which if read carelessly might imply that Irving had said Meier was his liaison with Hughes.

But the most pernicious article appeared in *Time* magazine on February 14. Meier's picture was set in the center of four others who were undeniably Irving's cronies or accomplices: Robert Kirsch, a long-time friend of Irving's; Gerry Albertini, an idle millionaire, according to *Time*, who apparently kept the manuscript in his safe; Richard Suskind (who like Irving would go to jail for his part in creating the manuscript) and Elmyr De Hory, art forger extraordinaire. Meier's inclusion in that lineup would hardly help his battered image and would increase, not dispel, suspicion about him. If the picture was damaging, the story beneath was devastating.

With Irving's claims of meeting Howard Hughes tarnished, said *Time*, there remained but one major mystery to be solved: whether Irving compiled his manuscript with the help of material stolen from Hughes' files. The article continued:

> As part of the same quest (to solve the mystery and presumably expose the thief)[2] an eclectic consultant, John Meier, appeared before the federal grand jury in New York which is looking into the possibility of mail fraud and fraud by wire (telephone). Meier, who worked for Hughes in the late '60s as a scientific expert in Nevada, is now seeking the Democratic nomination for the U.S. Senate in New Mexico. After his grand jury appearance, Meier told reporters: "I never met Clifford Irving or his wife and had not heard of either of them before I read about the Autobiography of Howard Hughes in the newspapers." Yet when he faced the grand jury, Meier pleaded the Fifth Amendment. In addition, Mrs. Martin Ackerman, the wife of Irving's former attorney, is said to have identified Meier as the key figure in the mystery, possibly the Hughes intermediary Irving called George Gordon Holmes.

After two weeks of constant denials and testimony under oath, the preeminent national magazine was calling him a liar. Having Mrs. Ackerman link Meier to Irving produced a press release from Wyshak saying that there was no basis for the innuendo attributed to Mrs. Ackerman in *Time* magazine. It said Irving's attorney Martin Ackerman would have his wife issue a public statement denying she ever told reporters that Meier was Holmes or that he was a key figure. It did no good. The story persisted.

As for Meier pleading the Fifth, he never refused to answer questions concerning Irving or his manuscript, but he would not answer questions concerning his dealings with Howard Hughes. Regardless, that charge was aired twelve times on the major Albuquerque radio station KQEO as part of the following editorial:

> We have running for the Democratic Senate Nomination in New Mexico a man formerly unknown in the state. The reason, naturally, is that he's a very recent import to the state. He picked up considerable notoriety last week though, in connection with the Howard Hughes autobiography caper when he went before a New York grand jury to testify as to what he knew. According to *Time* magazine, his contribution to public knowledge was to take the Fifth Amendment. It seems to us the last thing we need in public office is anyone who has secrets he needs to keep from grand juries.

Time magazine's story, and its fallout which contaminated the local press in New Mexico, ended Meier's political ambitions.

Stanley Meyer was the missing link between Irving and those Hughes anecdotes whose authenticity had so impressed McGraw-Hill. Meyer eventually sat in front of the grand jury and told his story. He was a Hollywood groupie — one of those personalities operating on the fringes of the movie business — who threw lavish parties, knew everyone who was anyone, but by the early '70s was bankrupt. He had a talent for insinuating himself into the affairs of others, which is how he came into possession of a copy of Noah Dietrich's memoirs of his days with Hughes compiled by writer James Phelan. It was this work containing the hitherto unknown anecdotes of Howard Hughes that formed the basis of Irving's phony manuscript.

Meyer visited Gregson Bautzer, the Beverly Hills attorney whose most important client was Howard Hughes. Bautzer was used by Hughes to keep anyone from publishing his biography. Meyer gave a copy of Phelan's work to Bautzer, who reported to Davis. Davis sent a letter to Phelan in December of 1970, threatening a lawsuit if he continued.

A dispute between Phelan and Dietrich — in which Meyer's hand played no inconsiderable part — ended their relationship and Dietrich gave Phelan's material to another writer, Bob Thomas.

While Thomas was bashing out his version, Meyer was meeting up with

Irving, an old pal he had not seen for years. They met in June 1971, at a pool side party in California. During their conversation Irving had said he was compiling material for a book on the four richest men in the United States, one of whom was Hughes. This led Meyer to hand over yet another copy of Phelan's manuscript and it was from this material that Irving eventually faked Hughes' biography.

Thomas, meanwhile, redid the Phelan material and by September 1971, had completed his first draft and had delivered a copy to Meyer. Once again Meyer tiptoed off to Bautzer and laid the manuscript on his desk. Although Bautzer denied Meyer was paid for his services, the authors of *Hoax* noted that Meyer's attenuated financial situation took a turn for the better in November of 1971 when he paid off $52,000 in promissory notes, bringing to an end bankruptcy proceedings undertaken against him a year before.

Shortly after Meier's grand jury appearance, Davis called him to gloat over his predicament.

"You son-of-a-bitch, Chester," swore Meier. "I know what you did to me with Clifford Irving."

"You like that, John?" crowed Davis. "Just wait till you see what else I've got planned. You made a big mistake thinking you could take on Chester Davis and the CIA because between us we're gonna fix you."

10

THE PLUMBERS

Nixon was a ruthless politician and attracted ruthless men, some of whom considered murder justifiable. In this pre-Watergate period the President was under constant scrutiny in the press, especially from columnist Jack Anderson whose associate, Clifford, produced stories showing the unsavory side of his administration. Several of these stories were based on Meier's information. The previous August, Anderson had stunned the White House when he disclosed that $100,000 had been skimmed from one of Hughes' casinos and paid to Nixon following his election.

Nixon's administration was among the most vindictive in the country's history. The record is replete with outbursts by Nixon against sworn enemies and talk of grinding them underfoot. He drew up lists of those to be taken care of in due time: politicians, actors, reporters, football stars — all to be undone by the IRS and/or other powerful federal agencies. His staff was likewise vengeful.

Under Nixon's sponsorship, a clandestine group, the Special Investigations Unit, was formed to be used against Nixon's political enemies. The team was under Ehrlichman's control.

Ehrlichman's unit, aptly named "the Plumbers," was created to stop the damaging information leaks that were hurting the administration. The impetus to form the team came in June 1971, when the *New York Times* began publishing the highly controversial Pentagon Papers stolen by Dr. Daniel

Ellsberg, a former Pentagon bureaucrat. These papers showed how cynical the military and political objectives of the Vietnam War were. Nixon was incensed by their publication and Ehrlichman added Ellsberg's name to his blacklist. A plan was devised to break into Ellsberg's psychiatrist's office in the hope that damning information could be found on Ellsberg. When the Plumbers proved not to have the expertise necessary, E. Howard Hunt was brought in.

Hunt, ostensibly retired from the CIA, was working for the Mullen Company, a CIA front which had replaced Napolitan and Associates as Howard Hughes' representative in Washington. Almost as soon as Mullen had taken over, Nixon's staff asked company president Robert Bennett to find evidence of misdeeds O'Brien might have committed during his time with Hughes. Nixon's baleful eye was on O'Brien, the mastermind behind Democratic Party election campaigns who would direct the party's 1972 campaign against him.[1]

While Bennett was rooting for dirt on O'Brien, Hunt went to Miami and visited old comrades-in-arms from the Cuban wars. Hunt was the first chief of covert operations for the CIA's mysterious Domestic Operations Division. This is of more than passing interest as Virgino Gonzales,[2] now doing surveillance on Meier, was part of that division.

During the night of September 3, 1971, Hunt's group broke into the office of Ellsberg's psychiatrist. Ehrlichman, who would go to jail for complicity in the burglary, would later write that he was convinced Nixon ordered the crime.

Meier and Humphrey's plot to unnerve Nixon appeared to be unfolding. Don Nixon telephoned Meier on February 2. He offered Meier, who was on his way to testify before the Irving grand jury, a meeting with Attorney General John Mitchell. Nixon said Mitchell was prepared to resolve Meier's problems with the IRS. But Meier, who knew the price of such help, turned him down.

Two days later Mitchell authorized the pivotal burglary of O'Brien's office in the Watergate complex and a burglary of publisher Hank Greenspun's office in Las Vegas. Hunt travelled to Las Vegas for a setup meeting with a Hughes security man who handed him a set of plans of Greenspun's office. This burglary did not materialize, although the planning demonstrates a casual working relationship among the Hughes organization, the White House and the CIA. Eleven days after targeting

O'Brien's and Greenspun's offices, Mitchell resigned as attorney general and joined the Committee for the Re-Election of the President, known by that most fitting of acronyms, CREEP.

CREEP's security director was another supposedly retired CIA officer, James McCord. McCord's highest rank with the CIA was director of technical and physical security sections of the Office of Security. Jim Hougan, author of a fascinating book called *Secret Agenda,* comments that the Office of Security is responsible for protecting CIA assets, operations and personnel but more importantly it protects CIA secrets. It is this responsibility that makes it such a mysterious component of the CIA with a mandate to react quickly and decisively to protect any breach of the agency's integrity.

The Office of Security is separated from the bureaucratic hierarchy of the agency and reports directly to the director. It is known to have carried out much of the agency's domestic dirty work, such as arranging for experimental mind control drugs to be secretly administered to unsuspecting "volunteers." Through Maheu, it recruited his friends in the Mafia for the planned assassination of Fidel Castro. It set up Maheu's company and the Mullen Company as fronts. It was probably agents from this branch who tried to recruit Meier into the deep-sea mining program as part of the Jennifer Project's operational cover. The Office of Security collected all the material from the domestic spying program, some of which came from agents such as Gonzales.

McCord's background is significant because of the Office of Security's involvement with Maheu's firm, what Meier had seen firsthand of the CIA's role in political payoffs and the threat Meier posed to a multitude of the agency's operational covers throughout the world.

On February 8, Don Nixon phoned Meier at his campaign headquarters. He asked if Meier would help recover the damaging information given to Larry O'Brien. Meier refused.

"But we're going to have to get it," Don blurted.

"Well, good luck. I'm in New Mexico, what can I do? You'll have to go through your contacts in Washington." It was a call that could have removed any doubts that Richard Nixon might sit tight, waiting for the Democrats to publish. Meier, however, simply took it as confirmation that Nixon was sweating. He couldn't see in that short conversation any indication that the

President's irrationality could lead to a burglary. But George Clifford certainly could.

On February 29, Meier arranged to meet Clifford for dinner in Washington. When Meier arrived in the lobby of the restaurant he was surprised to find Clifford sitting there with Louis Russell. As before, the discussion between them concerned Richard Nixon and his prospects of retaining the presidency. Clifford startled Meier by referring to his discussions with Don Nixon and the panic that must have paralyzed the President upon discovering the Democrats had information about the million dollar payment. Meier, who had been told to be wary of Russell, was flabbergasted. Russell began wondering aloud how they could be sure Don Nixon was passing the messages to his brother. He looked at Meier for an answer but Meier was still too stunned to respond. Clifford, however, said there was no doubt — Meier had overheard Don telling the President all about it. This crucial remark, delivered with such off-hand authority, forced Meier to nod in agreement though inwardly appalled at Clifford's indiscretion.

When Russell left, Clifford smiled and told Meier not to worry, he had news — the Republicans were planning to break into the Democratic National Committee headquarters. Meier found this incredible, but Clifford said that Russell was spying on the Republicans.

Meier remained dubious. He had been close enough to Humphrey's campaign in 1968 to know that no matter what else was in short supply, political campaigns abounded in rumors. The idea that the Republicans were preparing to storm O'Brien's office was too outlandish — even for them. Who was Russell and from whom was he receiving such specific information?

Hougan's research into the anomalies of the burglary and the backgrounds of those involved for *Secret Agenda,* came perhaps closest to uncovering evidence of the Democrats' plot. In *Secret Agenda,* Russell emerges as James McCord's right hand man. He is described as a tipster to Jack Anderson. He was a former guard at the Watergate complex who also worked as a night guard at Nixon's CREEP headquarters and who popped up after Watergate doing security work at the Democrats' election headquarters.

Russell was a double agent. A trafficker of information, he spied on the Republicans for the Democrats and undoubtedly spied on the Democrats for the CIA. Through Hunt and McCord, the CIA had infiltrated the White House Plumbers and CREEP — all it needed was a plant inside Meier's group to gain a complete insight into the the silent warfare the two parties waged. Russell, with his connections to George Clifford, was tailor made for that role. When Meier met him in Washington, Russell was employed by the company which guarded the Watergate complex. Shortly after, he quit and joined McCord and Associates.

It is obvious that McCord divulged the burglary plans to Russell, who left his job to aid the operation. To share so dangerous a secret shows how much McCord trusted Russell and McCord was no fool. His record with the CIA was sterling. In this instance he may have made a grave error, though he was sharing the information with a man he had known since his early service with the Company.

Russell knew his way around Watergate and was intimate with the security protocol protecting the premises. But Russell was potentially more valuable to McCord than that. Through his relationship with Clifford he was a connection into the Meier-Humphrey conspiracy cell which would have been of great value to the CIA, for whom McCord despite his retirement, was still operating.

Not only were these Democrat conspirators trying to prevent Nixon's reelection, a number of them such as Schrade and Haddad were also courtiers of the hated Kennedy clan against whom the CIA was still conducting a vendetta. Even after Meier antagonized the CIA by interfering in their scheme to embarrass Teddy Kennedy, they continued to seek that Senator's political destruction. Hunt, dressed in a wig and fitted with a voice-altering device supplied by the CIA, had been abroad during the summer of 1971 interviewing a former Kennedy campaign worker who purported to have lurid information concerning the Chappaquiddick scandal. When this failed to materialize, Hunt went to the CIA for a collection of scandalous political caricatures of the Senator which he planned to circulate.

Russell's connection to this influential group of Democrats was enough to ensure his value to McCord. But there was yet another dimension to his usefulness — a closeness to Clifford and through it a connection to Jack Anderson. Clifford, in early 1972, was coauthor of a book with Anderson which by all accounts had the CIA so thoroughly worried that by the middle of January Anderson and his associates were put under CIA surveillance.[3]

Not only was Anderson causing anxiety in the White House by publicizing the administration's dirty dealings, but also he had begun publishing information based on intelligence documents which the CIA believed originated within the agency. These were classified documents, a précis of which the CIA did not want appearing in the nation's newspapers — yet they did, week after week. As many as sixteen agents in eight cars were assigned by the Office of Security to shadow Anderson and his associates in an effort to discover how he was receiving his information. During this period Meier openly met with Anderson and Clifford, which must have added to the CIA's concern that the Jennifer Project could be the next operation compromised.

Abruptly in April, surveillance was stopped. A plot by Hunt to murder the columnist had been hatched sometime during the third week of March. It has been argued that the watchers were removed because it would not have done for a CIA surveillance team to become witnesses to Anderson's murder at the hands of people employed to re-elect Richard Nixon. During this period, McCord was conducting his own investigation of Anderson using Russell as an informant. His report was hand delivered to the Office of Security.

Considering Russell's involvement with Clifford and Meier, this report must have contained information pertaining to these two. If Russell repeated Clifford's remarks concerning Don Nixon to the CIA, the agency would have been fully warned that the Democrats were not only aware of Richard Nixon's indiscretion but were planning to expose it.

While Meier, through Don Nixon, was manipulating the Nixon forces at the highest level, Clifford, through Russell, was able to watch the lower echelons. In a way, Meier's group was the Democrats' equivalent to CREEP, with an important difference. It was tiny in comparison and more tightly knit. This was a conspiracy of friends against only one enemy, not a gathering of mercenaries and political appointees dressed for war against half a country.

A group of strange yet familiar bedfellows found their interests now focussed on Larry O'Brien's office. Likely, the Hughes faction were asked what documents could exist tying Hughes to Nixon and would have had as much interest in the answer as Nixon and the CIA.

It is author Jim Hougan's belief that McCord was operating on a secret agenda during his stint with the White House and that during the burglaries he was taking care of the CIA's interests, not the President's. There were suspicions that McCord had arranged for CIA personnel to be employed in the White House Secret Service detachment and in the Office of the President. The presidential taping system, which recorded all telephone calls and conversations in the executive offices of the White House and Camp David, would have been open to them. If the suspicions are to be given weight, then the CIA was eavesdropping on all the President's private conversations. The agency might have been as alarmed as Nixon when his brother telephoned to say that the Democrats had Howard Hughes' secrets locked away in Larry O'Brien's office.

Even if the suspicions of Nixon's staff were wrong, and his phones had not been tapped, Meier's were. He was under constant surveillance by the CIA and the phones in his Albuquerque office were bugged shortly after he announced his Senate candidacy. While the bugs were in place, Meier had received Don Nixon's plea for help and had talked to his fellow conspirators about their strategy to scare Richard Nixon. Although guarded — except with Don Nixon — these conversations would certainly have contained enough hints to conclude that the Democrats had the goods on the President's dealings with Hughes.

The CIA and the Hughes organization knew that their common interests were in danger. However the intelligence was gained, in early 1972 there was a coalition of interested parties representing the White House, the CIA and the Hughes organization, all staring fixedly at O'Brien's office.

While Meier was putting unbearable pressure on Richard Nixon, Chester Davis was subjecting Meier to some of his own. On March 20 the Hughes Tool Company filed suit in Salt Lake City against Meier, demanding an accounting of the millions of dollars he had spent purchasing mining properties for Hughes, properties which the Tool Company was now claiming were worthless. The suit alleged that Meier was a member of a conspiracy that had paid approximately $1 million for some two thousand or so mining properties in Nevada, California and Utah, which in turn had been sold to Hughes for $9 million. The $8 million in profits had been divvied up among the conspirators. In fact, Meier had no part in the cash transactions relating to the mining properties — his role was merely to negotiate the terms of purchase.

Meier decided to seek out Hughes who knew better than anyone his role in buying the properties and how the money had been disbursed. If he could see him, Meier was certain Hughes would put a stop to the charges.

On March 21, he and Jennie flew to Vancouver, British Columbia, and checked into the Bayshore Inn, where Hughes had been staying for the previous week. Then Meier set out to make contact with Hughes' aides.

The aides found him first. He was spotted in the restaurant by John Holmes, one of the inner circle who ministered to Hughes. Holmes asked why he was there.

"I want to see Mr. Hughes," said Meier.

Holmes shook his head and said it was impossible.

Shortly after this exchange, Meier went to the washroom and at the door ran into his old friend Dick Hannah, Hughes' chief spokesman. Hannah grabbed his arm and pulled him inside.

"John, for Godsakes don't hang around here. You're public enemy number one. You've got to stay away from here."

Hannah was nervous, even more so when Meier said he had come to see Hughes about the lawsuit. He brushed this aside, saying he considered Meier a friend and wanted him to stay away from trouble. Meier heard the door behind him swing open. Hannah's face turned pale. Meier half turned and saw two men. One pointed at Hannah and said: "Get the hell out."

Then he addressed Meier. "What are you doing here?" Hannah left swiftly. Meier tried pushing his way past but his way was barred by the two strangers. He demanded to know who they were.

"Howard Hughes' bodyguards," one of them replied.

"Oh, I didn't know he needed them."

Two others entered the washroom. One was an RCMP officer, who demanded to know Meier's purpose for being in Canada. "I'm on business."

The Mountie looked for guidance to one of the others, who told Meier to be out of the hotel the next day.

When he returned to his room Meier found it ransacked. The camera he used to take pictures of Hughes' penthouse earlier that day was gone and so was his briefcase. Meier left Vancouver the next morning.

Back in Albuquerque his continued absence from the state and lack of participation in the campaign caused the local press to dub him "the invisible candidate." A number of personal files were stolen from his campaign office and the telephones were discovered to be bugged. Meier was the common denominator in a rash of burglaries: his film office, his attorney's office — now his campaign headquarters.

Richard Nixon's troops, their equipment jingling and their trumpets sounding, approached the Democratic National Committee's headquarters with all the stealth of a medieval cavalry charge. Doubtless they thought they were being quiet, but the commotion roused the Democrats long before they arrived. Of the anti-Nixon conspirators, no fewer than four — Hubert Humphrey, George Clifford, John Meier and Bill Haddad — received accurate information of the planned burglary, right down to the names of those planning to commit it.

Haddad was told as early as December — six months before the burglary — that a small band of Republicans was planning something big and bad. The information came to him through A. J. Woolston-Smith, a New Zealand-born private investigator with links to both British Intelligence and the CIA. Hougan writes that Woolston-Smith possibly learned of the plot through the injudicious bragging of Louis Russell. What Woolston-Smith told Haddad could hardly have been news. George Clifford had already been dealing with the conspirators through Russell. What exactly passed between Russell and Clifford will never be known, as both are long dead. But it is an intriguing relationship, the private eye who found himself privy to the political secrets of the decade, and the investigative reporter searching for the means to sandbag a President.

Meanwhile, Don Nixon's last plea for Meier to retrieve what he had supposedly given O'Brien was made on May 11, 1972. Don sounded desperate and asked if Meier would attend meetings in Washington scheduled for May 13 and 14, in which he would be promised a solution to his problems with the IRS in exchange for his cooperation. Meier again refused. Then Humphrey called Meier with the news that Don Nixon had been heard fulminating against O'Brien and threatening that the administration was going to move against him because of his dealings with Meier and Maheu. This eleventh-hour warning came May 20 when the burglary plans were well advanced. By then, McCord had been operating a reconnaissance post from a hotel room opposite the Watergate complex for two weeks.

On May 26 came the first and unsuccessful attempt to break into

O'Brien's office. A second attempt a day later also failed. On May 28 McCord and his gang managed to pick the locks and gain entry. They planted bugs on the telephones and photographed some documents — obviously not the ones they had come for because on the evening of June 16 they returned, only to be captured at gunpoint by police alerted to their presence by a security guard.

One of Watergate's unanswered questions is whether the Democrats lured the burglars into their national headquarters in order to have them arrested — as the Republicans believe — or, as the Democrats maintain, they were arrested after disturbing the guard.

Even if one were to forget the parts played in the affair by Meier and Clifford, surely the actions of the Democrats in the months prior to the break-in clearly demonstrate their intentions. There is every indication that they were laying a trap. As to who sprung it, that is a matter for conjecture — Clifford is the most likely suspect.

The Senate investigation that followed Watergate revealed that Haddad reported to O'Brien in March that sophisticated surveillance techniques were being used against the Democrats. O'Brien ordered the DNC communications director, John Stewart, to meet with Haddad in New York on April 26. Haddad, accompanied by Woolston-Smith, told Stewart and some others that the DNC offices were going to be violated and that the Republicans were planning to break in and bug the phones. He named McCord as being somehow involved and even described the break-in team as consisting of Cuban exiles from Miami, information which in retrospect was astoundingly accurate. Senate investigators, and the minority Republican members of the Watergate Committee, were intrigued by the possibility of a plot to entrap the burglars and pressed Haddad as to why, with such information, he didn't do more to prevent the burglary. Haddad said he did — he sent a file on the matter to Jack Anderson, not just once but twice. Even more mystified, the investigators wanted to know why Anderson, who was never shy of revealing anything, did nothing with the story. Anderson later described the Haddad affair in his book *The Anderson Papers:*

> The arrest of the Watergate Seven was a chance fluke. But the plot might never have proceeded even that far if I had been a more diligent investigator. On April 14, 1972, I received a remarkable letter from

William Haddad, a New York entrepreneur who until a dozen years ago had been a prize winning investigative reporter. He wrote that a private investigator had told him of plans to tap the telephones of the Democratic National Committee. He understood the plan had been hatched by a group of advertising men... who had been recruited for the Nixon campaign.

I had everything but a road sign pointing to the story. I had been alerted to the Watergate plot two months in advance. I had personal ties with the Waterbuggers. Yet, I was quite oblivious of the conspiracy when on June 16 I was making my way through Washington National Airport to catch a plane to Cleveland. I recognized a familiar face and stopped for a chat. It was Frank Sturgis. (Sturgis, one of the Watergate burglars, had been a friend of Anderson's for years.)

George Clifford was co-author of the book. To talk of flukes and lack of diligence when Clifford was part of the conspiracy against Nixon is nonsense. Forgetting for a moment that Clifford was involved, Anderson's later excuse that Haddad's information was sloppy and vague was an unbelievable admission from the foremost investigative journalist of the time.

Meier was present when Haddad compiled the material to be sent to Anderson. It was a thick folder which even contained the photographs of the ringleaders suspected of having designs on O'Brien's office.

Looking at the situation in which the Democrats found themselves from March to April 1972, it is obvious that knowing what they did, they had three choices: to prevent the burglary either by exposing the plans or placing guards inside the offices; to allow it to happen and expose the culprits later; or — the most dramatic of all — to have the burglars nabbed in the act.

If Haddad genuinely had wanted to expose CREEP'S criminal intent he would not have been stopped by Anderson's failure to pick up the story. He was a journalist himself, publisher of the *Manhattan Tribune*,[4] of which Meier was a director. Other reporters would have killed for such a story, but Anderson was the only one contacted. The option of preventing the burglary by exposing the plot had a short life, if any at all.

Clifford, who was at the center of the plot, had no interest in publishing anything while his enemies in the Nixon camp were maneuvering themselves into position. Any publicity in advance of the burglary could well have exposed Russell and, trustworthy or not, Russell was well placed to spy on the Republicans. Clifford would want his mole left undisturbed as long as possible.

Thus, Haddad's motive in sending that dossier to Anderson was not to cause the columnist to expose the evil intentions of the Republicans. It makes more sense to believe that Anderson was being readied to expose the burglars after the fatal deed was committed.

It is tempting to think that Anderson was a part of the conspiracy. But he could also have acted as he did to protect Clifford. Perhaps Clifford asked him to look the other way while he slid a stiletto between Nixon's ribs. If so, one can hardly blame Anderson for standing aside given the beating he was taking from Nixon's administration. Meanwhile, despite the warnings, the Democrats did nothing to protect their headquarters. There is no record that the building's security was alerted or requested to put someone inside the DNC offices overnight — the simplest way to prevent entry.

This unwillingness to defend their headquarters demonstrates the Democrats' intentions more clearly than anything else. With nothing to lose and everything to gain, the conspirators could only hope the Republicans wouldn't suffer an attack of nerves and refuse to come looking for Meier's illusory documents. Any unusual activity would have scared McCord's team away, as would the slightest hint that their own security had been breached.

The main argument advanced against the whole business being a trap is that the Democrats would have sprung it the first time their headquarters was entered. As there were no arrests the first time, the argument goes, there was no trap. But letting them come in and escape so they could be exposed later, was just as much a trap. It could well be that Clifford, a fluid thinker who undoubtedly organized the game at this stage, kept an open mind as to which option to choose depending on the circumstances.

If the Democrats stood back and let the Republicans burglarize their headquarters and get away, Clifford, given his relationship with Russell and the information already in the conspirators' hands, was perfectly poised to expose it as the action of Nixon's re-election committee. It is plausible that Clifford could have wanted the personal satisfaction of skewering Nixon by "solving" the burglary.

Considering his collusion with Russell, one can presume that Clifford was informed of the burglary team's agenda, including the timing of the break-ins. When McCord's crew came back June 16, perhaps Clifford had a change of heart. He might now have wanted them arrested, or perhaps they were only captured because the burglary team's ineptitude roused a security guard.

What began with Meier and Humphrey plotting to scare Nixon into committing an irrational act led to this dramatic capture of the President's men inside Watergate, regardless of the Democrats' claims that they had done nothing to provoke it. Watergate was a masterpiece of political espionage that can be boiled down to a few important elements: the deliberate baiting of the Nixon camp; the laying of a false trail to the DNC headquarters; the use of an inside spy; the refusal to take protective measures despite constant warnings; and the collaring of the burglary team by accident or by design.

Richard Nixon's part in the whole affair is less of a mystery: He ordered the break-in. The evidence of his complicity is overwhelming. In the aftermath of Watergate, there arose an almost pathetic chorus from the majority of Nixon's people who went to jail — they didn't know why O'Brien's office was chosen as the target. Certainly in interviews or in their memoirs, they admitted to conspiring to cause the break-in, or to covering it up. However, when it came down to explaining what the operational target was, they were mystified — with the exception of McCord, who would have been informed by Russell.

A most illuminating book about Watergate is *Blind Ambition* by John Dean, Nixon's chief counsel. He describes how he and Charles Colson, Nixon's special counsel, sat in their cells wracking their brains in an effort to discover why O'Brien's office was the target. Dean quotes Colson as saying:

> It's incredible. Millions of dollars have been spent investigating Watergate. A President has been forced out of office. Dozens of lives have been ruined. We're sitting in the can. And still nobody can explain why they bugged the place to begin with.

Even though he was faced with a catastrophe, Richard Nixon could hardly call his staff together, ask each for an oath of loyalty, then confess to receiving an enormous payment from Hughes in the hope that they would feel obliged to come to his aid by attacking Watergate. He had to know what Meier's information was. Could it be plausibly denied? Was there a defense? Only he would have had the motive for ordering the break-in. Because he couldn't admit the reason, it went ahead with almost none of the participants knowing why.

As to the President's predisposition for ordering a criminal act, according to Ehrlichman he was more than capable on other similar occasions:[5]

> Nixon would not have restrained Hunt and his confederates (from burglarizing Ellsberg's psychiatrist's office). Nixon was demanding action. Once before, when Nixon was in such a mood, Colson had planned to firebomb the Brookings Institute to get at its cache of secret documents. Nixon knew about that plan in advance too, as I discovered after I ordered it stopped.

Nixon personally had nothing to gain from these criminal operations, one of which — a firebombing — smacks more of terrorism than intelligence gathering. How much swifter would his approval be for a burglary that might save his presidency?

Richard Nixon, entangled for the second time in a scandal with Hughes, brought disaster upon himself by panicking as Humphrey intuitively knew he would.

In 1960, in his first presidential campaign, he thought the Kennedy forces were going to ruin him by exposing the $205,000 "loan" from Hughes to his family. He also believed that reporters had the details and were ready to rush them into print. He was only partly right. The newspapers decided to sit on the information as the campaign was almost over and Nixon would not have had sufficient time to defend himself.

In an effort to strike first, Nixon's campaign manager placed a story with a friendly columnist, making the whole affair fragrant by avoiding the source of the money and by arguing that Nixon was ignorant of the transaction until much later. When reporters holding back the story saw this, they abandoned their qualms and publicized the deal for what it was. It cost Nixon the 1960 election, in his mind at least.

In 1972, frantic that the Democrats were about to expose Hughes' $1 million gift, he again struck first, when perhaps it would have been better to suffer the agony. Once again it would cost him the presidency.

A front page story in the *Los Angeles Times* on June 18, the day after the break-in, broke the news of Watergate to Meier. He was at home in

Newport Beach after leaving Nevada and the shambles of his political campaign. His first thought was of Clifford. He marvelled at his friend's dogged assurance that the DNC office would be attacked.

They had expected something later in the campaign when nerves were more apt to fail, but Nixon's nerve had given out early and his burglars, as Clifford had foretold, had targeted Larry O'Brien's office. They were described only as intruders by the *Times*. Looking at the story again and again, Meier wondered what would happen next. Nixon was finished, that much was obvious. To obliterate him, all the Democrats needed to do was release details of his dealings with Hughes and the motive for the break-in would become apparent. For the remainder of the morning Meier's spirits rose. He forgot his doomed senatorial campaign and the federal hounds that had been unleashed against him.

Since returning from Albuquerque, Meier had planned to take his family on vacation — the first they would have had in years. Not only were Meier's nerves ragged from the attentions of his enemies at the CIA, the White House and Hughes' Summa Corporation, but Jennie and the baby were ill.

Reading the *Times* story, Meier was desperate to speak with Clifford. He, more than anyone, would know what had happened. Meier was experiencing an almost narcotic desire for inside information mingled with an urge to luxuriate in the mutual satisfaction of what they had done. Although he phoned, he could not catch Clifford that day or the next. Clifford's attempts to reach Meier as he commuted between Los Angles and Newport Beach that week were equally unsuccessful. They failed to make contact before the Meiers left on June 24 for a holiday in Canada.

HUBERT HUMPHREY WAS TRAILING Senator George McGovern in the primaries, after losing California. The old campaigner would make his final stand in the convention hall in Miami on July 10 but his eclipse that night was not to take place before the Democratic Party as he'd known it. Out of the 1968 debacle in Chicago — when Mayor Richard Daley's police had billy-clubbed anti-war demonstrators and newsmen on the streets — had come revolution.

With blood still fresh in the gutter Humphrey had heeded calls from party dissidents to set up a Reform Commission to overhaul the party's delegate selection process in time for the 1972 convention and McGovern was in charge of the commission.

Four years later the Democratic Party woke up to find McGovern, the arch reformer, standing before them like some bashful Napoleon at the head of an army whose troops, drunk with equality, liberty and fraternity, were more than capable of scattering whatever opposition stood in their way. Reform meant giving women an equal say, the young a chance, racial minorities representation based on whatever percentage of a community population they constituted. Welfare recipients found their cause championed at the Miami convention, as did gays and lesbians. Reform meant taking power out of the hands of the old brokers who, with their myriad of alliances and affiliations, had molded the Democratic Party and the nation.

America watched as McGovern defeated Humphrey by this unprecedented sampling of race, age, gender and income. After cutting the unions down to size, McGovern enraged the old guard by first promising to reappoint Larry O'Brien as chairman of the Democratic National Committee, then reneged on the commitment. In keeping with the new focus of the Democratic Party, McGovern appointed a woman.

Happy to be away from it all, Meier and his family travelled across Western Canada. Occasionally, Meier called his lawyer Robert Wyshak in Beverly Hills to let him know where he was, only to hear complaints that he could hardly have picked a worse time to leave. Wyshak was besieged with calls from Meier's friends and acquaintances wanting to know why he had vanished. Clifford had sent Wyshak a telegram urgently requesting that he contact Meier. Meier finally reached Clifford on July 3, Joanne's tenth birthday. Clifford sounded anxious.

"Don't you know what's happening here?"

Meier asked if he meant the Watergate business.

"Yes, we've got to sit down and talk. Can you come to Washington?"

"George, I'm on holiday. Can't it wait?"

"No, I'll fly up there." But Meier dissuaded him by saying he would come straight to Washington once he returned home from his travels in Canada. By Independence Day, Meier had been away almost a month and felt the weight of the world lifted from his shoulders. For the first time in years he felt freedom. Richard Nixon seemed a million miles away. The

Hughes organization was like a bad dream and the CIA — once out of sight — was out of mind.

Meier grew increasingly disturbed by the thought of returning to the United States. By degrees he came to consider a life in Canada. His family would have to leave their friends and start anew in a foreign country, but the prospect was exciting. They stayed in a suburban Vancouver hotel for a few weeks enjoying the change of pace, the lack of racial tension and the generally relaxed way people conducted their business. On an impulse, Meier let a real estate agent show them a house on the bluffs above Georgia Strait. By noon they owned it.

Meanwhile, Gonzales and the CIA had lost track of Meier. His unexpected decision to leave the United States and his failure to return home caused the CIA to launch a search for him. But if the CIA was having trouble, British Intelligence in the person of a Mr. Johnson telephoning from Ottawa, managed to find him without undue effort. Johnson introduced himself as a representative of the British government and asked if he were planning to visit Britain any time soon and if he would mind meeting him. Meier said he would be passing through London en route to Zurich in September.

MEIER WAS WAITING to clear British customs when he heard — "Oh, Mr. Meier, Johnson here." Turning, he found a man offering to shake his hand. He took it and felt it gently tug him out of the line. They went to a coffee shop where Johnson waved some identification in front of him and quizzed him about his plans to move to Canada. Would he be there long? what were his intentions? — all with such charm that Meier found himself answering questions he would never have accepted from a stranger.

"I'm going to move my family there," he said.

"Well, yes. I can understand why. Our people in Washington have heard some things." Had he perhaps thought of living in England where he would be a little farther away? Meier said his family was planning to stay in Canada. Johnson didn't press but asked if he would be interested in talking, unofficially, to some people in London.

"About what?"

"Oh, this and that."

"Why not?"

Johnson escorted him to his Zurich flight. When he boarded, Meier found his ticket had been upgraded to first class. He was halfway to Zurich before he realized he had not gone through British customs.

In America, Richard Nixon appeared to be heading for a landslide victory. By the middle of September, the polls showed him 34 points ahead of McGovern. Nothing short of catastrophe could stop his re-election.

Despite the digging of the *Washington Post* and the *New York Times,* the Watergate investigation was only slowly uncovering the parts played in the burglary by the lower echelons at CREEP and the White House. Few Americans believed Nixon had anything to do with it.

The phone lines linking Meier, Schrade and Clifford buzzed. Schrade had already visited McGovern's headquarters, taking with him a dossier outlining Nixon's sins including Meier's information concerning the payment to Rebozo. Schrade gave McGovern an outline of how this had been collected and its relevance to the Watergate break-in. He urged McGovern to use it against Nixon. Meier, too, was pressing one of McGovern's advisors, Stan Steinbaum.

Had Humphrey been Nixon's opponent, there is no doubt that the Hughes payment would have been an issue, as he had vowed as much to Meier. McGovern didn't have the stomach. This "most decent man in the Senate" as Robert Kennedy had once described him, had come before the nation promising enlightenment in exchange for Nixon's darkness. Politically pious, full of rectitude and honorable to the point of primness, here was someone whose sensitivities wouldn't allow him to go poking about in black corners feeling for something disgusting.

What Meier and Schrade were expecting would take no small amount of courage, for once cast, such accusations are potent and can harm not only the victim but the accuser. On October 31, the eleventh hour before the election — and with the CIA listening in, Meier called Steinbaum at McGovern's headquarters and demanded to know why the candidate was letting the presidency slip from his grasp. He had spoken earlier that day with Schrade, who was beside himself with anger. Meier decided to try to convince Steinbaum that McGovern had nothing to lose and should act. But McGovern had neither the will, the inclination nor the courage. Instead, he hoped that some reporter would do his dirty work for him.

McGovern vented his bitterness at Nixon for escaping the consequences of Watergate and the failure of the press to save his campaign. After being humiliated by the size of Nixon's victory, McGovern complained that the press, while critically reporting upon his campaign, had not given Nixon the same scrutiny — had not even laid a glove on him.

"Not a single reporter could gather the courage to ask a question about the bugging and burglary of the Democratic National Committee..." McGovern complained. For those Democrats in the know, this was nothing short of hypocrisy. McGovern sat on the information which might have made him President and did nothing, to the great chagrin of Paul Schrade, who called him in his hour of defeat and mocked him for his faintheartedness.

11

HEAR NO EVIL

Richard Nixon had confounded the conspirators. His re-election must have seemed to them like the triumph of a superior, if malevolent, sorcery.

On November 7, 1972, while Nixon stood victorious, the conspirators were a scattered and fading force. Meier had gone to Canada. Humphrey was a broken man. Schrade was dispirited by the party's alienation of the unions. Clifford was left to contemplate being a known enemy of an administration which had just received an enormous mandate.

Eleven days after Nixon's victory, Meier was called by William C. Turner, an attorney for the Securities and Exchange Commission who was probing Hughes' purchase of Air West. Meier's name had come up during his inquiries and would he be prepared to aid the investigation? Meier agreed.

While Turner was trying to undo the Gordian knot Hughes had made of the Air West takeover, Meier was in and out of Europe pursuing business deals. A group of Arab investors wanted help setting up a processing plant in the Middle East to record Arabic pop songs. This presented an opportunity to visit Buhler. Unable to reach Hughes in North America, Meier wanted to see if Buhler would help. He saw him in Liechtenstein on January 25, 1973. Initially, the meeting was friendly. Over coffee Meier said he was concerned about Hughes' health. The newspapers reported that he was in London staying at the Inn on the Park — was that where he was?

Buhler was evasive. "I know you were a friend of Mr. Hughes and did a lot of work for him, but would you be interested in working with me? We could arrange for you to have an office here or in Zurich."

Meier refused to consider the offer until he had spoken to Hughes.

Buhler shook his head and said there was no possibility of that. He now worked for Chester Davis who wasn't too happy with Meier but would let bygones be bygones if Meier would work with them and drop his demands to see Hughes. The thought of working for Davis was repugnant to Meier and he made no attempt to hide it, which led to an argument. Faced with Buhler's refusal to help, he left empty handed.

When he returned to Canada he found his application for Landed Immigrant status, which he thought would be a formality, was becoming an ordeal. He was told to make himself available for an interview on February 6.

That day on the very steps of the Immigration office in Vancouver, Meier froze as eight men rushed and surrounded him and Jennie. One snatched his arm and shoved a sheaf of papers into his hand. The men were from Intertel. As Meier pushed his way through them, he could see yet another man off to the side taking photographs. The papers were service for the civil suit begun against him by Summa Corporation for his part in purchasing mining claims.

The meeting with the Immigration officer was as disquieting as the incident preceding it. Apart from wanting to know the extent of Meier's assets and bank accounts, the officer demanded to know what he had been doing during his years with Hughes and his part in the mine procurements. It was the kind of information that might have been sought in discovery proceedings. Meier was disconcerted by such interest, considering what had occurred on the steps of the Immigration office, and tried to fend him off with vague replies. What nagged at him too, was the question of how Intertel knew he would be at the Immigration office at that particular time. There was nothing of chance about the encounter, not considering the size of the ambush or the presence of a photographer.

Unknown to Meier, the Immigration Department in Vancouver was working hand in glove with Intertel. Among the gang who surprised him was a well-known immigration snitch, Robert Morrison, who was now employed by Intertel. Others included William Brendzy, another snitch who was a process server with a small-time bill collection agency in Vancouver.

Four days before the ambush, Brendzy had arrived at the main border crossing between Washington State and British Columbia and was given Meier's confidential immigration file. Earlier, an Immigration officer had refused to turn it over, but a call from Vancouver headquarters convinced him otherwise. Brendzy took the file, kept it over the weekend, copied the contents and gave copies to Morrison, who delivered them to Intertel. This was a fundamental breach of Meier's right to confidentiality in his dealings with the Canadian government. His confidential file was turned over to a professional investigator working for a foreign security company owned by friends of Richard Nixon.

Morrison was a career informer used by the Canadian Immigration Intelligence Service.[1] He provided them with information against persons he felt were undeserving of admission to the country, usually people of color. By his own admission Morrison — being paid by Intertel — wanted to prevent Meier from emigrating to Canada, as this would have provided him with protection against civil proceedings underway against him in the United States. Morrison approached his contacts in the Vancouver Immigration office to queer the pitch.

Here was a foreign company successfully manipulating one of the most sensitive of Canadian bureaucracies. Meier's application was delayed as Intertel requested but the collusion didn't stop there. The Vancouver Immigration office next delivered a transcript of Meier's interrogation. When this surfaced six months later, its existence in American hands caused great embarrassment to the Canadian government. The government scrambled to justify its actions by saying it was simply one government helping another, which ignored completely the fact that this blatant trafficking was done through Intertel to assist not a government but a private company, Summa Corporation.

Grant Carson, owner of the collection agency Brendzy was working for, admitted they had joined in pursuit of Meier after being told they were being hired by the "Canadian Secret Service." In reality, it was two Intertel men who showed them thick folders on Meier and Don Nixon full of photographs and documents likely created by the U.S. Secret Service.

The Intertel pair showed Carson and Brendzy a black telephone which reputedly cost $12,000, an eavesdropping device for conversations taking

place within the house. One said they had a contact in the B.C. Tel security
department and the phone was going to be planted in the Meier home. The
practical Carson asked what they would do if the Meiers wanted one that
wasn't black. Neither had considered this. With Intertel coordinating the
surveillance, Carson's crew kept a 24-hour watch on Meier's home. When
he went abroad, he was tailed by the CIA.

While the cozy arrangement between Intertel and the Vancouver
Immigration office was facilitating the transportation of Meier's confidential
files to his enemies in the United States, Meier was back in London dealing
with the Arabs and their taste for pop music. On the evening of February 22
he returned to his hotel room at the Skyline and found it a shambles. The
locks on his briefcase were snapped and his papers lay scattered about the
floor. Immigration documents and a book containing phone numbers were
missing. The lining was ripped out of a suit jacket.

Meier noticed he was being followed. During March 3 two men were
with him wherever he went. Hubert Humphrey had told him that if he were
ever in trouble in Europe to call Susi Wyss in Paris. Meier had been
introduced to Wyss before but only socially. She was a clothing designer and
intellectual who moved easily within the diplomatic circles of Paris.
Humphrey, who as Vice President had knowledge of such things, told Meier
that Wyss had intelligence contacts that crossed the Iron Curtain. She was a
trusted and able expeditor who had undertaken tasks on behalf of both
sides. He met with her two days later in Paris.

Meier mentioned the men following him and that he had been dealing
with Buhler in the hopes of getting to see Hughes. Wyss warned Meier to be
careful: "This Dr. Buhler is very dangerous. I wouldn't go near him at all."
Meier, who had supposed Buhler to be just another of Hughes' agents, was
disturbed to hear him described as dangerous.

Back in the United States, Nixon was given little time to savor his
victory. The Senate Select Committee on Presidential Campaign Activities,
better known as the Watergate committee, was being formed to investigate
the political connections behind the burglary. The White House knew it was
only a question of time before the Senate's investigators sniffed out Meier.

The Republicans made a half-hearted attempt to pin the blame for
Watergate upon the plotting of the Democrats, using — of all people — the
ubiquitous Louis Russell. Investigators for the Watergate committee issued a
subpoena demanding Russell's testimony. But on May 18, 1973, the very

day McCord began his public testimony before the committee, Russell suffered a heart attack. He would later claim to have been deliberately poisoned. John Leon, who was conducting the Republican's Watergate counter-offensive, was determined to prove that the break-in and arrests were entrapment.

In a memorandum to the party, Leon had said he hoped to show that Russell had been a spy for the Democrats and that Russell had tipped them and the police to the time of the burglary.[2] On June 2, Russell, whose testimony could have given weight to this theory, died after suffering a second heart attack. Leon was left without a witness but still had a story. He was to appear at a press conference with a statement expected to give the Watergate affair new perspective. On July 13, Leon too suffered a heart attack and died, taking the counter-offensive to the grave with him.

By the summer of 1973, Nixon's executive staff — those seasoned fighters who had twice brought him victory — were decimated. Ehrlichman, Haldeman and their subordinates were casualties, leaving Nixon virtually alone. During final meetings with his staff, as they were being hounded out of office by revelations of their illegal acts, Nixon revealed the existence of a sizeable nest egg stashed away in Rebozo's care. The first mention of these riches came when John Dean told Nixon shortly after the break-in that the burglars were demanding hush money. Nixon asked how much their silence would cost; Dean estimated $1 million. Nixon said he knew where it could be found.

When Nixon met Haldeman and Ehrlichman and asked for their resignations, he disclosed that Rebozo had a fortune secretly hidden away. In his encounter with Haldeman, Nixon lamented the fate of his two stalwarts but said he had the money to pay for their defense, which he estimated at $300,000.

Haldeman, stunned, asked where the money would come from. Rebozo had it, Nixon told him. "But I reminded him that Bebe had only $100,000 of the Hughes money. Where would the rest have come from? Nixon told me this interesting news. There was much more money in Bebe's 'tin box' than the Hughes $100,000..."[3] And so there was.

MEANWHILE, Meier was in London being introduced to Robbie Robertson by a business associate. Robertson offered to use his contacts in

London on Meier's behalf. He alluded to having friends in Scotland Yard who might give him information about Hughes and began making himself useful by doing odd jobs for Meier. He was suave and engaging with an endless supply of jokes.

Buhler was tenacious in his efforts to contact Meier, who was doing his best to avoid him. On July 12, while Meier and his family were in Hawaii, a man came up and told him to call Dr. Buhler in Liechtenstein before leaving for Canada. Meier was disturbed by the ease with which Buhler had found him.

It was August 9, 1973 and one of those sweltering mornings when the heat and stillness of the air are a warning against being too trustful of the weather. Meier was not planning to be away all day, a few hours at most. He put his children, Johnny, then sixteen, Jimmy — two years old that very day — and Joanne into his white Mercedes and headed towards the U.S. border. With them was a family friend from California, Floyd Hargan. Hargan had wanted to go crabbing in the tidal pools down at the Point in the interval between opening Jimmy's presents and lunch. It was a short distance from the Meiers' home in the Vancouver suburb of Delta to the peninsula of Point Roberts, a tiny digit of land attached to the Canadian mainland but American territory nevertheless as it lies below the 49th Parallel.

As Meier pulled from the driveway he noticed a car parked across the way. Inside were two men who seemed to be watching them. The Mercedes accelerated easily and the other car tucked in behind. Farther down the road another car pulled a U-turn as he passed and he found himself leading a small procession. Not wishing to alarm his party, Meier continued on but as he cruised past the Canadian customs shed he saw the cars stop and turn away. Just ahead was the small U.S. customs post. Crossing here was usually a formality. As the Point is surrounded on three sides by water, there is no way to reach the mainland of the United States except by boat or plane. All road traffic uses that one road in from Canada.

Normally the U.S. customs shed would contain only one official but as Meier coasted slowly up he could see four men inside: a customs officer in shirt sleeves, a man he took to be a member of the Border Patrol and two other men in dark suits, white shirts and ties although the heat that morning would have been best endured without a jacket.

Meier knew something was wrong. His sense of alarm was only heightened when instead of asking the perfunctory questions, the customs agent simply waved him through. His first impulse was to turn around but the children were thirsty and perhaps his imagination was too overheated. Quelling a sense of foreboding, he decided to stop at the store ahead and buy soft drinks.

They had hardly entered the premises when two other men, in suits, ties and dark glasses, walked in behind. Meier had seen this uniform before and knew something serious was about to happen. He reached for Joanne and the two boys and shoved them towards the door. Hargan seemed unsure what to do but followed Meier out as he hustled them empty handed into the car. Meier passed his wallet containing his phone numbers and identification to his eldest son and hurriedly turned the Mercedes towards the border, yanking it through a U-turn raising clouds of dust as it rolled over the gravel shoulders.

The main road cuts right through the peninsula and runs north and south. It is generally straight except for a blind curve at the border. As he came out of the curve heading north, Meier braked violently. Ahead three cars lay broadside across the road and behind them were a collection of bobbing heads and weapons. The tires screeched against the hot tarmac as the car lurched forward, throwing everyone against their seat belts.

Three men clutching guns sprinted the few yards from the roadblock to his stopping point. It was terrifying. He lowered the window to ask what they were doing but before he could open his mouth a deputy sheriff shoved his service revolver through the opening up against Meier's temple.

"Get out of the car."

Meier opened the door and stepped out. He noticed two others in plainclothes pointing pistols at him. They were IRS agents. He stood uncertainly beside the car while the deputy sheriff pulled his hands behind him and snapped on handcuffs. "What have I done?" he asked.

He heard sobbing and half turned to see looks of horror on his children's faces. Little Jimmy was crying and his brother was trying to comfort him. Hargan turned white. One of the men addressed Hargan by name and asked if he lived in Northridge, California. Hargan nodded in disbelief, clearly confused by the fact that he was known to the people who had just ambushed them.

Hargan was ordered to put the children in the car and drive it home. Meier was placed in the rear of a patrol car and driven to Point Roberts jail.

Inside, sitting at a desk, were the pair who had entered the store. They said nothing as he passed, but the black lenses of their sunglasses followed him as he was led to a small cell and locked inside.

He tried calling to the deputy sheriff, asking why he was being held but was ignored. A short time later one of the IRS agents came and said that the men in the outer office wanted to see him. Then he ordered the deputy sheriff out and vanished himself. When the pair arrived they showed Meier their shields through the bars. His heart sank. They were Secret Service. He was now in the hands of Richard Nixon's Praetorian Guard. Without further formalities, one agent announced their meeting was off the record. "You don't have to talk to us, Mr. Meier, but it's in your best interests to listen. Do you understand?"

"Yes."

"If you cooperate we will drive you to the border and you can go home. If not, things are going to get tough."

Meier asked what they wanted. They said he was under arrest for income tax evasion. The price of his freedom was the surrender of all documents in his possession or hidden away with his lawyer, Robert Wyshak, pertaining to Hughes, Nixon and the operation of federal agencies, particularly the CIA.

This was the shopping list the Watergate burglars had been given some fourteen months before. Incredible as it was, the search which had started in the nation's capital had now come to an insignificant corner of the United States, with the Secret Service replacing the CIA freebooters who had failed their commission and were now in jail. The White House was now hoping to prevent Meier from giving his information to the Watergate committee.

Meier asked if he could speak with his lawyer. The agents smiled at this. Wyshak had just left for a holiday to Egypt. Didn't he know? Meier said he imagined he was still at home. But they assured him he wasn't.

How long would they give him to make a decision?

"Five minutes."

"Can I call another lawyer or maybe my wife?"

"No."

"Where's the warrant for my arrest?"

"Just yes or no."

"No."

"Okay, if that's your answer, we're leaving. You'll regret this. That was the biggest mistake you'll ever make." They walked away and two of his captors returned. Again Meier asked to see the warrant and for permission to phone his wife. He could not see the warrant and their orders forbade his phoning home.

Meier could hear the phone ringing and the deputy answering. He could hear him say: "No, he's not here. He's been taken to Seattle." Callously he called out that it was Meier's wife; someone told him to shut up.

An hour later, Meier was led from the jail, his feet shackled and his hands still in cuffs. He was driven to a pier, where he was lowered into a small powerboat. By now the weather had changed; the wind had shifted to the southeast and the morning's clear sky had been replaced by a light drizzle. He shivered in his cotton shirt. He tried to steady himself and toppled over, falling between the seats. He tried to struggle upright but one of the guards put a foot into the small of his back and pushed him face down against the floor. There were a couple inches of water slopping around in the bilge and he was soon covered in a film of oil. He felt the boat swing away from the pier and the engines thrust the stern deeper as it picked up speed. From the corner of his eye he could see the drawn guns of the pair watching him while he listened to their nervous muttering to the pilot to be careful and not to risk trespassing into Canadian waters.

The charge on which Meier was arrested — income tax evasion — was still being heard by a grand jury in Las Vegas. The IRS and the Secret Service had placed agents in Point Roberts because they knew he would be indicted. Yet Meier was arrested before the indictment was in and there was no legal warrant allowing them to act. Having him cross the border into U.S. territory was too good a chance to miss. Had Meier learned of the indictment while in Canada, he could have avoided arrest by staying out of the United States, as income tax evasion is not an extraditable offense.

The boat which carried Meier away from Point Roberts that afternoon brought him to the U.S. border town of Blaine. Virgino Gonzales tried to lay hands on him there, arguing the CIA's proprietorship, but the IRS wanted him for themselves. From there, Meier was transported to Everett, a town north of Seattle. The next day he was arraigned in Snohomish County District Court.

Gonzales made sure newspaper photographers were on hand to take pictures of him being hustled into court. Meier appeared in Seattle before a

U.S. magistrate who — over the objections of the U.S. attorney who wanted him sent to the Las Vegas judge who had ordered his arrest — released Meier after he posted bail. There were no restrictions preventing his return to Canada. It was one of the few breaks he would get in court. Once free, he hastened home.

Meier's arrest broke an agreement between Ralph Kaminski, the chief IRS investigating officer, and Meier's lawyer, Wyshak, who was promised there would be no indictment without a conference between the parties. Wyshak had once been the U.S. Attorney for the tax division of the Justice Department, in Los Angeles. Pre-indictment conferences were not uncommon. Notwithstanding this agreement, the moment Wyshak left on holiday an indictment was handed down. The government charged that Meier had failed to report income of $2.3 million earned from 1968 to 1970 — most of it Meier's alleged share of money paid out by Hughes for mining properties. Kaminski would later say he, too, had no advance warning of the arrest.

This former agent's work on the Meier investigation made him the most travelled agent in the history of the IRS. Another distinction was that his investigation was orchestrated by the White House which gave him *carte blanche* to travel where he would to gather information on Meier.

The process used to indict Meier was a travesty. The judge who presided at Meier's grand jury and who ordered his arrest was the brother of an important witness who appeared against him. Judge Roger Foley heard evidence from his brother Joseph Foley — a lawyer who had done the conveyancing of the mining properties for Hughes — without so much as a blush. He issued the warrant for Meier's arrest and set bail at $100,000. (Judge Foley did discover his scruples when the government was later seeking to indict Howard Hughes for his conduct in the takeover of Air West. Then Foley remembered his brother and removed himself from the bench.)

Not only was brother Joseph allowed to give evidence — so was Meier's former lawyer, John Suckling. He arrived in court bearing confidential documents belonging to Meier — violating Meier's privileged relationship with his lawyer. Another federal judge had an opportunity to comment on the proceedings in Foley's court when Wyshak sought a restraining order against Suckling to prevent his supplying further evidence to prosecutors. Los Angeles U.S. District Judge Andrew Hauk, after listening to Wyshak's recital of the manner in which the evidence had been obtained, said the whole business was rotten "and you can tell Foley that." He further commented that Suckling's performance might make a case for disbarment. Resorting to language rarely heard from the bench, Hauk said: "Mr. Suckling, what you did sucks."

Meanwhile, statements from Buhler were entered into the files. Of course it was not mentioned that he was a paymaster for the CIA in Europe and associated with Nixon and Vesco. All those details would only come out ten years after Meier's indictment when the *New York Times* tumbled to Buhler and phoned Meier to ask for information on this mysterious European. When the story appeared Kaminski was quoted as saying the CIA prevented the IRS from interviewing Buhler about Meier. Regardless, information he had supplied to the IRS was collected and formed part of the indictment.

Buhler, according to the *Times,* had been subpoenaed in 1967 to testify before a grand jury investigating organized crime and the use of Swiss bank accounts and Liechtenstein financial establishments in fraudulent schemes. To escape, he called upon his contacts within the CIA and was immediately spirited out of the country. The newspaper said that Buhler, a lawyer and businessman, had been connected with stock and tax fraud, illegal arms deals, kidnapping and questionable overseas payments on behalf of American corporations. Kaminski described him as a "bagman, a courier and a paymaster" for the CIA in Europe. When Meier submits what he knew of Buhler's activities on behalf of Howard Hughes, Richard Nixon and his connection with Vesco, Dr. Buhler appears to have been sitting at some great crossroad controlling the transit of money and influence — a pivot for grand and secret alliances. Unfortunately none of this was known to Meier or his lawyers at the time of his indictment.

The manner of Meier's arrest and arraignment concerned Clifford, who arrived in Vancouver on September 8. This was the first time they had met since before Watergate and as usual Clifford had a plan. Meier would soon be contacted by the Watergate committee and asked to give evidence. Clifford advised him to give them everything but his actual documents, which should be withheld until his public appearance. Clifford then promised to meet Meier in Washington before his interview to brief him. He said he had a contact on the committee's staff and promised to arrange for reporters to cover Meier's arrival in Washington and to keep his name in print while he was giving evidence.

On October 12, Meier flew to Washington for his first Watergate interview. The flight was uneventful until the plane stopped in Chicago. A man came aboard and insisted he sit next to Meier, over the protests of a flight attendant who said his seat was elsewhere. Eventually, he took her by the elbow and walked her down the cabin and showed her something from a wallet, then came back and sat down. Later Meier went to the bathroom. When he returned his seat mate was putting Meier's briefcase back under his seat. Meier had no original documents. His diaries were hidden in a safe place. As he left the plane the flight attendant whispered he was being trailed by someone from the government.

Meier met Clifford in the terminal and told him he was being followed. Clifford said he too had been trailed to the airport. The next morning, Humphrey called, but said it would be unwise for them to meet. "I want you to know that whatever happens, John, I'm with you. This is our one chance to get rid of Nixon and by God we ought to take it."

That afternoon the Watergate investigators and attorneys arrived at Meier's hotel room. For seven hours, with Wyshak present, he was quizzed by Martin Lackritz, Terry Lenzner, Scott Armstrong, Robert Muse and Carolyn Andrade. Meier, without his diaries, referred to notes drawn from the journals and memos. When describing his meeting with Rebozo in Miami he withheld the date and exact location. But he did tell them of the briefcase full of money which was passed to Rebozo and of the conversation which ensued. He told of other payoffs in which the CIA had had a hand and said he possessed a list of dozens of politicians whose campaigns the CIA had asked Hughes to support financially.

Wyshak, a compulsive photographer, took a picture of the group catching them sharing a joke but the joviality vanished as the flash popped and one of the investigators angrily tried to get at the camera. The investigators protested they were supposed to be doing their work quietly and didn't want the snapshot appearing in the next day's papers. Wyshak haughtily assured them it would not. What did appear in print were Wyshak's remarks that Nixon would have to resign once Meier gave his testimony.

That night Meier, Wyshak, Clifford and their wives were at the Rue Gauche having dinner when Secretary of State Henry Kissinger strode in with a young woman on his arm. As Kissinger walked by, Clifford jumped up and buttonholed him: "Mr. Secretary, I don't know if you've ever had the chance to meet John Meier of the Hughes organization, but let me introduce you."

Kissinger hissed "son-of-a-bitch" in Meier's direction and went off muttering, causing Clifford no end of glee.

At 11 p.m. Clifford rang Meier and told him to meet him in the lobby. Meier protested that he was going to bed but something in Clifford's tone convinced him to dress and go downstairs. Clifford then drove him to his office. "Your conversation with the committee's investigators has already been passed to the White House. After we had dinner I was called by one of my contacts in the White House and he practically gave me verbatim what you told the committee."

Another of his sources in Chester Davis' law firm had told Clifford that they had been briefed. Meier had to be extremely cautious if everything he said was being given to his enemies. This strengthened his resolve not to hand over documents unless they could be displayed in public.

A week after the first interview, Meier returned to Washington. This time he met with Scott Armstrong, Robert Muse, Mary DeOreo and Sharon Kirby. They supplied him with a transcript of the first meeting and Meier was dismayed to find it incomprehensible. Names and facts were jumbled; he couldn't believe this mess was the official record of his statement. He asked why it was so garbled and was told they didn't have a proper stenographer working on it, which was hardly credible. Again there were renewed demands for his records and again Meier resisted and said he wanted to be sure his story would be made public before producing his documents. A few days later the evening news reported that Richard Nixon had once ordered his brother Don's phones to be tapped. Meier's name was floated out by the newscasters as being linked to the operation.

Meier was at the airport in Vancouver on November 26, to catch a flight to Los Angeles, when he noticed the U.S. Immigration officer stationed in the terminal had circled his name on the passenger list. Alarmed, he left the airport and called Wyshak. Wyshak petitioned Judge John Sirica, whose court was trying the Watergate defendants in Washington, and obtained an order protecting Meier from process servers while travelling to the Watergate hearings.

By now the Watergate Committee had amassed a formidable amount of data on the break-in. It is not surprising, therefore, that by December those most intimate with the investigation would have formulated some theory to explain the burglary. On December 11, the committee's chief counsel, Sam Dash, said he believed it all had to do with Don Nixon and John Meier.

Dash's remarks were given prominent but brief play in the nation's major newspapers. The *Los Angeles Times* reported that Dash claimed it was a credible theory that O'Brien's office had been searched to determine what he knew about Don Nixon's ties to Howard Hughes.

> The committee has privately questioned John H. Meier, a former Hughes official about his friendship and travels with Donald Nixon and about Meier's knowledge of a $100,000 campaign contribution from Hughes to the President's re-election effort. Dash said his theory... was based on closed-door testimony and other information gathered by the panel. He said it was not "inconsistent" with earlier testimony taken in public.

The newspaper quoted O'Brien rejecting Dash's theory but Dash held that O'Brien's files were the objects sought by the burglars. Dash argued that O'Brien's knowledge about campaign contributions and "any relationship between Meier and Mr. Donald Nixon... may have been the basis and reason for the break-in at the Democratic national headquarters..." The story then described Meier's reported firing from Hughes' employ and his trip with Don Nixon to the Dominican Republic. It repeated how Don's phones were bugged, then added yet a further dimension which should have elicited more response:

> Senate investigators also believe that a proposal by (E. Howard) Hunt and G. Gordon Liddy to break into the office safe of *Las Vegas Sun* publisher Hank Greenspun had been aimed at determining whether Greenspun had information relating to the relationship between Johnny Meier and F. Donald Nixon and Edward Nixon, the President's brothers.

It had always been said that the proposed burglary of Greenspun's office was intended to turn up any tidbits he might have had in his safe regarding Senator Ed Muskie, another Democrat presidential contender in 1972 whom Nixon wanted to embarrass. Dash and his investigators were dismissing this and drawing a line from an aborted operation in Las Vegas to the most infamous burglary in the history of the United States which they were now proposing had the same goal.

Incredible as it now seems, the Meier-Don Nixon connection became a forgotten subject. There was now little, if any, interest in what had precipitated the break-in. Given the complexion and bluntness of Dash's statement, Meier naturally expected to give testimony as soon as the hearings reconvened in the New Year. But a call from Clifford ended that hope. There would be no more appearances before the cameras. The Watergate hearings were going back into secret session.

"We've been tipped off that they've all made a deal. A lot of people are worried that by pushing the hearings into the realm of Howard Hughes a lot is going to be uncovered that involves more than Richard Nixon. The committee will get hold of you and insist that all your documents be turned over. They will want your diaries and papers."

Meier asked what he should do.

"Don't even think about it. Once they've got them you'll never get them back. There's not going to be any more investigation. The last thing they want is you on national television. Nixon's out. They are discussing immunity with him. It's the end of the ball game."

Within a matter of weeks Meier was called by the investigators. They wanted all his diaries and any material substantiating his allegations. Meier asked if he would be allowed to give public testimony. His testimony was not needed, he was told — just his documents. Meier refused.

In retrospect, Clifford might also have had another motive for wanting Meier's diaries kept in Canada. He was a bold man but not stupid; his instincts for self-preservation would demand that his part in entrapping Richard Nixon not be exposed unnecessarily. Notations of meetings, conversations, telephone calls, journeys undertaken and companions visited, provided the blueprint of conspiracy.

12

DAMAGE CONTROL

By January 1974, the Watergate hearings were entering their final days. Committee members had now fixed their attention on the mysterious Howard Hughes and his furtive commerce with the President of the United States through Nixon's intermediary, Rebozo.

When finally the theory for the break-in had been advanced by Dash and its focus narrowed to John Meier and Don Nixon, Meier was left to sit at home, thousands of miles from the hearings, while Don Nixon, Rebozo and a whole cast of bit players were invited to testify. As the transcripts show, Meier — like Banquo's ghost — was never far from center stage. His absence is inexplicable if the committee were serious about getting to the truth.

Perhaps the testimony Meier was prepared to offer was so frightening as to cause the committee to recoil. When asked to explain Meier's absence, Dash preferred that his former assistant Terry Lenzner answer. Lenzner said the committee was convinced by the IRS not to listen to Meier.

In the light of what is now known, that is an incredible admission. The presidential office lost more than it won during the Watergate wars but the coup of using the IRS to muzzle Meier must have been a handsome victory.

Had Meier's story of a CIA-protected payoff by Howard Hughes to Richard Nixon gone into the record, it would have been calamitous for all involved. To prevent this, the IRS destroyed Meier's credibility by whispering of his supposed thefts from Howard Hughes and his subsequent crimes of evading taxes on this illicit income. There is incontrovertible evidence that at this time the IRS was being manipulated by the CIA, the White House and the Hughes organization to Meier's disadvantage. The CIA, using Buhler, had secretly participated in bringing evidence against Meier at the grand jury hearings. Summa Corporation's security arm, Intertel, had supplied information to the IRS which led to Meier's indictment and had taken an active part in having him arrested at gunpoint in Point Roberts. Meier's IRS files were going to the White House via Ehrlichman.

Without the benefit of Meier's testimony, the hearings resumed behind closed doors as the Senators tried to unravel the details of Hughes' payment of $100,000 to Nixon. The fabled $100,000 payment was ancient news by the time of the burglary. Jack Anderson wrote about it a year before Watergate. To suggest that Nixon was afraid his election would be jeopardized if O'Brien publicized the payment is nonsense and could not possibly have formed a motive for the crime. However, the Watergate committee was apparently intent on getting to the bottom of this well-worn item while steadfastly ignoring reports of a payment ten times larger.

On March 21, 1974, the President's loyal friend, Bebe Rebozo, was sworn in and provided the most bizarre testimony heard during these historic sessions. On the surface what occurred seems normal enough. Anyone reading the transcript would likely give up from boredom. But if one considers the information the committee possessed about Rebozo, Meier and Don Nixon, there is no rational explanation for this remarkable interrogation other than that it was a piece of theatre with both sides reciting lines settled in advance. That the politicians on the committee sabotaged the proceedings, conspired to ignore any exploration of the $1 million payment and acted as tame inquisitors of the President's crony, is obvious.

Before Rebozo's appearance, the committee and all its investigators knew that the IRS had been attempting to track down a million dollar contribution that they suspected had been passed from Howard Hughes to Richard Nixon.

Meier had told them that he had seen the actual transaction. Ehrlichman had admitted to the committee that one of his contacts in the IRS, Roger Barth, had come to him saying that IRS agents wanted Rebozo for an interview. It was a sensitive matter because of Rebozo's relationship with the

President. Ehrlichman was asked by the committee if Barth told him why the IRS agents wanted to speak to Rebozo. His reply is interesting.

> It had to do with whether or not Rebozo had received funds from the Hughes organization, or an offspring or an entity or something. I have forgotten what it was, but they had representations from Maheu or one of those people, that they had paid money to Rebozo and they (the IRS) wanted to track it down and make sure it wasn't taxable...

Ehrlichman could not have been referring here to the $100,000 payment made to Rebozo. Details of this transaction had been common knowledge for months, if not years. Had this been the object of the IRS search, Ehrlichman would never have been so vague.

He then says that he contacted Rebozo and warned him of the IRS request and briefed him on what their interview would cover. "And is that the first occasion that you discussed the $100,000 contribution?" he was asked.

"I don't think even the number was used," he replied. He was being fed an easy answer but his lawyer's brain subtly avoided the offer. He knew the IRS were not investigating $100,000 and adroitly avoided perjury.

Bebe Rebozo's appearance before the committee aroused an unusual tension between the politicians and staff — an air of conflict and division which suffuses that section of the transcript. While the staff would occasionally run afoul of the Senators during the months of hearings, there now appeared an undercurrent of frustration which suggested they were being prevented from getting at Rebozo by the politicians. Like a pack of hunting hounds, safely chained, watching the fox being paraded before them, they yelped and strained but couldn't give chase.

Occasionally, committee staff earned themselves reprimands when their disrespect for Rebozo's testimony grew too obvious. When Rebozo was being questioned about some money he had taken from the Florida Committee for Nixon, which he had hidden in an account under another's name, he couldn't come up with a proper explanation for the maneuver. During his painful floundering his lawyer interrupted the proceedings as yells of derision arose from the investigators.

"Well, Mr. Chairman," his lawyer William Frates protested, "Mr. Bellino (Carmine Bellino, the committee's chief investigator) is hollering 'Oh Jesus' down there and I resent that and ask that you caution him and these other investigators to at least conduct themselves in a proper manner."

Bellino was an intimate of the Kennedy family, had handled personal matters for Jack Kennedy, had helped Attorney General Robert Kennedy to take on the Teamsters' Union and had scooped up Louis Russell right after the Watergate burglary. He debriefed Russell and kept him in the Democrats' camp during that dangerous summer immediately following Watergate when the Republicans were trying to sniff out the conspiracy they were sure had entrapped them. Given that he knew enough to neutralize Russell and that he had the benefit of Meier's story, there were probably few aspects of the Watergate affair that had escaped Bellino. He may have been Clifford's source on the committee.

Meanwhile, Frates fought every effort by the staff to question Rebozo on campaign contributions other than those made for the 1972 election, appealing constantly to Senator Sam Ervin to uphold his ruling that questions be restricted to that election. This tactic saved his client from having to answer questions about his financial dealings in 1969. Frates, bolstered undoubtedly by the support he was receiving from the politicians, was bold enough to define the committee's agenda for them when, after yet another tussle in which his objections were upheld, he said: "We all know why we are here — to interrogate on a $100,000 contribution. It seems to me he hasn't had any interrogation — we ought to go to the issue..." The committee was only too ready to oblige.

However, finding out just where and when this $100,000 was passed was no easy task. The money had been given to Rebozo by Richard Danner, one of his friends in the Hughes organization, but because of their different stories, their amendments to original statements, their inability to recall times or dates or in what part of the country the transactions took place, their failure to match even the year in which it happened, the whole affair remained clouded.

After groping for some time, the committee began asking Rebozo to name the persons with whom he had first discussed this $100,000 payment. After extensive probing, he named Richard Nixon, two lawyers and "a PR man, a friend of mine down South..." Asked to name his friend, Rebozo hesitated. "You know, I'm almost afraid to ever inject a new name in these (proceedings). My experience is they just get hounded and questioned and get involved. But he's just an innocent friend. His name is Hank Meyer who is one of the top guys down there and a good friend of mine." In the matter of Hank Meyer, Rebozo was being less than honest. A year before, when Meier was racing around Europe trying to meet Buhler in order to re-establish his contact with Hughes, he had been called by Hank Meyer on a number of occasions.

He had talked about having mutual friends and wanted to put Meier in the way of a unique investment opportunity. He would arrange for Meier to buy heavily discounted shares in Resorts International, a company of which Meier had never heard. Meier had no idea that this company was involved in looking after Hughes; nor that it had such chummy relations with Nixon and Rebozo; nor that its security arm, Intertel, was hot on his trail. There was something odd about a stranger offering him such a fabulous deal and, moreover, being able to locate him so easily while he was on the move throughout Europe. Meier declined although Meyer called him from New York, Florence, London and Miami, pressing for a meeting.

Rebozo's testimony dragged on until he spoke of the two IRS special agents who came to see him at Key Biscayne. They had assured him repeatedly that he wasn't under investigation. They were checking the tax returns of "Danner, Maheu, Hughes or (whoever)" and wanted to question him. Rebozo then stated:

> They asked me if Danner gave me any money or did he give me $100,000. I said "yes." They said, "what did you do with it?" Well, when I said "I've still got it," they did a doubletake because that was not expected. So he (one of the IRS agents) said, "What we're here for is to try to locate $1 million. We've searched all over. There's a million that we feel, perhaps, taxes have not been paid on and this is the first amount that we've been able to locate..."

Because of Rebozo's use of the phrase "perhaps taxes have not been paid," one can conclude that the IRS was not searching for a campaign contribution, which is untaxable, but hidden income, which the million dollars delivered to Rebozo for Nixon assuredly was.

Kenneth Gemmill, one of Rebozo's lawyers, added important nuances missing from Rebozo's testimony when he testified on May 29: "Mr. Rebozo called me on June 8 and said '(Leonard) Garment (President

Nixon's counsel) says I should come and see you about a problem.'" The pair got together three days later in Philadelphia.

> He told me basically that he had been visited by two revenue agents who upon questioning were intelligence agents and that they had told him they were not there investigating him, they were investigating the Hughes Tool Co. and Maheu, and I think Meier, if my memory is correct... I asked him to tell me what the agents had asked about and he said that they were looking for $1 million and he told them he could tell them where $100,000 was, that he had received two deliveries, $50,000 each in bills from Mr. Danner, he put them in a safe-deposit box in joint names at the Key Biscayne Bank with Mr. Wakefield, his lawyer...

Clearly, the IRS had intelligence agents tracking down $1 million which in some way involved Hughes, Meier and Rebozo and had come to Rebozo for an explanation. But there is a marked difference in the way Rebozo tells it and Gemmill's account.

Rebozo leaves out Meier completely, whereas his lawyer includes him. Then Rebozo attempts to make it sound as though the agents began the interview by mentioning the $100,000 and only later got around to the $1 million, when it seems more likely that Rebozo owned up to having the $100,000 while being interrogated about the elusive $1 million.

One might have expected someone within the assembled ranks of the Watergate committee to have shown some interest in the search for the $1 million and to have at least asked Rebozo or Gemmill what they knew of this payment which the IRS agents were so sure had been made. But the Senators showed a shocking lack of curiosity. That such openings were ignored could not have been accidental. The spectre of an unknown payoff appearing suddenly within the proceedings startled no one. Such inattention suggests premeditated and tacit agreement among the questioners; it could account for Rebozo's and Frates' cockiness on the stand and for the sullen frustration of the investigators.

The by now ritualistic examination of Rebozo continued until he was asked if he had had any discussions with Danner about John Meier. What followed was the party line on Meier which those associated with the Nixon White House recited repeatedly: Meier was suspected of buying fraudulent mining claims and selling them to Hughes for profit; he was patronizing Don Nixon and would likely lead him astray; Meier was a publicity hound.

Rebozo piously said that he didn't think "that Don Nixon should be consorting socially and otherwise with a representative of Hughes Tool Company," pharisaically seeing the mote in Meier's eye. It was Rebozo who had taken $100,000 from his friend Danner and it was he who had once offered Danner the use of his home during the time Danner represented Hughes.[1] Why didn't someone ask him to explain this phobia about Nixon and Meier's relationship, which compared to his admitted liaison with Danner seemed the height of innocence?

Rebozo conceded that he had met Meier once and admitted that he was part of the effort to break up the Meier-Don Nixon relationship along with Danner, Maheu and Ehrlichman. But he denied knowing that the IRS was investigating Meier, that the White House had requested Meier's IRS files, or that information regarding Meier and Don Nixon meeting at Orange County Airport was the result of a Secret Service operation, events of which others would say he had intimate knowledge. After a few more desultory questions, it was over.

Rebozo's lawyer, Frates, now became fulsome in his praise for the committee. In response to Senator Joseph Montoya's comment that he hoped the pair would leave "convinced that we have been as courteous as anybody could be with a witness or with his attorney," Frates replied: "(We) couldn't ask for anything more." His rhapsody continued: "Senator, I have no reservations. I think that the Watergate (investigation), the total picture, has been very helpful to the country, I supported it" — here he surely got carried away — "Mr. Rebozo has supported it... I feel and Mr. Rebozo and everybody in his office has indicated... Senators — we couldn't have asked for better treatment..." How right he was. Frates then went on to praise the committee members and staff with two notable exceptions. He singled out Armstrong and Bellino, whom he said had brought "no credit to the Senate of the United States," referring to their conduct during the pre-hearing investigation of Rebozo.

Bellino refused to sit still for this. Bitter words were exchanged, refereed by the rest of the gathering, until Dash came forward and defended Bellino and Armstrong, arguing that their zeal, if irksome at times, was honestly motivated. With that Frates delivered a general salute: "I'm sure Mr. Rebozo appreciates what the Senators have done and we didn't expect anything else from a Senator. Senator, when you walk in this room, you or anyone of the other Senators, I stand up and Mr. Rebozo stands up. That is the way we feel about a U.S. Senator..."

In this oration — delivered on Rebozo's behalf — the cynical might discern a measure of gallows relief, an unseemly embracing of the firing squad by the newly reprieved. The record is silent on how this valediction was received. Had they any shame, the Senators should have blushed.

There is one final detail that should not be overlooked. On Rebozo's second day of testimony, it was revealed that the committee had asked the IRS for its investigatory records concerning him but was getting stiff-armed by the service. This refusal gives yet another glimpse of that baffling relationship which existed between the committee and the IRS.[2] By now, the Senators had ample evidence that Nixon's staff had routinely read supposedly inviolable IRS investigatory reports — including Meier's — to which they had no right, and that the executive branch was using the IRS to abuse its enemies. Their own lawfully assembled committee, however, was refused access to those same files during an investigation into campaign irregularities. Eight months earlier, Richard Nixon's refusal to turn over the presidential tapes had provoked a constitutional crisis and caused a great deal of senatorial snorting, yet during a high-profile investigation the IRS was allowed to thumb its nose at these same Senators with apparent impunity. The committee had to content itself with digests of these files.

Roger Barth, a former assistant to the IRS commissioner, appeared before the committee on June 6. Barth was controlled by Ehrlichman. He arranged Rebozo's interview with the special agents searching for the missing $1 million. Using his access to special case reports, he kept Ehrlichman posted on developments in the Meier case and the investigations of Rebozo and Don Nixon, who was suspected of having received some of the Hughes money destined for the President.[3] His friend, Vernon Acree, another highly placed IRS official, was also supplying Meier's IRS files to members of CREEP.

Reading from a digest of Meier's IRS file, Armstrong quoted: "Bebe Rebozo, personal friend of the President, allegedly instructed Meier not to be available for interview because of Meier's alleged association with Donald Nixon regarding the acquisition of money and funds." He asked if that sounded familiar. Barth said it did. (This harkened back to Rebozo's use of the Secret Service to deliver Meier to a clean telephone so Rebozo could pressure him not to disclose details of the Hughes payment to the IRS.)

The committee wanted to know why Barth or others at the IRS did not do something about Rebozo purportedly telling Meier not to cooperate with their investigators. They asked if an obstruction of justice investigation had been undertaken. Barth didn't know of any. Armstrong asked if there were any concerns expressed by Ehrlichman or the Secretary of the Treasury "that a citizen, Mr. Rebozo, was advising another citizen not to meet with the IRS?" Barth couldn't remember if there were.

Former IRS commissioner Johnnie Walters added perspective both to the Hughes-Meier investigation and to Barth's testimony. Barth, his former assistant, was regarded as a White House spy, according to Walters. He had come to the service after "being the advance man for the Nixon girls and David Eisenhower in the 1968 campaign."[4] Walters, a career civil servant, was obviously not thrilled to have him.

Did he know Barth was passing on details of sensitive case reports covering Meier and Rebozo to the White House? No, he said, and it would have alarmed him at the time had he known. As for the Hughes-Meier investigation, it was "a mammoth undertaking," just a "great mass that rolled along like Old Man River," said Walters.

Walters had been in Nevada in the summer of 1972 to be briefed on the investigation and was astounded to find one whole wall of a conference room festooned with charts, flow diagrams and other data attempting to put together the puzzle of Hughes' holdings and what had happened during the mining transactions in which Meier played a part. The investigation was sucking up resources and agents and Walters was concerned that it would go on forever.

Walters said that at one time it was felt that Don Nixon might have been Meier's partner in receiving money from the mining sales. He said this might have been the reason for Rebozo's attempt to intimidate Meier into refusing to talk to the IRS. However, the business of the mining claims, as Walters makes clear, arose as a byproduct of an investigation undertaken into Hughes' empire and was not started until the spring or summer of 1972, months after Rebozo's phone call.[5] No one on the committee bothered to badger Walters — as they had Barth — as to why no one had investigated the allegation that Rebozo had tried to intimidate Meier into silence.

Walters was the last witness and the Senators seemed content to discover, among other things, that the Meier investigation had reached the top rung of the IRS and was being reviewed not only by Walters but also by his boss, the Secretary of the Treasury. Some of the other witnesses questioned about Meier included the brothers Nixon and their lawyer Stanley McKiernan. To Edward and Don Nixon, Meier's name was odium itself. Here were a couple of innocents abroad — especially Don Nixon — if their testimony is to be believed. Neither of them took money from Meier, Hughes, Rebozo or anyone, including brother Richard. Don Nixon even denied asking for or wanting a finder's fee for helping Hughes buy Air West, another lie, as Ehrlichman has shown. He starts by telling the committee that Meier insinuated himself into his company and that by 1969 Ehrlichman had warned him to stay away from Meier.

Nixon said he was employed in the food industry at that time and was trying to get contracts with Hughes; he was not about to "slap John Meier down when he was number two man with Hughes." He said Meier had once been given a "clean bill of health" by Ehrlichman, but Nixon had never been warm to him. Meier was forever trying to ingratiate himself, Nixon told the Senators. Then he produced the greatest piece of self-delusion recorded in the transcripts.

"He was pursuing us, pursuing me, my wife... and my kid brother, Edward. In fact, he was trying to move in, you know, typical, I guess, for someone wanting to do the job for his boss. But not at one time did he get through me — get to anyone in the White House — get to my brother."

In McKiernan's case, the committee discovered that at the time the President's brothers were being quizzed by Watergate investigators, he had been briefing President Nixon on meetings he had attended. The committee began probing McKiernan for a sense of where Richard Nixon's concerns lay. Asked if there had been any discussion with the President concerning the likes of Meier, McKiernan denied that Meier's name had been mentioned. Finding that hard to believe, the committee persisted.

"Did you discuss with him the interrogation with regard to Donald's trip to the Dominican Republic with John Meier?"

Probably he did, McKiernan admitted. In the context of the committee's task, there seemed little reason to pursue such questions. One is left with the impression that the committee was prying into Richard Nixon's psyche, taking his mental pulse, seeing if John Meier and the shenanigans of Nixon's brother Donald were still on his mind.

13

INTERNATIONAL INTRIGUE

As Nixon's political life disintegrated by degrees, the death watch became protracted and dangerous for Meier. By early 1974 Meier was emotionally exhausted. Clifford had called him with the dismaying news that federal Judge George Boldt had been given charge of his income tax evasion case to be heard in Reno, Nevada. Judge Foley had finally been forced out by Wyshak and as none of the federal judges in Nevada would take the case it was assigned to Boldt, who normally presided in Tacoma, Washington.

What disturbed Clifford was Boldt's background. He was a known friend of the Nixon administration who had taken on the highly politicized job of chairman of Nixon's wage review board, part of the apparatus created to keep wages and prices in check. It was a highly unpopular program, especially among unions who claimed Boldt was keeping wages down but not prices. By January 1972 even Nixon was saying: "Everyone wants to replace the board chairman, George Boldt."[1]

But Boldt was not fired as the unions demanded because his cause was championed by John Ehrlichman, who describes the judge as a friend of the family. Whether Ehrlichman's thoroughly jaundiced opinions of John Meier were kept to himself during this time, or shared with this family friend, is unknown, but what is on record is that the Nixon administration stuck with

Boldt to the bitter end. It was during the twilight of this administration that Boldt was appointed to hear Meier's case.

Pressed on all sides by the U.S. government and the Hughes organization, harassed in Canada by Intertel and the CIA, Meier desperately needed allies. He fell into the arms of British Intelligence and from there came his eventual recruitment by their Canadian counterparts. The British tumbled quickly to the possibilities afforded by Meier's political and industrial contacts and his knowledge of the mysterious Hughes empire, which was spreading within their sphere of influence like a virus. Meier presented an opportunity to unravel a problem which appeared to have worried the British for some time and came to a head in early 1974 during the mad dash to find oil in the North Sea.

When the Arab nations embargoed petroleum sales to the West following the 1973 Egyptian invasion of Israel, it convulsed the economies of all oil-dependent countries — none more severely than the United States. Overnight there were fuel shortages. Highway speeds were cut to conserve gasoline. Service stations closed by the thousands as they ran out of fuel. This land of plenty was jolted into recognizing that its industrial survival was dependent on Middle Eastern leaders. In the course of meetings with members of MI5, Meier learned that the oil-panicked Americans were turning their attention to the North Sea and attempting by subterfuge to gain control of this enormously strategic oil supply which the British naturally wanted for themselves.

The postwar antipathy that existed between the British and American intelligence communities is well documented. It has at its root the understandable American mistrust of British Intelligence, once it became obvious that both MI5 and MI6 had been infiltrated by Soviet spies. Arch-traitors McLean, Burgess, Philby and Blunt betrayed not only British, but undoubtedly American secrets. Compounding the almost irreparable damage caused by their betrayal was the fact that at this time the Labour Party was governing Britain under Harold Wilson, whose predilection for things Soviet had even MI5 worried.[2]

Meier's MI5 contact was Brian Boyce; they first met on April 3, 1973, in New Scotland Yard. Boyce began by giving a synopsis of Meier's situation in the United States, using information British Intelligence had gathered from its sources in Washington.

"Frankly, the Americans are going to do everything they can to eliminate you," said Boyce. "We can help you if you stay in Canada, but only up to a point. We could speak to the Canadian government but we consider that you should move yourself and your family to London."

Meier was unprepared for this and said that he was trying to settle down in Canada. "My kids are at school — it's become home for us — I don't know if I want to uproot everyone right now," he said.

Boyce apologized for his pessimism but said nevertheless Meier could expect little or no help from the Canadian government if the United States made concerted efforts to cause trouble. The suggestion was that Canada could not be considered autonomous when the national security of the United States was in question.

Boyce asked for an overview of the Hughes conglomerate and Meier spent considerable time, as he had done for Ludwig, explaining not only its various entities but also the executives who ran them. The intelligence officer then said he understood Meier had a number of contacts within the CIA and asked if it would be possible to have access to whatever information he was receiving from those sources. "Concerning what?" Meier asked.

"Well, would you be able to obtain any information relating to the North Sea?" At this time the east coast of Scotland was swarming with American roustabouts, drillers and geologists whose appearance might not have given the inhabitants of Hughes' native Texas pause for thought, but in conservative and quiet Aberdeenshire was viewed with astonishment.

The oil-rich North Sea had been tidily subdivided by the British government into exploration parcels and hastily formed companies were jostling with the major oil corporations for exploration rights. It was assumed that somewhere off the east coast of Scotland lay vast reserves of oil estimated to be 50 percent larger than those surrounding the continental United States.

The British, said Boyce, had learned that some of these new companies were in fact properties of the CIA, raising fears that the CIA might gain control of the oilfields which represented economic salvation to the British after decades of living on international credit. Wilson's government, carrying on a Labour tradition of nationalization, assumed that it would add North Sea Oil to the steel, coal and railway industries then under government control. But the entrepreneurs — and there are no more radical free-enterprisers than oilmen — threatened to pull out at the mere suggestion. The British did not share their expertise in off-shore oil exploration, so Wilson and the Left quietly backed off. But what if those firms which appeared to be British or British-European owned were in fact CIA properties? Boyce asked if Meier knew what companies Howard Hughes owned in Europe as the British believed that it was through Hughes fronts that the CIA was operating in the North Sea.

Meier said he had a contact in California who might be of some help. Meier's contact was a personal friend and a high-ranking CIA officer who worked in California supervising security in the aerospace industry and was responsible for protecting it against foreign agents. He gave security clearance to executives and high-level employees at Hughes Aircraft and other corporations involved in military contracts.[3] Meier delivered a dossier detailing Hughes' European companies with CIA connections to Boyce when they met at the Londonderry Hotel two weeks later. Boyce was grateful but clearly unsettled by the ease with which Meier had obtained this valuable secret information.

"I beg your pardon, John, but it's for reasons such as this," said Boyce "that we are trying not to give the American government any information. The CIA is leaking like a sieve. Anybody can get anything from them. While it's marvelous for us that you have obtained this, the implications are really shocking. You have no status with the agency and yet you are able to come up with this." Boyce promised the information would be presented to the British government. On Friday, July 12, Harold Wilson took control of the North Sea oilfields. Instead of nationalizing the industry, the Labour government promised to buy a 51 percent share in all companies developing wells in the North Sea. Overnight, the British had seized back the initiative.

Although the CIA's endeavors in the North Sea were being thwarted by the British, the agency was pulling off a dazzling coup in the Pacific where the Glomar Explorer — its cover as a Hughes deep-sea mining vessel remarkably still intact — was raising a Russian submarine from its grave 17,500 feet beneath the surface. The mission was compromised by the burglary of Hughes' Romaine Street headquarters in Los Angeles on June 5 during which some classified documents linking the CIA to the Glomar project disappeared.

Considering the ease with which the burglars broke in, and the circumstances surrounding the enterprise, it was generally assumed to have been an inside job. That Summa Corporation would benefit from the burglary was apparent the moment news of the raid became known. The Securities and Exchange Commission was pursuing an indictment against Hughes and Chester Davis for the Air West takeover and had received a court order the day before the burglary, allowing its investigators to seize records from Romaine Street. Maheu, seeking damages in a Los Angeles court as the result of Hughes' slur that he was a "no good dishonest son of a bitch,"[4] was claiming that documents stored in Romaine Street were germane to his case and he too possessed a court order to seize them. There was always a chance that some Senate or Congressional committee with more gumption than the Watergate committee might want to examine these archives one day. What better way to forestall any sifting of Hughes' secrets than to have them removed by robbers, thus allowing Summa's agents to easily avoid demands for incriminating documents.

Apart from the Glomar document, none of the papers appeared to have been of any great import. In the thousands of papers removed, no other incriminating documents have yet come to light.

Citizen Hughes, the book written by Michael Drosnin based on documents taken in the burglary, is a compilation of fragments of correspondence that passed between Maheu and Hughes, none of which was startling. As for the famous Glomar document, Drosnin states that no such document was stolen during the break-in. He bases this on the testimony of his unnamed collaborator — The Pro — who he claims supplied him with the documents two years after the burglary.

According to Drosnin, The Pro led the break-in team and flatly denied he had possessed or seen the Glomar paper. Drosnin concludes the Glomar document was not part of the booty taken by The Pro but was removed by a security guard Mike Davis who was on duty in Romaine Street that night. Davis told police that the four burglars bound and gagged him; after they left he freed himself and found the document lying on the floor. He stuffed it in his pocket. It was never properly explained why Davis kept this to himself for more than ten months and would only confess two weeks after a *Los Angeles Times* story disclosed that the Glomar memo was among documents stolen from Romaine Street. Davis told police that after reading the story he became worried and flushed the memorandum down the toilet.

However, when skeptical detectives asked him to submit to a polygraph test he declined. This was the second invitation for a lie detector test that Davis had refused. Shortly after the break-in he had let himself be fired rather than take a polygraph to confirm his account of that night. His story of finding the Glomar document lying on the floor was a piece of fantasy. On July 6, a month after the burglary, an infamous Beverly Hills private detective named Bobby Hall popped up at Meier's home with a briefcase full of loot from the Romaine Street heist, including the CIA contract for Glomar. He wanted to sell the haul. Meier, he supposed, would be in the market.

The inimitable Jim Hougan describes Hall thus: "Little Bobby Hall was a sleaze. You could describe him in other ways — as a private investigator, a father, a wiretapper, an informer, a dope peddler and a double agent — but mostly he was a sleaze."[5] Given such attributes, Hall could also be described as a hustler, likely a blackmailer and almost certainly a double-crosser. There were two burglaries against Hughes operations in the spring of 1974 and Hall was party to both. His part in the second burglary has never before been disclosed.

The first robbery occurred April 24 when Hall's two partners Jack Ginsburgs and Gene LeBell entered Hughes' Encino offices and removed a telephone scrambler unit.[6] (Encino was the nerve center of the Hughes communication network controlled by Bill Gay.) This unit scrambled voice communications between Encino and CIA headquarters in Langley and the CIA's Mullen Company office in Washington and was located in the office of Encino security man Vince Kelley, an old acquaintance of Hall's. Possession of the scrambler would enable anyone who had recorded their conversations to decipher the gibberish. This was a devastating breach of security. It is known that Hall, a virtuoso "wireman" who had used his telephone tapping artistry in the service of Vesco and the Hughes organization, was given the scrambler. The implication is obvious. Hall, for whatever reason, had been tapping the lines in Encino and needed the scrambler to decode the results of his labors.

Two weeks after the robbery, Hall placed a newspaper ad offering a reward for the return of the voice scrambler with no questions asked. Ostensibly he was attempting to lure the thief into surrendering the equipment so he could return it to its rightful owners.

A week later he returned the scrambler to Kelley. When seventeen Hughes employees were ordered to take polygraph tests following the Romaine Street burglary, Kelley was the only one who failed, leaving the examiners to assume he had guilty knowledge of the event. In an effort to convince investigators otherwise, Kelley went to Hall, who arranged for a second test to be administered which Kelley passed easily.

Hall arrived at Meier's home on the morning of July 6. Opening a briefcase he said that he understood Summa Corporation was out to crush Meier. The memos would help, said Hall, and he laid out a sample of what he had. He was prepared to sell Meier the complete contents of the Romaine Street robbery.

Meier asked if he had been involved in the break-in and Hall admitted he had. What immediately caught Meier's eye was a dossier marked "Government Activity." After leafing through a couple of memos, he came across a copy of the Glomar agreement between the CIA and Hughes. Realizing the sensitivity of it, Meier asked if Hall wasn't worried about having it in his possession.

"Worried about what?" asked Hall.

"The government," replied Meier.

"The government? No way. They don't care about any of this stuff. Summa's the only one who cares. Forget the government."

Meier realized only then how truly ignorant Hall was about what he had stolen. Meier didn't know of course that the ship had just sailed and had yet to reach its destination. The CIA was nervous that at the eleventh hour the Soviets would discover the mission and order a warship to intercept and prevent the Glomar Explorer from dredging up the wreckage of the lost submarine. Meier said he wanted time to consider the offer but wondered if Hall would mind if he copied just a couple of the memos and papers for study.

Hall raised no objection so Meier leaned forward and grabbed a few memos and slipped the Glomar memorandum between them. He left the house immediately, drove to a store which had a photocopying machine and copied the papers. When Hall left, Meier promised to consider the offer, but he was really only being polite. He had little interest in the stolen papers as they were mostly "Dear Bob" and "Dear Howard" letters and he already possessed enough of them in his own files.[7]

Realizing the enormous news value of the CIA contract, Meier sent it off to George Clifford for use in Jack Anderson's column. Anderson held onto the information for almost a year. It could be that the columnist's patriotism outdid his urge for a scoop.

Had the police known of Hall's trip to Meier and its purpose, it would have added a remarkable perspective to both burglaries, for Hall was not supposed to have had any part in the second job, the Romaine Street robbery. This robbery had not been previously linked to the theft of the voice scrambling unit from Hughes' Encino office. This knowledge might also have opened other avenues when it came time to investigate Hall's murder.

In July 1976, as Hall stood in front of his refrigerator, someone slipped behind him and fired a .38 calibre slug into his head. He rocketed forward, hit the refrigerator and dropped lifeless to the floor. Hall's partners, Ginsburgs and LeBell, with reputations to equal his, were found guilty of killing him. Their conviction relied on circumstantial evidence and what purported to be confessions — statements the accused claimed were nothing more than the results of trickery.[8] Regardless, there was a neatness to the fates of Hall, Ginsburgs and LeBell who, among them, had broken into two Hughes strongholds, compromised CIA communications and almost ruined one of the most important intelligence operations ever mounted.

MEANWHILE, Boyce had been pulling strings to help Meier and his family achieve landed immigrant status in Canada. He arranged for Meier to meet with members of Canadian Intelligence in Toronto. Like their British counterparts, these officers from the RCMP's D-Division were interested in Meier's international contacts. They asked if he was contemplating citizenship. Meier replied that he had not thought that far ahead; what he needed was permanent residency in Canada. A few hours later one of the officers called to say they had taken care of it. A week later Meier was officially landed.

While he could now feel less like a refugee, the sheer mass of his problems in the United States exerted an unsettling gravity which tugged at him from across the border. He was facing charges of conspiracy[9] and income tax evasion before Judge Boldt in Reno relating to his 1969 income tax return, while a second set of charges against him for his 1970 taxes was before a judge in California.

Richard Nixon, the totality of his crimes hidden from the American public, resigned on August 8, 1974, rather than endure the shame of impeachment. Meier was being interviewed on a Vancouver radio station when the news of the resignation was spewed from the network wire.

Had Nixon's political demise taken place two years earlier, Meier might have felt giddy. But his world had drastically changed since he and Humphrey had connived to frighten Nixon out of office. Then they had been fueled with the high octane of politics. Humphrey had his heart set on the presidency; Meier was seeking to win a place in the Senate. Far from being a member of the U.S. Senate, he was now living in a foreign land, his reputation in tatters, his lawyers in the United States fighting a rear-guard action against the tandem litigation of Summa and with the IRS trying to ruin him. Meier could not even have felt encouraged by Nixon's replacement, Gerald Ford, considering that his name was on that list of CIA-approved politicians he had received years ago with a request for Hughes' financial support.

By the winter of 1974, Meier's health was failing, undoubtedly from the stress of his years with Hughes, and in these latter times, from trying to keep one step ahead of the CIA and Intertel. He was now acting as a consultant for a company called Trans Continental Video (TCV), whose president Alfred Wayne Netter had come to Canada from Israel some years before. The company held the rights to a video machine. (In those days these machines were expensive and designed for use in mini-cinemas in small communities.) The snag was that film distribution companies wouldn't release movies for conversion to video. Meier, with his film industry contacts, was hired to get around this. Robbie Robertson, on the strength of his supposed contacts in the English movie industry, become involved with Netter also. Robertson had accompanied Meier from England to Canada and had been living in his house.

On the evening of November 30, while Meier was in Edmonton on company business, Jennie phoned to tell him she'd heard a radio report that a TCV executive had been murdered. Netter's brutally stabbed body had been found in a hotel room in Beverly Hills.

Meier was on his way to England on other business but before he left he called a number of TCV investors, some of whom had not yet heard of Netter's death. Meier was suffering from high blood pressure and from ear problems he had suffered since childhood which had been aggravated by his war injury. When he arrived in England he felt dizzy and ill. He checked into the Carleton Towers Hotel and called a specialist, Dr. Martin Raynor, who diagnosed Meniere's Disease — an infection of the inner ear — and hypertension. His advice was that Meier should rest and not travel by air until he was well.

However, Meier's income tax evasion trial before Boldt in Reno was to begin December 2. His lawyer, Wyshak, attempted to have it delayed, but was unable to reach Boldt before the trial started. When he came to court without Meier, the judge was so incensed he ordered Meier's $100,000 bail seized. Wyshak argued that Meier was ill; Boldt ordered that he present himself for a medical examination in London. Meier called the U.S. Embassy and William Kish, the legal attache, told Meier to come to the embassy for an examination by a U.S. Navy physician. Meier raised no objection but asked for it to be done outside of the embassy. Kish refused. Meier asked if he could bring his own doctor. No, he was to come alone, said Kish.

With the memory of his arrest in Point Roberts still vivid, Meier was afraid of being kidnapped. He said he would only go to the embassy if his doctor could accompany him.

The next day Meier's hotel room door suddenly opened and in walked three men. Raynor, who was there treating him, demanded to know who they were. One identified himself as James Lindsay, the hotel security man.[10] The others were from the American embassy. The trio backed out without explaining what they had intended to do. Frightened by this, Meier called Boyce, who sent an intelligence officer to spirit him quietly out of the hotel. Despite his medical condition, they went to the airport. There were no boarding formalities. Meier was simply driven to the side of the plane and put aboard.

His hasty return to Canada was taken as further proof that Meier was lying about his condition. If he could fly to Canada, argued the authorities, he could fly to the United States for trial. But the prospect of travelling to Reno was now too daunting. He had no intention of going anywhere near Ehrlichman's crony Judge Boldt or of risking the kind of treatment he had already received from Judge Foley.

On January 3, 1975, Boldt declared Meier a fugitive from justice.

14

THE GONZALES AFFIDAVIT

On May 2, 1975, in Mexico City, Virgino Gonzales — a member of the CIA's ultra-sensitive Domestic Operations Division — did the unthinkable. He walked into the law offices of Goodrich, Dalton and Rigueline and signed what was tantamount to a confession.

The agent carried a 10-page affidavit which he requested be translated into Spanish so it could be filed in the Tribunal Superior de Justicia del Distrito Federal — the federal court in Mexico City. Once completed, the Spanish version of this remarkable document was stamped and placed in the court registry.

The Gonzales Affidavit was a comprehensive account of state-directed spite, intimidation, mischief and even contemplated murder.

These were the disclosures of a field agent who worked for the mysterious DDP (Deputy Director of Plans). He painted a picture of a sinister America where a hidden bureaucracy dedicated to eradicating political problems like John Meier and Edward Kennedy, worked unfettered by conscience or decency. It meant nothing to suborn, bribe, trick, pander, prostitute, threaten or to commit murder.

But the CIA was not alone. Gonzales attaches the Hughes organization and the Nixon White House to their activities in simple, dispassionate prose. Virgino Gonzales was part of domestic operations and he acted mainly within the United States, where the CIA's operations are supposedly limited if not verboten.

Virgino Gonzales is an alias.[1] Possibly his name is Max Gorman, or Max Gorman Gonzalez. Hougan, in his encyclopedic compendium of America's spooks, says as much, but gives no basis for his supposition.[2] He notes that the CIA would not comment on whether it ever had a Virgino Gonzales on the payroll and that Gorman denies ever having written the confession.

Such denials would be expected. The CIA would hardly want to dignify the affidavit by admitting it had been written by a retired agent.

The Gonzales persona says at the beginning of his affidavit that he is Cuban born and a naturalized American who is also known as Frank or Gerry. He was recruited into the CIA in 1959 and resigned in December 1974. He served in the field in various parts of South America before joining the Domestic Operations Division.

A little more is known about Gorman or Gorman Gonzalez. He is a friend of Frank Sturgis, the CIA man captured at Watergate. Sturgis has led a colorful life. He was running guns for Castro when he was recruited into the CIA. When Castro later defeated Fulgencio Batista, Sturgis ran Cuba's air force intelligence section. While in this capacity, he plotted to murder Castro but Washington denied him permission to carry out the assassination.

When the *New York Daily News* ran that story on Sturgis in April 1975, his friend Max Gorman Gonzalez confirmed it and added that the CIA had asked Sturgis to participate in assassinations in Cuba and elsewhere.

Sturgis was bitter and disillusioned with the agency after serving 15 months in prison for his part in Watergate. At the time of the *Daily News* story, Gonzales was disaffected for reasons of his own. It is likely that by then he had drawn up his affidavit, whose tightly typed admissions would be filed less than two weeks after the Sturgis interview.

Gonzales' motive for producing his affidavit may have been exculpation, revenge or a combination of the two. By 1975 Gonzales had discovered the CIA had betrayed him and his friends while on active service in Cuba. This apparently was related to a plot by Cuban exiles to kill Castro which the CIA allegedly scuppered in 1968 by informing the Cubans what was afoot. Gonzales was one of the few who escaped being killed or captured during the mission which the expatriates believed was sanctioned by the agency.[3]

However, he makes no mention of this in his affidavit which, after giving only a few personal details, begins in earnest with an affirmation that he was making the statement of his own free will, knowing full well the personal risk involved. The document continues:

> I love the United States and am grateful for all that it has done for me... It is not my intention to place the security of the country at risk and to involve any of my colleagues in this statement. My intention is simply to show that the agency is a tool of the President and those close to him in power and is used in a wrongful way to harass people for personal political purposes.
>
> I am also aware of the dreadful future awaiting the country with the bid for ultimate power now being made by the Rockefellers, with their policies geared to fear of so called outside forces, a Red in every bed.
>
> Attica was an example of the Rockefeller belief that force must be used to the full at all times to keep the establishment on top. Carl Valone knows better.
>
> The administration is and, has always been, aware that the balance of terror is on America's side, not Russia's, and we use it anywhere to help the war and arms lobby, but cloaked, as if fighting for freedom. Others have tried to show the truth by writing books but this I cannot do and the truth is always denied and I would be accused of being Red.
>
> The harassment of people causes suffering and is a waste of time and tax money when there are things for which the agency was founded which are left undone.
>
> In this statement I try only to show that an individual was harassed by surveillance without reason and the way in which I and others, blindly followed orders from all sides.
>
> During 1968-1969 I had been told to drop all investigations in Sinclair Weeks and his movement of monies abroad for political funding and first came into contact with John Meier in April, 1969 in Las Vegas. At about 1500 (hours) on April 25, Senator Edward Kennedy arrived in Las Vegas and was to give a speech that night. With other agents I arranged for Jack Entratter of the Sands Hotel to fix a girl for Kennedy and for pictures to be taken for future use.
>
> Kennedy fell for the situation but the full use of the operation was ruined when Meier heard something of it. I learned later that he had contacted Bill Haddad, Larry O'Brien, Joseph Napolitan and Steve Smith

and warned them of a problem. Though the story appeared in one paper Meier annoyed the company.

At the end of 1971 I was ordered to an assignment that included monitoring the activities of John Meier and was shown a file on him, along with other agents.

From memory this file showed that Meier came from New York, his early business life and how he joined Hughes and evaluated the underground testing in Nevada. He was giving the AEC a hard time on behalf of Hughes.

Meier was shown as a leftist and surveillance had taken place (on him) since 1968. He had been followed during visits to Max Palevsky when he met with Daniel Ellsberg for whom he was trying to set up funds for his defense at trial.

On file were photographs taken at Orange County Airport in July 8, 1969, showing Meier with Don Nixon and others. These were taken by the Secret Service and had been passed to Bebe Rebozo at the President's request. Rebozo was to contact Robert Maheu to have Meier fired or kept out of things.

During 1968 and 1969 Meier met with several CIA agents in Nevada. It had been thought by them that Meier was informed regarding agency cooperation with the Hughes organization and Maheu's company. It seemed that Meier had stepped into the Ecuadorian situation as well as obtaining a list of politicians whom we wanted funded through Hughes. It was believed that Meier had lists of cover organizations and business operations which were intended for Hughes' personal use only.

It was also thought that Meier may enter political race in Nevada and run for Senator Howard Cannon's hold on the state. This upset Hughes as Cannon was his man all the way. Meier was known to have close contact with President Balaguer of the Dominican Republic and this area was sensitive to us and the President. This caused a backing off in our plans.

Meier was listed as being seen in Hawaii with Donald Nixon and his wife and Mike O'Callaghan (Governor) of Nevada and his wife in late 1970.

My own surveillance of Meier, with alternate agents, started in January, 1972. On January 9 Meier went to the Balboa Bay Club at Newport Beach and lunched with Congressman Dick Hannah and two others. They discussed Korea, Singapore and the Far East. That evening Meier went to Albuquerque where he had an apartment at La Buena apartments and it was our intention to place bugging aids (there). This became urgent when Meier announced his run for the Senate seat in New Mexico on January 11.

During January we know that Meier had many calls with Donald Nixon and Donald Nixon Jr. The President's nephew called from Nassau 28568 and talked politics. Meier also contacted Hubert Humphrey and met with Jerry Landreth, who was on Humphrey's staff. This was in L.A. on January 25.

We were informed that Arthur Blech, Meier's tax consultant and also the President's was a leftist and speaking to friends against the President. We noted a number of meetings between Blech and Meier in L.A. at this time. This became part of my FIRs (field intelligence reports).

In the last week of January I was told that Meier's name had been passed on to reporters by friends of the agency. This was in relation to the Clifford Irving book. This I was told was part of the general buildup to sabotage the New Mexico campaign. It was arranged that Meier be served with a subpoena on January 30 at his New Mexico apartment. I waited outside to see that service was carried out by the postal authorities and then, with others, contacted the New Mexico papers to make sure they knew about the service to appear in New York.

I was watching Meier at L.A. airport when he met a Western flight on February 1. He met with Senator Mike Gravel and they went to NBC where Meier was interviewed by Roy Neal about the Irving case. This was no worry as the Hughes side were in touch with Neal.

February 2 Meier flew to New York and we photographed him sitting with Marvin Kratter who had been involved with Boston Celtic basketball team and had a home in the La Costa Club.

The Irving case showed that we had the wrong man but Meier was kept from New Mexico and his campaign. Stanley Meyer was involved not Meier. This did not matter to us at the time.

Right after the case Meier went to Washington DC to have dinner with Jack Anderson and his assistants. During this dinner other agents entered Meier's room at the Marriott Hotel but found nothing as Meier had his papers with him. In the restaurant we photographed Meier and Anderson and were convinced that information against the administration was being passed. This was confirmed when Anderson wrote stories on Donald Nixon later that month.

On February 18 Meier was seen meeting Paul Schrade of the Auto Workers Union at their headquarters in L.A. Present was Harry Evans who was Schrade's assistant and became campaign manager for Meier. Meier had also met with known leftists of the United Auto Workers, including Pancho Madrano who helped Meier's campaign. Also on the 18th Meier met Robert Kahan on Wilshire. Kahan was a known leftist and had communist friends. We worried where Meier's information would finally land.

February 19 Meier was seen and photographed at the L.A. Hilton with Harry Evans and Edward Kennedy. On the second floor there was a meeting of the UAW's community action program. Many Mexicans were there including the brother of Cesar Chavez. Meier was with a woman most of this time and I ordered a check. She was Wanda Russell, a private detective employed by Meier, and she told the New Mexico police of our bugs and of certain threats to Meier.

These threats did not come from us but I learned that Intertel, the Hughes people, were involved. This annoyed me and I made a complaint to the company. In reply I was told that the Hughes group were preparing a lawsuit on Meier for getting fees over his salary. This would be used during the campaign. I was told to cooperate by informing media friends. I was not happy with this.

Two of us were with Meier when he went to New York on April 16. It turned out he was attending his mother's funeral. During this time he made calls from pay phones. I felt he was aware of us when we returned with him on April 19.

The Hughes people, I was told, were still worried about the campaign but I was then told that the IRS would release a story on Meier in May. This they did on May 11 saying they were investigating his affairs in Nevada.

May 29 we followed Meier and Harry Evans to L.A. where they went to the Humphrey campaign HQ. At 1300 (hours) we photographed Meier with Robert Humphrey at the HQ. Surveillance was relaxed after June 6 when Meier lost his campaign.

By June 25 we were aware that Meier had been lost and not until the 29th was I told that he was somewhere in Canada. He had called Paul

Schrade on (202-554-7417) and had been heard discussing the presidential campaign. They also talked of a man called Stan Sheinbaum and of Richard Nixon at length. They talked of Richard Nixon's involvement in the Bahamas and the Hughes-CIA ties. Intertel agreed to help find Meier as they were already heavily involved in Canada. They found Meier in the Vancouver area.

On September 5 we found that Meier had traveled to Nassau with Donald Nixon Jr. and his brother on Pan Am 405 out of Miami. Nixon Jr. took Meier to the Bahamas Commercial Bank in the Bahamas but they had flown by the time I reached there. October 16 Meier again called Paul Schrade in California. And when he talked to Stan Sheinbaum at McGovern's HQ (213-469-9061) on October 31 the call was traced and we knew Meier's new home.

The call to McGovern was to indicate that Meier felt that the candidate had been too lenient on Richard Nixon during the campaign in view of the information available to him.

During the year Meier had passed stories to Norman Pearlstine of the *Wall Street Journal*. It was felt that we should fund another contact at the paper to stop this writer's Hughes-Nixon stories. Pearlstine was later transferred to Tokyo, Japan.

I learned that Meier had applied to be an immigrant in Canada but was told by Intertel that they could block this easily. I was warned to be careful about involvement because the contacts were at low level in immigration.

After the November 7 election surveillance was still kept on Meier but at a lower key. On November 29 he was picked out in L.A. when he lunched with John Dodson of *Newsweek*. Dodson was a black with leftist feelings and anti-Nixon leanings. They lunched at the Brown Derby and discussed the President and his administration. I also handed to the IRS some of the files we had taken from Tom Benavides' office in Albuquerque included were Meier's own tax files and letters to and from politicians. During a meeting in early 1973 I was told that Meier was talking to William Turner of the SEC about the Hughes-Air West deal and that the President wanted to know about this. It was considered delicate.

January 24 we followed Meier from Vancouver to Seattle on flight 144 and he took the 12:15 Pan Am to England, London. I was told by the COS[4] — brought home early this year — that Meier was making enquiries about Hughes' stay at the Inn of the Park. This seemed to worry Intertel more than us.

Intertel told me that they had arranged a meeting for Meier with Vancouver immigration on February 6 and that this was to be used to serve Meier with a writ outside the offices, before his meeting. Meier was followed with his wife and baby and the Hughes people had men around the area to take photographs.

The timing was chosen by Intertel to embarrass Meier with immigration. This could have come back to us if the senior immigration men had realized it was a setup with the help of a funded immigration man. Bob Morrison was a help but there was a problem with his drinking.

February 19, 1973, Meier again went to England and stayed in the Potmen Hotel in London. Little could be done to enter the room because of the television security hookup and the security officer Mr. Deecon. I was told that Deecon drank at a nearby public place and during this time I was able to put in a listening aid. Meier had meetings with Arabs about consulting work in the Middle East.

February 23 he moved to the Churchill Hotel and on March 4 went to Paris in France and stayed at the Meridian Hotel. There he met with motion film people. Among them Serge and Christian Marquand and a Susie Wyss, friend of Joseph Napolitan, campaign advisor to Humphrey.

I was told that Meier would visit Tahiti in March with actor Marlon Brando. This was learned as the result of a telephone call with Brando in L.A. (CR5 3217). Subject was a real estate deal. In L.A. Meier had medical treatment with a Dr. Shapiro in Beverly Hills and Shapiro's records showed that Meier had a high blood count and hypertension.

It was assumed that Meier would go from L.A. to Tahiti but (following) a call from Brando on the evening of March 26 both decided against going. Brando turned down his academy award on the 27 and this attitude convinced us that Meier was dealing with kooks and leftists with no thought for America.

May and June of 1973 Meier made a number of visits to England and kept asking about Hughes. London station and Intertel told us that he had no success trying to reach Hughes.

August 6 I flew to Vancouver when it was decided with the IRS and Intertel to do something about Meier. We were told by Intertel that he had been visiting Point Roberts with his children.

On August 9 Meier made the journey with three children and a man called Floyd Hargan. He was followed and the local law officers told to prepare to block the road if Meier attempted to leave before we were ready. As Meier left two armed officers arrested Meier. Arrangements had been made for a secret grand jury to hand down a tax charge indictment that day.

Meier was held at Point Roberts jail for some hours while I debated with the IRS but they wanted to keep him themselves. I had not realized the IRS was working closely with Intertel and was unable to lay hands on Meier without a smell. Meier was taken to other jails and August 10 I arranged for some photographers to be at the jail to wire out pictures of Meier in shackles.

I know that Meier's lawyer Robert Wyshak was in another country and out of contact. I was told Judge Foley in Las Vegas would be with us all the way and that the judge's brother was a lawyer with the Hughes group in Las Vegas. The judge set bail at $100,000. I was angry to hear that Meier raised the bail and that a Seattle judge released him without being made aware of our needs.

Meier went for arraignment in Vegas on September 7 and I was again told that Foley had everything in hand and would not release Meier. A deal had been made with Meier's former lawyer John Suckling of L.A. and we had Meier nailed.

But lawyer Wyshak told the court that Meier had been under surveillance and bugged and wanted the government to answer questions.

We did not want this as it could have raised other questions about the bugging of Hank Greenspun of the *Vegas Sun* and former Governor Grant Sawyer. Meier returned to his home on the 7th (of September) with me as company.

The following day he met George Clifford, Jack Anderson's assistant, at Vancouver airport. It later showed from the stories coming out that Meier had talked about payoffs, the President, Air West, and other things bad for the administration.

In October I was told that Meier was to give evidence to Senate Select Committee on the Presidential Campaign Activities. October 12 he flew by United to Chicago and then to Washington DC national airport. He was met by George Clifford and checked into room 689 at the Mayfair Hotel. The lawyer Wyshak was already there and at 11:15 I photographed Meier with Senator Gravel, his wife and daughter at the hotel.

My contact on the committee told me that Meier was to be seen in his room and I could not get in. At 13:00 on October 13 Martin (he must mean Meier) was seen by Martin Lackritz, Terry Lenzner, Scott Armstrong and Robert Muse. It lasted until about 20:00.

Meier had reserved that evening at the Rue Gauch for himself, George Clifford and wife, Wyshak and wife. Henry Kissinger was dining there with his future wife and I was known to some of Kissinger's party so it was awkward.

Meier next appeared in Washington on October 22 when he was seen at the Jefferson Hotel by committee people Scott Armstrong, Robert Muse, Mary Deoreo and Sharon Kirby. I was assured we would see every word of the transcript. At 17:00 that day he met William Turner of the SEC.

At 10:00 on October 24, Meier and lawyer Wyshak visited David Grace in New York after flying Eastern. Grace, with a Tom Murray had told Meier that Air West was for sale in the first place.

Meier left New York for England where he again asked about Hughes. Intertel took over this.

At this time I was told by Intertel and Jack Cromar (of Hughes security) that a Bruce McInnes was in regular touch with Meier in the Vancouver area. I tried to recruit him but he seemed not to understand. Or the sugar was not enough. Later a colleague Abbott, formerly Abbes, was to try and I do not know the result.

On November 27 a story came out in Canada about IRS operations there and I was annoyed and complained as I was not happy working with Intertel and the IRS who were both clumsy and could blow us up.

December 8 I again entered Canada and this day Meier met Canadian MP John Reynolds at his office. At 21:30 Meier met Tom Pettit of NBC at the airport. December 9 Pettit and Meier met all day. I could not close because I had been in Pettit's company before and he may have noticed me. I did not want to call on Intertel for help. Meier had a house guest from December 23 through 29. She was Marjel DeLauer whose house we had entered in Arizona when she was writing about Hughes in novel type.[5] January 3 in 1974 Meier left for London, England, and I was told from there that he stayed at the home of Sarah Churchill, Winston Churchill's daughter. She was in New York but Jack Cromar told me that Meier was with a Robby Robertson whom he had met the year before.

I was told that Robertson was a writer and worked under other names so little was known of him. There appeared to be a block on official facts on him but he was a member of a London club and entertained in the Stork Room. Even here there was no one to talk and then nothing was known except he seemed to have a private bank abroad. It was known that he had contacts with the detective division of Scotland Yard because we had our own contacts there. His description was average everything and there were no photographs.

Meier and Robertson traveled to Europe until January 11 when Meier left on Flight Air Canada 853 for Vancouver. On January 24, Meier picked up Bruce McInnes in a suburb of Vancouver and they went to Nanaimo (on Vancouver) Island to meet Tom Douglas of the NDP party. Douglas we found to be a socialist with a daughter living in California who was also a leftist.

Meier was again in London, England, from January 31 to February 7 when he left for Toronto via Montreal. Robertson was with him and on the morning of the 8th they went to see Andrew Brewin an NDP member of parliament.

It was arranged that we should have our own Conservative contacts pull Reynolds away from Meier but this did not work out. I again blamed Intertel and Ralph Winte for interfering like amateurs.

During February it became clear Meier and Robertson had talked a lot. Robertson gave radio interviews and television talks on the supposed death of Hughes and was anti-Nixon. March 2 Meier and Robertson drove to Seattle and were followed in cars. They then went on 852 Flight to San Francisco where they met Harry Evans. We were unable to get a clear picture of Robertson who always seemed aware of surveillance.

March 4 the two men flew to Burbank and on the following day Meier was seen at the courthouse where the Maheu trial was taking place. Intertel told me they spotted Meier but lost him and could not keep him in sight.

Trace was lost until March 7 when Meier was spotted in Circus Circus, Las Vegas. He appeared to be alone but when he left for Canada the next day Robertson was with him. March 13 Jack Cromar saw Meier at Meier's home in Canada. We felt to call the Hughes people to tell them to keep Cromar out as I was not happy he was aware of our aims. I became uneasy at the events at one meeting when we thought how to stop the possibility of involved information coming out from Meier or Robertson.

It was getting serious to the administration and the Hughes group. It was suggested that Robertson be removed from the picture absolutely and Meier would get the message because he was married and had children.

The matter was not dropped but there was worry about the British attitude if Robertson had stored any data in England or Europe or if Meier would not accept the warning. There was discord with the IRS, Intertel and ourselves. All wanted to be chiefs and I was nervous of the Intertel man in Toronto, Hill, who had missed Robertson there when he had been chasing around the Bahamas and Miami. He was too loud and made too many slips for safety.

I asked to be put elsewhere and was put onto Hugh Hefner for a time.

Gonzales describes the operations of a police state. His affidavit is a simple monograph explaining the elements of that system and shows the involvement of everyone from the head of state to the lowest policeman.

It amounts to this: the state security system is turned loose against a political enemy of the head of state. Apart from using its own formidable resources, it commandeers the police, the courts and other state agencies to wage war on the victim with only one prohibition — that what is done has to be done in secret. Thus the appearance of law and order is maintained as is the illusion that the victim has full civil rights. What is chilling in this case is that once the victim managed to put a buffer between himself and the state — as Meier did by going to Canada — murder is eventually contemplated.

Gonzales traces the CIA's annoyance with Meier to his penchant for interfering in the agency's schemes, beginning with the Kennedy episode through to his meddling in Ecuador and the Dominican Republic where he caused "a backing off in our plans," presumably those to assassinate Balaguer.

The agency suspected that Meier had lists of CIA cover organizations and knew that he had obtained a list of politicians that the agency wanted elected. It obviously worried that Meier's information would land in the wrong hands.

There are two periods of intensive surveillance noted in the document. The first and longest, covers about a third of the affidavit and runs between

January and November of 1972, the period immediately before and after Watergate. The second ranges from August 1973, when the Watergate inquiry is heading inexorably towards the Hughes connection, and March 1974 when it is scrutinizing this connection and Nixon is on the brink of resigning.

Gonzales leaves no doubt that Nixon was behind the surveillance. On one occasion the President can be seen directing it when he asks the CIA to bring him the substance of what Meier told the SEC about the Air West takeover. It is obvious too that the agency not only tapped Meier's various phones but Schrade's and those at McGovern headquarters.

The Gonzales affidavit surfaced in May but a month earlier Meier had been told that he might be receiving help from an unexpected quarter. This was conveyed to him by that sympathetic CIA officer who had given him the list of Hughes' fronts that was turned over to the British. This officer phoned Meier in early April 1975, and said he would be receiving a call from a person who might be of help. There was no mention of an affidavit being provided. Then, someone called and introduced himself to Meier as a friend of a friend.

"It is difficult for me to explain everything to you, Mr. Meier, but perhaps you could give me the name of your lawyer, his phone number and his address,"[6] said his new friend. Meier complied and repeated it slowly, giving the caller time to copy it down. In response to Meier's questioning, the mystery caller said he was calling from Miami, and going by the name Virgino Gonzales at present.

"Mr. Meier, let me ask you a question. Do you remember having dinner a month ago in Vancouver?" — and he named the restaurant. Meier asked how he knew and Gonzales said he had been there. Sensing Meier's puzzlement, Gonzales said he had only mentioned it to show he had some knowledge of Meier's movements and to vouch for his own credibility. Gonzales said he would be going to Mexico within the month and would call from there.

When he phoned, Gonzales said he was leaving Mexico City and would drop off a package to Wyshak which might be helpful. Then on May 3 Gonzales called from Los Angeles and said he would leave a package for Wyshak at the International Hotel on Century Boulevard. Meier called his lawyer who went and retrieved it.

Attached to the affidavit was a note from Gonzales to Wyshak which read:

I do not know if this will be of any help at all. All I can do is to show some idea of the surveillance work kept on Meier and others. It goes on all the time and still goes on. People can not know the extent of this kind of thing.

Copies of my original notes and credentials will be in a deposit for safety and can be released on my death or note. The agency will of course deny this as they always do and I only hope soon others will come forward and show the amazing power game behind all that is happening in America and how the agency is a tool of the President's and the Rockefeller's (sic). Not just in America but all over the world, and not just for intelligence reasons.

It may not be possible but protection is needed for me and when you get this I will remain on the move until I hear that this is coming. For others in the business who want to get out as well.

Consulting his diaries, Meier cross-checked Gonzales' dates, times and places. What the agent had recorded was accurate. His editorializing, on the other hand, was something else. Meier would hardly have described Blech as a leftist but he might have been persuaded that Brando, if not a kook, was certainly eccentric.

This was not the first public manifestation of this CIA operative. His presence had been noted in early January when Bruce McInnes told reporters that he had been approached by two CIA agents, Virgino Gonzales and a "Mr. Abbott" and asked to spy on Meier.[7]

McInnes was a freelance journalist and broadcaster who knew Meier and was aspiring to make a documentary of Hughes' life. He had been in Las Vegas in August 1974 to meet with officials of Summa when Gonzales and Abbott came to his hotel room and offered him a commission. Purportedly representing an oil company, they asked if he would consider doing research. This involved gathering information on Meier's knowledge of Summa, his connection with Jack Anderson and Donald Nixon — peculiar research even for an oil company. McInnes said he declined. Abbott arrived in Vancouver in November and McInnes rejected his offer a second time. McInnes contacted Andrew St. George, a freelance writer who lived in New York and was considered close to the CIA (too close by some).

From St. George, McInnes learned that Gonzales and Abbott were with the CIA.

Publication of the Gonzales affidavit put Meier under siege. Reporters, politicians, Canadian Intelligence officers, lawyers for the Senate Select Committee on Intelligence (which was probing CIA activities in the United States), St. George and even McCord's lawyer — all wanted Gonzales and imagined Meier could produce him. But Gonzales had prudently retired and was content to watch the show from a safe distance.

Meier's Member of Parliament, John Reynolds, brought the affidavit before the Canadian House of Commons, where it caused consternation. If Gonzales were to be believed, CIA freebooters were operating in Canada as though the place were little more than a banana republic. This was at a time when the government was peddling the fiction that Canada was a CIA-free zone and that if the CIA really did need to do something in Canada, the RCMP would be in on it. The Mounties weren't in on this. The Solicitor General ordered the RCMP to track down Gonzales and find out what was going on.

Two of the RCMP security service officers given the assignment, Paul Ouellette and Mitch Mitchelsen, had been working with Meier for some time and were — whether the government knew or not — already trying to discern the scope of CIA penetration into Canadian affairs. They had one major handicap in finding Gonzales — they were not allowed to leave the country. The Americans didn't want the RCMP carrying their investigation across the border, which ruled out any possibility of ever finding Gonzales since by then Gonzales was nowhere near Canada. His movements were designed to put some distance between himself and the United States because he feared for his life. Although he filed his affidavit on May 2, it wasn't until May 15 that the newspapers got hold of it.

After dropping off his package for Wyshak he arrived in New York and paid a brief visit to a lawyer's office in the bowels of Harlem. Ruben H. Mack's law practice is on the second floor of a dusty old building on West 125th Street, surrounded by the debris of a neighborhood that looks as if it had been fought over by armored divisions. Burnt-out and abandoned buildings, old car wrecks and the ever-present smell of marijuana gave it a most melancholy air.

Why Gonzales would pick a lawyer in the ghetto, only he knows. But he climbed the few flights of well-worn stairs, pushed open the stout front door and stepped inside the attorney's office, unannounced and without an appointment. Mack didn't know what to make of his visitor, who flashed a CIA identification card, gave him $500 in cash, said he needed representation, and then vanished. Gonzales had been in the office for barely two minutes. Mack never saw him again.

A man telephoned Meier from Miami on May 16 identifying himself as Max Gorman.[8] He gave Meier a phone number to call thirty minutes later "because a friend of yours wants to talk to you."

When Meier called the same person answered the phone. With no attempt to disguise his voice he now identified himself as Gonzales. He had seen nothing in the papers (the first story had been published in British Columbia only the night before) and was concerned that Meier had not received the affidavit. Meier assured him he had and that his lawyers were working on it.

"Good," said Gonzales, "I am leaving for Europe and I wanted to make sure all was well with you before I left. I'll be in touch."

Gonzales wrote two letters to Mack from Europe, one on May 29 and the other on June 2. In his first letter he asked Mack not to let Washington have his CIA identification number as "it will give the Agency a big working advance on me." He was heading for Spain and Germany to be with friends and to "get more facts to back my case about what has been happening through the past years." He wrote:

I do not feel safe, as you can imagine. But these things must be done. I have my papers from Mexico and when this is over I will settle there because I have lawyer friends who can help me more than anywhere else. Certainly, I can testify if I am given personal protection because there is no doubt my life is on the line.

From this Gonzales appears to be saying that the affidavit was just the first installment of a grand expose of the CIA which he was preparing. His reference to testifying concerns the proceedings of the Senate committee on Intelligence, under Idaho Senator Frank Church, which was probing the CIA.[9]

In his next letter he promised to come back and visit Mack but said he was still on the move collecting information. He said he would arrange for a friend to give Mack more money.

I gather the lawyer Wyshak has had some kind of contact with the Church people and that the committee has a copy of my affidavit.[10] Really what I need first is for you to arrange that I will be interviewed abroad, if required, but only if I can be certain of protection because my evidence about the political side will cause me to have many enemies on all sides. Even now I am taking the greatest care as I am known to many of the people I need to contact here and who knew me in South America and in the States. It is easy to do a job without caring, but now I do care and believe that what I did for others was wrong and I want to put it right.

Whatever became of Gonzales' desire to collect the necessary evidence to "put it right" is unknown. His last contact with Meier came almost a year after he filed his affidavit. He gave no reason for the call other than to ask how Meier was doing. They chatted for a while and Meier asked if he would like to talk with people in the British government. Boyce had asked him to steer Gonzales his way if he could.

"Do you know him personally?" asked Gonzales of Boyce. Meier said he did and that he could be trusted. Gonzales said he was planning another trip to Europe and would meet Boyce. Later, the Intelligence officer thanked Meier for his help with Gonzales. Meier asked if the meeting had been fruitful.

"Yes, very," said Boyce without elaboration. Perhaps that is where the mysterious Gonzales material ended up after all — in the hands of the British.

ON MAY 23, 1975 Meier received an offer of assistance that was more a threat than a comfort. It came in the form of a mysterious call from a man offering to set up a system whereby Meier would be able to tape his telephone calls. The man introduced himself as Reice Hamel but Meier could not place him, nor the mutual friends Hamel claimed that they had. Meier gave a vague promise to consider the offer.

Hamel was one of the best wiremen in North America. He was a gifted sound technician who had recorded many stars including Frank Sinatra, Joan Baez, Barbra Streisand and The Who. Now he was living in Point Roberts and apparently wandering the backroads of British Columbia soliciting menial recording jobs working out of a van full of sophisticated equipment.

Some days later, Meier discovered Hamel in his living room after he had talked his way past the children at the front door. He claimed to have been inspecting the room to find the best location to install the equipment. Meier got rid of him but a few days later he tried to get in again to make the installation. Meier turned him away but later Hamel called him warning that Meier's phones were bugged.

Concerned, Meier called the telephone company and was put in touch with the head of their security Gordon Mackie who, upon hearing Hamel's name, immediately left for Meier's home.

Mackie confided in Meier that Hamel had been caught in Nanaimo with an illegal box which allows callers to make long distance calls without paying the tolls. The security chief then crossed the border to Point Roberts where the local police told him that they had noticed Hamel was armed with a .38 automatic and kept a large Doberman in his van.

Mackie, after scouting around the outside of Hamel's house, returned to headquarters and checked the telephone line installed there. It showed that illegal equipment was attached.

Within minutes, Meier received a telephone call from an irate Hamel demanding to know who had come on his property and protesting that his phone lines had just been checked.

Meier, realizing the significance of Hamel's ability to have his lines monitored against interception, called Mackie and repeated the conversation. Now fully aware that he was dealing with a sophisticated professional, Mackie placed a tap on Hamel's line knowing that it would be immediately detected.

On July 18, Mackie and three Whatcom County deputy sheriffs arrested Hamel. His home was searched and his black and blue boxes seized. An array of state-of-the-art bugging equipment was left untouched as it was not covered by the search warrant, as was his van — which turned out to be a highly sophisticated mobile surveillance unit. One of the seized pieces of equipment was capable of tapping any phone simply by dialing its number. This technology was so advanced that the local police envied its capabilities. Some of the equipment was rigged to self-destruct if tampered with.

Hamel was charged with possessing toll fraud devices and damaging county property. He was set free after posting $250 bail. He called Meier upon returning home, interrupting Meier's interview with a *Playboy* reporter. "I'm gonna come round there and kill you," he raged.

Meier called his RCMP contacts who arranged for the Delta police to grab Hamel as he crossed the border. They seized a handgun and escorted him back to the border warning him to stay away.

The incident so disturbed the RCMP that they changed all the phones at their Vancouver headquarters.

ON AUGUST 3, 1976, Meier's father died in New York. For the first time since being declared a fugitive, Meier felt the corrosive frustration of being unable to travel freely within the United States. He called Wyshak and asked if he could secure an amnesty from Boldt's court on compassionate grounds in order to travel unmolested to the funeral. The justice department flatly refused but he decided to risk the trip anyway. None of the border crossings in the West were safe so he would attempt to cross back East, hopefully unnoticed.

He flew to Windsor, Ontario, rented a car and was waved through the Detroit border crossing without examination. From there he flew to New York and went to the cemetery, making sure to arrive well in advance of the funeral procession. He watched the funeral from a safe distance. Two men stood apart from the party at the graveside, in case he should come blundering in. But Meier bided his time and waited till the mourners and watchers left and when the workmen arrived to cover the coffin, he walked over to pay his respects.

When he returned home his security contacts, who had been attempting to reach him, were furious when they found out what he had done. In order to give him a cover in the event his work with the RCMP security service was accidentally disclosed, Meier was introduced to members of British Columbia's Coordinated Law Enforcement Unit, known by the acronym CLEU.

CLEU had been set up to coordinate and organize police intelligence efforts against organized crime operations in the province and international drug smuggling. Meier's contact with CLEU was Eddie Hameluck, a retired RCMP intelligence officer who had worked with some distinction on the Soviet desk. In November, CLEU formalized Meier's cover by sending him a letter inviting him to become a consultant for a study it was doing about gambling. The letter was placed on file in case Meier was spotted with RCMP officers by some of the crime figures in Vancouver for whom Meier, with his Las Vegas connections, was something of a celebrity.

He was still under CIA surveillance. An RCMP team photographed three men following Meier and asked if he could identify them. He recognized one as a friend of Merhige.

Perhaps now that the year was almost over, surveillance was slackened and the CIA and Intertel's interest was suspended while the spooks and shadows assigned to Meier went home for Christmas. If so, they chose a bad time to relax. On New Year's Day, 1976, Meier began a journey which his enemies would surely have thwarted had they known his destination.

John Meier, age 2, with his mother Hedwig, taken in Astoria, Long Island, New York.

courtesy Meier Entertainment

John Meier, age 4, with his sister Mildred, age 3, taken in Astoria, Long Island, New York.

courtesy Meier Entertainment

Meier in 1952 in Korea where he served in the U.S. Army. He was an American Legion Chaplain and later served in the U.S. Marine Corps Reserve.

courtesy Meier Entertainment

Above:

In 1954, John Meier as U.S. Military Fire Chief of Tokyo.

Opposite:

Howard Hughes, billionaire industrialist and legendary entrepreneur. After moving to Nevada he became obsessed with the effects of nuclear radiation and had Meier organize an anti-testing campaign. Hughes' $1 million payment to President Nixon was the reason for the Watergate burglary. From the time that Meier advised Hughes of the infiltration of the CIA into the Hughes organization, Meier was targeted by various government agencies and Hughes himself left the U.S.A. Months before his reported death on April 5, 1976, Meier saw his body encased and frozen on a secluded island off the coast of Cuba.

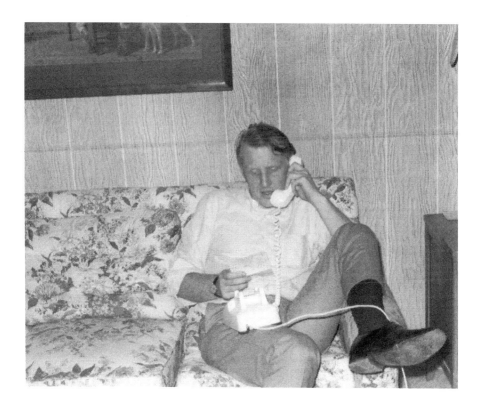

George Clifford, journalist, associate of columnist Jack Anderson and leader of the group plotting President Nixon's downfall. With Meier, he provoked Nixon into ordering the Watergate burglary. Wrote numerous anti-Nixon articles based on information supplied by Meier.

courtesy Meier Entertainment

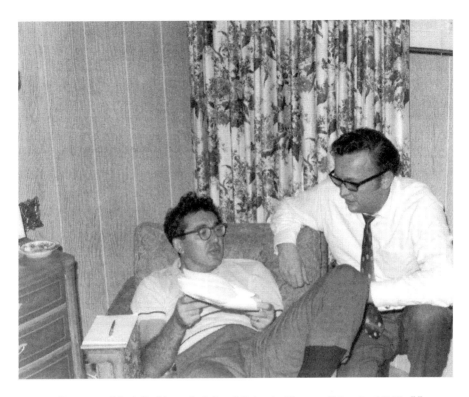

William Haddad (left) with John Meier in Puerto Rico in 1968. He was a former journalist and power broker in the Democratic party, and long-time political associate of the Kennedy family. He was instrumental in organizing the disinformation fed to Richard Nixon.

courtesy Meier Entertainment

To John H. Meier - with best wishes - Hubert H Humphrey

Above:

John Meier, in 1969, (left) with President Joaquin Balaguer of the Dominican Republic (center), Don Nixon and interpreter Rolando (far right), presenting a bust of John F. Kennedy from President Nixon and John Meier. Don Nixon had left the selection of the gift up to Meier. When Richard Nixon learned that it was a bust of JFK, he swore at Donald and cursed Meier.

courtesy Meier Entertainment

Opposite:

Hubert H. Humphrey, Vice President of the United States, close personal friend of John Meier and his family. Humphrey helped direct the group which planned against President Nixon's re-election in 1972. This group's activities ultimately led Nixon to panic into ordering the Watergate break-in.

courtesy Meier Entertainment

President Joaquin Balaguer of the Dominican Republic (right center) toasts Meier (left center) after awarding him the coveted Christopher Columbus Award, the highest decoration the Dominican Republic could bestow on a foreigner. Donald Nixon (left) and Senator Mike Gravel (right) look on.

courtesy Meier Entertainment

Donald F. Nixon (center), the President's brother, with his wife Claire Jane (to Nixon's right), Jennie Meier (front right) and Jeannie Meier (front left) in Honolulu, 1970. Meier was forwarding information from Howard Hughes to the President through his brother. Hughes was anxious for a reply.

courtesy Meier Entertainment

Michael O'Callaghan, after being elected Governor of Nevada, with his wife and John Meier, Jennie Meier, meeting in Honolulu. Meier was carrying important information from Howard Hughes and Hughes wanted to know the results of the meeting. When Meier tried to contact Hughes after returning from Hawaii, he was shocked to learn from Las Vegas Sun publisher Hank Greenspun, that Hughes had been kidnapped from the Desert Inn.

courtesy Meier Entertainment

Senator Edward Kennedy meeting with John Meier at a Democratic function in Los Angeles in 1972. The two were discussing Meier's U.S. Senatorial campaign in New Mexico. Meier had previously interfered with a CIA plot to embarrass the Senator.

courtesy Meier Entertainment

Mayor Sam Yorty (left) presents a plaque to John Meier, president of the Nevada Environmental Foundation, for his work in the field of ecology.

courtesy Meier Entertainment

John Meier, candidate for the Democratic nomination to the U.S. Senate for New Mexico, 1972. This photograph was taken just prior to the Nixon White House, the CIA and the Hughes organization's successful destruction of Meier's political career. He was the victim of a prearranged mistaken identity being confused with the source for Clifford Irving's faked biography of Howard Hughes — a Stanley Meyer. The publicity killed his Senatorial campaign instantly. The motive for stopping Meier was Nixon's fear that Meier would use the position of Senator to expose the Nixon-Hughes connection including the million dollar bribe to Nixon via Bebe Rebozo.

courtesy Meier Entertainment

Autographing his book Speaking for the Earth, the official book for the first Earth Day, John Meier engages in conversation with Mrs. P. Seymour, wife of Howard Hughes' aide, John Seymour.

courtesy Meier Entertainment

Mayor Oran Gragson (center), Mayor of Las Vegas, his wife Bonnie (left), Senator Mike Gravel of Alaska and John and Jennie Meier (standing). Senator Gravel was involved in trying to halt the AEC testing program and ultimately paid a high political price for his efforts. To the credit of Gravel, Meier and Preston Truman, the nuclear policies of the United States were changed.

courtesy Meier Entertainment

Left to right: Robert Humphrey, son of Vice President Hubert Humphrey, Governor Goodwin J. Knight of California, the Hon. Milton Polland, now the Marshall Islands' ambassador to Mexico, and John Meier. The group were the principals of Radiarc Industries Inc., a high tech company.

courtesy Meier Entertainment

Susi Wyss, a high-level intelligence connection in Europe introduced to Meier by Hubert Humphrey. She revealed to Meier that Dr. Buhler was the CIA's paymaster in Europe.

courtesy Meier Entertainment

Robert Wyshak, noted U.S. tax attorney, with John Meier in June 1973. The two were discussing the politically motivated IRS charges brought against Meier on orders from the White House. Ralph Kaminski, the lead investigator for the IRS, later stated that after the extensive investigation that he conducted, he was unable to find any wrongdoing by Meier and that "his case was obviously motivated by people that must discredit Meier in order to survive."

courtesy Meier Entertainment

John Meier with the King of Tonga, Taufa'ahau Tupou IV, at the ground breaking ceremony to begin the airport construction project funded by Meier's efforts. The U.S. government did not wish to see this kind of development in Tonga and were furious with Meier's involvement.

courtesy Meier Entertainment

Perhaps the only photo ever taken of the Watergate Committee investigators shows Meier swapping a joke with Terry Lenzner, Scott Armstrong, Robert Muse and Martin Lackritz. Washington's Mayflower Hotel was the scene of this secret meeting between John Meier (far left) and the Senate committee's staff investigators in Oct. 1973.

courtesy Meier Entertainment

James Barber at his desk. He was the Salt Lake City lawyer who represented Meier when he was accused of obstruction of justice.

courtesy Meier Entertainment

Robert Robertson was the government's key witness against Meier. Much of the evidence used against Meier in the murder case actually suggested that Robertson committed the murder. A paid informant who, along with former RCMP Cpl. Pat Westphal and prosecutor William Halprin, (who has since met mysterious death) distorted evidence, contrived allegations and concealed facts for the U.S. government in order to destroy Meier.

courtesy Meier Entertainment

Alfred Wayne Netter, Vancouver stock promoter, president of TCV, found murdered in a Los Angeles hotel room. U.S. authorities fabricated evidence to frame Meier but after serving two years in prison for allegedly participating in the murder, Meier was cleared.

courtesy Meier Entertainment

Under tight security, Meier is escorted from the Vancouver jail to the airport by U.S. police officers five days before Christmas 1983. Larry Leffler (seated in front of Meier), a Beverly Hills policeman, was also executive producer for Paul Pompain Productions, a company preparing to do a negative film about Meier — an astounding conflict of interest.

Photo by Mark Van Manen, courtesy of the Vancouver Sun

The Meier family, John Jr., Jeannie, John, Jim, Joanne and Jennie, paying a surprise visit to John at Mission Prison, outside Vancouver, in 1980, after his transfer from the United States. Instead of being released, the U.S. charged Meier with conspiracy to murder and again sought his extradition from Canada to face another false allegation.

courtesy Meier Entertainment

John and Jennie at the Federal Prison in Englewood, Colorado, January
23, 1980.

courtesy Meier Entertainment

Albert DeBlanc, Los Angeles lawyer who agreed to represent Meier on the murder charges after he read Brenner's bigoted comments about African-Americans. Ultimately, DeBlanc destroyed the government's framing of Meier.

courtesy Meier Entertainment

Over the years John Meier made many connections with celebrities, some of whom became friends. Here he is with Mickey Mantle in 1986 at Mantle's home in Dallas.

courtesy Meier Entertainment

John Meier, with his wife Jennie and daughter Jeannie after obtaining bail at his extradition hearing on the obstruction of justice charges laid in Salt Lake City Utah.

courtesy Meier Entertainment

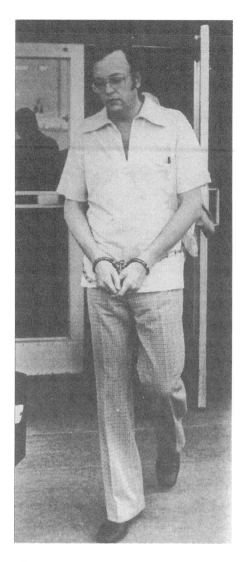

For five years, John Meier was a political prisoner. He remained an exile for over a decade later, before being able to return to the country of his birth.

courtesy of Bruce McKim, the Seattle Times

15

THE SECRET OF CAY SAL

S omewhere off to the west lay Cay Sal. Meier couldn't see it but the fishing boat skipper stabbed a stubby finger at the chart then pointed confidently into the thickening night air, indicating where it would lie.

"Soon," he said.

Chuck had asked the skipper to pace his approach with the fall of darkness and so for the past hour the engines had been throttled back and now ran with a low mutter, a decided change in pitch, Meier thought, from the roar of the past three days.

Behind them it was dark but to the west the air still plucked at the elusive last glowing of the fallen sun. Meier left Chuck and the skipper in the small wheelhouse and climbed down onto the deck where he sat and, as he had many times that day, pondered what he was heading into.

The quickening of the engines caused him to look up. Now the horizon had turned a uniform black and the boat was heading towards Cay Sal, a tiny islet some 30 miles off the coast of Cuba — the most westerly and remote of that necklace of cays and islands stretching almost from Florida to Hispaniola.

After a while Meier could see lights ahead and Chuck tapped his shoulder and whispered, as if afraid to say it aloud — "Cay Sal."

The fishing boat, all its running lights extinguished, slowed down and then coasted to within a couple of hundred yards of the shore whose line was now visible from the phosphorescence of breaking waves. Chuck threw Meier his leather jacket and a baseball cap, then went forward to help the crew launch the dinghy. Meier put on the jacket, zippered it and pulled the cap down hard.

Here he was, at the end of a 650-mile voyage from Port-au-Prince, boarding a dinghy with a man whose surname he didn't know, and whose first name probably wasn't Chuck, being surreptitiously rowed to a sand dune in the dead of night to avoid detection from unknown forces ashore — and still he didn't understand why. But he did have faith in Dick Hannah. Dick had said to come, so here he was. What was it on Cay Sal that Dick had so much wanted him to see? He had thought about nothing else for two days.

The last time he had seen Hannah was at Vancouver's Bayshore Inn when his old friend had warned him against pressing his luck with Intertel. He had always regarded Hannah with affection even at the height of the Hughes organization's campaign against him. Hannah played a part in this campaign by virtue of his position as Hughes' chief spokesman but had done so without enthusiasm, Meier knew that much. From time to time Hannah would phone to apologize and try to give whatever information he could to help.

Hannah had represented Hughes for two decades and was a vice president of Carl Byoir and Associates of New York, one of the country's leading public relations firms. His journalistic credentials were impressive. He had worked as a reporter and editor for the *Los Angeles Times,* did public relations for Paramount Pictures and Republic Studios and spent three years as correspondent with the U.S. Marine Corps' Second Division in the Second World War. Meier had known him since first going to work for Hughes in the fifties.

Towards the end of his career with Hughes, Hannah was disturbed by something about the organization. At least that was the impression Meier got from his infrequent phone calls.

Hannah had told Meier that he wasn't proud any more of what he was doing. Once he said that he wasn't even sure if he was working for Howard Hughes, that strange things were happening with the organization. But when Meier asked for an explanation Hannah would go no further.

At the age of 60, Hannah underwent open heart surgery. He survived but the prognosis was not good. Six months later, at the beginning of

December 1975, he called Meier. He was dying. The fragility of Hannah's voice alarmed Meier.

"You sound awful, Dick. What's wrong?"

Hannah had more on his mind than his health: "John, I am going to do you a big favor. Take down this number, it's in Miami." Meier obeyed and Hannah said that when he called he was to ask for Mr. Moody. Meier wanted to know why, but Hannah was evasive.

"You're going to see what I haven't been able to tell you about for some time," Hannah said. "Someone in Miami will make arrangements to take you to Cay Sal." Meier persisted in trying to force an explanation but Hannah asked for forbearance.

"Listen, John, just trust me. I don't know how long I've got but please believe me, I'm doing you the biggest favor anyone has ever done. I always liked you and your family, just do as I ask."

Meier phoned the number and asked for Mr. Moody. The man who answered told him to wait, then someone else picked up the phone.

"Mr. Moody?" Meier asked.

"No, you've got me. My name's Chuck."

After a pause he asked: "Who told you to call?"

Meier said Dick Hannah.

"What's your name?"

"John Meier."

"Uhuh. What's your wife's maiden name?"

"Cravotta."

"Okay. What's your telephone number?"

Meier told him. There was a long silence and Meier could hear Chuck breathing down the phone as if trying to resolve some inner conflict. Then he said abruptly: "When can you come down and see me in Florida?"

Mindful of his status as fugitive, Meier asked if they could meet in Canada.

"Nope. That's no use. I've got to take you somewhere."

Meier blurted out "Cay Sal?" and half-caught an oath in the swift intake of breath before the line went dead. Intuition prevented him from ringing back.

Chuck phoned the next day and apologized. "I didn't want to talk on that phone. Listen, we're doing Dick a favor. That's all I can say. I'll make arrangements for you to go to the island." Meier again asked what was so important about Cay Sal but Chuck was as evasive as Hannah had been. Meier asked if he could make his own arrangements, but Chuck said the island was out of bounds to strangers.

Meier said he would try anyway. He phoned people he knew in Miami who operated a charter seaplane service to the Bahamas. When he mentioned his destination, he was told it was impossible. The Bahamian government forbade any unauthorized landings anywhere near the island and his contacts refused to take him.

If he couldn't fly to Cay Sal then he would have to go by boat. He phoned an old government contact in the Dominican Republic and told him he needed to reach Cay Sal. Yes, of course, said his contact, but it would be far easier to sail from Haiti, as a glance at any map would show.

"I'll talk to some of my government friends in Haiti and see what can be done," he told Meier.

Meier was passed on to a government contact in Haiti. As he had done substantial business in Haiti and had met the infamous Papa Doc Duvalier on a number of occasions,[1] the Haitians were only too glad to help. Within a few days a boat had been set aside for Meier. He and Chuck agreed to meet in Port-au-Prince.

On January 1 Meier began his journey to Port-au-Prince, flying to Toronto, then on to Kingston; from Jamaica he flew to the Dominican Republic where he made his connection to Port-au-Prince. Chuck was already in Port-au-Prince. Together they inspected the fishing boat that was to take them to Cay Sal and found it a dilapidated craft with powerful engines and a good cruising speed. Chuck said it would do. They sailed on the afternoon of January 3 with a small crew. Meier and Chuck shared cramped quarters with the crew in the cabin below the wheelhouse.

During the voyage Meier found Chuck personable, yet guarded. He talked a lot about flying, a passion he shared with his friend Dick Hannah, and asked Meier a few questions, more out of politeness than inquisitiveness. He was a large burly man — not quite Meier's height — and Meier guessed him to be somewhere in his forties. His companion made hardly any reference to Cay Sal on the outward trip and now that they were heading for the island, Meier found this sense of mystery disturbing.

In 1957 Howard Hughes had leased the island from the Bahamian government for reasons never disclosed. A tiny speck of land — hardly more than a couple of hundred acres above high water — it lies below Key West and because of its proximity to Cuba, has reputedly been used by the CIA as a forward base for sending parties across the Nicholas Channel into Castro's stronghold. In 1971, Hughes' lease was renewed and according to testimony given at the Watergate hearings it was renegotiated by Dick Danner. At the time of the renewal there was talk of building a private fishing retreat on the island.

They hove-to off Cay Sal at about midnight on January 5 and within minutes the dinghy was unlashed from the foredeck and launched. Meier clambered in behind two crewmen who sat together athwartship each grasping an oar. Meier was directed to the stern while Chuck sat up front. He warned Meier to say nothing in the event they were discovered coming ashore.

"Let's hope that doesn't happen," he said as one of the oarsman pushed off. It took about five minutes to row to the beach. Chuck jumped out first then motioned Meier to follow. As they waded ashore the dinghy pulled away and disappeared into the darkness.

With Chuck leading, they ran at a crouch up the beach towards some shrubs. They pushed their way in through the branches and lay hidden while catching their breath. Meier's heart was pounding. Chuck whispered that armed native guards patrolled the island and that if they should come across a patrol Meier should attempt to hide in the bushes while he went to speak with them.

While lying there, Chuck nudged him and pointed. In the light thrown from one of the buildings Meier could see two figures, rifles slung across their shoulders, making the rounds. Through the bushes Meier could make out what appeared to be a group of cottages, some of which had lights burning inside, and a large shed with tractor equipment parked beside it. Behind this little settlement he could see the outline of a small hill.

Meier asked Chuck how anyone got on to the island and Chuck growled: "No one gets on here without Moody's permission." When the guards had moved on, he told Meier to follow him, then started off at a run towards the shed. Chuck ran faster than Meier and was fiddling with the lock as Meier came up. The shed appeared to be windowless. As they stood at the door, Chuck showed nerves for the first time. He was fumbling with the lock and he muttered to Meier: "I hope I know what I'm doing. A lot of people owe Dick favors but godammit, mine's settled after this. "

The lock yielded and both stepped inside as Chuck closed the door. It was pitch black and the air was stale. Chuck removed a small flashlight from his pocket and aimed the beam down the room until it settled on the burnished sides of what Meier at first took to be a large molded trophy case.

It was about seven feet long and perhaps three feet high. Chuck made no attempt to move closer but Meier, for whom the case had begun to take on a familiar appearance, went forward quickly.

Here was the cryonics chamber that he and Buhler had purchased for Hughes five years before. He had arranged its shipment from Germany to the Medical Institute in Miami. In the pale beam of the light he could see the dials with the German inscriptions beneath. His companion came up beside him, went around the casket, quickly lifted the lid and lowered the flashlight to give Meier the most fleeting glimpse inside. Swiftly closing the top, he whispered "That's it. You've seen it, let's go."

Meier hadn't seen anything. "No, let me see it again." Chuck grabbed his arm and tried to drag him away but Meier struggled free and yanked up the lid. Cursing, Chuck dipped the light downwards a second time.

Meier saw that within the casket was an inner container — a tapered, translucent cylinder which contained a body. He grabbed the light and shone it directly onto a plexiglass screen. Through a slight mist he could clearly see the frigid features of the corpse.

"Good God," Meier muttered. "It's Howard Hughes."

Hughes was lying there in his hermetically sealed coffin, frozen stiff, his eyes closed, his beard neatly trimmed, awaiting the day of his resurrection. His body appeared to be wrapped in a metallic sheath which ended at the upper chest. Meier could see bare flesh as far down as the top of his shoulders. There was a slight hum coming from the chamber.

Meier was transfixed. He was vaguely aware of Chuck tugging at him but still could not move. Then he felt himself being lifted bodily off the ground as Chuck held him in a bear hug and began dragging him away.

"No, not yet," pleaded Meier, but Chuck cursed.

"Godammit, Meier, we've got to get out of here. You've seen it all."

By the time they reached the door Meier had stopped struggling and they both tried to compose themselves before stepping outside. Chuck slowly opened the door and glanced around. He pulled Meier outside, set the lock and sprinted to the shore. The dinghy was waiting and Meier scrambled in while Chuck pushed off. He sat in the dinghy shivering at the thought of what they had done. Chuck said he was glad it was over. Meier apologized for the scene inside the building.

Chuck shrugged it off. "I've just done you a big favor. I don't know why and it's none of my business. I did it for Dick. Frankly, I don't know if you are working with us or not." He looked at Meier who said nothing. "Well, I guess it's too late to worry about that now."

Their voyage back to Haiti was uneventful. When he made his farewell in Port-au-Prince on January 8, Chuck warned Meier never to call him again.

According to the Hughes organization, Howard Hughes was alive and well at the other end of the Bahamas in Freeport.

Meier attempted to talk to Hannah after he had returned to Vancouver but no one would put his call through. On January 16, Dick Hannah died.

Meier reported Hughes' death to Boyce in England and to his intelligence contacts in Canada. Boyce warned that he had penetrated the most closely guarded secret of the Hughes organization and that he should say nothing, as the consequences of possessing such knowledge could be drastic. Meier heeded the warning.

Meier was called again by Chuck on March 4. "Keep an eye on the first week in April, around the fifth or sixth," said Chuck. "That's when they're going to announce the old man's death."

Following the announcement of Hughes' death on April 5, he kept calling Chuck's number in Miami but no one would acknowledge they knew him. Meier checked the number and found it belonged to a company called Cay Sal Ltd.; when he checked the company officers he found a C. Osmond Moody listed as a director.

BEFORE HUGHES WAS OFFICIALLY DEAD, the pre-trial wrangling between Wyshak and Chester Davis continued unabated before Judge Aldon Anderson in Salt Lake City as Summa's civil suit against Meier moved inexorably towards trial.

Summa's suit demanded that Meier account for the money he had spent on Hughes' behalf buying mining claims and sought the return of any of that money it felt was ill-spent. Davis had been demanding that Meier submit to an examination for discovery, a pre-trial hearing in which lawyers are allowed to question the opposing party before meeting in court. Wyshak had refused, arguing that Meier had bought the properties at the direction of Howard Hughes and had not worked for any of his companies, and that if Meier was to submit to examination so too must Hughes.

Davis stunned the court by agreeing to make Hughes available. For years Hughes' lawyers had doggedly protected his person from being involved in any litigation, criminal or civil, or of being hauled before such bodies as the Senate Watergate Committee which sought his presence. Yet after all this stonewalling, Meier's lawyer was now being promised an audience. Well, there was one catch — Meier would have to submit to the ordeal first. Davis would produce Hughes once Wyshak had produced Meier. Davis said they would conduct their examination of Meier on April 5.

On April 3, Jennie became seriously ill and Meier called Wyshak and asked him to put it off. Wyshak tried but Davis was adamant. Fulminating about his court order and Meier's evasiveness, Davis browbeat Wyshak into agreeing to make Meier available in Vancouver at the agreed time. Realizing that Hughes' deposition couldn't be taken — at least not on this side of eternity — Meier presented himself for examination in a Vancouver law office on the morning of April 5. Chester Davis was not present, so Meier's deposition was left to another Hughes lawyer. Among their party was Jack Cromar, the Hughes security chief.

When the examination was over and they were about to leave, the Hughes lawyer was called outside. When he came back it was to announce that Howard Hughes had just died.

"How unfortunate," said Wyshak dryly. "We give you everything. You give us nothing."

"Too bad, counselor," said Cromar with a smirk.

All evening Meier was besieged by reporters begging for comment. Without explaining why, Meier told *Vancouver Sun* reporter Lew Thomas that the time of Hughes' death was "very convenient" and that he hadn't died that day but some time before.

The world was now agog as purported details of Hughes' death were trickling out. The official story was that he had taken ill in his hotel room in Acapulco, Mexico, where he had been living since leaving the Bahamas. Afraid that he would die, his aides summoned a private jet and rushed him back to Houston. Then, he died as eccentrically as he had lived, in the air thousands of feet above land — like an eagle extinguished in the element it cherished most. If nothing else, it was poetic.

There were witnesses to it all, naturally, and doctors who performed an autopsy, the results of which were later admitted to be inaccurate in that the codeine levels reportedly found in tissue samples — said at the time to be within therapeutic level — were in fact a 1,000 times greater.[2]

The death announcement extinguished the growing suspicion that Hughes' demise was being concealed. The IRS had suspected for years that Hughes was dead and by February, 1976, was on the verge of declaring him legally deceased. This suspicion was aired during the Watergate testimony of former IRS Commissioner Walters, who said that he was worried as far back as 1972 that Hughes might have died and that the IRS should be trying to assess what was owed in estate taxes.

Walters never said what made him suspect this. But he obviously believed it, despite the fact that following Hughes' departure from Las Vegas — where he saw no outsiders — the hitherto reclusive Hughes had become gregarious. He was apparently seen by half a dozen people including U.S. Ambassador to Nicaragua, Turner Shelton, and Nicaraguan dictator, Anastasio Somoza, who gave glowing accounts of his mental and physical state.

On February 27, 1976, Jack Anderson published an internal IRS memo saying IRS agents speculated that Hughes had died in Las Vegas in 1970 and that his organization had been using a double to maintain the fiction that he was still alive, traipsing the double around various countries and passing him off to visitors as the real thing. Hughes' death in Las Vegas seems unlikely (but not impossible), if only because of the fact that Meier was speaking to him almost up to the time he left Nevada. Nevertheless by February 1976 the IRS was quite right in thinking Hughes dead.

The day after Hughes was declared dead, Boyce called Meier from England. After expressing astonishment at the story the American authorities were issuing, he warned Meier again to be careful what he said about the death and asked him to reconsider his decision not to come to London.

Meier was inundated with calls from all quarters in the days following. Movie stars Jane Russell, whose bra[3] had so taxed Hughes' imagination, Cary Grant, and Catherine Grayson, called seeking inside information. Was the body really Hughes? Had he actually died in the fantastic circumstances reported by the newspapers? Was there anything Meier could tell them that wasn't in the papers? Meier was unwilling to satisfy their cravings. The Hughes mystique, so potent in life, lost none of its power in death.

Some months after Hughes' announced death Rick Harrison, the assistant Attorney General of Texas, came to Meier's home seeking information to advance the claim that because Hughes was officially a Texas resident, the state was entitled to death duties. The Texas authorities were assessing taxes on Hughes' estate, while in the courts mountebanks with fake wills contested the fortune. Hughes was supposed to have died intestate, or with a will that could not be found. But his will, composed and witnessed in 1968, was resting in the vaults of the Commercial National Bank in the east Texas town of Victoria. The will was placed into the safekeeping of the bank's chairman A. B. J. Hammett.[4]

Meier had met Hammett in Las Vegas a number of times during his career with Hughes and knew Hughes had money in Hammett's bank. Hammett was an expert on gold and had written books on the subject urging the development of America's vast gold resources. As Meier was Hughes' main agent in purchasing mining properties, he spent many hours in consultation with Hammett.

Hammett was aware of Hughes' wish to be frozen after death; he and Meier had often discussed the topic. In the fall of 1968, as Hammett and Meier were having dinner, Hammett said he was returning to Texas to place Hughes' will in a safety deposit box. He opened his briefcase and pulled out a manila envelope. Hammett briefly displayed the contents but all Meier could see was that the will was typewritten and that Hughes' and Hammett's signatures were at the bottom. There was no time to make out the other signature. Hammett said this would replace an older will which he also had in his possession. Hughes was leaving everything to his Medical Institute. There was another envelope in Hammett's case which contained the names of the three executors Hughes had appointed.

Given Hughes' preoccupation with cryonics it is not too difficult to imagine what the will contained. His wish was to survive death. By composing a conventional will he would be giving away all he possessed. His fabulous wealth would be taken by the government and what was left would fall into the hands of distant relatives.

The new will must have stipulated the way his body was to be stored and treated and how his estate should be managed until he returned to claim it. Such a will would have caused an uproar on all fronts — from governments, which had had a hard enough time getting taxes from him in life; from his companies, which would not want their profits stored away for eternity along with Hughes' frozen remains; and from his relatives, who had a claim to a share of his fortune.

Meier told Harrison of a conversation he had had with Hughes' body servant John Holmes following the April 5 announcement. Holmes had joked about the body buried in Houston not being that of Howard Hughes. Would it be possible to find out? Harrison said it would be impossible.

"Texas is one of the few places where when they bury you, you stay buried. It's probably one of the reasons they brought him back. Exhuming bodies down there is a tough one. In this case it'll never happen."

Not only couldn't they dig up the body, Harrison said, but the state of Texas couldn't convince the Mexicans to let them see the piles of secret papers that the Federales had seized at gunpoint from Hughes' suite in the Acapulco Princess Hotel upon news of his death.

These papers may have thrown some light on the Hughes will but the Mexicans, with historic scores to settle with the Texans, were turning a deaf ear. Meier could barely disguise his excitement. "You mean they seized the papers while they were putting them in the shredder?"

"That's right. They've got cabinets full of the stuff but they won't let us have it."

Meier thought that perhaps he might achieve what the Texans could not. If he didn't act soon, Summa or the CIA would beat him to it and the papers would vanish back into their maw.

While the public believed that Hughes lay under six feet of solid Texas earth, beside the remains of his mother and father in the family plot at Glenwood Cemetery, Houston, a furious fight erupted over his estate.

During this celebrated melee, Summa's attention was diverted by such absurdities as the Mormon Will which Melvin Dummar[5] and lawyer Harold Rhoden made so notorious. The clique which was running Hughes' empire took their eyes off the documents in Mexico at approximately the time Meier fixed his firmly upon them.

Since these files had moved from country to country to match the supposed wanderings of Hughes, they potentially contained answers to the questions that perplexed Meier and a host of others. When did Hughes die, and where — in Nevada, the Bahamas, Nicaragua, Canada, England?[6] Provided he was alive when he left Nevada in 1970, under what circumstances did he live the remainder of his life? Did he have control of his affairs or was he incompetent, disabled by frailty and mental disorders, mad and deranged, prematurely entombed behind the curtained penthouse windows of luxury hotels?

For weeks Meier pondered how he might pick the Mexican lock. As far as he could judge, it was the Mexican's antipathy to things American — particularly Texan — which was making them so obstinate.

It occurred to him that they might not be so unyielding if they were approached by another government. What if the Canadian government requested the papers? After all, both Canada and Mexico had been victims of American expansionism and forced at times to arms to defend their sovereignty. From this perspective, Canada and Mexico had much in common and relations between the countries had always been cordial. The more Meier considered it, the more he became convinced that if approached properly, the Mexicans might do for the Canadians what they were unwilling to do for the Texans. The major difficulty was arranging for the Canadian government to make the request.

Meier had earlier that year been introduced to Terri Clemens-Trevillion, an accountant in Vancouver who was a friend of the Mexican Attorney General Dr. A. G. Manero, who, by this marvelous coincidence, was now sitting on top of the Hughes Papers.

Meier again sought out his Member of Parliament, John Reynolds. Reynolds had introduced the Gonzales affidavit into parliament and was later made the Conservative Party's coordinator of investigative research into the activities of the CIA. This was a non-parliamentary function which carried no official weight; by September 1976 the Gonzales affair had long blown over and with it most of the investigative research. Reynolds agreed to lend his support. On September 27, Trevillion left Vancouver for Mexico City, where she met Manero and asked for his assistance. Manero balked. Did Miss Trevillion have any official documents explaining why such a request was being made? What was the purpose of having the papers copied? And on whose authority were these requests made?

Trevillion went to the Canadian Embassy in Mexico City and talked a secretary into giving her a letter saying she was representing John Reynolds, a Canadian MP investigating CIA activities in Canada. Any assistance the Mexican authorities could provide would be appreciated.

Back she went to Manero, whose response indicated he felt it was a lot to ask and he didn't want to be obstructive but could she please provide some sort of letter from the Canadian Justice Department or the RCMP saying why Mr. Reynolds wanted the papers, *por favor?*

She returned empty handed to Canada and reported her failure to Meier. On October 2, Meier, Reynolds and Trevillion met to draft a letter to Manero. There was no hope of getting the Justice Department or the RCMP involved. The letter to Manero was written on House of Commons stationery, dated October 5 and read as follows:

> This note is to follow up the visit of Miss Trevillion to your office. As you are aware, I have been investigating some matters pertaining to the CIA in Canada and Mr. Howard Hughes' connections.
>
> Attached you will see the minutes of a committee hearing where the solicitor general of Canada authorized an investigation into this whole matter based on documents that I presented to the committee.
>
> In discussing your request to have a letter from our justice department or the RCMP I have been advised by all departments that I have talked to that any letter to a foreign government must come from External Affairs which is our embassy in your country. Therefore, they felt that the letter which you have in your possession from our embassy represents the government of Canada and would suffice.
>
> I trust this meets with your approval as we are quite anxious to review the documents that you have in your possession and see if they can assist us in our investigations.

Cleverly the letter hints that the RCMP and the Solicitor General were consulted and felt obliged to defer to External Affairs. However, a close reading shows that Reynolds is not saying he has actually approached either of those government bodies. He could have gone to someone in Fisheries or Agriculture.

Regardless, when the indefatigable Trevillion presented this to Manero on October 22, the Attorney General opened the vaults, guards staggered out with stacks of boxes and wheeled in a Xerox machine. She spent two days photocopying 3,428 documents. These proved to be the last major cache of Hughes' personal papers to fall into public hands. To describe it as a brilliant coup is no exaggeration. Trevillion returned home with her boxes of plunder and after half-heartedly flicking through them, Reynolds turned the lot over to Meier on October 26.

Amid the dross were nuggets of pure gold, memos showing that Hughes was befuddled with drugs, desperately ill, and had hidden away a will which his keepers were frantically trying to find.

Logs of his daily activities for a portion of May and June, 1972 — while he was in Vancouver — showed him constantly being shuttled between the bathroom and a movie screen on which he watched the same movies again and again. Some days he hardly ate. On June 12 all the nourishment he had was one helping of dessert and he dawdled over it for an hour. But he did get his drugs, his "bombers," as they are noted in the log, to help him sleep.

What emerges of Hughes' last days is a picture of stupefying inactivity, as though Hughes were living in an indulgent asylum where his whims were permitted even if they caused him harm. If one accepts this portrayal of Hughes in 1972, in which he is staring vacantly hour after hour at the same movie, not eating, mainlining drugs, spending hours each day attempting his only physical exertion — a bowel movement — can one candidly expect that the CIA, which had tied itself so tightly to Hughes' industrial empire, would allow their joint affairs to be presided over by anyone in this state?

This pattern of starvation and drug abuse was made vividly obvious by the condition of what was supposed to be Hughes' corpse when it was turned over for burial. It was little more than a skeleton — shrunken, dehydrated, wasted, with broken hypodermic needle tips embedded in the arms.

Even if nothing more than these still-frames of Hughes' existence had been found, the effort by Meier and the others would have been worth it. It totally refuted the persona that Summa had cultivated for Hughes during the years of his exile; he had been described as walking about, piloting airplanes, even getting ready for a big birthday bash to mark his seventieth birthday.[7]

The news that Meier had the papers must have been a blow to Chester Davis, Bill Gay and Nadine Henley, the triumvirate now ruling Summa. The organization was still reeling from the September edition of *Playboy,* which savagely exposed Summa dealings with the White House and the CIA and showed Meier had been on the receiving end of dirty tricks because of his knowledge of these connections.

Entitled "The Puppet and the Puppetmasters," the article concluded that Watergate was an attempt to discover what Meier had told the Democrats about Nixon and Hughes and that Bernstein and Woodward had missed the boat in refusing to investigate these associations as a motive for the burglary. *Playboy* promised to publish a second installment concerning Hughes' death, his will and how Summa had tried to make peace with Meier.[8] Shortly after the appearance of the article, a team of government security agents arrived in Hollywood and began questioning people in the movie industry about Meier's contacts and his activities during the time that he ran his motion picture company.

George Clifford called Meier in November after stories based on the Mexican documents ran on all the major wire services and said both he and Anderson were worried what might happen to him. Clifford's White House sources told him an investigation was underway to determine how Meier had retrieved the papers and what role had been played in the affair by the Canadian government, as Washington was furious. Clifford also said his contact with the CIA had told him that the agency was growing nervous about Meier's relationship with the Canadians.

Playboy's proposed second part never ran. When Meier inquired of the writers he was told the magazine had been placed under such pressure by the government that it had killed the feature. By that time Meier had the Mexican documents in his possession. When he suggested *Playboy* run a story based on them, the magazine agreed.

"The Puppet and the Puppetmasters" had appeared just in time for the 1976 Republican National Convention in Kansas City and was read with great interest because part of the story detailed the CIA request that Hughes put money into the 1968 election campaigns of various Senators and Congressmen.

The most prominent name on that CIA list was that of Gerald R. Ford, a congressman from Michigan in 1968, who had become President after stepping up from Vice President subsequent to Nixon's resignation. Among those ready to contest Ford's nomination was Ronald Reagan. Reagan was intrigued by the story of Ford's place on the list. By coincidence, Reagan was using the services of Hughes psychic Peter Hurkos. Hurkos' wife Stephanie phoned Meier and asked if he would meet Reagan's aides. Reagan wanted to get to the bottom of the *Playboy* story. Was it deliberately done to embarrass the President? What further information could Meier provide on Ford? Did he have any material on Reagan himself or Jimmy Carter?

Meier gave Reagan's people copies of two stories that were published March 27 of that year showing that despite the hype and *Playboy's* claims of breaking the story, the list was old news and was not released to embarrass Ford at the convention. As for other information, Meier said he had none. Reagan's people returned to Kansas.

From the thousands of Mexican documents, Meier had placed a small pile to one side. These memos showed there was an in-house forger working away in the Hughes organization reproducing Hughes' signature,[9] not an altogether remarkable discovery considering Hughes' incapacitation.

One signed by John Holmes to Nadine Henley dated June, 1975, read:

> I have signed HRH's signature (to) the three (3) promissory notes from the First City National Bank of the Southwest and the Texas Commerce Bank. He had not been well enough at this time to sign. We will also get a certification to you. Destroy this after reading.

Another showed the copy of the back page of an affidavit that Hughes was supposed to have signed in England relating to Summa's case against Meier. The affidavit was witnessed by Levar B. Myler, another Hughes aide, and had been presented in Anderson's court during the course of the litigation. However, under the signature of Howard R. Hughes was the caption "No good cannot use — Levar" with an arrow indicating the signature, thus showing it to be the result of some experimentation which would not pass muster.

There were two other memos of note, the first from "Howard re: Meier" which said:

> HRH wants you to drop the pressure on Meier and Greenspun. You told him that this was done and he has found out otherwise. He says that Greenspun has had enough and Meier was entitled to money he had received because HRH had agreed to it. He does not want a big noise about this but says it is to be a priority matter now.

As if by way of answer — although it was a year later — came a memo dated August 2, 1975.

Chester says Meier will have to be destroyed and now that we have Judge Anderson in our pocket in Utah we should not let him get away. Meier exposed our flank and still gives trouble. Look what he did to Dick Nixon when there was no need. We must continue to say that you did not know Meier was getting any money on the mining deals. If Meier has any memos from you available on the subject we will go in and deny that they were from you. We can destroy his credibility and he cannot financially hold out against us forever. It will also be a warning to Maheu and Greenspun that we intend business all round.

At the bottom was "Ans" presumably — answer — followed by "Ok." This final memo was a neat encapsulation of the tactics used against Meier: financial exhaustion and the annihilation of his credibility.

16

THE CANADA FILES

S hortly after Hughes' death was announced, Meier was invited by a Justice of the British Columbia Supreme Court, Angelo Branca, to his chambers. Branca said he was speaking on behalf of a friend in government.

"He tells me that you can lay your hands on documents — sensitive documents — that would be of interest to our government, documents concerning politicians, that sort of thing. Might I arrange a meeting between yourself and this person? Would you attend?"

The documents to which Branca was referring had been delivered to Meier by his contact at CIA headquarters in the hope they would be of assistance in his dealings with the Canadian government. Meier had given them to the Security and Intelligence Branch which was quietly probing the CIA's infiltration of domestic affairs. Meier was disturbed to hear that Canadian politicians knew of their existence.

The papers covered topics ranging from the habits and financial affairs of leading Canadian politicians, including Prime Minister Pierre Trudeau and members of his cabinet; to an assessment of the Canadian military, the country's defense systems and defense industries. They also identified the leading CIA agents in Canada, Cleveland Cram and Stacy Hulse. The dossier on Trudeau was about thirty pages outlining his schedules, personal contacts, business interests, telephone numbers and gossip about his personal life.

Two days later Meier arrived at Branca's chambers with a collection of the documents some three inches thick. He was introduced to Ray Perrault, a Liberal Senator from British Columbia who claimed to represent the Prime Minister. The government wanted the documents for evidence that the CIA was operating in Canada without permission. Meier had no objection. He was a landed immigrant and he intended to apply for full Canadian citizenship.

However, he asked Branca to seek an assurance from Perrault that the files would be handled carefully and that his part in obtaining them would not be disclosed. Perrault swore he would speak to no one except the Prime Minister. After delivering the files to Trudeau he rushed back to Vancouver to see Meier. Perrault produced a notebook and popped the questions he had flown 3,000 miles to ask. Who was Meier's source and could he arrange a meeting with him?

"No," said Meier. "I wouldn't even ask."

Perrault persisted. What would be the harm? The government needed to talk to him. It would be very quiet. Meier was adamant. He wouldn't do it.

On August 14, Perrault met Meier and told him that Trudeau had been startled by the files and was grateful for his assistance in providing them. He promised that the government would protect Meier. Perrault then said the Prime Minister would be sending a confidential investigator, Pierre Genest, out to see him. Genest had been given the task of studying the CIA's activities in Canada. By now Meier was beginning to be alarmed by the incessant demands for more information, particularly the name of his CIA source, so he called his intelligence contacts. When Meier told them he had given the file to the government, he was told there had been no requests made to the security branch for its assistance. Trudeau and the Liberals wanted Security out of this one and were going it alone. Naturally, Security didn't like this and began its own investigation of what the Liberal politicians were doing. Its advice to Meier was to break off contact as politely as he could — the Security Service didn't believe any politician knew how to keep a secret. The type of information he had turned over would undoubtedly raise the ire of the United States if his part in obtaining it were leaked.

When they met in September, Meier told Genest that he couldn't help him any further. Although Meier was given his citizenship as a reward, none of the promises made to him was kept.

In the midst of these discussions with the Liberals, the two lawyers trying to prove the validity of the Mormon Will arrived in Vancouver to see Meier. They were representing Melvin Dummar, who had spun a most bizarre tale of meeting Howard Hughes one night out in the desert near Tonopah. Their encounter resulted in Hughes' will being delivered to Dummar, a service station attendant. This will left the bulk of Hughes' estate, minus a portion for Dummar, of course, to the Mormon Church.

"The last thing on God's earth Hughes would leave money to was the Mormon Church," Meier told the lawyers. "His intention was to leave everything to the Hughes Medical Institute in Miami. That will is a hoax. Furthermore, Hughes would never have been wandering around the desert at night." Not liking Meier's response, they left.

As for Hughes' authentic will, Meier phoned Hammett in Texas out of curiosity when the furor over the Mormon will was at its height. He wondered when the real thing might be produced. Hammett just laughed and said he expected there would be a lot of wills produced before the question was settled, leaving Meier with the impression that he was biding his time. However, when he phoned him again some months later Hammett sounded flustered and told him to stay out of the business.

ABOUT THIS TIME, Meier was approached by the Peruvian consul in Vancouver who asked him to meet a Lorenzo Montali, whom he described as the personal representative of the President of Venezuela, Carlos Andres Perez.[1] Perez had come to power thanks to the assistance of Meier's old friends Joe Napolitan and Clifton White who for the first time in the region's history carried North American electioneering techniques south of the Rio Grande. In office, Perez was reputed to have spent the country's oil wealth extravagantly as he did billions of dollars in loans from European banks.

Upon meeting Meier, Montali said the President had a collection of diamonds which he wanted to sell. He wondered if Meier could help. Because the President was trying to sell diamonds secretly and well away from his own backyard, Meier wondered if what was being proposed was legal. He said he didn't have any expertise in the diamond business but he would make some inquiries. That night they met for dinner and Montali pulled a small velvet pouch out of his pocket, undid the string and tipped it up. Out waddled the largest diamond Meier had ever seen. It was the size of a duck's egg and would have made the centerpiece of a maharajah's crown.

Seeing the shock on Meier's face, Montali said the President had "lots more like this" he needed to sell. "I have spoken to the President," said Montali, "and he asked if I would give you the diamond so you can have it appraised."

Meier put it in his pocket. Later he took it to Hameluck who measured and photographed it. Hameluck was curious why the President of Venezuela was unloading diamonds.

When Meier presented the diamond to a jeweller friend, the jeweller refused to believe it was genuine. "That can't be real," he said. "This must be a joke." Meier, who had been known to play practical jokes on his friends, assured him he was serious and said he would leave it with him overnight for an appraisal. When he returned the next day the jeweller rushed towards him. "Where did you get that diamond? It's the biggest I've ever seen." Meier asked what it was worth. It weighed almost 19 carats but the jeweller couldn't put a price on it. "There's no one in Canada who could accurately estimate its worth. You'd have to take it to Switzerland or maybe London or New York."

Meier returned it to Montali with the observation that Canada wasn't the place to sell diamonds. He would have to take it elsewhere.

As this eventful year ended, Meier's litigation with Summa ballooned with the infusion of the Mexican documents. Launched in 1972, the suit came to trial in Salt Lake City at the end of 1976, with Wyshak seeking to show that Hughes was *non compos mentis* for much of the time after he left Nevada and unsuccessfully arguing that the case should be delayed while handwriting experts examined some of the documents to see if the signatures were genuine.

Hank Greenspun, using his column in the *Las Vegas Sun,* came to Meier's aid. Unfortunately, he chose to throw him the anchor, not the life ring. It was a Thanksgiving Day column and Greenspun — who was also being sued by Summa — used it to lambaste Summa Corporation, the government and every federal agency on the horizon, especially the federal judiciary.

...I don't know how many of our citizens are not embroiled in a lawsuit with the Howard Hughes interests, but if there is no bread in the house and no clothes on the back, just being free of Summa Corporation and its vengeance is cause for gratefulness. Some of us aren't so lucky, but still being alive after having been threatened many times by Summa people with burial is cause for thanksgiving. Bob Maheu was number one on Summa's list for destruction and he wound up with a court judgment for close to three million dollars. So whether he collects it now or in the next 30 years, he is alive and hopeful, which is more than can be said for those who placed him on the list for extinction.

John Meier is a fugitive in Canada from the wrath of Summa, but he too is very much alive and fighting back even though he is under a million dollar bond if he ever returns.

On yesterday's ABC's *Good Morning America* show two men on *Faceoff* discussed unequal justice in the United States. Bill Rusher asked his opponent, 'Other than Patty Hearst what other individual has ever been placed on a million bond?' I almost climbed through the TV set in my desire to yell 'John Meier' which happens to be one of the most unique court cases because it is probably the first time in history that any citizen has been placed under this unconscionable bail for an alleged minor income tax violation.

Meier had evidently displeased the upper echelon of the Hughes empire which immediately caused the entire federal bureaucracy to gang up on him. And if Hughes with his two billion dollars isn't formidable enough, try tackling the IRS, SEC, CIA and the entire Justice Department who live only to do Summa's bidding.

Even John, in his Vancouver lair is thankful on this day, for he has come into possession of all the Hughes documents from their secret files which the Mexican government grabbed before the Hughes aides could shred them all after disclosure that Howard Hughes died of criminal neglect in Mexico. With this kind of information, the Summa people are not too thankful today, for their position has suddenly reversed and all their incestuous relationships with the IRS, SEC and the federal judiciary might soon come to light. It now appears that when a federal judge declared Meier to be a fugitive and subject to arrest and held on a million dollar bail if he ever returns to the U.S. the intention was to keep him out of the country so he could not give testimony before the Senate committee, the courts and the federal agencies on Hughes' activities.

So if you are not on Hughes' list for destruction give thanks in your hearts because it's tough competition to be singled out...

On Thanksgiving Day 1976 Meier was up to his neck in federal judges, and while thankful for the moral support, he quailed inwardly at the thought of what effect this outrageous challenge to the federal bench would produce.

But that wasn't the half of it. Judge Anderson was aware of the questioned documents found in the Mexican papers but Wyshak had obviously not dared present the Chester memo in which the judge's name had been used. It took a call from another judge — the judge trying the case between Summa and Greenspun — to alert him to that document's existence.

On December 6, Brian Greenspun, the publisher's son, came to Vancouver to examine the Mexican papers to see if there was anything that might be used in his father's defense. Spotting the Chester memo, and its implied corruption of the court, Greenspun copied it and returned to Las Vegas where he gave it to his father. It was then presented in his case as evidence of the type of justice one could expect when faced with litigation involving Summa Corporation.

It didn't take long for the contents of this document to be brought to Anderson's attention. Furious, he hauled Wyshak before him and demanded that all copies of that memo be recovered and produced in his court.

17

TROUBLE IN TONGA

Tonga is so small as to be generally hinted at on maps by a few random dots placed between Fiji and French Polynesia. Even on a large scale map it requires considerable squinting to pick out Tongatapu, the largest mass of sand and coral to be found in the tiny, far-flung collection of reefs, islets and volcanic mountains which form this romantic kingdom of the South Seas.

In total Tonga comprises about 173,000 acres, much smaller than some ranches in Texas but far more populated, being home in 1976 to some 90,000 people.

Formerly ruled by the British, it achieved independence in 1970. Like Great Britain, it is a constitutional monarchy, except in Tonga's case the monarch plays a more active role in directing the nation's affairs. King Taufa'ahau Tupou IV, ruler of this South Sea paradise, having reached the conclusion that his kingdom was living in the 1930s while the rest of the world was forty years ahead, took it upon himself to close the gap.

His majesty is enormous in stature, weighing almost 400 pounds and endowed with a jovial good nature. He read law at Sydney University. Tupou realized the answer to his country's chronic problems of unemployment was to end its isolation and establish a tourist industry.

The way for outsiders to reach Tonga was by boat or by flying to Fiji and taking a small plane over to the capital Nuku'alofa on the main island of

Tongatapu. The airport at Tongatapu was too short for international jets and couldn't handle the weight of large aircraft.

The harbor at Nuka'alofa was too shallow for large ships. Radio communication between the islands was primitive, using Morse code between the capital and the seven substations scattered through the chain. International calls went via radio telephone to Fiji or Wellington, then into the Commonwealth cable system or fed to a communications satellite.

The King had unsuccessfully tried to get the harbor deepened and the airport runway lengthened. The U.S. government, within whose sphere of influence the kingdom lay, was full of promises but little more. It was more interested in developing Samoa to the north. So the King sat in his quaint palm treed islands watching his people migrate to Australia and New Zealand for work or remain poor and unemployed at home.

One day the Soviets arrived with an offer. They would put money into Tonga's development in exchange for refuelling and layover rights for their fishing fleet on its journey to the Antarctic. The King opened discussions for construction of an 11,000-foot runway. Any such plan was an anathema to the U.S. which didn't want a Soviet base in the region or a military-size airport in Tonga. Before long, efforts were made to dissuade the King from letting the Soviets in. The Americans promised to build the airport if the King broke off negotiations with the Soviets, which he did, causing them to take their business to New Zealand. However, the U.S. reneged on all the promises as soon as a Soviet presence no longer threatened. Frustration and disappointment led Tupou to go it alone and stop waiting on the whims of foreign governments to bring Tonga into the modern age.

Bill Waterhouse, the Australian bookmaker, was a mutual friend of Meier and the King. The King asked Waterhouse how private capital could be attracted to the islands to build the airport and lay the foundations for a tourist industry. Waterhouse consulted Meier in October of 1976.

To raise sufficient capital for such an ambitious proposal, Meier conceived the idea of founding a merchant bank. This bank, holding a royal charter, would solicit funds from private investors in return for stock. Using this as seed money the bank would float a large loan from a Swiss bank. The money would be committed to building an airport in Tonga and an industrial park. The Tongan government would issue long-term government bonds which it guaranteed. Money raised from the bonds would be deposited with the bank to finance the completion of the airport, a new satellite communications system, a large condominium and hotel development, and the ancillary supports necessary for sustaining a modern tourist industry. Revenue from landing fees and profits from the hotels and condominiums which would be owned by the bank, would be used to redeem the bonds.

To carry out these ambitious plans, Meier would need to travel internationally. In April, 1977, Meier met Ouellette and the Intelligence officer suggested he apply for full Canadian citizenship. He said the government would support his application and Meier would thus have a Canadian passport. Meier next began meeting with consular officials of various governments laying the groundwork for trips to the Orient and Australia where he was planning to sell Tongan bonds. One of the countries he contacted was the People's Republic of China which has its consulate in one of the posh areas of Vancouver.

On May 5 Meier was visited at his home by two members of the security service. They knew of his meetings with the communist Chinese and asked if he were going back to see them again.

"For what reason?"

"Could you think of something?"

"I guess so, why?"

The officers looked at each other, then one produced a small box. "Could you do us a favor," he asked. "Could you get this inside the building?"

Opening the box he showed Meier what appeared to be a speck of dirt — perhaps a millimeter across — lying on a bed of cotton wool. The officer picked up the tiny object between his forefinger and thumb and laid it in the palm of his other hand. Then he moved it with his index fingernail displaying a minute spike on the back. Meier could only imagine it was a bug, but he had never imagined them so small. "Is that what I think it is?"

"Yes," said the officer. "Once they let you in they'll take you to a meeting room. Just find a way to push this into the wall or if the coffee table is wood, stick it in the leg or the frame."

Meier asked if it were really important and they both nodded. He didn't like the idea but he took the bug.

Meier phoned his contact at the consulate and arranged a meeting for the next day. When he arrived with the bug in his coat pocket, he was taken to a meeting room and served tea but not left alone. An interpreter arrived accompanied by the vice-consul. Meier chatted about the plans for Tonga and the opportunities for the participation of the Chinese government.

Because the table was metal, Meier began glancing at the walls wondering how he could implant the bug under the noses of the Chinese who were obviously not about to leave him alone. Finally, as Meier got ready to leave, he put his hand in his pocket and felt around until he had the tiny bug between his finger and thumb. Just before leaving the room he let his papers drop near the doorway and, as he bent down to pick them up, he thumbed the bug into the wall near the door frame. The wallpaper was patterned, nicely camouflaging the device. Sweating slightly, he was shown out.

Meier became a Canadian citizen on November 2. He picked up his passport five days later and flew to Japan, the first of the countries he planned to visit to sell Tongan bonds. Among the people he saw was Ryoichi Sasakawa, one of Japan's richest industrialists. They met at the Ship Building Industry's Foundation in Tokyo and Meier asked if he could persuade his government to buy Tongan bonds. He needed to raise $50 million to get the airport underway.

Sasakawa promised to speak well of it to the government. He inquired into Meier's background and finding he had worked for Howard Hughes, displayed great curiosity about Meier's former boss. He thought it a great joke that the Japanese had stolen Hughes' patents for a fighter aircraft and from these created the Zero, the most famous Japanese fighter of the Second World War.[1]

Meier went to Tonga next, where he arrived on November 21 to find the country suffering the effects of a large earthquake which had collapsed homes and damaged what few roads there were. Before meeting the King he was introduced to his cabinet and the heads of various departments including George Aakau'ola, the chief of police.

The King had a good grasp of business. In their discussions Tupou said he expected the Americans would not be happy with what was planned since they obviously wanted Tonga to remain backward. But he didn't want to remain a dependency of the United States and the airport offered independence.

At one of their meetings the King mentioned the abject state of communications in the islands. Meier pressed him to have the British company Cable and Wireless Ltd. put in a modern system as well as a communications satellite for international lines.

The year ended on a sour note. Judge Anderson, having tried Meier in absentia, ruled against him on December 21 finding he had breached his position of trust and profited by diverting monies from the sales of five mining properties.

He found Meier liable for losses and would later decide the extent of damages. The case itself was curious as it had started with ten defendants named as conspirators. By the time it came to trial Meier was the only one left, causing Wyshak to ask in court how one was supposed to conspire with one's self. In making this finding, Anderson rejected the facts that Meier had never worked for Summa, that he had negotiated the purchases at Hughes' direction and that none of the checks for any of the properties were made out to him.

Undoubtedly the mining ventures were, in part, a laundering operation. Money was siphoned off through the Hughes Tool Company to buy mining claims. The money would go into a bank account, some of it would be used to pay off the owners of the mining properties while the rest was run through various international accounts until it vanished.

Anderson decided that it vanished into one of Meier's bank accounts when it was actually credited to one of Hughes' European accounts, where it was used for such things as the purchase of cryonics equipment.

When the suit began in 1972, Summa emphasized that Meier had purchased worthless mining claims and made sure such stories were kept in print as he fought for the Senate nomination in New Mexico. But in 1976 it was apparent that these claims were not as paltry as Summa would have the public believe.

In Tonapah, on a hill at the back of the historic old Mizpah Saloon, Summa had opened a secret gold refinery and was processing tailings removed from around the Manhattan Claim, fifty miles north. The operation, which began in 1974, was conducted without fanfare and doubtless because of what the company had been saying about Meier, the whole thing was quite furtive.

Using a cyanide leaching process, engineers at the heavily guarded plant had taken out 4,000 ounces of gold in the first 18 months of operation and were expecting to recover 60 ounces a day once they had the refinery operating smoothly. In 1976 the Manhattan Mine was producing $2.9 million a year from a claim Hughes had paid only $243,000 to acquire.

If Anderson's ruling was bad news, more would follow. The *Salt Lake Tribune*, on January 6, 1978, reported the existence of the memo in which the judge was said to be in Summa's pocket. If that wasn't bad enough considering Anderson was in the process of assessing damages, another of Meier's self appointed champions was on the warpath, right under the judge's nose in Utah.

Doug Wallace, whom Meier had never met, called from Salt Lake City saying he was publishing a paper concerning the conspiracy against Meier. Meier was aghast. He was waiting to see what Judge Anderson would do and was not about to inflame him. Wallace was persistent and despite Meier's best efforts to dissuade him, Wallace published his *Millennial Messenger* — an inflammatory monograph aimed at the Mormon Church — in which he hammered Judge Anderson's ruling against Meier. The monograph said this was the judge who had conveniently declared Hughes to be a citizen of Texas six weeks before his death and that Meier was the victim of a criminal conspiracy. The conspirators, Wallace said, were the Mormon Church, the CIA, the Hughes organization, Intertel and just in case that didn't quite cover it, unnamed "others."

On March 6, Wallace went even further. He sent a letter to the Senate Judiciary Committee requesting the impeachment of Judge Anderson for corruption, complete with a verbatim rendering of the Hughes memo containing the judge's name. He circulated the letter to all the news outlets.

When a copy of Wallace's petition arrived in the mail, Meier begged him not to involve him in his war on the Mormon Church. The appeal fell on deaf ears, for on March 25 Wallace expanded the mailing list and sent letters demanding Anderson's impeachment to Chief Justice Warren Burger, U.S. Attorney General Griffin Bell, the acting director of the FBI and President Jimmy Carter. Copies, naturally, went to all of the media.

Judge Anderson brought in his decision at the end of March: Meier was going to have to pay every cent Summa demanded — all $7.9 million. Then Anderson asked the FBI to do something about the memos which he claimed to be forgeries.

At this time Paul Schrade heard rumors that the government was about to move against Meier. He and Meier's other friends were afraid something awful was about to happen. Schrade arrived in Vancouver to warn Meier. He said his contacts in Washington were telling him to expect the worst.

"I know the government is furious about you getting the Hughes papers and frankly we're worried. We think it's time you came back down to the United States..."

That prospect had little appeal. Meier said he couldn't possibly do that with $1 million in bail hanging over him.

"We know, but we think we can help you better if you are down there. While you're up here there's not a hell of a lot we can do. Nobody in Canada will help if the going gets tough," Schrade said prophetically.

That afternoon Meier spoke to Wyshak, who advised him not to leave. He would be better off having the protection of Canadian citizenship.

What Meier and his friends didn't know was that a grand jury in Salt Lake City was being convened to hear evidence that Meier had actually forged a number of those Hughes documents presented in Anderson's court. At least this is what Meier's former friend, Robbie Robertson, was alleging.

Robertson had attached himself to Meier during Meier's stay in London four years earlier. He had returned with him to Canada and had stayed as Meier's house guest for months at a time. Thereafter the pair journeyed together and Robertson mixed himself readily into Meier's affairs.

He had involved himself in Netter's video company while supposedly writing a book about Howard Hughes. After Netter's murder Robertson bought a house a couple of blocks from Meier's. However, through financial hardship, he lost the house and his car. As his fortunes declined so too did his relationship with Meier. By the time the Mexican papers surfaced their relationship was in its final stages but still Robertson had appeared in Anderson's court giving evidence on Meier's behalf.

He had testified to seeing the Hughes documents Summa claimed were forgeries while sorting through the boxes shortly after they had been turned over to Meier by Reynolds. Hence Meier could not have forged them.

Anderson chose to disregard this. Robertson returned to work on his manuscript and in June he and Meier went to a meeting with a publisher's representative in Vancouver. This publisher's view of the manuscript was that much of what Robertson had was already known, as there had been a veritable spate of books on Hughes since his death. She turned it down and suggested instead that the company might be more interested in a story with new material. Meier, by now, was in no mood to collaborate with Robertson.

Unable to sell this first version, Robertson would rework the manuscript and turn it into an expose of his former companion. In this edition, he accused Meier of forging the Hughes documents and of forging the infamous list of politicians the CIA wanted elected in 1968.

In a newspaper interview Robertson said threats had been made against his life and that he was dealing with the FBI and would soon be placed into protective custody in the United States — likely the first time that anyone going into protective custody felt safe enough to trumpet the fact. However, it wasn't just protective custody, but a paid berth in the Witness Protection Program that was being made ready for him.

The story Robertson was now telling was described by Salt Lake City FBI special agent Loren Clyde Brooks on May 16, 1978, when he appeared before a Grand Jury. According to Brooks, the FBI were advised by the RCMP that a fraud had been perpetrated upon the court in Utah which prompted the Bureau to "open a case for investigation in the matter of Hughes Tool Co.... that involved a civil suit against John Meier." This would lead the jury to believe that the initiative came from Canada, whereas it is obvious that Judge Anderson instigated the investigation. It had bogged down only to be revitalized by Robertson. This is how Brooks described Robertson and his story:

> Mr. Robertson refers to himself as a freelance writer and journalist. His current work includes the writing of a book on the life of Howard Hughes. He described how he became acquainted with John Meier and how it was his intention to gain as much information as he could from Meier to even possibly write a story about Meier. This led to frequent visits and subsequently a visit to the residence of John Meier where he was allowed to examine certain Hughes documents that had been acquired by Meier from Mexican authorities. He said as he entered the room in the basement of Mr. Meier's home he noticed a Xerox machine. He noticed an electric typewriter with various types of golfball-type settings that could be exchanged within this machine. He seated himself on the chesterfield (and) he noticed that Mr. Meier was preparing some documents in the typewriter and frequently he would make a mistake and crumple up the document and throw it in the fire... Then he noticed Mr. Meier would take

some of the documents that had Mr. Hughes'(s) handwriting and it would appear that he might be tracing or at least glancing at the document and then doing some copy work on these originals that he would type. As the meeting went on Meier offered to obtain some coffee for the two of them. So he excused himself from the room and Mr. Robertson took advantage of that time and examined what was going on at this table. He noticed certain documents in the typewriter and on the table and in fact used the copy machine and copied one of them. And this document that he copied on the machine he made available to the FBI. Now the significance of this is the fact that this copy machine had some characteristics that are identifiable. It seems that the glass on this copy machine had not been cleaned and therefore certain dust particles appeared on this paper as it would be copied from the machine...

Robertson's eye for detail — dust on the Xerox and a multiple-head typewriter to change type faces — was apparently all that was necessary to construct a case for forgery and obstruction of justice.

Brooks continued singling out the damning dust dots and even invited jurors to compare the location of the dots on the various forgeries that Meier had brazenly created in front of Robertson, who appears to have popped into his house by chance. One of the jurors, incredulous someone would commit a crime so casually in full view of a witness, said the obvious.

"That doesn't make sense..."

"Yes," replied Brooks, "that's a surprising thing to have a witness observe..."

The juror, sensing there was more to this, asked: "Were they close, or how close were they?"

Brooks didn't want to go into that: "Well, if..."

Assistant U.S. Attorney Max Wheeler helped out: "Do you recall Mr. Robertson's explanation of that, Loren?"

Brooks: "Well..."

Wheeler: "I asked him that question in my office. Do you recall his answer?"

Brooks: "I don't recall. I don't know if it's in this affidavit or not."

However, what Brooks could remember without any difficulty was that someone on Meier's behalf had threatened to kill Robertson. Later, when Robertson met Meier, the RCMP who were monitoring the meeting identified Meier as being accompanied by a known hit man. (This person would later be revealed to be a barber, a mutual friend of theirs, whose Sicilian birthplace appears sufficient grounds to label him an assassin.)

After all this, Brooks' memory of the relationship between Robertson and Meier suddenly cleared and he recalled that Robertson had said that he was writing a book in which Meier was expecting to be mentioned favorably. Lulled by this, Meier had taken Robertson into his confidence.

"They met in England," said Brooks, "He tried to hire Robertson for $50 a day as his personal consultant. Robertson said he wasn't interested in being a consultant at $50 a day but he would be interested in writing a book about Meier and about Howard Hughes and that could compensate for any service he could render Meier..."

Brooks told the grand jury that during his investigation he had studied the transcript of the Meier-Summa case, in which a former FBI document expert declared the questionable documents to be forgeries and those telltale spots to be from a dirty photocopy screen. This opinion, combined with Robertson's story to the FBI, had led to the grand jury hearing. It must have slipped Brooks' mind that Robertson also appeared in those same transcripts telling a totally different tale. Robertson in those transcripts is busy explaining why Meier couldn't have forged the documents.

While Robertson was describing dust dots to the grand jury, Meier was busy with the affairs of the bank in Tonga. If Tonga were to have an international airport and an international bank, there would have to be an international level of security on the islands. The Tongan government had no security system remotely capable of coping and Meier was asked if he could recommend a Canadian officer who might become Tonga's security advisor. Without hesitation Meier recommended Hameluck. Subsequently, Hameluck quit CLEU and joined the embryonic Bank of the South Pacific as its security chief.

Hameluck had already met Baron Vaea, Tonga's Minister of Labour, who earlier that year had called Meier from Saipan asking for an urgent meeting with Canadian Intelligence. Meier said he would ask for someone to go to Tonga but Vaea preferred to meet them in Canada. Vaea arrived and Meier introduced him to Hameluck. The baron was hesitant but eventually told a tale which caused the imperturbable Hameluck to start scribbling in his notebook.

He described how on one island the American Peace Corps had

erected a warehouse through which parcels and shipments arrived to be cleared to and from the United States. The Peace Corps had been active in Tonga for a number of years and so the Tongans paid little attention to what was going on in the warehouse. One day a box arrived in Nuku'alofa and was stored in a small customs shed before being routed to the Peace Corps center. It fell off a shelf and landed at the feet of a customs officer. The box split open and showered the floor with cocaine. Immediately the Tongans fixed their attention on the activities of the Peace Corps and the numbers of parcels passing through the shed from all parts of the Orient en route to the United States. Vaea said that they were now paying more attention to ships transferring their cargoes to other vessels within Tongan waters. Some of the ships involved were of American registry and had sailed for Vancouver, causing the Baron to wonder if the information might be of use to the Canadian government. Hameluck promised to pass it on.[2]

By the spring of 1978 interim financing was available to start construction of the airport so Meier left for Tonga. An American contractor was going to do work on the runway. Meier was with this contractor in Auckland having dinner when he noticed a man at an opposite table take a small camera from his coat pocket. He placed his coat across the table to cover the camera. After a time, Meier watched him slowly lift up the coat and aim the lens at them.

A few days later the Minister of Police, Aakau'ola, told Meier that the United States was seriously alarmed by what was happening. He said there had been numerous phone calls to Tongan officials and American residents on the islands seeking information about Meier's activities. Aakau'ola said there had been some unofficial representations made to the King expressing American displeasure and the King wanted to see Meier privately.

The King told Meier that he would be safer from American antagonism if he had diplomatic status when he travelled outside Tonga. He made Meier his financial advisor and issued him a diplomatic passport.

By May 15 the machinery had been assembled for building a new runway. The King, watched by representatives of the Australian, New Zealand and United States governments, ceremoniously dug the earth with a silver shovel. It was a signal for the engines to start and in line abreast, bulldozers and tractors came through the tall grass. The diplomats who likely never thought he could pull it off looked askance.

Two days after the ceremony, Meier was indicted in the United States on two charges of obstructing justice. A warrant was issued for his arrest.

Meanwhile in faraway Tonga, Princess Piloleou, the King's daughter, had a sense of foreboding. She told Meier at a lunch meeting that she was worried that her father, who was then celebrating a big victory, would almost certainly feel some repercussions for defying the Americans.

Later, Meier accompanied the buoyant monarch to visit the West German Navy's training ship, *Deutschland,* which was anchored off Pangaimotu Island, about 150 miles north of Nuka'lofa. They were entertained aboard the cruiser, then went ashore with the ship's company for a feast.

Less than a week after the grand jury brought in its indictment, the British sent a messenger from New Zealand to see Meier. He was attending a ball in the British residency on May 26 and dancing with Queen Mata'aho when she whispered to him that there was a man in the royal party who wished to speak with him. As there were a number of Americans at the ball, the introduction had to appear casual. The man greeted him like an old friend. The stranger led him away from the royal party and once out of earshot said Boyce wanted to warn him to be careful while travelling.

Meier asked what he meant but the stranger said he was only a messenger. Something was underway in Washington and Boyce was suggesting that Meier fly to London prior to returning to Canada, or leave Tonga and call him. "It's the bloody phones here, old boy, can't trust 'em," said the messenger with a wink. Meier caught a plane with the Queen and the Minister of Police to Fiji. From Suva he phoned Boyce on the evening of June 1. Boyce's message was simple: now that Meier had a diplomatic passport, he must use it in every country he visited.

"Make sure you get it stamped on entry. Don't present your Canadian passport anywhere," said Boyce. "We don't know for sure what's going on in the United States but there is every indication that even more trouble is brewing and that you are being watched." He told Meier that if he encountered any problems in Commonwealth countries he should phone him. For the next couple of weeks Meier hopped all over the Pacific, was in and out of Japan, Australia and New Zealand, diligently using his diplomatic passport.

In the midst of all this came a terrifying phone call from home. Three strangers, two men and a woman, had been stalking Jimmy for kidnapping and the family feared he was about to be snatched. The police had been called and now the seven-year-old was under constant guard by the family. At night someone always slept with him; during the day he was escorted to school and the teachers were warned not to let anyone near him.

Before Meier left Canada there had been attempts to intimidate him, which now seemed to be escalating. He had thought that his departure would spare his family any further harassment. For instance, on March 24 he and Jennie had been out for dinner with some friends, leaving Jimmy at home with his sisters. The boy was sleeping in the front room under the window when someone tossed what appeared to be a Molotov cocktail at the house. It was thrown with considerable force, shattering the large sliding glass window and showering the boy with glass. He woke up screaming. The projectile travelled the length of the room and hit a wall twenty feet away. It was a coke bottle filled with a colored liquid and a piece of singed rag jammed into the opening. Later Meier received a phone call and an unidentified male voice said "the next thing that comes through the window will level the house..."

On May 27 — almost a month after Meier flew to Tonga — Jennie learned from a woman working in a local bowling alley that strangers were inquiring about her son. They were asking staff for the times Jimmy usually bowled on Saturdays. One woman saw them hanging around the alley on three occasions. When the gang finally started to walk up and down the aisles looking for Jimmy she called Jennie and warned her to keep him away. Jennie called the Delta Police and an officer came to the house while another picked up the strangers. He examined their American identification which later proved to be phony. Unable to charge them with anything, the police escorted them to the border and warned them to stay away. Jennie meanwhile called Hameluck, who alerted Security and Intelligence. They tracked the suspicious Americans to the U.S. Army base in Fort Lewis, Washington, through a rental car they had driven and fixed a proper identity on them. An armed policeman slept in the Meier house that night.

Canadian security told Meier it was unlikely any further attempts would be made against Jimmy. When Boyce was informed, he cursed and said it was barbaric; he used the opportunity to warn Meier again about travelling. Spooked by all this, Meier decided to bring his family to Australia.

He was leaving the Japanese Embassy in Wellington on the afternoon of June 20, when a limousine pulled up and a man rolled down a window and called his name. Meier went over and the man introduced himself as Z. P. Benyukh, First Secretary of the Soviet Embassy, responsible for information. Benyukh asked Meier to join him for coffee. Meier replied he was on his way to the airport to catch a flight to Auckland and accepted Benyukh's offer of a lift.

The Russian chatted about Tonga and asked Meier how the airport plans were progressing. Meier said he was organizing the financing, which led Benyukh to say that his government would become involved. He gave him a post office number in Wellington — Box 27246 — where he could be contacted.

Meier boarded the plane in Auckland on his way to Tonga and, although there were plenty of empty seats, another passenger made a point of sitting next to him. When they were aloft the man said abruptly "John Meier." Meier, merely nodded. "I'm Captain Semple, United States Navy." It was an announcement made with no warmth whatsoever. "I'm representing the government from our embassy in Wellington."

"What has that got to do with me?"

"I'm going to Tonga for a meeting with the King and I wanted to talk to you first."

"What about?"

"Well, we're going to do everything in our power to stop what you're doing in Tonga. And we will."

Meier said what he was doing had nothing to do with the U.S. government. He was a Canadian citizen and didn't appreciate being threatened.

"Listen, Meier, you're just lucky we're doing it this way," said Semple.

The captain got up to use the washroom and Meier took a look at the briefcase he had left lying on the floor. It was open. Meier quickly leafed through the files and saw that it contained papers on surface ships, nuclear submarines and military bases — one folder contained pictures of himself. Meier closed it before the officer returned.

Later, the King told Meier that Semple had been dispatched by the State Department to discover what Meier was doing in Tonga and the scope of the airport development. Semple had argued that Meier's proposal wasn't in Tonga's best interests. The U.S. didn't feel it was appropriate for Tonga to have an expanded airport.

From then on the surveillance on Meier increased markedly. Meier and

Waterhouse were followed from Tonga to New Zealand to Australia and the tail stayed with Meier all the way to Tokyo, where he arrived on the first of July.

FOR SOME TIME, a cadre of FBI agents working in the Los Angeles office had been immersed in what was arguably one of the most sensitive political investigations in the Bureau's history. These officers, dismissive of the whole Watergate investigation undertaken by the politicians, were probing Richard Nixon's relationship with the late Howard Hughes and financier Robert Vesco hoping for an explanation as to why Nixon was apparently spending far more than he should have earned. Showing an equal disdain for the public record, they were determined to get to the bottom of Hughes' death, for here too, they found the official explanation too incongruous to accept.

Meier was approached by Jay Walker, a friend and businessman from California who was a highly placed agent in the U.S. State Department. An acquaintance of Walker's was Alan Copeland, a curious character whose exploits on behalf of the FBI and Treasury Department were the stuff of novels. He was a businessman but he acted as an undercover civilian agent and had infiltrated various criminal organizations in the U.S. and England. In the early days of July, Copeland had come to Walker and asked if he could put him onto Meier.

Copeland was working with the Justice Department's Organized Crime Strike Force and the Los Angeles FBI office and told Walker he wanted Meier's help in bringing back Vesco. The FBI agents reasoned that as Meier knew Vesco and was on friendly terms with Donny Nixon, Vesco's aide-de-camp, he might be able to exert some influence over Vesco.

The approach had been so casual that Walker hadn't attached much importance to the request, but Copeland came back and impressed Walker with the urgency of the matter, saying they had limited time to put the deal together.

Walker called Meier's home and spoke to Johnny who told him that Meier was in Tokyo at the New Otani Hotel. He contacted Meier and relayed the FBI's message. Meier was non-committal and complained about the pressure he was getting from the U.S. government. Walker said he had a friend in Tokyo, Masatake Takahashi, a reporter and author who might be of some help. He offered to call Takahashi and have him visit Meier at the hotel. Before Takahashi went to see Meier, he called Walker back.

"How good a friend is this man?" asked Takahashi. Walker said he was a close friend.

"Well, he is in a lot of trouble here."

"What do you mean?"

"I have checked with some people I know in the government and the Americans are planning to go to any lengths to remove him from Japan and get him back to the United States." Walker naturally assumed this meant extradition, but Takahashi said there was more to it than that.

"If they can't do it that way they are going to put out a contract with the Yakuza." Walker imagined he was hearing things. Did he say the Yakuza — the U.S. government was planning to use the Japanese Mafia?

Takahashi asked what he should do and Walker told him to warn Meier.

Meier, unaware of the danger, was meeting with the industrialist Sasakawa who had sent his secretary to bring him to Sasakawa Hall. After the usual formalities, Sasakawa told Meier that he was hearing of American displeasure with what was occurring in Tonga.

Through an interpreter Sasakawa said: "You are under surveillance in Japan from the Americans. They have asked the Japanese government security forces for assistance but they have been turned down. Our government has said it will not get involved as you are on a mission from the King of Tonga. If you wish to stay in Tokyo I can assure you nothing will happen to you. Perhaps you would like to leave your family here while you travel?"

Meier thanked him, but was beginning to feel frightened. This was not the type of surveillance he had learned to live with all these years. The British had detected an ominous shift in intensity and now the Japanese felt obliged to warn him. Surely the Americans could not be that serious about preventing an international airport in Tonga.

When Meier returned to his hotel that afternoon, he met Takahashi. When he heard the story of the Yakuza, he thought of his small son being stalked and his stomach churned. After Takahashi left, Meier called Charlie Onadera, who represented various Japanese firms and who had contacts within the Japanese government and the U.S. Embassy.

Without telling him Takahashi's story, he said he was experiencing difficulties in Tokyo which he felt were emanating from the U.S. Embassy.

Could Onadera check with his contacts and find out what was up? A few hours later Onadera came rushing into Meier's hotel room.

"John, you've got to get out of here," he said. "Somebody at the embassy is dealing with the Yakuza. You'll have to leave Japan." Meier said he couldn't believe the U.S. government would deal with such a group. Perhaps it was a joke? "Trust me. They are serious," pleaded Onadera.

Onadera said he had some contacts within the Yakuza and he would speak with them in an attempt to forestall any action on their part.

Takahashi returned with Kazuyofi Hanada, editor of the *Shukan Bunshun,* a weekly magazine. Alarmed at the prospect of what might happen to Meier, the pair came to interview him about his background and his troubles with the U.S. government. If anything happened, at least the story would get out.

But Meier wasn't about to give the Yakuza a sitting duck. The next day he hustled himself and his family out of Japan and flew to Australia. Somehow he felt safer in a Commonwealth country, though the feeling lasted only as long as it took to spot the car with four men inside watching him as he walked along Bligh Street in Sydney.

The King of Tonga was in New Zealand and wanted to see him. Meier travelled to Auckland and made his way to a house in Epsom where the Tonga government had a residency. "I'm getting a lot of calls from various people who represent the Tongan government in different places telling me that the United States is asking an awful lot of questions about what we are doing," said the King. He was worried that the United States was more committed to disturbing Tonga's plans than he had imagined. He would check with his contacts in Britain and would see Meier the next day.

Whether from constant tension or bad food, Meier became ill. The King sent his physician to treat him and told him the next day to return to Australia and regain his health before tackling any more business.

As he went off with Baron Vaea that evening for dinner, Vaea told him something the King had failed to mention — the Americans were gearing up an international press campaign against the King, to force him away from Meier.

A few days after returning to Australia, Meier was walking with Jimmy when he noticed a car filled with men following slowly behind. Meier took the boy to McDonald's for lunch, then ducked into a cinema to see *Star Wars.* When they came out the men in the car were waiting. That night he phoned the King who was greatly agitated. The King had been told by the police that he had been followed while in New Zealand and that the phone in the Epsom residency had been tapped. He said he was preparing a letter of complaint to be sent by courier to the White House. Then Waterhouse told Meier that his friends in the Sydney police said there were a number of CIA men in town closely watching him.

Meier called his intelligence contacts in Ottawa and they reported everything calm in Canada — perhaps he should forget the South Pacific for a while and return home. Waterhouse tried to reassure him that his diplomatic passport would prevent any sudden moves against him but the situation was so threatening that he called Hameluck who told him to come home immediately. They could go to Ottawa and ask the Canadian government to get hold of the Americans and sort it all out.

The next day, July 25, he met with reporter Kevin Perkins who had information that as many as six CIA men were in Sydney for some purpose relating to Meier. Perkins advised that Meier return to Canada. That evening Perkins drove Meier to the Qantas cargo building to pick up a package that had been sent by the King.

It was a code book which would allow Meier to communicate with the King by letter or telegram. When he picked it up he noticed the package had been opened. Turning to the clerk, he showed him the broken seal. The clerk stammered that it hadn't been opened there, it must have been tampered with in Tonga. Cursing, Meier stormed out. He burnt the code book later.

That evening he decided that his family should return to Canada. He was entertaining doubts about his ability to carry on. If the CIA could free-wheel in Australia, what might it do to him in the Philippines, South Korea or Taiwan where the local authorities could be counted upon to look the other way? For the first time the thought of failure crept into his mind. If he couldn't sell bonds there would be no chance of building the airport and the bank was finished.

On Thursday, July 27, Jennie and Joanne decided to do some last minute shopping, leaving Jimmy with his father for the afternoon. Meier had been trying to reach Hameluck for hours but couldn't get a line from his hotel room to Canada. He was assured the hotel phones were working and the trouble must have been with the overseas connection.

In the afternoon he decided to go out and call from the street. He took

Jimmy's hand and stood waiting for the elevator. As they entered it two men rushed out of a suite and jumped in before the doors closed. On their way through the lobby Meier spotted two men and a woman sitting reading newspapers. From the corner of his eye he saw the woman nudge one of her companions as he and his son walked by. Then they all rose and made their way to the elevator. Jimmy said: "Daddy, where are we going?"

"Just down here to make a phone call, son."

He looked around and the two men from the elevator were a few paces behind. They had gone a couple of blocks when a car suddenly veered off the road and pulled across the pavement ahead of them. Before Meier had time to think two men leapt out. The first shouted: "John Meier — Detective Sergeant Haynes — you're under arrest." Jimmy, who had seen this before in Point Roberts, started to cry and Meier tried to comfort him while demanding to know the reason for his arrest. "You are going to be returned to the United States. You are wanted for obstruction of justice. Get in the car."

He placed Meier and Jimmy in the back and returned them to the hotel. They found their room swarming with police searching luggage and drawers. Meier asked to see their warrant and Haynes refused, saying he was being taken to a police station. "My family's out. I have to take care of my son," he protested. Haynes said the boy would be looked after and the woman from the lobby came into the room.

Meier asked to make a phone call but Haynes refused. Haynes said they had seized his passport. Meier said he was not travelling on a Canadian passport and produced his diplomatic passport. "I've got diplomatic protection. I'm on business for the King of Tonga and I want to call Bill Waterhouse who is the Tongan Consul." Haynes was not prepared for this. He looked perplexedly at the Tongan passport. He changed his mind and let Meier call Waterhouse while another policeman ran quickly to another phone to tell headquarters about the diplomatic passport. Waterhouse promised he would inform the King.

With Jimmy in the care of the policewoman, Meier was led away to a police station where he was placed in a large room which contained only a mattress and toilet. The police treated him with courtesy.

That evening Waterhouse arrived with another police officer. This officer said the Australian police had been told Meier was armed and dangerous and connected with the Mafia. "We were told you were an

American citizen who was working with the Russians and were a subversive." Meier asked him the source of the information and was told it had come via a telex from Washington.[3] Waterhouse assured him that he would be released the next day.

Meier appeared in the Phillip Street court before Judge Rex Butler. Herman Woltring, acting for the United States government, began by arguing that Meier was wanted in Utah for obstruction of justice and that he should be given to the U.S. authorities who had a plane waiting to fly him back to the United States.

Meier's solicitor Andrew Rogers interrupted, saying Meier had a diplomatic passport and was therefore immune to arrest, and furthermore that he was a Canadian citizen. If the Australian government didn't want him in the country he could be asked to leave, but the United States had no right to demand that a Canadian citizen be given to them.

That afternoon Judge Butler ordered Meier released. It was now imperative he get Jennie and the children out of Australia. On July 29 the family parted. While they could fly back with ease, for Meier any journey was perilous. The U.S. government had displayed a grim determination to seize him and was not likely to be deterred by a setback in court. Any plane he boarded in an attempt to escape to Canada could easily be diverted to Hawaii or Alaska. This had happened on his family's flight to Tokyo from Vancouver. Their flight was supposed to be non-stop, but for some reason it had put down in Anchorage, Alaska. Jennie had watched two men come aboard and walk down the aisle scanning the passengers. Looking at the tickets she saw Jimmy had been put down as J. Meier and supposed this was the reason for the inspection.

Meier couldn't simply book a flight to Singapore or any other destination in the Far East and attempt to hop back home by working his way west through Europe. Once started on that route his progress would be easily monitored and the U.S. could have him arrested as he changed planes in some country where the authorities and the courts would be more compliant.

Meier was trapped. Boarding a plane would be tantamount to surrendering. The Americans had him on the run; outside Canada he was vulnerable. When he returned to the hotel, his mind was whirling. How could he throw the CIA off the trail long enough to get safely back to Canada? Confused and irresolute, he was sitting despairing when Perkins phoned and said he was sending a driver over. Meier was to pack up and go with him. Meier was brought to the *Sunday Telegraph* offices where Perkins warned he had been tipped the U.S. was still trying to have him extradited.

If he could find a sanctuary he might be able to plan an escape. He stayed at Perkins' home for two days until Perkins arrived and said the police had questioned him about Meier's whereabouts. The CIA's efforts to get Meier had made the news and this was causing them embarrassment.

"I don't think it's safe for you to stay here any longer," said Perkins. "I've got a couple of Irish friends who will look after you."

Early the next morning Perkins drove Meier to John and Avril Harvey's home in Mossman. Meier hid there for three days, not venturing out until August 3 when he left with Avril's brother, Eric. They drove to Manly where Eric rented a flat under an assumed name.

Eric, who was on holiday from Ulster, had seen more than his fair share of intrigue in the war between the British and the IRA, and was likely as good a watchdog as any in Australia. Perkins sent word his house was under surveillance and for Meier to exercise caution in attempting to reach him. Meier hardly moved from the flat. He was lonely, dispirited and homesick, and for once, quite incapable of formulating any plan that had the slightest chance of working.

The next day, Meier went to Waterhouse's home in Manly, leaving Eric parked outside keeping watch. Waterhouse was back from Tonga and Meier was anxious to see how things stood. Waterhouse was pessimistic. The development had been trashed in newspapers where a combination of disinformation about the bank and details of Meier's notorious background were being effectively used to embarrass the King. With Meier in hiding and unable to sell the bond issue, the whole enterprise appeared on the point of collapse.

By August 12, Meier was beginning to worry about involving his friends any further. He told Perkins and his Irish bodyguard that he would no longer compromise them and would take care of himself. Perkins wouldn't hear of it, and Eric — who probably would have chauffeured the Pope through Protestant Belfast — just shrugged. Meier called his State Department friend Jay Walker in California. "John, don't tell me where you are but I've been trying to find you for days," said Walker. "The Bureau is trying to organize a deal to get you out of this. They've asked me to tell you to try and make your way to Canada and they'll be in touch once you get home."

In an effort to keep the banking project alive, Meier sent his friend John Lester, who had been appointed acting Governor in his place, to Hong Kong to speak with investors. Feeling unsafe in Manly, Meier went back to the Harveys on August 23. The police had given up watching Perkin's home so on the 25th Meier went there and stayed overnight. Eric then rented another flat, this one at 5A Gower Street.

The next day Eric drove him to the main post office in Sydney and watched his back while Meier called Boyce in London. It was obvious he couldn't get out of Australia under the noses of the police and the CIA.

"Brian, I'm trapped here," Meier told him. "I can't leave Australia by boat or plane. I wouldn't make it home."

With unruffled English efficiency Boyce said: "Call me in fifteen minutes, I'll see what I can do." While Eric scrutinized the post office concourse, Meier rang Boyce, who told him to go to the Peking Palace Restaurant on Military Road the next day and ask for Wally.

Accompanied by the redoubtable Eric, Meier went to the Peking Palace at noon and asked for Wally. He was shown to a table where a smartly dressed man was finishing lunch. "Well, Mr. Meier, some friends of yours in England have asked me to help you. Perhaps you could tell me what it is you need."

Meier said he simply wanted to get out of the country and home to Canada. Wally asked about his passport and Meier showed him the two he had.

"Okay," said Wally. "Where can I get hold of you?"

Meier gave him the Gower Street address. Wally said he would be in the Peking Palace having lunch for the next four Sundays if Meier needed him. In an emergency he could leave a message at the restaurant using the name John.

For nine days nothing happened. Then, early one morning while Meier was asleep, Eric was startled by a noise at the door. He ran and pulled it open only to find the hallway empty. As he was closing it he noticed an envelope had been pushed underneath.

When Meier opened the envelope he found a note from Wally instructing him to attend the Cuban Embassy's Ministry of Foreign Affairs office, September 7, where he should ask for Olga. Later that day he called

Walker, who told him that the FBI was prepared to send Copeland out to see him.

"Would you like him to come out?" asked Walker. Meier said that that would only complicate things. He was working on getting home and would rather see Copeland in Canada.

Lester went with him to the Cuban Embassy. Meier asked him to come and get him if he had not reappeared within an hour. Once inside, he asked for Olga; a secretary led him to an office and introduced him to Olga Chamero Trias. After shaking hands and offering him a chair, she opened a folder, placed a small mound of newspaper clippings detailing his various escapades in the South Pacific on her desk and cocked a Latin eyebrow at him.

"You have been very busy?"

Meier said he hadn't been doing too much lately and she smiled and asked if he could be in Australia Square at 4 p.m. that afternoon where he would be met by a Mr. Bass.

"Go with him please. He will make arrangements for you to get the proper documents to get you out of Australia."

She then gave him a list of countries in which he would be safe from American pressure. Most of them, Meier saw, were in the Middle East. Naturally, he would be welcome in Cuba, but she didn't recommend that as it would only harm him in the long run. The Cubans would help while he was in Australia. He was to use the name John Banfield when dealing with her.

Meier stood in Australia Square in the pouring rain for over an hour waiting for Bass. Shortly after five, with Meier despairing of his arrival, a man and a small boy appeared. The man introduced himself as Bass; taking Meier's arm, he wheeled him around and walked him a couple of blocks to an apartment complex. They went up a flight of stairs, then Bass pushed open a door into one of the suites. Inside, smoking a cigarette, was a photographer. Meier stood against a wall and was photographed.

Bass suggested they have dinner and Meier found himself sitting in Pips International restaurant with Bass and the boy. His companion asked no questions but regaled him with tales of his playing days in the Australian football league. He was big, burly and tough-looking and Meier had the impression he had been a professional. Bass told him to be back in Australia Square in four days' time.

At the appointed hour Meier saw the shaggy form of Bass ambling towards him, holding a newspaper. He seemed about to walk by without any look of recognition, but when he was barely a stride away, he quickly switched the paper from his left to his right hand. Meier felt a slight knock against his stomach as a small packet appeared just long enough for him to grasp at it. Bass carried on without breaking stride.

When he opened the package Meier found a New Zealand passport bearing his picture but made out in the name of John Banfield, who was, according to the document, about 10 years younger and a good six inches shorter than Meier. He decided to shave off the beard he wore in the passport photo in order to make himself look younger. As for the difference in height, he would just have to remember to stoop when he presented it.

This whole episode shows a curious side to the workings of the international intelligence communities. The spectacle of the British and Cuban (if not Australian) security and espionage services cooperating in Australia for the purposes of preventing a Canadian citizen from falling into the hands of the CIA would need Le Carre to do justice to all its convolutions.

But even those with no understanding of this esoteric world can make some sense of the situation. If Meier was to be helped by the British, then it would have to be done through a cover in case of failure, as the British would not want the CIA to wonder why Meier was so important to them. Not only that, the British would not want the Americans to discover they had thwarted and deliberately sabotaged an American operation. They were, after all, allies.

If anything went wrong, the CIA would be led back to the Cubans and would naturally assume Meier had friends in the Communist Bloc. One could speculate that the British, using the labyrinthine connections which apparently exist between intelligence networks, simply asked the Cubans for a favor. If the Cubans would front Meier's extrication, the British — in all likelihood assisted by Australian security officers with leanings more towards London than Washington — would do the actual work. Meier's rescue demonstrated a surprising but nevertheless effective alliance.

On the 14th Meier called Olga Trias at the Cuban Embassy.

"Oh, Mr. Banfield," she said, "I hope you are still coming at 4 o'clock to remove this furniture. You said you would do it before but you didn't show up."

Meier apologized for his tardy behavior and said this time he would keep the appointment. When they met, Trias warned him not to delay leaving Australia any longer.

"You have the documents, don't talk to any more people than you have to, and leave quickly. If necessary go to the countries I gave you and you will be safe. But our strongest advice to you is to leave. Now do you need any more help?"

Meier thanked her for all that she had done and said he would be leaving soon. The next day Perkins told him that the police were redoubling their efforts to find him. He doubted Meier could stay hidden much longer. Meier went to Lester's flat in Point Piper and began sorting files in preparation for his flight. Some documents concerning the bank he destroyed, others he boxed to be sent to Canada. His personal papers and diaries he placed in his briefcase. That done, he watched the Ali-Spinks fight on television.

The next day Meier called Jennie, who was worried sick. She and the children were crying. Meier comforted them by saying that he would make it home in time for his birthday on September 28 — eleven days away.

He moved to an apartment in Chatswood and said goodbye to Eric, who was visibly moved by the prospect of Meier's departure. For days now, Meier had been studying the routes and timetables for trains, planes and buses leaving Sydney. He asked his companions for details of the different airports in Australia, how passengers were segregated, how they were boarded and where they were kept. Then he looked at the international routes and decided to take the long way home. It was essential, too, to cause a diversion — to make the authorities think he was going somewhere other than his intended route.

His first move was to lay a false trail. On September 20 he picked out a small travel agency in Chatswood and went in to purchase a ticket for a flight to New Zealand. He told the travel agent his name was John Meier and asked her to book him a flight to Wellington. The woman entered his name in the computer and took his passport. Something appeared to be out of order because she looked hard at the screen and typed another command. Something else popped up. She cleared the screen and, then excused herself. She got up and walked around a divider. Meier followed but stayed hidden behind the partition. He could hear her speaking on the phone — "he's here now buying a ticket to New Zealand. Yes, I have his passport..."

Meier returned to his seat. A few moments later she appeared and sat down to make out the ticket. She was making no move to produce it so Meier, judging he had stayed long enough, picked up his passport and said: "Excuse me, I've got to go to the car, I'll be back in a minute."

He stepped out into the rain and had hardly gone a couple of yards when two police cars came racing down the street. He turned a corner before glancing back. The cars stopped outside the travel agency. Meier spent the night at the home of Dean Wentworth, Lester's partner. He had kept the false passport hidden, as to be arrested with that in his possession would have meant ruin. Meier now asked Wentworth if he would hold it "just until you hear from Lester and then do everything he asks." Wentworth was game.

Lester had offered to accompany him to Canada so Meier asked him to pack his bags and be ready to leave in the morning. The next day they loaded their belongings into Wentworth's car and Meier had them driven to Strathfield train station.

"What do I do now?" asked Wentworth after unloading their bags.

"Just go home and wait for a call," said Meier.

He bought two tickets to Melbourne. They arrived there about twelve hours later in time to catch the Adelaide train, arriving there the next morning.

Meier's spirits rose; he was on the move after weeks of hiding. Meier had refrained from providing Lester with the details of their itinerary and Lester was too British to ask where they were going. He merely said he hoped Meier would let him make a phone call to his wife in case he disappeared along the way. They had coffee in the Adelaide station then caught a taxi to the airport where Meier booked a flight while Lester took care of the luggage. Standing in the terminal Lester finally let his English reserve slip and asked where they were going.

"I'm taking you home, John. We're going to Perth."

Lester was overjoyed. His family lived in Perth and he hadn't seen much of them in recent months. They rested in Lester's home for two days. On September 24 Meier told Lester to phone Wentworth and tell him to fly to Perth on the 26th and not to forget the package. He was to board the plane in Sydney and, using the name on the passport, was to buy a ticket for Singapore Airlines on the Perth-to-Singapore run with connections to Frankfurt via Colombo-Dubai-Zurich. When he disembarked at Perth, Wentworth was to go to the Singapore Airlines counter an hour before the flight and check through Meier and Lester's luggage which would be left near the counter. He was not to bring luggage of his own.

Wentworth was to take the envelope with the forged passport and put the ticket to Singapore inside. Then he was to go into the pre-boarding area and enter the nearest men's washroom to the Singapore Airlines kiosk. There he would see Meier washing his hands. Meier would lay down a ticket for a return flight to Sydney and he was to place his package alongside. He was not to acknowledge Meier.

The Singapore flight was to leave at 2:30 p.m. About an hour before the flight Meier went to the ticket counter and asked for a ticket for the Sydney 4:30 p.m. flight. The agent asked his name and handed him a ticket without a reaction, which was not what he wanted. He asked if she knew anything about visas. "I'm a Canadian and I think mine's run out. Will I get into trouble?"

It sounded serious. The clerk said she didn't know but he should check with the Immigration office as soon as possible.

"Well, I don't know. I've had so much trouble this trip with the arrests and everything. I hope they don't kick me out of the country because of this."

That got a reaction. The woman was now staring at him. He said that he'd be back half an hour before the Sydney flight to check in his luggage, then slipped away and, showing his ticket for a flight to Sydney, was allowed to enter the pre-boarding area. He had settled on Perth airport for his escape because its pre-boarding area mixed international and domestic travellers together.

Meier got into the men's room just ahead of Wentworth and the exchange went smoothly. Wentworth was handed a ticket in Meier's name for his return flight. Meier noticed Wentworth's hands trembling. When he left the washroom he found Lester looking helplessly at Meier's luggage piled high near the check-in counter. Wentworth in his haste had forgotten to check it through. Lester had to leave the boarding area and put it through on his ticket.

When their flight was called, Meier and Lester walked on and flew out of Australia. While they were heading to Singapore, the unfortunate Wentworth was being arrested by Sydney police, who boarded the plane as

soon as it landed looking for the passenger going under the name John
Meier.

In Singapore Meier stooped to disguise his height as he went through
Immigration but the officer didn't give him a glance. Neither did the
officials in any of the other places he stopped. Even the efficient Germans
waved him through, though he was six inches taller and ten years older than
he should have been and affecting the most peculiar New Zealand accent
imaginable.

In Frankfurt Meier and Lester collapsed of exhaustion and stayed the
night of September 27 in the Park Hotel. They caught a flight to Montreal
the next day. While in the air, Meier went to the bathroom, tore up the New
Zealand passport and flushed it down the toilet. When he arrived in Canada
he produced his Canadian passport.

18

CANADA SELLS OUT

Now that Meier had broken cover, it would be a race to get to him. The FBI office in Los Angeles had been patiently waiting for him to surface and so, too, had the U.S. Justice Department. His reappearance in Canada caused a flurry in both camps.

The FBI agents sent Walker and Copeland[1] to see Meier on October 10. Copeland was in many ways an oddity, also something of a wonder. American born, he spoke English with a chiming Cockney accent, a legacy of a childhood spent on the streets of London. He was a civilian who for the sheer thrill of it became an unpaid undercover operative for a number of U.S. police intelligence formations. He had even been loaned to Scotland Yard when the British were desperate to stamp out a particularly vicious gang of murderers and criminals in London. Copeland infiltrated the gang, impressed them by giving them a machine gun and collected the evidence which eventually led to their conviction. His part in the affair can be found in John Pearson's book, *The Profession of Violence: The Rise and Fall of the Kray Twins.* He practiced his dangerous pastime in various parts of the United States where, as a result, a number of Mafia personalities unexpectedly found themselves in federal penitentiaries.

Copeland was sent to give Meier a briefing on the concerns of the Los Angeles office. He told him that the deeper the agents dug into Hughes' death, the greater the pressure from the CIA to lay off. The agents had talked about coming to see Meier but someone at a high level had strongly suggested they not do this. Meier told Copeland he would help if the agents were serious about pursuing what had happened to Hughes and the nature of Hughes' relationship with Richard Nixon. Copeland assured him they were. Meier said that it was because he had such knowledge that he was under so much pressure from the government and Summa Corporation. Would these agents be able to do anything about that?

Copeland could not say what help might be given but said the agents were sincere and could be trusted. He asked for someone in Canadian security to act as a liaison with the FBI. Meier suggested Hameluck, and Copeland returned that afternoon to Los Angeles.

Two days later Walker called Meier and said he had met with FBI special agent Bradley Maryman and a high official from the Justice Department. He asked for Hameluck to fly immediately to Los Angeles for a meeting. Hameluck returned with encouraging news; the agents appeared sincere. They had already talked with security people in Ottawa and were briefed on what Meier had been doing in Tonga.

"John, they are trying to see if they can work something out so that all the outstanding matters in the U.S. can be fixed up. But I've got to tell you, they are under a lot of pressure from some people in the Justice Department."

On October 16 Meier was driving Hameluck home when Hameluck noticed they were being followed. Meier phoned Maryman and asked if the U.S. was planning to act against him. Maryman said something was going on but the Los Angeles office was being kept in the dark.

Four days later the Vancouver RCMP Commercial Crime squad working with the U.S. Justice Department beat the FBI to Meier. On the night of October 20, a group of officers led by RCMP Corporal Pat Westphal forced their way into Meier's house and arrested him in front of his family. He was taken to the city jail in Vancouver and held under the Extradition Act on charges of obstructing justice.

Three days after being arrested, Meier appeared before British Columbia County Court Judge Ray Paris seeking bail, but Westphal put a stop to that. A telegram had arrived from England saying that Meier was presently wanted on a U.K. warrant for forging a passport application in the name of an Ivor Arthur Robertson. It took Meier's lawyer John Taylor five days to get him out.

Meanwhile, Hameluck paid another visit to the Los Angeles FBI and returned to tell Meier the agents were going to fly to Washington to confront whoever was attempting to thwart the investigation. They had promised not to stop until they had answers to the questions raised by Hughes' death and Nixon's surprising wealth. The agents would be coming to Vancouver November 20 to meet Meier despite orders from Washington to stay away.

Copeland arrived first; Meier was called to meet him November 19 at the Bayshore Inn. Copeland took him aboard a 40-foot cabin cruiser and they sailed into the Georgia Strait. On board were two men dressed in matching slacks and jackets as if crewing a luxury yacht. Copeland described the pair as FBI; Meier had the impression they were stationed in Canada.

Copeland told him that the Los Angeles office was prepared to offer him protection. If he wanted they could sail that minute for American waters where he would be met and escorted all the way to Salt Lake City. That proposal panicked Meier. "Or you can stay here and fight the case," Copeland quickly added, seeing the look on his face. "These guys are risking their jobs for you," he said, of the agents in Los Angeles. He expressed his misgivings about the whole enterprise, saying he, too, was worried about the pressure being exerted on them to stop.

Copeland picked up a briefcase and removed a sheaf of papers. The first was his letter of authority from the FBI, the next was an internal FBI document listing the people being investigated. They included Richard Nixon, Donald Nixon, Howard Hughes Medical Institute staff, a number of Summa employees and an equal number of U.S. Senators.

"This is what I'm working on, but frankly the whole thing makes me nervous. Look at the names. I think I'm in way over my head."

The next day Meier met Brad Maryman, Dick Garbutt and another agent and discussed the matter of his extradition to Salt Lake City.

"There is no question you are receiving special treatment. If any country makes enquiries about you this is what they will be told," one of the agents said. He was shown an FBI criminal intelligence dossier bearing his name. There was a short biographical description, an outline of the charges against him and his fugitive status, followed by allegations that he was involved with an international organized crime syndicate and was to be treated as armed and dangerous.

The report was on file in FBI headquarters in Washington, placed there by James Golden, Nixon's former personal Secret Service agent and friend who had worked for Intertel and Howard Hughes; he was now a power in the U.S. Justice Department's Organized Crime Division. Golden's personal interest in Meier showed when he came to British Columbia and visited CLEU's office in Victoria. He wanted to know why the organization was dealing with Meier and what information he was providing. Golden asked if Meier had discussed the Hughes will and attempted to convince CLEU to sever its relationship with Meier.

Faced with Golden's report, Meier said he would tell the agents all he knew.

"If you really want to get to the heart of the matter you should exhume Hughes' body," Meier told them. When they asked why, he replied they would either find that the body buried in Texas was not Hughes, or — if it were Hughes — he had not died in April 1976. He described what he had seen on Cay Sal and of finding Hughes' frozen remains lying in a shed. At the end of the interview they warned him to speak to no one about what had been discussed.

Later that day, the agents received a call from Washington ordering them to break off contact with Meier and return home. They flew out of Vancouver on November 22, after being accosted at the airport by the RCMP. Due to the nature of the investigation they had not cleared their visit with Ottawa and the RCMP commercial crime section had been tipped to their meetings with Meier.

A couple of RCMP officers approached them as they were about to board their flight and demanded to know what they were doing in Canada. Garbutt told them to mind their own business. One officer asked them to stay in Vancouver until they could brief commercial crime on their discussions with Meier. When they refused, they were threatened with arrest — which would have created a remarkable incident had it actually taken place. Instead, Garbutt and Maryman pushed by and boarded the plane. An official protest was lodged in Washington, resulting in Garbutt being sent back to brief commercial crime. But he so distrusted the unit that the briefing he provided was a waste of time.

When he came before Judge Paris in early December, John Meier was being tried for a crime not covered by the Extradition Act. The allegation was that he did "corruptly endeavor to influence, obstruct and impede the due administration of justice by submitting documents which he knew to be fabricated..." None of this matched any of the obstruction of justice offenses described under the treaty, which proscribes acts such as dissuading a witness from giving evidence, jury tampering or using bribes or threats against the court. Meier's counsel, John Taylor, sought to convince Paris he had no jurisdiction to hear the case but the judge accepted the argument from Bill Halprin, a Canadian Justice Department lawyer acting for the United States, that forgery, which is covered by the treaty, was a component in the offense.

Meier was being tried for forgery although the grand jury in Utah had not charged him with that. Further, the section dealing with forgery in the treaty — as Wyshak[2] had unsuccessfully pointed out to Paris covered forgery and counterfeiting of state instruments, bank notes, government bonds, stamps and letters patent. It did not cover forgery of civil documents as was being alleged.

Trevillion and Reynolds were called by Halprin to explain their parts in acquiring the documents from Mexico. Reynolds' testimony was marked by an attempt to distance himself from Meier. The former MP had abruptly resigned from Parliament, then was identified by the Canadian Broadcasting Corporation[3] as an associate of organized crime figures in Vancouver. He was now a radio talk show host and none of his earlier chumminess was now to be found in his story about his dealings with Meier. If Reynolds was suddenly aloof, Robertson was venomous. What emerged was a vastly different statement from the one he made in Salt Lake City in front of Judge Anderson.

Initially, Robertson had told Anderson that he had gone with Meier to Reynolds' office and had carried out the box of documents. He had then accompanied Meier to his home and they had both looked through the box, at which time he had seen the documents whose authenticity were in question.

In Vancouver he changed his story and testified that this delivery-examination phase had happened over two days, not one as he had said previously. He said he had helped recover the box on November 4, 1976. The next day, in the evening "around five-ish" Meier called him to his home and while there, he had seen Meier barefacedly forging documents. At one point he said that Meier had even displayed his handiwork to him and commented "Not bad, eh?" In his new testimony, Robertson replies: "Not too bad."

Then Robertson said he noticed the dust marks on the photocopier and the multiple-headed typewriter that Meier was using to forge the documents. He ran a couple of papers through the machine to capture the tell-tale dust marks for future use, then left. In this account, Robertson is alleging the forgery took place on November 5 after 5 p.m.

Meier never testified to this effect, but in fact, Robertson was not at Meier's home on either November 4 or 5. By coincidence, he had been in Meier's home much earlier than that, on October 22 — the very night Meier picked up the documents from Reynolds. Meier's diary clearly states "Robertson stays at house" as a notation for that day. Even more enlightening is the entry for the following day: "Robertson reviews memos." It was Robertson who examined the Mexican documents. He stayed in Meier's house for three days sorting through them. It was Robertson, left alone with the box, who chose the documents he imagined would be of special interest. Robertson returned on October 29 and Meier's diary records "Review Robbie's list."

Robertson told the court he had secretly watched Trevillion deliver the papers to Reynolds. He said he just happened to be driving past Reynolds' constituency office on October 21 and spotted Trevillion in a Rolls Royce. The car was parked and Joe Romano — a prominent member of Vancouver's organized crime fraternity — was carrying a box into Reynolds' office.

He was cross-examined by Taylor, who wanted to know if he had been driving his own car when he saw Romano's parked outside Reynolds' office. He couldn't remember. Hadn't his car been seized that October for non-payment of bills? He couldn't remember. There were other things he couldn't remember, including his mother's name.

Taylor took him back over his Salt Lake City testimony and showed him his account of opening the box on November 4 and checking the files against the documents. Robertson refused to agree that this was "diametrically opposite" to the testimony he was now providing.

Taylor plodded along, reading all Robertson's replies to questions given at the previous hearing, taking them apart word for word as Robertson argued over the interpretation and attempted to reconcile his differing stories.

Typical of their exchanges is the following extract, in which Taylor questions statements Robertson gave Summa's lawyer Edward Clyde, pertaining to the contents of the box he said he opened with Meier.

"Again Mr. Clyde... is wanting to know what you saw in the box November 4, 1976, and you're referring to the fact that you indicated to the judge in Utah that the two of you opened the box, went through the box and you saw some logs and they weren't of interest to you?"

Robertson: "The logs weren't at that particular stage."

"But in no way in this court have you indicated that the two of you opened the box together."

"No, I haven't, sir."

"Have you a witness?"

"No, I haven't, sir."

"So you either misled the courts of Utah or you've misled this court?"

"No I didn't mislead, sir. I said what I understood and remembered at the time, at that short notice. I have since been able to review my whole files, my whole notes, etcetera."

When Taylor pressed Robertson on why he had remained silent in Utah if he had been so astounded by Meier's blatant counterfeiting, Robertson said he had mentioned it.

"Yes, sir, in that transcript should be the fact that I stated that there were false signatures."

"...Did you comment upon that to the courts?"

"Yes, I did, sir."

"That there were false statements?"

"Yes, I did, sir."

"In your transcript?"

"Yes, I did, sir. In fact I repeated it."

"And that the false signatures were the work of Mr. Meier."

"No I didn't say that. Nobody came back and questioned me upon it."

"So that because of the fact you weren't questioned on it, you led the courts to believe that you went and opened the box together with Mr. Meier, which was an outright lie?"

"It wasn't an outright lie, sir."

Robertson's testimony, taken by court reporter Ronald Hubbard in Salt Lake City, is 33 pages long. Nowhere in that transcript is there the slightest hint by Robertson that false statements were made by anybody. It is beyond imagining that a counselor as experienced as Clyde would not have been alerted by even the vaguest suggestion from Robertson that Meier had committed some impropriety. It simply could not have happened.

The final prosecution witness was Lyndal Shaneyfelt, a retired FBI document examiner who was prominently used by Summa Corporation to defeat the Mormon Will. Shaneyfelt had examined the questioned Hughes documents and declared them forgeries. He too subscribed to the belief that some of the marks on the photocopies showed unmistakable signs of being caused by dust. He classified himself an expert on photocopying and went to great pains to show the court the specks on the pages which he said were reproductions of dust present on the glass plate. He added up ten such dots which the questioned documents had in common. Had Meier's legal advisors been sharper and had their own expert look at these dots the outcome might have been different, but Shaneyfelt's testimony passed unchallenged.

Taylor's defense was solely designed to attack Robertson's credibility. He began with Eugene Ehrenholz, who owned the golf-ball IBM typewriter which Robertson said was used to produce the forgeries. Ehrenholz was a lawyer Meier had known for a number of years. He was also an engineer and had done some work in Tonga. He testified that Meier could not have had the typewriter in his basement in November of 1976 because he had borrowed it in January or February of that year and had returned it within a couple of days.

Halprin tried to shake him, saying Ehrenholz had told him that he had loaned the machine to Meier a day or so before November 5th.

"When I spoke to you," replied Ehrenholz, "you tried to suggest to me that the typewriter was loaned in November of 1976 and I said, no, it was earlier than that. It was late January or early February…"

Next came Vincent Zolfo, an Italian hairdresser who Robertson said had threatened his life. Zolfo denied this and said the root of Robertson's unhappiness with Meier was that he felt Meier had not done enough for him when he was hard up.

Robertson had made much of his English journalistic background, especially his work for Granada Television in Manchester, but Alan Jay, a former Fleet Street journalist working in the Manchester area during the time Robertson claimed to have been there, testified he had never seen nor heard of him. He had met him in Vancouver, where Robertson, for some unknown reason, insisted he knew him from the time they had met while covering an air crash at Winter Hill in Lancashire. Robertson told Jay that he remembered spending hours with him in a pub at the foot of Winter Hill while they were filing stories on the crash.

"I didn't challenge him on it," Jay testified, "because there was no pub at the foot of the hill and I don't recall Mr. Robertson being in... any pub... The nearest town is Bolton, some twenty-seven miles away and the nearest village was thirteen miles away. There was no pub. In fact, there was no building of any kind at the foot of the hill." As for Robertson's claim that he supplied Granada with news of the crash, Jay found this confusing. "... Granada was not in existence as it is today. In fact... I was supplying news to Granada Television..."

Of the other stories Robertson had supplied about his past, Jay said he had been highly entertained by Robertson telling of his escape as a Royal Navy officer from HMS *Amethyst,* a British warship which in a celebrated incident had been trapped up the Yangtze River by Chinese Communist shore batteries. Robertson said he had walked hundreds of miles through Communist territory in full uniform wearing his dress sword. Jay didn't believe a word.

Robertson denied ever telling this story and when pressed had said he once missed his ship in Shanghai. Taylor wanted to know if he had walked anywhere from Shanghai but Robertson invoked the British Official Secrets Act. The judge reminded him he was giving testimony in Canada and would have to answer, but to all of Taylor's further questions concerning his romp through China, Robertson replied that he couldn't remember. As for Robertson's credibility, Jay said he wouldn't have believed Robertson "no matter what he told me."

On December 11, Paris decided that it was not his function to weigh the evidence or to rule on whether or not Robertson was a liar — that being for a jury in Salt Lake City — and ordered Meier's extradition.

After Christmas, Copeland called to say yet another team of agents was being sent to see Meier as the others were working on the case in Los Angeles. This meeting had been cleared with Ottawa. Copeland said FBI agent Joe Charles would be accompanied by Sterling Epps of the Treasury Department and Jim Henderson of the U.S. Justice Department's Organized Crime Strike Force. Meier met with them at the Vancouver RCMP headquarters. Around the table were the American contingent, including a customs officer from the U.S. border station in Blaine, and Westphal.

Meier was disturbed that Westphal should be there after the work he had done with Robertson to have him extradited. Meier decided not to speak openly in Westphal's company. He not only mistrusted Westphal, he detested him. The meeting was supposed to explore the possibility of a settlement, but predictably, it went nowhere.

At the end of January, 1979, Copeland vanished. Someone had tried to kill him but the bullets had gone wide and Copeland disappeared. A week later he popped up again. He called Meier to warn him that one member of the party that had visited him — Henderson of the OCSF — was unsympathetic and could not be relied upon to help.

What Meier needed was political help. The federal government could prevent his extradition by refusing to hand him over. With that in mind he flew to Ottawa with Hameluck on February 14. While Hameluck visited his old friends in the security service, Meier went to the Parliament buildings. Late in the afternoon he met with Trudeau in Senator Perrault's office.

The Prime Minister said he had come to thank him for his assistance in supplying the government with the CIA dossier. He asked how the extradition business was going and Meier said he was not sure. He was still negotiating with the FBI and was hoping this would resolve his problems. Trudeau asked if he was in Ottawa to meet the security people and Meier said no. Well then, said Trudeau, showing how firm a grasp he had on affairs in Ottawa, what was Mr. Hameluck up to? Meier said he had no idea. Trudeau reached into a pocket and retrieved a small piece of paper.

"I do hope you realize that those documents you supplied on the government and myself are strictly classified. You are a Canadian citizen and I hope you understand that the only person you should be talking to regarding them, is this," and he handed Meier a paper containing the name of his confidant, Genest. Trudeau told him not to worry and left. Tommy Douglas was not so sanguine. He told Meier not to rely on Trudeau. Douglas, a former leader of the federal New Democratic Party, said he had spoken to the Prime Minister and it was his belief that no matter what Trudeau might say, the government would not help.

Preston Truman called and said that members of the AEC had been meeting with the prosecutor's office in Salt Lake City concerning the case against Meier. This brought back many bitter memories. Perhaps they were only there to gloat, but Meier didn't like the sound of it.

His appeal to the Federal Court of Appeal was rejected and Meier was held in custody while the matter went before Cabinet in Ottawa. Notwithstanding all the promises, the federal Cabinet refused to intervene and Meier was extradited on May 17.

If there had been nothing more to the case than what the public saw, it would have been bad enough for Meier. But the Canadian politicians knew that there was a sinister element to the affair that had never been made public: Meier had committed a grave political act against the United States by supplying Trudeau and his Cabinet with a secret CIA dossier. Knowing this, the Cabinet could not be ignorant of the implications of turning him over to the Americans, nor pretend that there was nothing special about this extradition.

What Meier didn't know was that someone close to the Prime Minister knew precisely what he was heading into. That person had sold him out to the CIA.

19

PRESUMED GUILTY

The cell was nothing more than an iron box measuring about six feet by nine, containing only a steel cot and a sink. The two U.S. Marshals who had escorted Meier from Canada stayed until he was placed inside and the steel door banged shut. They had taken custody of him on the afternoon of May 17, 1979. He had been handcuffed and chained to another prisoner being delivered to the United States; and both were driven to the Blaine border post. There Meier was unchained and taken to a small room to see two CIA agents who had flown in from Washington to meet him as he crossed the border. They promised that he could be home within a week if he cooperated. They spoke of obtaining information concerning his Hughes days, his political associates, what he had been doing in Canada and elsewhere, and with whom.

"I'm on my way to trial. I can't speak without my attorney," protested Meier. They pressed him to change his mind but he refused. The Marshals came in and they continued to Utah.

Instead of being taken to Salt Lake City Jail, the Marshals placed him outside of the city in the Davis County Jail. This came much to the surprise of the jail's supervisor, Jan Cunningham, who had received no warning of his arrival. Cunningham asked for an explanation but the Marshals were unwilling to talk until Meier was locked up. Meier pressed an ear against the steel door but could hear only snippets of the conversation. He heard them say "high security case... must be kept segregated... and... the office will be in touch."

He stayed locked in the cell for two days, seeing only the guards who passed his meals through the metal shutter in the cell door. On the third day he asked to make a phone call. The guard wouldn't allow it without permission.

Meier asked to see Cunningham, who came to his cell. Of all the jailers Meier would meet in the United States and Canada, none measured up to this Mormon for integrity or compassion. Cunningham addressed him by a strange name and Meier said he was John Meier. Cunningham asked if Meier was an alias. "No," he said. "That's my real name."

While Cunningham puzzled over his being given a prisoner under a false name, Meier asked if he could call his family in Canada. Cunningham shook his head. His instructions were to keep him incommunicado.

"But, why?" asked Meier. "I'm down here facing obstruction of justice — not mass murder." Cunningham said he would talk to the sheriff's office. He returned later looking perplexed.

"It's none of my business, Mr. Meier," he began, "but could you explain what this is all about? Frankly, I've never had a situation like this before in my jail. I don't know why they haven't taken you to Salt Lake or why every time I ask questions about you the sheriff's department keep saying they'll have to call Washington." He sat down on the bunk while Meier gave a precis of the obstruction of justice charge and vaguely referred to his work for Hughes and his meetings with investigators from the Watergate Committee. After listening, Cunningham opened the cell door and said: "Why don't you phone your wife. I'm sure she's worried."

It was a kindness Meier had not expected. He phoned Jennie at home and asked her to get hold of Jay Walker. He said he was locked up in a small steel cell and being denied his blood pressure medicine.

Jennie had been phoning Salt Lake City for days trying to find him but no one knew where he was. He sounded quite ill, so she phoned Walker who sent a doctor to visit Meier the next day. The doctor told Cunningham he must be given his blood pressure medicine and arranged for an attorney to represent him.

While this was underway, Cunningham was protesting to the U.S. Marshal's office who again ordered him not to let Meier have visitors, not to give him any medication, pencils, books, or telephone calls and not to let him out of his cell. Cunningham's office was across the hall from Meier's cell and through the metal shutter he could hear the jailer shouting into the phone. "He needs medication. Now either you give me permission to get it, or I'll do it myself. He's in my jail and while he's here he's going to be treated like a human being."

That afternoon, as the sweat oozed and stained Meier's prison greens, actress Terry Moore, who had been close to Howard Hughes, came breezing through the jailhouse as though it were little more than the naughty boys' room.

"Oh sergeant," Meier heard her say as he stumbled to his feet, "what a lovely place you have here..." The door swung open and she came in talking and waving an enormous bunch of flowers — "And, oh John, just look at this" — with not so much as a hello — "You have it all to yourself, too. Oh, it's so cozy. You lucky thing." She was perfumed, manicured, wearing an expensive dress, not a hair out of place, twirling around this iron box as though it were a penthouse overlooking Central Park. Cunningham stood at the door, abashed.

"Oh John, I'll bet you didn't know Sergeant Cunningham was a fan? Sergeant, there you are" — and she gave a big pout — "Be a dear and get a little table and a vase for John's flowers."

Cunningham did as he was told and returned with an old bottle and a battered packing case, resulting in her sigh that it would probably do but —"Sergeant, dear, could you find us a little doily to go on top, just to make it look pretty for John?" And off he hustled again. "Now, John don't you worry about a thing. I'm down here to see my friends the Osmonds and I'm going to talk to them about you — Oh, there you are sergeant, that's very nice" — as a piece of old gauze was slung across the top of the box.

She placed the back of her hand against her forehead and spied the cell door. "Am I imagining things or don't you think it's awfully hot in here, sergeant? Now wouldn't it be a lot better if that silly old door was left open till you fixed the air conditioning? And my goodness I'm so thirsty I could die. Could you find us a couple of cokes? — Oh, and don't forget the ice!"

Meier had hardly managed a word before she was on her feet and leaving. "Now sergeant," she lectured Cunningham, "don't you go believing all those nasty things the government says about my friend John. If you have any questions, here's my private number, you just give me a call." She handed Cunningham a card which the flustered and perspiring jailer put in his wallet.

With that, Terry Moore vanished from the cell in a puff of expensive perfume.

That evening Cunningham told Meier that he was giving the U.S. Marshal's office until the next day to do something about his medicine. The following morning the cell door opened and Cunningham stepped in.

"Okay Mr. Meier. I'll tell you what we're going to do. Man to man, if you give me your word you won't abuse the privilege, I'll keep the door open."

Meier said he wouldn't do anything to embarrass him.

"Fine — can you cook?"

Meier, who had never been near a stove in his life, said he could.

"Good. The cook's been released and there's no one here to take over. You go down to the kitchen and get lunch ready. If this works out we'll see if we can make things a bit easier for you."

"Can I make phone calls?" Meier asked.

"Sure, as long as they're collect."

Meier was taken to the kitchen where he found the cook's assistant, newly promoted to cook looking helpless among the pots and pans. Meier was just as lost. Faced with cooking meals for 40 prisoners, he did the only sensible thing: he phoned home.

"What can I give them?" he asked Jennie.

"Try grilled cheese sandwiches."

"How do I do them?"

She told him and he turned them out by the dozens. They had hardly finished cleaning up when he realized that within a few hours the prison would be expecting dinner. He was back on the phone. Jennie advised him to try something he knew — bacon and eggs — but to throw in sausage and grilled tomato so it wouldn't look too much like breakfast.

And so it went on. Every day he would call home and she would tell him how to make soup or salads or casseroles. Before long he ran out of food and one of the guards told him to make up a grocery list and a guard would go to the local supermarket and buy what he needed. Eventually, he was allowed to do his own grocery shopping. He would stroll down the street to the store, where he picked out the groceries while the guard signed the chit.

Naturally, he began to tire of dishing out hamburger and chili, and began browsing for steaks and chops and fresh produce. The food bill soared. The guards carrying the food began grousing about being loaded down but Meier ignored their complaints. Cunningham protested about the expenditures but Meier argued that the prison was overcrowded and many of the inmates were not getting proper exercise and needed a high protein diet to keep healthy. Meier offered to make extra meals for the guards. One day Cunningham said he didn't mind if he went out without a guard to the store. "Just go out and get what you want and sign for it," he said.

Next, Meier was removed from the cell and given a berth in the trustys' room. These were larger, better quarters with a TV set and more comfortable beds. In the afternoons between lunch and dinner Meier would join the guards playing touch football outside the jail.

In the middle of June, John Lester arrived from Australia to work on Meier's defense, but could only speak to him when he had time off between meals. Cunningham generously offered them the use of his office. Sometimes Meier would have to dash off to the kitchen and Lester would follow. Not being one to work while others watched, Meier soon had this very proper Englishman up to his elbows in soapsuds.

On the day of his court hearing Meier had put on a three piece suit and was in the kitchen directing lunch when two U.S. Marshals glanced in. They left, only to reappear a short time later, looking anxiously around. "Excuse me, brother," said one, "We're sorry to interrupt but could you tell us where we can find Mr. Meier?"

Meier looked at them and said: "Yes, that's me."

The two Marshals stepped back in astonishment. Then one lunged forward and grabbed his arm while his companion went running off to get a guard. Meier was being dragged from the kitchen when the guard arrived and the Marshals began berating him for letting Meier out of his cell. The guard protested that Meier was a trusty and the cook to boot, but this only incensed them further. They hauled Meier off, handcuffed him, and dumped him in their car.

When they returned from court they had Meier placed in solitary confinement. Cunningham had been away that day, but someone must have called him because he came back to the prison that evening. He took Meier with him while he phoned the U.S. Marshal's office.

"Listen, I've got John Meier here. He's a trusty and as long as he stays in this prison that's what he'll be unless someone with the proper authority comes and takes him away. If not, don't interfere in my jail."

Cunningham was curious about what passed through Meier's mind while he was out taking his solitary strolls to the stores. Did it not occur to him to just hop a bus and go home? Meier said it had, but he had given his word he wouldn't escape. Also, he was innocent — if he ran it would make him look guilty.

On June 20, Jennie, Joanne and Jimmy arrived in Utah for the summer. Lester had rented them a cabin but it was quite a distance from the prison. When Cunningham heard where they would be staying he said it was too isolated. He arranged with his sister to let them have her house in town rent-free. His sister was with her husband who was posted away for a couple of months. Since her house was behind his own home, Cunningham promised Meier he would keep an eye on his family.

Meier asked permission to give the inmates cakes and cookies.

"Sure — just bake them." He said he didn't know how. Could he bring in his wife? Cunningham just about choked on his coffee.

"John," he spluttered, "you've got an Englishman passing himself off as your legal assistant in there cleaning dishes, and now you want your wife?"

He went off muttering, but he didn't say no. Jennie arrived in the kitchen the next day, and the inmates found cake on their trays that night with their steaks and salads.

Meier's trial began July 25, 1979, in Salt Lake City.

Forgetting all the conflicting times and dates which make Robertson's account such a preposterous farrago, it essentially boiled down to this: Robertson was present in Meier's basement when Meier forged a number of memos. Then, said the prosecution, Meier took these forgeries and sprinkled them throughout the thousands of Hughes' company documents procured from Mexico by Trevillion. As Trevillion had consecutively stamped each document using a six-digit stamp — the first being 000000 and the final document being 003248 — Meier must have removed a dozen or so from the pile and replaced them with forgeries. In order to preserve the sequence, and to cover what he had done, he had re-stamped the forgeries with the numbers of those documents he was discarding.

Unfortunately for Meier, it was only after he had been convicted that his lawyer, James Barber, tumbled to the significance of those discarded documents. If Meier had made such a switch, then the originals of the jettisoned documents must still exist among the government's copies of the Hughes Mexican papers.

Prior to the trial, Barber had discovered that microfilms of the Mexican documents were in the hands of the IRS and had asked that the defense be allowed to view them. He was forced to proceed to trial without the benefit of examining the files. However, three months later Preston Truman, acting as Barber's agent, was permitted to view them. He later told Meier that Trevillion had copied only a fragment of the files and that the IRS microfilms contained other documents that would have been invaluable in his fight with Summa.

If the prosecution's argument had been correct, there should have been a number of documents in the IRS files which the Trevillion set no longer contained. These would be the documents Meier would have removed to make way for the forgeries. Unless the prosecution provided these documents, its argument that Meier had salted the files could not stand. No such documents were ever produced though the prosecution's theory depended on their existence. As well, Trevillion had used a special stamp only detectable under ultra-violet light and the originals had remained in the same order as the copied set.

At trial the indictment against Meier covered only two documents, although a number of others whose origins were questioned were introduced as exhibits. Of those in the indictment, one purported to show that Hughes' signature had been forged by one of his own people on a document entered against Meier in his civil suit. The other was the document which said Hughes wanted to stop the pressure against Meier and Greenspun. The Judge Anderson memo was dropped off the indictment.

Robertson was the prosecution's first witness. Others would be called — Trevillion and Reynolds, to date the arrival of the documents in Canada, and the old guard from Summa Corporation to disavow any knowledge of the documents and to declare them false. But the trial would really come down to a contest between two witnesses: Robertson and an expert familiar with Xerox machines.

The story Robertson now told was a carefully edited version of his previous testimony in Canada. During his examination by Stephen Snarr, the Utah Assistant Attorney General, there was no talk of seeing Rolls Royces or dirty copies, just of Meier busily toiling away in his basement perfecting the forgeries on a multi-headed typewriter, then making copies capable of blending in with the Mexican documents.

The strategy of limiting Robertson's testimony to its bare essentials was designed to prevent Barber from examining the contradictory stories the witness had previously told and using these variations to attack his credibility. Generally, under the rules of cross-examination, a witness can only be questioned on matters raised in his direct testimony. If Robertson did not recite any of the tales he told in Canada, then Barber would be prevented from forcing him to account for the discrepancies among versions he had given various courts. As soon as Barber attempted to steer Robertson into his previous testimony, Snarr was on his feet objecting. He told Judge Bruce Jenkins that Barber was canvassing areas left silent during direct examination and this could not be allowed.

Barber argued that in Canada, Robertson was asked a series of questions similar to what had been asked by Snarr and had told a story which he now omitted. "He omitted it for a reason... he knows a substantial amount of (his) credibility is going to be damaged by which story is told."

As an example, Barber said, he wanted to ask Robertson about seeing Trevillion and Romano in a Rolls Royce outside Reynolds' office on the night she delivered the papers — the story he had told in Canada. Barber said that before trial, he had informed Snarr that Trevillion would testify that she and Romano were in a Mustang that night. Snarr must have passed this on to Robertson, which explained why the issue was now avoided.

"It is my contention that Mr. Robertson flatly fabricated the business of the Rolls Royce and it is an indication of his lack of credibility... it is merely one incident where the man has apparently fabricated an event to make his story about Mr. Meier saleable..." said Barber.

Jenkins allowed him to proceed.

Barber then led Robertson through his former testimonies trying to get an explanation as to why he had told so many differing and contradictory stories. Robertson's standard replies were that he been confused about dates, or had forgotten details which he had since remembered after consulting his notes. But the matter uppermost on Barber's mind was Robertson's story of the Xerox machine which he had described to such effect in Canada.

In Vancouver he had said that while Meier was away from the basement he had gone to the copier and made copies of some of the forgeries Meier had concocted, which he later turned over to the RCMP. In the process of running the copier, he had noticed the platen was dirty and these dirty marks were showing up on the forgeries Meier was running off the machine. In this way, he neatly linked the copies, which Judge Anderson had previously declared fraudulent, to the very Xerox machine Meier had had in the basement.

Barber now asked Robertson if he had noticed there was dirt on the platen, and Robertson — despite his testimony in Canada — denied noticing anything of the sort. It was the paper which was dirty, he said.

Was he saying the paper had dust on it?

"I wasn't in a position to look for dust, sir."

Barber produced the testimony he had given in Canada where he was definite about the dust marks leaving tell-tale patterns on the copies. Did he remember saying this?

"Yes, I think I was over-assuming because I am not really an expert in that…"

Robertson steadfastly refused to say there was dust on the platen. He would only go so far as to say that he presumed the platen was dusty.

"Did you observe it was dusty?"

"I didn't particularly notice it when I was making my own copy…"

"You said in Canada, did you not… that the glass on the machine and the machine generally was dusty?"

"Yes."

"Was that statement true or not true. Did you notice that on the glass or not?"

"That was my general impression."

"Do you feel, Mr. Robertson, that it is all right to come in court and raise your right hand to testify to your impressions?" But the judge ruled that question inappropriate. The story about dust on the platen and corresponding marks on the exhibits, was the heart of Meier's defense. Using the anomalies, Barber was about to show that Robertson's story was utterly false.

As with the prosecution steering him away from his Rolls Royce observation, there appeared in this refusal to admit to dust marks a foreknowledge of what a Xerox expert would likely say.

Steven Thompson, a senior technician with the Xerox Corporation, was Barber's main witness. Thompson provided the court with an explanation of the various technical processes used to produce photocopies, expounding on the silicon sand cascade method — used in early machines — to the magnetic brush method found in more modern copiers. He said the two processes were so different that they produced their own characteristics.

The machine in Meier's basement was a Xerox 3100 copier using the magnetic brush process. Of that there was no question. When shown the two offending documents, Thompson said they could not have been made on a 3100 copier. They were unquestionably made on an older machine from the 914 family using the silicon sand process. Asked how he could be so sure, Thompson said: "When you look at the copies there is a high amount of background... these vertical lines."

"Are those vertical lines found on the Xerox 3100 type copies?"

"No."

"Why is that?"

"Because the paper travels in a different direction. In the 3100, the copy is placed on the paper from side to side. (In) the 914 family, it is placed on the paper from top to bottom."

Based on this expert testimony, Meier could not have committed the acts of forgery. The case built on Robertson's denunciation should have fallen right there. However, the prosecution didn't let this fatal testimony stand in its way. When it came time for Snarr to argue his case to the jury, he simply tossed Robertson's testimony overboard and told the jury it could disregard what his star witness had said and still find Meier guilty.

"...even excluding any testimony from Mr. Robertson, it is a case which presents a strong case on physical evidence... that would indicate that the only person who could have conceivably forged or fabricated those documents was Mr. John Meier," said Snarr, blithely gliding over the fact that there was no proof at all that Meier had done such a thing.[1]

The case which had been started by, and in fact, founded on, Robertson's "eyewitness" account, was now transformed into one of circumstantial evidence. Snarr said Meier was the only person to have had access to the documents between October 22 and November 5. The prosecutor made an amazing statement: "I am not sure we have provided a definitive answer in terms of time, place, machine, person, on that question, but let me focus that we have presented evidence to you... that should indicate that they had to be forged after John Reynolds provided them to Mr. Meier."

Simply put, the prosecution couldn't say how or when or even if Meier had committed forgery, but he was guilty anyway.

When the jury returned, two women jurors averted their gaze as Meier scrutinized their faces for the verdict. When the foreman pronounced him guilty, his daughter Jeannie broke down and sobbed. Hearing her cries, Meier vaulted the bar and took her in his arms. The guards jumped from their seats and were about to drag him back, but Judge Jenkins held up a hand to restrain them.[2]

NUMBED BY THE VERDICT, Meier was escorted back to the prison he had left with such fond hopes that morning. He returned in chains and handcuffs, dazed by the fact that he had just been found guilty of a crime he had not committed. The U.S. Marshals insisted he be placed in his old cell with the door locked.

The guards obliged. After an hour he was called out to see Cunningham. Fully expecting the sergeant to revoke his privileges now that he had crossed the threshold from prisoner to convict, Meier spoke first. "I guess this changes everything," he said. "I'll stay in my cell until they move me out."

Cunningham said he didn't think that would be necessary. "I've gotten to know you and now I've met your family. I've been speaking with some friends of mine in Salt Lake and as far as I'm concerned you've been persecuted, not prosecuted. You don't need to promise me anything. If you want to stay a trusty and work in the kitchen, you're welcome."

They shook hands and Meier thanked him again for the kindness he showed his family. Faced with a long separation from them, Meier took solace in correspondence. Many of his letters were saved to provide a chronicle of a family's despair, resignation, determination and perseverance. The most intimate correspondence was between Meier and his youngest daughter, Joanne, who in the fall of 1979 was sixteen years old. She would inundate him with letters — as many as three a day on some occasions — faithfully recording the family's triumphs and tribulations while Jennie and the older children put up a brave, if brittle, front.

In the aftermath of his conviction, when Joanne was railing against providence, Meier wrote:

Joey, don't take things too bad, and don't be bitter. You are a good and loyal daughter and I love you very much, but you must be strong, and don't blame God. Everything will be okay...

To Johnny, who was left with the task of working to help his mother take care of his younger brother and sister he wrote:

...I am pleased you are looking at the real estate field (as a career). Merlin's advice to King Arthur when the King was feeling low was "The best thing for being sad, is to learn something." And never feel bad, Johnny, if you fail at something. Henry Kaiser said before he died "Seventy-five percent of the things I try fail." He became the world's largest producer of cement. He was the third largest producer of aluminum. He built 1,500 merchant ships during World War II, etc. Not bad for a failure. You just have to be persistent. And never underrate yourself or feel inferior. You're a good son. I only ask you to watch after your mother. Let no one hurt her. I'm proud of you...

A couple of days after his trial, one of the hardest guards in the prison came to see Meier. He was a former navy lieutenant who Meier understood had been transferred to the prison shortly before he arrived. He identified himself as being with the CIA and handed him a card bearing the CIA's logo and the name and phone number of another agent in the Langley headquarters.

"You spoke to this person once before," said the guard. Meier looked at the name but couldn't remember.

"I've been put here to keep an eye on you. If you ever want to talk to us directly this is the person to call."

He said all Meier's phone calls had been monitored and his mail checked. However, unlike the U.S. Marshals, he made no move to restrict Meier's freedom or prevent him wandering out to do the prison's shopping.

When the Marshals came to relocate Meier to a federal prison they couldn't find him. It was early afternoon and they inquired where he was. Cunningham said he was out but would be back shortly.

"Out? Out where?"

"Down at the store."

"What's he doing there?"

"Buying dinner."

"Who's with him?"

"No one."

"What?" they screamed. Meier was strolling back, enjoying the sunshine, when the U.S. Marshals' car came racing along the road. It did a U-turn and before it came to a complete stop one of the Marshals dove out brandishing his gun.

"Meier!" he screamed. "Get in the car!"

With his arms full of groceries, Meier was shoved headlong into the vehicle while the Marshals kept up a constant stream of curses about what they were going to do to Cunningham. They dragged him to his cell and were stuffing him inside when Cunningham intervened.

"John, you just put down the bags and go and get your stuff ready."

The Marshals stood glowering while Meier collected his gear. He shook hands with Cunningham and was led away.

Meier had been told he was to be sent to the federal prison in Englewood, Colorado. Instead of going east, he was driven north into Idaho, where he was placed in solitary confinement in the federal prison in Boise.

On his second day in solitary, two CIA agents came to see him. "Well, Mr. Meier," said one, "now that you have been convicted and sentenced we'd like to talk to you." He produced a file about four inches thick. From it he pulled a sheaf of papers and asked Meier if he recognized them. Meier looked and saw it was part of the CIA's Canadian file which he had turned over to Trudeau. "Now that you're facing some time, perhaps you would be interested in working out a deal?" They showed him photographs of himself in Tonga and Australia and files containing notations of his activities from surveillance teams.

"If you help us, we can promise to have you out and back home with your family." Meier asked what they wanted.

"We'd like to discuss a number of areas: Howard Hughes, Tonga and what you have been doing with the Canadian government. We would like to know how you got these documents," he said pointing at the Canadian file, "and where the rest of them are." Meier said he would like advice from his lawyer.

"No, we'll get back to you, because right now, if you don't cooperate you're going on the merry-go-round."

They returned the next day. Meier still insisted on talking to Wyshak but was told that it wouldn't be allowed. Furthermore, until he cooperated he would be kept in solitary.

The agents possessed only a part of the Canadian file, indicating the source from which they had obtained it. Meier had given the full file to the Security and Intelligence Branch, but only selections of it to Trudeau's group. Since it was these same selections that the CIA had, they must have received them from a source in the Trudeau circle. This meant, in effect, that the CIA had penetrated the very apex of political power in Canada and was able to lay hands on the most sensitive documents passing through the Prime Minister's Office. Further, someone, in or close to Trudeau's inner circle, knew what Meier would be facing once he was extradited. Meier was betrayed by someone within the group that had come seeking his assistance. Considering what he had done for the Liberal government, Meier should have been protected as a political refugee. Instead his deeds were exposed to the CIA and he was hand-delivered to them. As for receiving help from friendly FBI agents, the CIA operatives were quick to disabuse him of that hope.

"We know who you have been talking to in the Bureau, but it's not going to work. We have control of this project. They don't."

Meier was kept in solitary in Boise for almost two weeks until October 11, when guards put him in handcuffs, leg irons and waist chains and he was flown with other prisoners to Seattle. A group going to the McNeil Island prison disembarked while 27 additional prisoners were taken aboard. Then the plane took off for Los Angeles where they were all unloaded and placed in Terminal Island jail in Long Beach.

Again while the other prisoners were allotted cells in the general prison population, Meier was led away to D block — The Hole — still wearing all the apparatus of restraint and performing the jailhouse shuffle, that curious stammering gait forced on prisoners who are expected to walk while bound in leg irons. It is degrading and offends the dignity more deeply than simply wearing handcuffs. On the way to D block, his guard apologized for putting him in solitary.

On Meier's second night he was put in leg irons and handcuffs and taken to a room in the administration wing where the two CIA agents were waiting. Again they repeated their demands. Again he asked to talk to his lawyer. Again they refused. "This is between you and us."

He asked if he could contact his family and they said if he cooperated he could be home with them. He asked for his blood pressure medicine and some of his belongings but they shook their heads. He asked if he could take a shower or get some clean clothes but these simple requests, too, were refused.

They came to see him once more in Terminal Island and warned that if he didn't cooperate he wouldn't see Canada again. On October 18, he was allowed an hour's visit with his brother-in-law from Los Angeles, then was strip-searched and placed back in his cell.

He was removed from Terminal Island on October 22, after eleven days in solitary. The next stop was the prison in El Reno, Oklahoma, where he arrived dirty, unshaven, tired, dispirited and unwell. He came with a party of thirteen other prisoners who stood outside the classification office waiting to be assigned a cell. Meier was the last man called in to hear that once again, he was going into solitary. This was too much. He complained that he had been found guilty of obstruction of justice and nobody had ever said he would spend all his time in maximum security. One of the officers showed him a card bearing his picture, containing the notation: "Hold until further investigation." Then the two CIA agents came in. This was his last chance to make a deal, they warned him. After this they would wash their hands of him and he'd likely never see home again.

"What exactly is it you want?" he asked. One said they had made it clear a number of times, but Meier said he wanted the precise details.

"You have files belonging to the U.S. government. We want them back."

The agents then spoke of other files. Meier could see they were confused as to the extent of the information they believed he had. In talking about the Mexican documents Meier could tell they were not quite sure what he had received. Also, they were unsure which White House documents he had and what documents taken from the Romaine Street burglary had ended up in his possession. After giving him the list, they said he would also have to sign a number of documents but they didn't elaborate on what those might be.

The agents said they knew Meier had documents hidden away with his lawyers in Canada and the United States, and had placed some documents in Switzerland. They had recovered some of the documents from a number of places, including New Mexico, which led Meier to believe they were talking about material burglarized from Tom Benavides' office during his election campaign. "If you help us you'll be home in 48 hours."

Meier asked them how they could possibly recover all his documents in

48 hours. One man smiled and said: "Mr. Meier, you just let us know where the files are and I can assure you we'll have them in 48 hours. Believe me."

Meier wanted a lie detector test to convince them he was innocent of obstruction of justice. One of the agents said that was unnecessary.

"I insist," Meier said. "You bring someone in to give me a lie detector test."

Again they said there was no reason to do that. Meier obstinately said he would do nothing without the test. "If we do it, will you talk to us?"

"Yes."

At 6 a.m. the next day Meier was brought from his cell and shown into a room which contained the agents, three guards and a man sitting before a polygraph machine. They removed his handcuffs and leg irons and sat him at a small table. On the table was the polygraph; the operator sitting across from him fixed the sensors to his fingers and calibrated the machine by asking a number of questions. Then the interrogation on the subject of the forged documents began. When he was finished, the operator undid the sensors and began studying the printout. Meier's restraints were replaced and he was taken from the room. Fifteen minutes later he was brought back. The polygraph operator was gone and Meier was told to sit down.

"Okay, Mr. Meier. What else is it you want?"

"I want the results."

"You passed the test, as you knew you would — and as we knew you would." For a second Meier thought he misheard him.

"Did you say you knew I'd pass?"

"Mr. Meier," the CIA agent said without emotion, "isn't it obvious that we can charge you and convict you and sentence you for anything we like? We know you didn't commit forgery, but let me tell you, if you don't cooperate your life will be a disaster..."

The enormity of this admission acted on Meier like an electrical charge. He leapt from his seat, and before the guards could intervene, he hit the agent a double-handed blow across the face, knocking him out of his chair. The agent, who had been caught by the edge of Meier's handcuffs, toppled to the floor just ahead of Meier, who had been attacked swiftly by the guards. The two nearest punched and kicked him while another guard waded in to hit him across the side of his face with a billy-club.

When Meier regained consciousness he found himself handcuffed to the metal frame of a bed in the dispensary. He had a violent headache and his whole body hurt. He remained awake for an hour until a doctor arrived and shone a light in his eyes. He told him he had a head injury but no concussion and would be sore for a couple of days.

"Have you ever been in prison before?"

Meier shook his head.

"Well, let this be a lesson. No matter what, don't ever — and I mean ever — hit a guard. You're lucky this is all that happened."

Meier said he didn't strike a guard.

"You probably don't remember, but they came to take you for a shower and you jumped a guard. They had to call the others to subdue you."

"That's not what happened. I hit a government agent."

"You're delirious. You hit a guard in the shower."

There was no point arguing. The next morning, battered and bruised, he was placed in a double cell in the medical unit. Helped into his bunk by his kindly cellmate, he lay there for two days spitting up blood.

He was finally transported to the federal prison in Englewood, Colorado, on November 2. He was sickly, thin, and had been held in solitary almost all the time since beginning the merry-go-round 35 days before.

At Englewood he was brought before an official who had a large folder on his desk. It was full of clippings from Canadian and American newspapers and magazines, including the *Playboy* articles. The official asked for his version of the events leading to his imprisonment; Meier spent an hour relating the details of his conviction and his travels since being removed from Davis County Jail at the end of September.

"I have a note here from Washington about you," said his jailer, handing it to Meier. It said he was to be held in maximum security. "That's what they want, but where would you like to go? Would you like to be in the general population?" Meier said he would, given his choice.

"Fine. I'll decide where you go once you're in here, not Washington. You can go with the other guys."

He ripped up the note and had Meier's chains and handcuffs removed.

It was now November 1979. If he could not get parole, his release date would be May 1981. It all seemed so distant.

One of his biggest challenges was to settle into the aimless life of a prisoner. Much of his career had been spent crisscrossing time zones, being in the center of some whirlwind or other, party to an endless series of intrigues — if not on Hughes' behalf, then with his friends in the

Democratic Party or with the British Secret Service or their counterparts in Canada. By any standards it was an unusual career. Now, his activities had shrivelled from a global scale to the few acres of Colorado hemmed in by the perimeter walls of Englewood prison.

What was there to do in such a place? Not much: Eat, write letters, watch the seasons change and dream about getting out early. Naturally, his first Christmas in jail was the hardest to endure. To Johnny he wrote:

> Wish that I could have been there with you this Christmas. I know that with you there, the rest of my family is safe. I think of you always, and love you for what you are. Make sure that your mother does not work too hard this Christmas...

Meanwhile, Alan Copeland had been dealt with by the Justice Department. He, too, was finding his feet in prison after being charged and convicted of fraud, despite efforts by his friends in the FBI to help him at his trial.

Copeland had no doubts he was being made to pay for his association with Meier. He went to jail convinced he was being persecuted for attempting to coax Meier back to the United States. "I never had any trouble until I met Meier. Then everything went wrong," he later said.

The charges laid against him involved the swapping of a painting of dubious heritage for the deeds to a house in Arizona in 1973. These charges, which had been left dormant for years and were about to expire, were suddenly activated shortly after Meier was arrested. Before going to trial in Phoenix, Copeland received a phone call warning him to keep Richard Nixon's name out of the proceedings, or things would go even harder on him.

The FBI and Treasury Department agents who acted as Copeland's controllers on the Meier case appeared in court on his behalf. Over the years, they testified, Copeland had been responsible for recovering millions of dollars worth of contraband, including paintings and stolen bonds, and had turned down offers of reward money. They agreed that Copeland had opened negotiations on their behalf with Meier.

The following exchange took place between Copeland's lawyer Steve Slepian and Special FBI agent Bradley Maryman.

"Was it felt that John Meier, if he wanted to, could name payoffs (made) to high United States government officials and that is why it was important to see if Meier would make a deal in Canada to come back to the United States?"

"I'm not at liberty to discuss that."

"How far can you go in discussing that, Agent Maryman?"

"The fact that the government did have an interest in his return."

Later the district attorney asked Maryman if any of his superiors had ever instructed him not to seek Meier's return.

"No, they did not." Slepian sensed a half answer in this reply so he asked if anyone had instructed him not to bring Meier back.

"Yes, sir, they did."

And there the matter hung. Was Maryman limiting his first answer to his immediate FBI superiors then, by his second, broadening it to include influential persons in government technically not his superiors? For who, except someone with power in government, could order around an FBI agent? Slepian had no doubts as to what Maryman was saying.

"It was quite shocking to hear that there were people in the Justice Department that said not to bring him back," he told the court, as the case wandered away from Copeland's perceived fraud into a strange landscape peopled by individuals as divergent as Meier and Vesco.

Copeland was sentenced to eighteen months.

Meanwhile, Joanne wrote to her father that her friends all thought he must have done something awful for all this to have happened. Her father replied:

...You say a lot of your friends are saying that I must have done something bad to be put through all this. They are right. I got the U.S. government mad at me because I exposed some of the CIA's activities, I tried to prove that Howard Hughes did not die in Mexico and I tried to develop an international airport in Tonga and the U.S. did not want one there. So, you see, as far as the U.S. government is concerned I am bad...

His letters sometimes gave an insight into the world of prison life. To Joanne he wrote:

Yesterday, the president of the Jaycees was sent to the hole and I have taken over as president. The Jaycees is the most powerful group in the

institution. What happened to the last president is interesting. A few
months ago he and five others got hold of the camera that belonged to the
Jaycees. They took pictures of themselves smoking grass, with $20 bills
sticking out of their ears and noses. Then they got the film out of the
institution to friends.

A few days ago a pound of marijuana was found near the fence. When
the guard opened it up he found photos in with the marijuana. The person
who threw the marijuana over the fence was the same person who
developed the photos. Anyway, these dummies not only committed two
crimes here — having marijuana and having money in the institution —
they also took photos of themselves committing them...

In a series of letters they discuss her part in the school's production of
H.M.S. Pinafore. He wrote that he had pictures of his family pinned above
his bunk, including ones in which she was decked out as a midshipman.

I tell everyone you are in the navy fighting overseas for Canada. Next week
I was going to tell them you were wounded and may not live, that way I
can get extra dessert when we go to chow...

He went before the parole board on January 22. He was told he could
bring an advocate — he chose Jennie. The couple sat across a table from the
board members. She attempted to tell them what it was like at home
without her husband. She was interrupted and told all prisoners' families
suffer. Reduced to silence, she could think of nothing more to say. The
board next asked Meier if he had learned anything and he said he had.
Expecting a confession, one of them turned up the volume on the tape
recorder which sat in the middle of the table while the rest leaned forward in
anticipation.

"I've learned never to get into politics."

"You admit you are guilty?" asked one.

"No, just wish I'd never gotten into politics."

"So you're sorry this happened?"

"Sure I'm sorry."

"So you're sorry you committed a crime?"

"I never committed a crime. I didn't forge documents or obstruct
justice."

"Wait outside."

After a few minutes he was called back.

"If you tell us you are guilty we'll grant you immediate parole. Are you sorry for committing these crimes?"

Meier protested he had committed no crime.

"Well then, you are to serve 15 more months. Request denied."

When he left the room Jennie could see by the look on his face what had happened; her knees buckled. As he tried to hold her up, one of the women librarians working in the prison rushed up to help.

"Oh, Mr. Meier — you got your parole, didn't you?"

"No."

"But we were all told you'd be getting parole."

"They turned it down."

Meier was taken to his cell, where he met his living unit manager, who also assumed he was going home. When Meier said he wasn't, the officer appeared astounded. "I drew up the report on you for the prison. It recommended parole."

Meier asked what he would have done, if he'd been offered release in exchange for a simple admission of guilt. The officer said if he were guilty he would admit it — "but if I was innocent, and had a long time ahead of me in here, I don't know if I'd stick to my principles. It would be fifty-fifty."

"Well, I told them I was innocent. And they told me another 15 months."

At one point even Joanne would pressure her father to say he was guilty if it would get him home earlier.

In answer to her, he wrote: "Now as far as my pleading guilty is concerned, firstly, I am not guilty so I would never plead guilty. Secondly, I am doing everything I can to get to B.C. soon..."

Further bad news followed. Judge Jenkins refused to lessen his sentence or allow him a new trial after Barber argued that what Truman discovered in reviewing the IRS files showed Meier did not tamper with the Mexican Hughes documents. His request for a transfer to a minimum security prison in California was also denied.

Jenkins was also refusing an extraordinary request from Meier's son Johnny who, unknown to his father, had written offering to serve his father's sentence in his stead. The judge praised Johnny's obvious love for his father but said guidelines established by the U.S. Bureau of Prisons prohibited him from taking his father's place in prison. Without mentioning his appeal to Jenkins, Johnny then sent a long and gloomy letter to his father saying he had failed his real estate exam. (As it turned out he had passed.) Meier replied:

> Sorry to hear about your real-estate exam. We've all had rough weeks. As you know I lost my appeal to the regional parole commissioner, lost my appeal to the judge on a reduction of sentence and lost my transfer to an institution in California. Besides that I am having a rough time trying to get (a transfer) to Canada. You think you have problems? Oh yes, one more negative point.
>
> On Saturday night while I was sleeping something landed on my face at three in the morning. I jumped up and found a bat flying around my room. I had left my window open that night. I chased it around the room for 30 minutes. It kept trying to land on my head for some reason. Anyway, I finally got it to fly out the window in the door of my room. Then I went back to sleep.
>
> At four, I heard this shouting and this black homosexual was running up and down the hall in his baby blue nightie screaming. He drew everyone out of their rooms to tell them a big vampire bat landed on his face. We all told him he was crazy and it was probably one of his boyfriends. I went back to my room and laughed with my face in my pillow for 15 minutes. So keep your chin up and your windows closed...

Meier asked to be repatriated to Canada to serve out the remainder of his sentence. While this request was being processed, he was given a three-day pass, which he spent with his family. It was the first week in July, 1980, and Jennie, Joanne and Jimmy had come to be near him in Colorado. He had not spent a night outside a prison cell in fifteen months. When he returned to prison, he realized somewhat guiltily he was thankful to be away from the noise, commotion and activity of the real world.

Finally Meier was told he was going to be repatriated, but would have to go to Lewisburg, Pennsylvania, for transfer to Canada. The prison authorities gave him air fare, cash to cover expenses and instructions to make his way from Colorado to Pennsylvania. Then they opened the door and let him go.

When he finally got to Lewisburg in the dead of night, they refused him entry. It was a maximum security prison and unheard-of for anyone to show up late at night seeking admittance as though the place were little more than the YMCA. Prisoners entering those massive old walls always came in chains under armed escort. No one had ever arrived by cab before.

Unable to go anywhere because the taxi had left and he was miles from the main highway, he roamed around the prison wall, holding his cheap suitcase like one of Dante's bewildered souls patiently awaiting advancement through Purgatory.

In his letter to Jennie he explains it best:

The driver then took me to Lewisburg and dropped me off at 12:30 a.m. Lewisburg is surrounded by a 40 foot wall. I couldn't find the front door. As I stood there with all my luggage under my arms a window opened up 30 feet above me and a guard yelled down to ask me what I wanted. I told him that I was here to check in. He said that no one comes here by themselves to check in, so he asked me to stand there until someone came out. I waited 15 minutes until a guard came out and asked why I was standing there with all this luggage. I told him I was supposed to check in and he told me that no one comes here by themselves. So I gave him my transfer papers and he went back inside. I waited another 30 minutes outside. By now I figure that the only way to get in was to commit a crime. But there I was two miles from the main road standing like an idiot trying to get into a penitentiary. The window 30 feet up then opened and someone yelled down to ask me if I ever heard of a Mr. Noah. I said yes, that was my counselor at Englewood. That satisfied him since he had just called there to ask them if they had ever heard of me. Finally at 2 a.m. I was let in.

They put me in a cell with a bed, a toilet and a few hundred cockroaches crawling around. I couldn't sleep. The next morning they put me here on the second floor. At least I have a window and no roaches. There are 1,100 inmates here. The place looks like some old museum, 20 foot ceilings with red shining tiles and heavy thick doors. It's also the toughest prison I've been in. I also found another bit of information. They told me that I was a CMC-5 (central monitoring case five). That means that my letters and phone calls have been monitored all along, even though Englewood said I was not a CMC. I don't know what the five means. But it explains why my mail was always delayed...

On his second day in Lewisburg, he was taken into an interrogation cell, four solid walls pierced only by a solid steel door with no windows. Inside were three men sitting at a small table. Two he didn't recognize, but the third was the more pleasant half of the CIA team which had dogged his footsteps on the merry-go-round. Meier was relieved to see that his partner wasn't there. The agent said the agency had a dilemma.

"We have a serious problem with you. Three things can happen. We could have you released right now and you could go home to your family. We could do our best to stop you being transferred to Canada, or, alternatively, you could get yourself to Canada but we'd get you back."

"This, though, is the last time we will deal with you. After this meeting you'll never hear from us again. All I'm going to ask is that you sign your name to these three documents and that's the end of it." He then introduced his companions: a CIA attorney and a notary public to witness his signature.

He passed three single sheets of foolscap to Meier and said they would give him time to read them and contemplate a decision. Before they left Meier repeated his request to talk to his attorney, but the agent shook his head. Could he make a phone call to someone in Ottawa, then?

"No. This is your own decision. You can sign or you can refuse. Either way, you'll never hear from us again."

Alone, Meier picked up the top paper. Under his name was a short statement to the effect that he had set up a bank account for the King of Tonga in Hawaii and that he had also been instrumental in obtaining funds from Libyan President Moammar Gadhafi. This money he had deposited into the Hawaiian account on orders of the King.

The second document said he had obtained certain classified documents from — there was space for him to add the names — who were members of the Central Intelligence Agency. Further, he was now directing whomever held those documents to surrender them to authorized agents selected by the federal government.

The third would prove to be the most intriguing. This said he was giving up all documents in his possession pertaining to Howard Hughes, his companies, his agents and any related businesses with which Howard Hughes had been associated. Further, he was granting the federal government complete access to his files for the purpose of allowing the government's agents to remove whatever documents they desired. He would be permitted to be present during the search or, if the documents were in a foreign country, it could be done in the presence of his agent.

After a decent interval the trio returned. The agent carried a cup of coffee and a sandwich for Meier. They all sat down and Meier was asked if he had any questions. Meier began with the Tongan document. He knew the King had a bank account in Hawaii used only to exchange currency when he was abroad. Petty though it was, its existence had not escaped the CIA.

"How are you going to say this?" asked Meier, pointing to the paragraph concerning the payoffs by Gadhafi. "There are no large deposits in that account. The King only uses it when he travels. There's hardly anything in there at all." The agent told him not to trouble himself.

"We'll see the money is deposited into the account when we're ready. All you have to do is sign the paper and we'll take care of the rest."

Picking up the CIA document, Meier asked what would happen to the people he named?

"You don't have to worry about it," said the agent, evading the obvious. "No one will know you've given us the names. I'm sure, if we spent the time, we could find out who you are dealing with. There are many ways to do it. This is the easiest. You tell us and we'll take care of it ourselves."

Meier pointed to the final document and asked how the agency could be assured that he had surrendered all of his files?

"Well, Mr. Meier, we might not know everything you have, but I'm sure we could tick off 99 percent of what's in those files. For example, we know you have a lot of documents taken from Hughes Productions.[3] We know you handled a lot of sensitive assignments for Hughes, not only ones made public but others still private. We also know that you had supplied to you the so-called Gemstone documents and files pertaining to John F. Kennedy and his family."

The mention of the Gemstone Files and the Kennedy material made Meier sit up. The Gemstone Files, or as they are more properly known, the Gemstone Charts, were drawn up by the CIA graphics department for Howard Hunt to be used on Richard Nixon's behalf. They were a master plan for the disruption of the Democratic Party's presidential campaign in the 1972 election.

Various clandestine operations were assigned the names of precious stones in an attempt to dignify their skullduggery. For example, Ruby was the codeword for placing an agent within the Democratic Party; Sapphire, the use of prostitutes to entice Democrats onto a houseboat fitted with video cameras loaded for blackmail; Crystal, the electronic surveillance of candidates, which, combined with Quartz, Emerald, Garnet, Turquoise, Topaz and Opal[4] would demoralize and destroy the political opposition to Nixon's reelection. The charts were such a shocking schematic of political interference and manipulation that John Mitchell ordered their destruction when they were presented to him at the time he was ordering the Watergate burglary. (This didn't prevent the resourceful George Clifford from obtaining a copy.)

Shocking as they were, the Gemstone Charts were insignificant compared to what the CIA imagined Meier possessed concerning the Kennedys.

Although Meier didn't enlighten the agent, the CIA was mistaken in this thinking. He didn't have the file, but he knew full well what it contained as he had once read it.

In the aftermath of John F. Kennedy's assassination, Robert Kennedy had amassed a file from many sources, but mostly from the FBI, which indicated that his brother the President had been killed as the result of a plot enacted by a number of leading industrialists in the United States including Howard Hughes. A member of the Hughes entourage was suspected of being involved in arranging the assassination in Dallas. Robert Kennedy had kept the file close to his chest in preparation for the day if, and when, he gained the political power to find out who had ordered his brother's death.

While Paul Schrade was recovering from the bullet wounds he received when Robert Kennedy was assassinated, he and Meier had discussed what might have happened to that file. Schrade told Meier he would ask Ted Kennedy when the opportunity arose. When he did, the surviving Kennedy brother turned white and told him never to mention the file again.

While these reflections ran through Meier's head, the agent opened his briefcase and took out two piles of documents and photographs to emphasize how intimate was their knowledge of Meier's files.

One stack contained nothing but telephone transcripts of Meier's conversations. He was invited to look through them. Each contained the date, time, location of the call, number dialed and what was said verbatim. Here before him were the transcripts of conversations long forgotten. Next he was shown eight-by-ten glossies of himself in various parts of the world.

There he was with Don Nixon at the Eiffel Tower and with Ted Kennedy walking the halls of the Senate. There was one taken in Nanaimo of him having lunch with Tommy Douglas; when he saw it, it occurred to him that it was likely Gonzales' handiwork. Did he have any questions?

"Just one. Tell me again what will happen if I do sign and what will happen if I don't?"

"Well, it's simple. Sign and we'll have the documents notarized. You can walk out of here and go back to Canada. As long as you fulfill your obligations, that's the end of it. If you don't sign, we'll just walk out of here and that's the end of this phase of your life."

There was something ominous about what might happen if he refused and what the next phase of his life might bring, but Meier had made up his mind. "I just can't sign them." The agent showed no emotion and made no attempt to argue. He merely sat still, giving Meier space for an explanation.

"The letter concerning the King is not true. I can't hurt someone like that just to save myself possible problems. And the CIA letter — again I can't name people who are loyal Americans who were just helping me out of friendship because they felt I was being persecuted by a few people in the U.S. government. The files you ask for are the least important, but I can't sign these." He handed the papers back.

A guard was summoned and they all stood up. Then, unexpectedly, they shook Meier's hand. The lawyer and notary left and the CIA officer stopped at the door. He told the guard to give Meier whatever he wanted from the canteen before returning him to his cell. He shook his hand again and wished him luck — Meier has never seen him since.

After Meier had spent six days in Lewisburg, a bus manned by Canadian prison guards drove up and took custody of him and five other Canadian prisoners. They were driven across the border and taken to Kingston Penitentiary in Ontario, a maximum security prison on the northeast corner of Lake Ontario.

By Canadian calculations he was eligible for parole and had expected to be released once he reached Kingston. Instead, he was kept there for the remainder of July, then August and most of September. Finally on September 26, 1980, he was transferred to Mission Institution, a medium security prison in British Columbia about an hour's drive from his home. Again he expected to be released but instead was shown to a cell and prevented from leaving, even under escort.

Within days of his return to British Columbia, an RCMP party organized by the ever-persistent Corporal Westphal turned Meier's home inside-out looking for evidence to support his suspicion that Meier had committed murder.

Robbie Robertson, the professional witness, still in the U.S. Witness Protection Program, now told a story of murder and greed that made his former musings about Meier and the dusty Xerox seem even more banal. With Robertson being readied for yet another grand jury, what had been left unsaid in Lewisburg was now, ominously, in the open.

20

FRAMED FOR MURDER

Whoever killed Alfred Wayne Netter, a Vancouver stock promoter and business associate of Meier's, had patiently awaited the opportunity.

Sometime during the evening of November 29, 1974, Netter let a visitor into his room at the Beverly Hilton Hotel. The guest avoided being seen by anyone entering the room. At about 9:30 that evening, a waiter delivered two prime rib dinners to Netter's room. As the waiter entered Room 405 he heard the distinct click of the bathroom door being closed. Netter directed him to lay the tray between the twin beds.

When the waiter returned with an order of tea, half an hour later, this unseen party once again ducked into the bathroom. Netter ate what would be his last meal but his visitor left his tray undisturbed.

Netter was only in his underwear when sometime after midnight his room guest — warily circling behind him — moved in swiftly and plunged a large, broad-bladed knife into his unprotected back.

The knife penetrated four inches into his lungs. Although the blow missed his heart, Netter would have bled to death from this wound. The murderer struck a second blow, this one less forcefully with the blade sinking just a couple of inches into Netter's back. In these last minutes of his life Netter rallied and turned to face his attacker, who thrust the knife into his chest. Twice, as they stumbled across the room, Netter warded off frontal blows, suffering deep cuts to his right forearm in the process, and then in the scuffle an errant swipe lacerated his scalp and caused his toupee to fly off.

The blow that killed him was either of two tremendous thrusts delivered to the front of the chest, one of which transversed the heart and lungs and sank deep enough to nick the back wall of the chest while the other, an inch below it, was equally ferocious and fatal. The two wounds were parallel and may have been inflicted as Netter lay on his back. The murderer then drove his knife twice into the abdomen, lacerating his liver and lower lungs to a depth of four inches. He left the room as unseen in his departure as in his arrival.

The body lay undiscovered until the following afternoon when a chambermaid finally ignored the Do Not Disturb sign on the door and let herself in. To her complete horror, she found Netter in a pool of blood, wearing only his underpants, his toupee askew, his right arm pointing to the closet.

Given the semi-nude state of the body, the fact that a knife had been used and that the Beverly Hills police discovered a local sex magazine in the room with a number of massage parlor listings circled by a pen, there was every indication that the murder was a sex-slaying of the kind that routinely occurs in the Los Angeles area when prostitutes have a falling out with their tricks. Contradicting this theory was the fact that nothing appeared to have been stolen. Netter's credit cards, money and watch were found in the room. And while it is a possibility that the unseen visitor was a male prostitute (or a strong female one) it is just as likely that the person who murdered Netter was someone he knew, trusted, and could never have imagined as a killer.

He had let the visitor into his room, had ordered him a meal (an unusual extravagance towards a prostitute) and felt comfortable enough to walk around in his underwear — all of which bespeaks ease and intimacy.

Meier, who was doing consulting work for Netter's company, had last seen Netter in the Hotel Vancouver four days before the murder. When they bumped into each other, Netter said he was going to Florida. Meier in turn said he was off to meet three investors in Calgary who had put money into Netter's company, Trans Continental Video, and from there would fly to England.

On November 28 Meier flew to Calgary and registered in the Four

Seasons Hotel. The investors came to see him the next day — the day of the murder — and Meier spent the afternoon and evening with them. During that fateful day Netter phoned and said he was in Florida.

Because the investors hadn't booked rooms, Meier offered to share his room. Gordon Nyen accepted while his two companions shared a room nearby. Nyen stayed with Meier that night and sometime between noon and 1 p.m. the following day, November 30, the three investors drove home.

Meier's plan was to drive to Edmonton, stay overnight, then catch a flight to England for a meeting with British Intelligence. However, that morning he had received a call from Robertson, who said he was in Seattle. When Meier told him of his plans, Robertson said he would fly to Calgary, accompany him to Edmonton and then on to England.

Meier met Robertson at the airport. He looked unkempt and had a deep cut across his hand which he said he had suffered while opening a can of beer. They drove to Edmonton and stayed the night in the Sheraton Caravan Hotel.

That evening Jennie called Meier with the news that the radio was reporting a TCV executive had been killed in Los Angeles. The next day Meier flew to England with Robertson tagging along.

Meanwhile, in Beverly Hills, the police began probing Netter's background. The contents of his wallet identified him as a Canadian; a telex was sent to Vancouver's RCMP headquarters where it was read by Sergeant Robert Siddle, the duty officer. Siddle opened a file and began inquiries to see if anything in Vancouver could explain Netter's death. Finding nothing, the crime was listed as unsolved and stayed that way for four years until Robertson, fresh from immersing Meier in charges of forgery and obstruction of justice, gave information to Westphal which now implicated Meier in murder.

The gist of Robertson's story was that Meier had guilty knowledge of Netter's murder before the body was found or before news of his death was made public. How could he be so sure? Well, as surely as he'd been in Meier's basement watching him work wonders with a dirty Xerox, he was now claiming to have overheard a phone call to Meier's Calgary hotel room in which Meier was told of Netter's death hours before the body was found.

Meier had passed Netter on to contacts in Switzerland where a $250,000 loan was secured so that TCV could finance the purchase of movies. As collateral, a life insurance policy worth $400,000 was taken out against Netter. This covered the amount TCV had to repay the lenders.

In the midst of all this, Netter's marital affairs threatened to sink the company. He had started leading a double life going under the name of Alfred Baron, a persona he adopted once he received the $250,000 Swiss loan. It was a ruse to hide assets. As Alfred Wayne Netter, he was purportedly broke and on welfare, and said so in court during an acrimonious fight with his former wife. But as Baron, he was not so badly off and had a condominium in Florida purchased with money taken from the loan.

When this was put to him he denied using the alias. The perjury was exposed and in September, 1974, Netter was sentenced to four years imprisonment. This curtailed plans to have the company listed on the Vancouver Stock Exchange, as the exchange declared the company tainted and investors such as Abe Froese who had banked on the company going public, lost heavily. Netter was released on bail pending an appeal, but the prospects didn't look good. After his release, he confided to his lawyer that he planned to flee Canada for Los Angeles and there catch a tramp steamer to Israel.

On November 26, Netter asked a friend to take him to the airport in Vancouver, saying he was going to Florida. Instead, Netter flew to Los Angeles and checked into the Beverly Hilton. Three days later he was murdered. After an investigation, the insurance company paid the proceeds of Netter's life insurance policy to a company formed to handle the Swiss loan — TCV closed.

An outline of Corporal Westphal's case is contained in the information he drew up to obtain a search warrant. It discloses that Robertson was providing police with information in April, 1978 that alleged that Meier, along with TCV's Vancouver lawyer Gordon Hazelwood, conspired to have Netter murdered to lay hands on the proceeds of the insurance money. He allegedly hired an American union official, William McCrory of Los Angeles, to do the deed.[1]

Westphal took pains to go into the company's background and to explain how the players came together and how by November 1974 there appeared little hope of the $250,000 loan being repaid. The following are extracts from Westphal's unproven hypothesis:

Netter and Liebich were still unable to obtain software or financial backing. This caused Meier to become increasingly unhappy... Meier stated to Liebich that he was tired of the delays and threatened Liebich and Netter and stated that "if Netter gives me any more trouble, all I have to do is make one call to Los Angeles and have that son-of-a- bitch bumped off. No one gets in my way." Meier had an associate and confidant by the name of Robbie Robertson... Sometime prior to the fall of 1974 Robertson was with Meier... in Las Vegas when Meier... had a discussion with a man introduced to Robertson as Bill. During this conversation, Meier stated that Bill was a good man to know because he was a hit man and could travel all over as an official of the Teamsters union.

In October, 1974, Robertson was advised by Meier that a William McCrory was coming to visit him and that Robertson should not be around.

On or about November 29, 1974, Meier, accompanied by Robertson, flew to Calgary and checked into the Four Seasons Hotel. Also present (there) was Ralph Buchmann a (TCV) sales promoter... I do not know why Netter went to the Los Angeles area... but I have been informed by TCV employees who knew Netter personally that it would have been easy for Meier to direct Netter (there) by telling Netter there was a secret source of money in Los Angeles who would meet him when he got there...

On or about November 30 a hotel housekeeper entered Netter's room and found him dead... The homicide investigators removed all Netter's personal effects from the room including an item recognized by them to be what is commonly known as a smuggler's pouch, a item used to secret items of jewelry on a person's body to get them through customs undetected...

Immediately prior and during November 30 both Buchmann and Robertson noted that Meier appeared to be unusually nervous. Then during the same morning of November 30 Meier received a phone call... from an unknown person... Meier turned to Buchmann and Robertson and stated: "Ha, ha, Netter was killed in Los Angeles." Neither Robertson or Buchmann noticed any shock or bewilderment on the part of Meier at this news but that after the phone call Meier calmed down.

Later that date, Robertson answered the phone in Meier's room... and spoke to Jennie Meier (who) told Robertson that she had just heard on the radio that Netter had been found dead. Meier got on the phone... and Robertson heard Meier state "yes I know."

On or about December 5 Robertson was again advised by Meier that he had another meeting with William McCrory for which Robertson was not to be present. A few days later Robertson was informed by Meier's children that Bill McCrory had been present at their house... and had entertained them in their back yard by displaying his prowess with a large knife by repeatedly throwing it at imaginary targets in the back yard.

Shortly after the death of Netter... Hazelwood... submitted a claim against (Netter's) London Life insurance policy. London Life delayed payment due to the unusual circumstances surrounding Netter's death and the possibility of the involvement of his business associates in his death. Pressure was then placed on London Life by Meier... accordingly London Life paid $410,367.12 to Hazelwood...

Sometime prior to May 1975, Robertson was made president of TCV by Meier and Hazelwood for the sole purpose of handling the insurance proceeds.

On February 10, 1975, Hazelwood wrote to the Los Angeles County Coroner... requesting a very large expensive diamond ring which Hazelwood claimed... Netter had been seen wearing before he left on his trip to Los Angeles. No such ring was found on Netter's person although the smuggler's pouch was found.

In November, 1976, Meier called Tony Parford, jeweller... requesting an appraisal of a large diamond....

Westphal's report describes how the proceeds of the insurance were divided and changed into British Columbia Hydro bonds, some of which were given to Robertson to deliver to the mysterious Swiss lenders. Robertson then lost three bonds worth $15,000 and had to repay the money but claimed that Meier likely stole them out of his briefcase. It ends with more threats issued by Meier, these against Robertson. Meier would appear to be a minor league Al Capone if this collection of disinformation, falsehood, innuendo and dissembling were in any way correct.

Westphal was the Canadian investigator of Netter's murder in 1978 but Siddle had done the initial investigation, during which he interviewed Robertson. Siddle had received a vastly different tale from the one Robertson later provided to Westphal. There had been no mention to Siddle of hitmen or damning phone calls; in fact Robertson professed to know nothing about the murder. Moreover, it was he who asked to meet Siddle and when they met, tried to pump Siddle for details of the investigation. What evidence had been gathered at the scene? Were there fingerprints, blood samples from the murderer or other traces of the assassin's presence?

When Siddle saw Westphal's account, he was so shocked that he signed an affidavit attacking Robertson's story and Westphal's investigation. He asked for a government inquiry into the whole affair, and that it be kept out of the hands of the police as he had grave doubts about the RCMP's handling of the Netter-Meier investigation.[2]

Meier did not have the kind of relationship with McCrory that Robertson described and the whole theory of the murder depended on. There was more to McCrory than either could possibly guess. McCrory was a valued advisor to the Central Intelligence Agency. Most damning of all — Robertson did not travel with Meier on November 29 or fly with him to Calgary. Robertson and Buchmann were never together in Meier's hotel room on November 30, eavesdropping on Meier's phone calls, listening to him cackle at the news of Netter's death. Buchmann was 600 miles away at the time.

The diamond Meier took to Parford belonged to the President of Venezuela and was not looted from Netter's dead body. Nevertheless, its inclusion in the story, like Meier's presumed murderous relationship with McCrory, swelled out the case and made a neat bow out of the loose threads left by the discovery of an empty smuggler's pouch and a supposedly missing diamond ring.

Westphal was apparently believing everything Robertson told him. That he would place Robertson with Meier in those two crucial November days shows he didn't check Robertson's story to ensure its accuracy. It would take a sustained and dogged pursuit by Meier's lawyers, especially Gordon Dowding, a former Speaker of the British Columbia legislature, to track Robertson's movements. What he found cast a very different light on the whole business.

While Meier sat in prison, Westphal interviewed Froese and John Yee, who was president of TCV (Canada) in 1974. Both Froese and Yee later signed affidavits describing the interview. Froese said that prior to the meeting he received a telephone call from Westphal in which the officer said that Meier was guilty of murdering Netter and that there "was an open and shut case against him."[3] He told Froese he wanted his evidence to put Meier in the electric chair. Froese asked how he had reached his conclusion and Westphal said he had been collecting evidence on the murder for two and a half years.

According to Yee's affidavit, when he and Froese met Westphal, the officer began the proceedings by saying that Alfred Netter had been murdered and John Meier was responsible. This must have provoked some reaction from Froese, as Yee's affidavit notes the following exchange: "Westphal then said: 'You wouldn't want to see a murderer go free,' referring to John Meier and Abraham Froese said: 'Granted, but you'd want to be sure you got the right man.' The Corporal said he was 'positive.' He then said he had spoken to John Meier and that John was a 'liar.'"

Froese's affidavit says that at this point he asked Westphal why he believed Meier was responsible and Westphal replied that he received the information from "company president Robbie Robertson."

"I asked him: How would Robertson know? and he said because Robertson was with Meier at the Four Seasons Hotel in Calgary." This reply evidently caused some astonishment because both Froese and Yee knew Robertson was not with Meier in the Four Seasons in Calgary.

"I immediately pointed out," said Froese, "that three members of the Canadian TCV company — Gordon Nyen, Ross Chalifour and Danny Mah[4] — had been with John Meier, not Robert Robertson..."

Furthermore, they told Westphal that Robertson was in Los Angeles the week of the murder. Westphal was so startled that he spilt a drink over his shirt.

Froese asked if he knew who had murdered Netter and the officer replied: "Yes, we have him under wraps right now in L.A."

Froese then inquired about Robertson's current whereabouts and was told that he was being paid, had a new name and "reports in regularly."

Froese and Yee told Westphal they would be prepared to give evidence concerning Meier's and Robertson's movements as "it appeared that John Meier was being unjustly accused by Robert Robertson."

"Westphal told us 'I'll get back to you' but he never did," said Froese. "I further told Corporal Westphal that Robert Robertson had conceived a bitter grudge against John Meier over a manuscript and had circulated vindictive and libelous letters attacking Mr. Meier which I had kept. The Corporal was not interested in seeing them. "

While all this was going on Meier remained in Mission, his requests for release denied. There was a parole board hearing on December 17, 1980, but prison officials refused to let his lawyer attend.

In Los Angeles, the Deputy District Attorney, Michael Brenner, who was responsible for the prosecution, phoned the board to prevent his release on the grounds that California was moving to extradite Meier for murder and he should be kept in custody because he would present a danger to his witnesses if released.

Meier spent Christmas in prison. In many ways he would rather have spent it in Englewood. Since repatriation he had been more closely controlled than ever. To be so near and yet so far was worse than being a thousand miles away in the mountains of Colorado.

To get parole, Meier's lawyers appealed to the Supreme Court of British Columbia and a judge ordered the parole board to convene another hearing. On January 19, 1981, the board relented and gave him his freedom — such as it was.

Michael Brenner convened the grand jury in Los Angeles on February 2 to seek the indictment of Meier, Gordon A. Hazelwood and William Raymond McCrory for the murder of Alfred Wayne Netter. Knowing it was coming, Meier had attempted to have a lawyer appear on his behalf to place exculpatory evidence before the jurors.

Hameluck flew to Los Angeles with a lawyer to meet Brenner and Larry Leffler, the Beverly Hills police detective in charge of the investigation. Hameluck asked why Leffler had not talked to Siddle and Leffler said he had disappeared.[5]

When Hameluck protested Siddle had not disappeared but was working with him, Brenner said if that were the case they certainly would not be interested in talking to him. Ignoring the insult, Hameluck argued Netter's death had been investigated by Siddle and that nothing was found linking Meier or Hazelwood to it. Further, when Robertson began telling his revised story his allegations were discounted by the RCMP because they contradicted what he had said to Siddle in 1975. He then asked if they knew Robertson had been in Los Angeles during the week of Netter's murder and advised them not to proceed until Robertson's story had been thoroughly checked. However, Brenner said they had other evidence besides Robertson's.

Indeed they did. Although it wasn't disclosed to Hameluck, they had an ace in the hole, an intelligence agent named John Ross, who would put Meier together with McCrory in circumstances totally independent of Robertson's story. Brenner had never met this agent but he had little doubt he could be summoned in due course. His name was found in Meier's files in CLEU's Vancouver headquarters. The files contained pictures of Meier walking with McCrory and indicated that these pictures were the result of information provided by Ross. He appeared to be an informant with intimate knowledge of Meier's activities.

Hameluck then tried to persuade them that Westphal's information justifying the search warrant was fatally flawed in placing Robertson with Meier in the Calgary hotel when in fact Meier had been with three other men. Further, there were witnesses who had seen Robertson in a Beverly Hills hotel — the Beverly Wilshire — the evening of the murder at the very time he was claiming to be in Calgary. Brenner was uninterested. None of this was placed before the grand jury, nor was Meier allowed to send an advocate to attest to his innocence.

The twenty-three citizens who sat for three days listening to evidence could hardly have had a more confusing mass of information thrust upon them. Mixed in with witnesses such as Robertson and Liebich, and their recital of death threats from Meier, were a parade of insurance agents, bankers and lawyers, as the District Attorney's Office attempted to create a scenario of guilt which mingled high finance and hidden dealings with blunt and bloody murder. When evidence was lacking, speculation filled in the gaps.

Robertson's testimony was crucial. If Meier knew in advance of Netter's death then he could only have received such information from the murderer. But with no cross-examination in grand jury proceedings, Robertson's story was allowed to stand unchallenged.

The financial theory advanced to the grand jury was designed to show how Meier and Hazelwood gained control of TCV and maneuvered Netter and Liebich to the sidelines — but not before Meier loaned them $250,000, which Hazelwood secured by convincing Netter to agree to a $400,000 life insurance policy. No shred of evidence was presented to show Meier was the mysterious lender; it was just assumed he was. It was similarly assumed that he received the proceeds from the insurance settlement, again in the absence of any proof.

The jury was led to believe that after Meier and Hazelwood had everything in place, Netter was lured to Los Angeles and McCrory directed to his hotel room to commit murder. There was no evidence capable of identifying the lender, or the final recipient of the insurance proceeds, nor was there evidence showing McCrory was in Los Angeles that night.

Westphal's information had stated that Liebich was present when Meier threatened he could make a phone call to Los Angeles and have Netter killed. However, in front of the grand jury that dire threat lessened considerably.

"He was sort of laughing along with it, so I didn't really take it, you know, (as) serious or it didn't even, you know, make any impression on me. It was a sort of figure of speech more than anything else..." said Liebich.

Buchmann, the TCV salesman, said he had heard Meier talking big about having people fixed if they didn't perform, but put it down to "childish... silly remarks" and that "any man having real connections like that would certainly not be talking about it to anybody, least of all a relative stranger like myself."

Although pressed by Brenner, Buchmann could not remember any instance of Meier making threats against Netter. Most surprising of all, Buchmann said he was not in Calgary with Robertson on November 30, 1974, overhearing Meier laugh raucously at the news of Netter's death, as Robertson had said.

Robertson, when he arrived, made the most dramatic entrance of all. When summoned to the stand, Brenner interrupted and insisted that he be surrounded by U.S. Marshals. In he came, flanked by bodyguards, in a piece of high theatre staged no doubt to impress the jury with the possibility that even in the confines of the grand jury room he risked assassination.

His testimony began with an account of what he was doing during that fateful November. On or about November 14, he was staying at Meier's house but had been asked to find alternative accommodation, as Meier was expecting McCrory. He went and stayed with his friend Tony Parford, the jeweller.

Ignoring reports that Robertson was in and around Los Angeles the week of the murder, Brenner advanced the narrative to November 29 and asked if he were in Calgary on that date. Yes, said Robertson, he had arrived the day before and was sharing a double room with Meier in his hotel. Meier asked him to leave the hotel on the evening of the 29th so he could give his bed to one of the three investors.

This was a profound change from his statement to Westphal in which he made no mention of clearing out to make way for someone else. This amendment came after the police were told Robertson could not have been in Meier's hotel room on the night of the murder. Dropped by the wayside, too, is Buchmann.

Robertson said he returned to the suite Saturday morning, November 30, in time to hear Meier receive a phone call at about 12:30 p.m. He didn't repeat the story that Meier turned around and said Netter was dead before breaking into ghoulish laughter. All he said at this point was that Meier's foul mood changed to euphoria.

When a second call came, Robertson had picked up the receiver to discover Jennie Meier on the line. He gave the phone to Meier, who said "I know, I know" before hanging up. He then turned to Robertson and laughingly said: "Al Netter is dead... He got killed in Los Angeles... Jennie heard it on the radio..."

Asked if he could set a time to the call from Jennie, Robertson — whose ability to affix small details to immensely important events makes his testimony so fascinating — said that it came before 2 p.m. How did he know? Well, after the call, he and Meier had left the hotel and were walking in the street. He had slipped on some ice and "cut my thumb just a little, and it was at this time I noticed it was just on 2 o'clock in the afternoon."

The rest of Robertson's testimony compiled a collage of corruption and viciousness which depicted Meier hiring a contract killer, threatening Robertson's life if his book failed to portray him sympathetically, stealing bonds from him and committing such flamboyant crimes as forging a British passport application in the name of Ivor Robertson.

The story of Ivor and the passport was repeated. However, now Robertson elaborated upon the mysterious Ivor. He said he had never met this Ivor but knew him to be president of a company associated with TCV. He said Meier once told him that Ivor lived in Spain. But he had tricked Meier into providing a sample of his handwriting and by comparing this with a sample of Ivor Robertson's handwriting he could see it was one and the same.

Another circumstance which left a damaging impression with the grand jury concerned the timing of the news of Netter's death. Brenner contended that news of the death did not reach the public on November 30 — the day Meier received the call from his wife telling him of the murder.

The police officers involved in the initial investigation said they weren't involved in making press releases November 30 after finding the body, leaving the impression that it was likely the next day, December 1, before the news broke. The grand jury was left with the impression that unless the police officially released news of Netter's death it would not become public knowledge — a patently ridiculous argument, as any journalist knows.

To prevent the media from discovering and reporting on Netter's death, the police would have needed to undertake extraordinary measures. As there was nothing particularly extraordinary about this murder, there is absolutely no reason why they should have. It had all the trademarks of a sordid sex slaying involving nobody of consequence.

Radio scanners are standard equipment in newsrooms — photographers routinely equip their cars with them. Even supposing there was no over-the-air chatter from the police about a murder in the Beverly Hilton, newsrooms — especially radio station newsrooms — check hourly with police and emergency departments to see if anything worth reporting has happened. It would be almost routine for someone to mention there was a body found in a hotel and the death appeared suspicious. Even if the police had kept it quiet for some reason, there must have been dozens of people who knew someone had been murdered within a short time after the discovery of Netter's body. The news would spread like wildfire through the hotel.

How could the mob of police and coroner's staff who arrived to examine room 405 — to take photographs, check for fingerprints, remove the body — have accomplished all this without guests or staff being aware of it? How long would it have been before a call was made to a radio station or a newspaper? Netter was not found in a remote location; his body could hardly have been found in a more public place.

One person who remembered hearing a radio broadcast on November 30 was Siddle. The commercial radio was giving out details of the murder before the communication department's telex machine began chattering with a request from Beverly Hills police for RCMP assistance in notifying Netter's next of kin.

The murder itself was now being tarted up as a contract killing. McCrory was described to the grand jury as a man with a remarkable military background who served in Korea as a weapons expert. He had often operated behind the lines during commando operations. According to testimony of a former friend, McCrory loved guns and knives and was known to carry a long, thin, double-bladed stiletto. The medical evidence disclosed that the knife which killed Netter was broad and single bladed. Moreover, Netter was butchered. McCrory was an expert with a knife and had used this skill in killing enemy sentries with one thrust to the heart or throat.

Had Netter's death been at the hands of a paid assassin he would have been quickly shot or killed more cleanly. Why would the killer stay in the room with his victim, let him order him a meal when every second he remains in contact compromises his chance of a successful escape? The whole thing was just too laborious and the investigating officers never for a moment imagined, when they saw the scene, that it was the handiwork of a paid killer.

At the conclusion of this one-eyed evidence, the grand jury took about fifteen minutes to reach a decision. It ordered all the defendants to be indicted. Bail for Meier was set at $750,000; for the others, $500,000. Extradition proceedings to have Meier and Hazelwood delivered to California were set in motion and a warrant for McCrory's arrest was issued. Warned in advance of the grand jury's deliberations, McCrory vanished while his lawyers gathered evidence to show his whereabouts on a single day seven years before.

It would not be until August 28 — a Friday, the RCMP's favored day for arresting Meier — that he was seized and held on the extradition warrant.

Earlier that day he and Jimmy had gone to West Vancouver. Jimmy bought a whoopie cushion on their way out for lunch. On the way to a movie, Meier noticed he was being followed by two cars. He and his son went to a matinee, and then Meier drove home. Instead of going straight home, they stopped at a friend's house which the Meiers were keeping an eye on until she returned from holiday. Once inside, Jimmy, now nine, said he was sleepy and went for a nap.

Meier was in the living room when the phone rang. He picked it up. A woman said: "John Meier?"

"Yes."

"The house is surrounded. Come out with your hands up."

"Who is this?"

"It's the police. Put your hands over your head and come out."

"Are you joking?"

There was no answer so Meier placed the receiver on the table and went to the front door. He was in the act of turning the latch when he heard an awful crash — the sound of the back door being smashed off its hinges. Jimmy had leapt out of bed and was running towards him when two RCMP officers burst into the room, guns cocked and levelled at Meier's head. He pulled open the front door to find another man pointing a gun.

Father and son were taken to the Richmond RCMP detachment and placed in an interview room. One of the policemen had begun telling Meier he was being held on an extradition warrant, when Jimmy sat on the whoopie cushion. The policeman stopped and looked at the boy with disapproval. The boy looked at his father who grinned despite the obvious seriousness of their situation. The policeman cleared his throat and began to address Meier a second time. He had hardly begun again when Jimmy shuffled and the whoopie cushion sounded again.

"That's it," snapped the policeman. He hustled Meier away from the boy. Instead of moving him elsewhere, they put him in a squad car and removed him to Vancouver City Jail.

Meier had been free for barely seven months. By some cruel coincidence Jimmy had been present on every occasion of his father's arrests — Point Roberts, Australia, at home in Delta and now here.

Meier made legal history when he appeared with Hazelwood before Justice Samuel Toy of the B.C. Supreme Court on January 13, 1982. No Canadian had ever before been the subject of two separate extradition applications.

Before the hearing got underway, Leffler, the Beverly Hills detective in charge of the investigation, had come to Vancouver. Ostensibly he was on official business, but there appeared to be another dimension to his activities. A gossip columnist for the Vancouver Province, Joy Metcalfe, ran into the detective at the opening of a Vancouver restaurant. Metcalfe spotted Westphal, whom she knew, and during a conversation was introduced to Leffler. She was told that Leffler was an executive movie producer for Paul Pompain Productions in Hollywood. So what was Leffler doing in town, asked the inquisitive Metcalfe? The answer was carried in her column: "...doing research for a film to be built around John Meier, an aide to the late Howard Hughes and the fellow the U.S. government would like extradited from his home... Leffler will be here for a week..."

Such a blatant conflict of interest would be hard to match. Metcalfe, who erroneously tagged Leffler in her column as an ex-policeman, had casually uncovered his vested interest in Meier's extradition. No Meier, no movie — hardly a model of police objectivity. Following the publication of this tantalizing tidbit, Metcalfe ran into Westphal at another function. Westphal caught her in a painful headlock and told her she shouldn't be telling tales.

As in Meier's previous extradition, Robertson, Westphal and Halprin assumed their customary roles of accuser, investigator and prosecutor. The case presented to Toy followed the general lines of what had been offered to the grand jury. However, there was one important difference: Halprin would not call Robertson to testify. His evidence was entered by affidavit, thus preventing Meier's lawyer, David Crossin, from challenging Robertson's story or from attacking his credibility as Taylor had done four years before.[6]

Before the hearing began, Meier had called Boyce in London and told him that the perennial accusation of his forging a passport application was going to be used in this extradition as it had in the last. Did he have any advice? Boyce asked for a little time. When he called back, Boyce told him to get a handwriting expert to compare the passport application to Robertson's hand. Crossin needed the actual document and asked for it to be produced. The prosecution complained that it would have to be escorted by courier from England and the State of California wouldn't bear the cost. Crossin said the defense would pay to bring it but if Meier was not found to have forged it, the other side would have to pay. Accordingly, the passport application was delivered and given to a handwriting expert along with examples of Robertson's and Meier's writing.

Meanwhile, Halprin could no more make the financial wheeling and dealing of TCV comprehensible than could Brenner before him. At times, Toy — a notably sharp and nimble-minded judge — complained that he was getting a headache trying to follow Halprin's argument.

Neither Meier nor Hazelwood's lawyers put many obstacles in Halprin's way as he sought to tie it all together — likely from a belief that it was all totally incomprehensible and hardly worth arguing. There was simply no evidence that it was Meier's money which had financed TCV.

Brenner was called as an expert on U.S. law when Meier and Hazelwood's lawyers argued that neither could be extradited because the alleged offense occurred in Canada (and presumably should be tried in Canada). If the jurisdictions were reversed and a person in California had counselled someone to commit murder in Canada, that person could not be extradited under U.S. law. It was an argument Toy rejected but later he had second thoughts.

While waiting in the corridor Crossin asked Brenner why he was pressing so dreadful a case. Crossin would never forget Brenner's reply — "That may be, but as a result of Netter's death Meier may have gotten some money and all we will do in Los Angeles is get twelve niggers on the jury and talk about the money because if there is anything niggers understand, it's money and if Meier got money, those niggers will convict him of murder regardless of anything else." This so shocked Crossin that he wrote a letter to Meier's MP in Ottawa, Tom Siddon, complaining of the prosecution's tactics.[7]

(This racist observation seems to have been a standing joke among those prosecuting Meier. Jessie McNeil, the lawyer who later handled Meier's appeal against extradition, also complained to Siddon that the case against Meier was virtually nonexistent and that when she had met Halprin to try and get it halted he "smiled and said 'You never know what a jury of 12 black people in Los Angeles will do.'")

To link Meier, Hazelwood and the supposed murderer, McCrory, Halprin produced various witnesses who remembered seeing a large bulky man — one described him as over six feet tall and close to 200 pounds — either with Meier or outside Hazelwood's office, whom they readily identified from photographs as McCrory. McCrory was described as a shade smaller than Meier. Halprin said that Robertson's affidavit described how he was introduced to a person whose size would conform to the coroner's description of Netter's assailant — a large, powerfully built man.

None of this described McCrory. McCrory is shorter than average, standing only five feet six inches. And he is wiry, not bulky. The person being described was not McCrory but Ed Fleming, a local businessman and pilot who often accompanied Meier in Vancouver. Fleming was with Meier in Tonga and visited him in Australia when he was on the run from the police. The only thing Fleming and McCrory had in common was that they both looked tough and undoubtedly were.

From Westphal's testimony some startling facts emerged. His original search warrant had been drawn up using Robertson's unverified account of his movements. This uncritical acceptance of Robertson's statements by the RCMP and the Beverly Hills police — regardless of the startling amendments he made as he went along — is the most alarming aspect of the whole affair. Westphal admitted that he had never spoken to Buchmann and when asked why, said he couldn't find him — an interesting admission from someone with all the vast resources of the RCMP at his disposal. Then he admitted that while Robertson was claiming to be in Calgary on the night of the murder there was absolutely nothing to corroborate this. Crossin asked where Robertson said he had been that night:

"He said he went out and got drunk, or had been drinking quite heavily, and met up with a friend and spent the night with a friend at his place."

"And then you contacted the friend?"

"Well, he didn't recall who the friend was, sir."

"He didn't recall who the friend was? Did he recall where the friend lived?"

"He did not, sir."

The man who could remember the precise time he fell and cut his hand on Nov. 30, 1974, could not recall the name of the friend with whom he had spent the previous evening and most of that morning. Westphal admitted he was unable to corroborate Robertson's account of his whereabouts not only on the night Netter was murdered but for the three days preceding it.

Given Robertson's conflicting statements, had he attempted to find out where Robertson had been from November 26 onwards?

"No, I — as far as I'm concerned, he was — he told me that he had been in California prior to the 28th and he returned to Vancouver and on to Calgary. He didn't have anything to — any receipts again, airline receipts or anything to show me that he had been in California..."

"He had nothing to indicate he was in California?"

"Nothing."

"...have you anything to indicate he took a flight from Vancouver to Calgary on the 28th?"

"I have nothing, sir, no."

Crossin asked if Robertson had been asked if he had been in contact with Netter during the time he was in Los Angeles.

"I think that question was put to him and he replied 'No.'"

Meier's lawyer wanted to know, in view of Robertson's revised statements, if Westphal had attempted to find out for himself if Robertson had met Netter in California or for that matter what he was doing there.

Westphal said that he was no longer active in the investigation since the grand jury verdict and he didn't have access to Robertson. "I don't know where he is and it would be very hard for me to question him on his affidavit, sir."

Next came the matter of the hotel records for the time Meier stayed at the Four Seasons Hotel in Calgary. These records would have been invaluable in comparing Robertson's story with Meier's. Westphal said the hotel didn't keep records longer than two years and by the time he got around to seeking them, they had been destroyed.

However, lawyer Gordon Dowding, who had worked on Meier's case for months, had also gone hunting for these records. In an affidavit filed after hearing Westphal's testimony Dowding said in August, 1981 he went to Calgary and questioned a hotel employee about the records and was told that the hotel kept records not for two years but for seven.

The hotel's November 1974 records had been destroyed in March of 1981. When Westphal began his investigation in April 1978, those records, according to what Dowding said, would have been available to him then and for three years afterward. They would have still been there when Froese startled him in October of 1980 with the news that Robertson was not with Meier in Calgary on the night of the murder.

Dowding returned to the hotel in August 1982 and spoke to another employee who said that the hotel kept a microfilm copy of guest transactions including telephone calls. Dowding was delighted. The employee went off to retrieve the records for the week of November 24, 1974, "and returned to tell me in bewilderment that the only microfilm record missing in the files was for that period from November 24 to December 1, 1974."

When Crossin asked Westphal if he had attempted to secure hotel records showing that Meier and Robertson stayed in Edmonton on November 30 after driving there from Calgary, Westphal said he had taken Robertson's word for it that he and Meier had flown out that day for England.

How that flight can be reconciled with testimony from witnesses who said Meier called them at various times that evening to talk about Netter, is beyond imagination. Meier would have been in the air somewhere between Edmonton and London when those calls were made. The police interview shows Robertson didn't say he flew out right away. Robertson, in the extradition hearings affidavit, said he stayed over in Edmonton on the night of November 30. He just didn't say where. Clearly the police knew of this vital stopover. They did not check where Meier and Robertson stayed that night so they could seize hotel and telephone records. It was a stunning lapse in police procedure.

Meier was at the Sheraton Caravan with Robertson, where he received a call from Jennie with the news of Netter's death. This call would have been made hours after Netter's body was discovered as Meier didn't check in until well into the evening. Once he received the call he began calling others in the company — one of those calls being made to Buchmann in the early hours of December first, when Westphal had Meier on a plane to England.

But Robertson said that Meier received the incriminating call in the Calgary Four Seasons before they left for Edmonton. The long distance records of Meier's home phone, which the authorities seized but never produced, would have settled this question.

Westphal's suppositions aside, there is no doubt where Meier and Robertson were that night. Dowding obtained records from the Caravan showing Meier stayed there November 30 and left December first. There were other records concerning a guest, a Mr. Robertson — supposedly of Geneva, Switzerland — and a phone call he made which even the most inexperienced police officer would have wanted to pursue.

As Westphal had the pair leaving Edmonton for England, he couldn't be expected to have discovered that a Mr. Robertson had phoned the Beverly Wilshire Hotel hours after Netter's body was discovered. Nor could he be expected to tax his brain for an explanation as to what it might suggest, such as the possibility — raised by Meier's lawyers — that Robertson had left the Beverly Wilshire in such a hurry that he had not checked out and was attempting to rectify the matter by telephone.

Crossin only called two witnesses for the defense, a handwriting expert and Abe Froese, who had little to say except that Meier and Netter seemed to have had an amicable relationship. As Boyce predicted, the handwriting on the Ivor Robertson passport was found to be Robertson's. Meier's lawyers demanded that the State of California pay up.

Hazelwood gave evidence on his own behalf and denied any part in scheming to murder Netter, that he had ever met McCrory or that he was gleeful at making $400,000 from Netter's death.

Reporters covering the trial usually dozed off when the evidence dealt with money being moved here and there, but Hazelwood woke them up with his tale of how Robertson confessed to murdering Netter. Hazelwood recounted how Robertson became appointed president of TCV to replace Netter after his perjury conviction and how he maintained an office in the same building as Hazelwood. Around June 1975, a short time after Netter's insurance money had been converted into B.C. Hydro bonds, Hazelwood said he noticed Robertson was showing the effects of alcohol when he came to work. He decided to have a word with him.

"When Mr. Robertson came in I told him I wanted to speak to him privately," said Hazelwood, "and he ushered me into his private office and asked me what it was about." He confronted Robertson with his excessive drinking, which Robertson denied until Hazelwood upbraided him for breathing whisky fumes on him as they spoke.

"He looked at me and he started to tremble and finally he said: 'You had better sit down.'"

Hazelwood said he would rather stand but Robertson said he had better be seated.

"So I sat down in the client chair... and he sat on the desk and started talking... He said, 'I can't sleep at nights.' I asked him why. He said... 'Netter put up a hell of a fight.' And I said how do you know? I thought you were in Calgary at the time? And he said 'I wasn't. I was in Los Angeles. I was there.'"

"I said tell me more about it and he said 'It's all Meier's fault.' And I said how is that? And Mr. Robertson said: 'Meier introduced me to Netter and I got involved with Netter and that is how it all came about.' I said did Mr. Meier have anything to do with Mr. Netter's death and he said 'No' but he says: 'I'm going to get Meier'" Hazelwood then described a rambling monologue in which Robertson told him that the pen was mightier than the sword and he was keeping notes of what Meier was doing and would concoct a scenario implicating Meier in the killing if it were the last thing he did.

Returning to the topic of Netter's murder, Hazelwood asked for more information. Robertson replied that he was a trained killer who had worked with British Naval Intelligence. While reporters in the courtroom struggled to keep up with this amazing testimony, Hazelwood recounted how Robertson had reached into his pocket and pulled out a garrote.

"It was a device that looks a little bit like a small tape measure and it had a little — it was silver with a silver cross on it and he pulled it out and it made a little zinging sound. I said what's that? And he said: 'This is what we use. It's a stainless steel thread and we just get behind somebody and go.'" and Hazelwood mimicked the gurgling noises of one being choked. Robertson threatened Hazelwood with death if he ever repeated the story, saying he had friends in the Mafia.

Hazelwood said that he had not told anyone the story. He had not told Meier because Meier was overly talkative and he was afraid it would get back to Robertson who might have been tempted to carry out his threats. He had considered giving Leffler and Westphal the information when they interviewed him in 1980 but he never quite got round to it. No one asked if he kept quiet to prevent London Life from rushing back to recover its $400,000.

In his final argument Crossin said there were no facts to support allegations that Meier had counselled anyone to murder Netter nor that he had any part in having Netter insured. Like Hazelwood's lawyer, he argued that the State of California had no jurisdiction to extradite Meier because he was in Canada at the time of the crime.

On March 1, Toy rendered judgment. Firstly, he rejected arguments that the conspiracy to murder Netter was not an extraditable offense. Turning to the evidence, Toy said it was not his function to assess credibility of witnesses or weigh evidence. "It matters not if I categorized Robert Robertson's deposition evidence as perjured or grossly misleading... it matters not if I consider Robert Robertson's deposition false in any particular, mistaken or true," said Toy.

He said that he had been invited by the defendants' counsel to penalize the State of California by refusing to commit because they were attempting to "rely on the evidence of a man who may have given false testimony or left a false impression."

"The state, when it moves in to prosecute those who have allegedly committed crimes, does not have the luxury of picking and choosing their witnesses. The state may have to rely on drunks, prostitutes, criminals, perjurers, paid informers as well as solid citizens," said Toy.

However, dealing with Hazelwood first, he said there was not sufficient evidence to show he was connected with the murder and ordered his release.

While there were just as many innocent as guilty explanations for

Meier's financial involvement in TCV, there was an added dimension to the case against Meier which was not present in that brought against Hazelwood, said Toy.

The difference was Robertson's story of Meier being involved with McCrory, of Robertson being present in the Four Seasons listening to Meier repeat "I know, I know," upon being told by his wife that Netter was dead, and the threats Meier had made against his life. If a jury accepted Robertson's evidence it could infer that Meier was guilty and so Toy ordered his extradition.

That afternoon Meier was taken to Oakalla, the provincial prison in British Columbia which has since been demolished. He remained in that old and uncomfortable jail from March first until August 20, when he was released on $150,000 surety pending an appeal against Toy's decision to the Federal Court of Appeal. Then California dismissed all the charges against McCrory. Trying to put the best possible face on it, Brenner, in a letter to McCrory's lawyer Earl Boyd, said the decision was due to "our re-evaluation of the evidence on which this indictment was based."

It was a re-evaluation which became necessary when McCrory proved he was nowhere near Beverly Hills on November 29, 1974. Boyd, who had travelled up to see Meier, had told him this much. When Meier asked where McCrory was, Boyd had said that was "too sensitive" to discuss. Meier took this as indicating McCrory was engaged in CIA business.

With Hazelwood and now McCrory gone, Meier stood alone. The marvelous conspiracy, so deftly crafted by the prosecuting authorities — eager to advance every detail of Robertson's recollections — was in tatters. But it had not unravelled to the point that Brenner was about to rethink the case against Meier.

Justice Toy, however, was having second thoughts. On December 1, in a remarkable letter to Justice Minister, Mark MacGuigan, Toy said he might have erred in ordering Meier's extradition by failing to accept the contention that the crime was non-extraditable (as Meier's lawyers had argued from the beginning). The judge said he was basing this on the outcome of an extradition case in Quebec in which the same principles were argued.

"If the *obiter dictum* (opinion) in that judgment accurately reflects the law in this country, the conclusion I arrived at, which was adverse to the interest of John Herbert Meier, was incorrect," wrote the judge with great humility.

His petition to the government was made to no avail. The Canadian government clearly had had enough of John Meier. The Liberal Party's amateur attempt to investigate CIA operations against leading party members during 1976 had been exposed some months before while Meier was in Oakalla.

Opposition MPs armed with details had asked embarrassing questions in the House. What had the CIA been up to in Canada? Had it been engaged in supporting political parties? Why had the Liberals attempted to spy on the agency without calling on the RCMP for help? Had the RCMP and the Security Service been penetrated by the CIA?

NDP member of parliament Svend Robinson, who had been fed the details by Meier's lawyer Dowding, wanted Meier to be brought before the Commons Justice Committee to testify. Robinson went as far as to claim he could produce five RCMP security officers who would give details of CIA intrusion into Canadian affairs and institutions. He claimed Meier would provide details of the CIA paying to elect two provincial politicians in British Columbia and of interfering in elections within the ever volatile province of Quebec.

Not surprisingly, Meier was never invited to appear in Ottawa. The same Canadian government that wanted Meier's information so desperately in 1976, now saw that it was in its interests to suppress the whole matter.

21

IN SEARCH OF JUSTICE

A cavalcade of police cars roared up to the portals of the Los Angeles County Jail late in the evening of December 20, 1983, bulging with riflemen drawn from the city's police elite.

Anyone who watched this parade tear through Los Angeles, heralded as it went by sirens wailing and its passage splashed with the garish flashing lights of a dozen patrol cars, might have been excused for thinking some awful disaster was taking place.

It was only John Meier's long-awaited arrival. After 28 months he had finally been extradited. His escort, large enough to have fought a battalion of terrorists, was simply taking him from the airport to the jail. Had Meier been a *boss of bosses* no doubt he would have felt complimented by the attention. As things stood, he was terrified by the speed at which they all roared through the city.

The Supreme Court of Canada refused to hear an appeal against extradition on December 6, 1983. The Justice Minister signed the extradition papers a week later and five days before Christmas — with no warning to his family — Meier was told to collect his belongings for the journey south. A lifelong diarist, Meier kept a record of what happened:

December 20: Had an interview with CKVU television and (the reporter) tells me that everyone in the media seems to know I am leaving on CP Air at 7:30 p.m. tonight for Los Angeles. It's unbelievable to me that this could be so. My poor wife had been calling Ottawa everyday to speak to someone at the department of justice. As of today she has not been told that I am to leave soon. In fact, only yesterday did one of my attorneys find out that an extradition order was signed last Thursday by the minister of justice. This was done after being told for the past year and a half by the minister that he would give myself and others a chance to present new facts to him or evidence that showed the reason behind the extradition was political in nature. It is obvious that I was lied to by the minister. My lawyer Jessie MacNeil is still waiting for an answer to her telegram of two weeks ago asking when she could have a meeting with the minister.

After my interview with CKVU I was asked by a guard to step into another room before my interview with Alyn Edwards of BCTV. I was told they had received word I was to leave at 11:30 a.m. which was in another 15 minutes. I could have my interview but would be unable to telephone my lawyer and my family to say goodbye. I stood there stunned. I planned to have my wife and children come to see me today. Christmas is coming and I still did not believe they would be cruel enough to send me away from my family in so heartless a fashion.

After my interview a dozen guards and inmates offered to call my family for me. I was led to a room to meet with Larry Leffler of the Beverly Hills police and a Lou who never gave me his name. Also there was Bill Halprin, the Canadian justice department representative and an RCMP officer who was to drive us to the airport and six representatives of the remand center where I was staying.

All of the remand center personnel shook my hand and wished me well. Halprin sneered and said "Well, Meier another Christian goes to the lions." I was then handcuffed and led to the car in the garage...

He was driven from the Vancouver city jail to an RCMP detachment near Vancouver airport, pursued by reporters and photographers. The RCMP tried to shake off the pursuers by weaving up and down alleys and side streets. When they left that evening for the airport they were again followed by journalists while three RCMP cars ran interference. As they were weaving in and out of traffic, Meier asked why the RCMP were so concerned about a couple of reporters.

Leffler's answer was: "You never know what they'll do." I started to think I was going stupid. What the hell could they do? I could see some reporter paid $100 a week being gunned down by the RCMP because he was trying to get a story.

The persistent reporter was Alyn Edwards, who subsequently caused consternation by trying to board Meier's flight with a cameraman. In Leffler's haste to avoid Edwards, Meier found himself being rushed onto the airplane where he collided with a stewardess who mistook him for the police and asked what she should do next. Meier says.

I lifted up my arms to show her my handcuffs and tried to point behind me to the U.S. agents who looked like a couple of hoods from New York and told her I was the victim — she needed to talk to them.... They then stood in the aisle looking for Edwards and frantically tried to decide if I should be put in the food galley or the toilet so that Edwards would not film me. The doors shut without Edwards and they were ecstatic...

At 10 p.m. we landed at Los Angeles. I can now relax, I thought, but as the plane stopped I looked out of the window and there sat at least a dozen police cars and at least 30 policemen with automatic rifles at the ready. The pilot asked everyone to remain seated. The two agents pulled me up and shoved me down the aisle and down the steps from the plane. An officer yelled from behind a car "in here" and we ran 50 feet and I was shoved into the back seat. In ten seconds we were off, sirens blaring, lights blazing. Leffler said: "Welcome to L.A. How do you like our SWAT team." I sat there hoping I wouldn't have a heart attack. What normally takes an hour to drive from the airport to Los Angeles County Jail took us 25 minutes. We never stopped for a light. I am convinced the people we almost drove off the road thought Los Angeles was under attack or some major catastrophe had occurred. I am impressed by how the SWAT team works but my God, can't anyone see what this is — it's a Hollywood movie.

Sunday, December 25. It's Christmas and I miss my wife and four children so much. I am tired and ill. There is an old proverb that I'll never forget — to cause anxiety is the secret of the torturer. This is all the U.S. has to do to its political prisoners. At 50 years old and under pressure since 1970, how much more can my family or I take?

Upon arrival here I was put in what they call the High Power Section, in other words maximum security. In my section are 16 cells. I am in a cell with a metal bunk that sits four feet off the floor and I have about four by five feet to walk around in. The cell is 10 feet high and the neon lights stay on all night. Outside the cell bars, five feet from my cell, is a one-way mirror going the length of the 16 cells. Every so often employees bring their family and friends in to see the prisoners. The inmates feel like animals on display in a zoo. It's depressing when you can't even relax going to the toilet. There's no privacy.

When I came here I had no money. Leffler gave me $1 to spend. The problem is you even have to buy your own soap, you get absolutely nothing. Every day we are allowed out of our cells to take a shower for 10 minutes. We get no sun, no air and no exercise. I had to have my attorney Regis Possino get a court order so that I am able to at least get my medicine.[1]

On December 21 one of the inmates hanged himself. There is no way anyone on the outside can understand how inhumane a place this is. Anyway last night on Christmas Eve we all received a present from the Sheriff, Sherman Block, along with a card that said no public funds were used to purchase the gift. We received an apple, an orange, three walnuts and 20 candies. We have no TV or radio or newspapers. I have no idea what is going on in the outside world. I have tried to get someone from the Canadian consulate to see me but I was told that they are too busy. I just hope and pray that somewhere in the Canadian government is someone who has compassion for a Canadian citizen and his family who are suffering so undeservedly...

Meier was not as alone as he imagined. His local Member of Parliament, Tom Siddon, was not convinced of Meier's guilt and championed his cause. Through Siddon, the Canadian government was prodded to approach the U.S. authorities and ask that Meier's health not be allowed to deteriorate.

Meanwhile, Brenner, in an interview with the *Vancouver Sun* shortly after Meier's arraignment in Los Angeles, did not sound overconfident about his chances of having Meier convicted. "Maybe we'll win, maybe we'll lose. I'm not saying it's a deadbang thing," said Brenner. "After we've presented the evidence I don't think anyone's going to say he didn't do it. But there's a question of being able to prove it beyond a reasonable doubt. I can see some of the jury coming out saying we know he did it but maybe there's not enough proof..."

Meier's grand arrival had impressed even the prison's hardcases, those who wore the red wrist bracelets marking them as the most dangerous people in the institution. Sporting his own red bracelet, Meier was placed in the high power unit, which contained an assortment of murderous psychopaths such as Angelo Buono, the Hillside Strangler, some lesser known mass murderers, an Armenian who had shot and killed a Turkish diplomat and Jamie Villa, a professional killer considered one of the most dangerous men in the United States.

At the end of January 1984, Meier appeared in court seeking bail. His friends and relatives from the Los Angeles area, including Schrade and Hargan, offered their homes and property as surety. But Leffler told the judge that Meier had millions of dollars stashed away in Europe, had purchased valuable paintings as recently as 1981 and owned property in the Canary Islands, all of which came as a great surprise to Meier.

Halprin told the judge that Meier had used excuses such as poor health to delay extradition proceedings in Canada, had fired lawyers to accomplish the same purpose and that if he were granted bail and fled to Canada, the extradition processes would have to start all over and might take years.

The judge denied bail. Meier's lawyer wrote an angry letter to Ottawa asking what business Halprin had giving such evidence. Meier was returned to L.A. County and the daily drudgery and haphazard violence of prison life. Later the prison administration took off his red bracelet and moved him from maximum security to the general population.

Dear Jennie:

It's Tuesday (February 7)... Regis (Possino) came today. He looked totally dejected. It seems to me I always have to spend my time cheering up my lawyers. Since I have no money I have to do most of the legal planning myself. The problem with this case is the serious consequences if you plan wrong. Anyway it seems the prosecutor asked Regis if I would plead to a lesser charge and get six years. Then I could get out in four. Would you believe it? But that is how they convict an awful lot of innocent people. Some people get tired of fighting. And if you face life without parole or have to do 20 years, four years look good, even if you are not guilty. This is what they call justice...

Now after telling you all that, I want to repeat what I have told you before. I am not going to let myself get so depressed I am going to give up. Every time I get a setback obviously I am upset but then I pull myself together and go on. What grieves me is that my problems cause so much anxiety to my family... it would make me feel better if I thought you were thinking of your own futures more...

Saturday (February 25) I'm in the medical pill unit. There are about 300 inmates in this unit but there is no treatment on weekends. Unit 2400 is next to us with another 300 inmates. We line up for our medication at 9 a.m. They take us into the day room where we are given a paper cup. There are benches all around the room but no one is allowed to sit down. If you are very sick you are in trouble because you have to stand in line. If you talk in line a guard, who carries a flashlight, shines the light on you. If he wants, which is 50 percent of the time, he drags you out of line and has another guard handcuff you. Then they put your face against the wall and beat you up. The other inmates say nothing...

March 10. A big day for me today. At 2 p.m. they took everyone to one of the two yards on the roof. They marched us up to the roof and I was so excited I couldn't wait to get there. When we got there I had to squint. The sun was out and there was a slight breeze. I walked to a corner of the roof and just sat there and closed my eyes. I was elated. I hadn't been in the sun like that since December. I tried to think I was home again, sitting on our back upstairs patio...

Monday (March 19) the start of another letter to you. I just returned to my cell from breakfast. Angry as usual. I looked at the clock on the wall and saw that we had exactly five minutes to eat. You see inmates eating from their tray as they are leaving their table to dump the leftovers in garbage cans. Then they walk back to their cells still chewing food. Now I realize why we are so hungry at night. We eat dinner at 3:45 p.m. and by seven o'clock you are starving. Most riots in prison are because of food and I can see why...

...The demeaning things that happen here everyday astound me. As we all walked to breakfast this morning — all lined up with our right shoulders to the wall — there sat an inmate on the floor in front of the chow hall cutting his toe nails with a nail clipper. One guard was standing over him with the toe nail clippings scattered at his feet. Last week I asked a guard if I could cut my toe nails as they have grown so long in the past four months that they bother me when I have my shoes on. I was told the only way was to ask the deputy in the control booth outside the chow hall and if he wants to he will let you have nail clippers. But you must sit in the hallway and do it so that they can keep an eye on you. I declined. There is no way I'm going to let the system degrade me more than I have to. I'll let my nails break off by themselves...

Another thing you see a lot of is inmates selling various items. Up and down the freeway they come at all hours yelling such things as "Milky Ways on the line, a dollar a holler" or "Short dogs on the line, name your price." Short dogs is enough coffee to make two cups. You are not permitted to have any food or drink in your cell but inmates buy tin cans and burn paper or parts of their blankets to cook up a cup of coffee. If you get caught they charge you. One trusty is now yelling "flying A's fifty cents." These are pills with an A on them that are used for inmates who get seizures. One inmate asks if they would get rid of his headache and the trusty selling them says they are great for headaches. The other night an inmate was selling nitros[2] and saying they had codeine in them...

April 5: I have been here since December and am still struck by the severity of the system. I feel I am watching a play and that it is not real. The appalling scene of an inmate standing naked in the hall being searched because of trying to sneak a slice of bread out of the mess hall, a guard five feet tall standing on a bench in the pill room yelling that if anyone is caught talking no one will get their medication, another guard telling a line of inmates, some of them waiting days on and off, that there will be no telephone calls while he's on duty because all they wanted to do was call their whores.

The guards open the cells yell chow, pill-call or visits and give you 10-to-15 seconds to jump out of bed, get dressed and get out the cell before he closes it. You see inmates stuck inside their cells or standing outside half awake with clothes or shoes in their hands. At times an inmate gets stuck in the cell door and pulls a shoulder or breaks an arm or leg. It goes on daily...

April 9. Last night they put a new inmate in my cell. His name is Floyd Lokken. He is nearly 70 — looks 90 — weighs 90 pounds, has had a stroke, has only a third of his stomach, limps because of a broken leg, is senile and has various other ailments. His wife is ill and on a portable lung machine.

He was driving home and was stopped by the police. They asked him to get out of the car and saw that he couldn't walk too well so they charged him with drunk driving and he was sentenced to six months.

In here he is not going to get the medical treatment he needs. They put him on a top bunk. This means I have to help him get up and down as I did in the middle of the night and this morning and assist him getting around as he is completely lost in here...

I took over taking care of Lokken as of yesterday (April 10). He is senile and couldn't find his way to the chow hall, gets lost when he has to get his medication, forgets our cell number, doesn't know why he's here or when he will get out. He gets his medication four times a day and five minutes after taking it he forgets. I have to keep track of his medication and listen all the time in case they call out his name. I even have to roll cigarettes for him and tell him when to sit down, stand up or even sleep.

...Regis came in today (April 12) and I finally got a chance to discuss strategy with him. Brenner told him that since I had been in jail so long it would be best if we hurry and get this case over with. He knows that I have not had a chance to properly prepare a defense. He has had his shot. It's my turn next. You and the children just have to hang in there. I'll be alright.

I was called out again to meet two FBI agents. They were interested in Brenner and that mining company.[3] In return, they said that they would see that I got more freedom — roof, stores etc. — At this moment it is very difficult to evaluate the situation.

...Old Floyd came back again. He was taken to another unit and put in a cell with five blacks. Within five minutes he was robbed of his pillow, his towel, and two pairs of glasses. They had to bring him back...

Today, (April 21) the head trusty was able to get one of the deputies to approve my working with him. He is going to be moving to another unit and he got permission to break me in. There are over 50 requests from other inmates in the unit to become trusty. There are many advantages including access to phones without permission, you can stay out of your cell from 6 a.m. to 10 p.m., stores three times a week to buy newspapers and candy, showers every day and clean clothes every week...

May 8. I don't think a day goes by here that I don't shake my head. This afternoon an inmate, Howard Williams, started to complain that he was very ill and felt he was going to have a heart attack or seizure. Deputy Delhauer did the right thing and asked him to sit down until he felt better.

A few minutes later he was called away then the inmate fell over on his side. As I got up to walk over to him a deputy from another area happened to come in and told me to stand back. All of a sudden the inmate went into a violent seizure. As his body shook and his head kept smashing on the floor the deputy started laughing and said: "That should knock some sense into him." Other inmates, seeing I was being blocked by the deputy ran past us to try and hold Williams down. Deputy Vogel came running up and, seeing what was happening, ran to the telephone to call the clinic. It took them 15 minutes to respond. When they arrived the deputy who was laughing said: "don't worry he's only faking it, and if he isn't it was a good show. I've had a dull day."

Two nurses and a medic tried for another 10 minutes to form a chair device into a stretcher. They then tried repeatedly to put him on this contraption. Since he was having convulsions they kept dropping him again and again on to the floor which he struck with his head. An inmate suggested they put something in his mouth so that he didn't bite his tongue which someone did. I went and got a blanket and suggested that he be carried to the hospital this way. Four inmates then carried him away...

May 14. Melvin Jones died today. Melvin was a black man in his early fifties and a friend of mine. He complained of sharp chest pains for an hour but was told that he had to wait for pill call. At pill call he collapsed. Two nurses and a deputy were there at the time. The nurses claimed that they were busy and had to continue handing out pills to the other inmates. The deputy did nothing for five minutes and then decided to call the clinic. When the medical team finally arrived, Melvin was dead.

On May 19 the guards arrived, handcuffed Meier and took him back to the high power unit. They cut off his white bracelet and fastened on the red band. He would find out later that an informer had told guards that he was planning to escape. He was returned to his old unit once the authorities determined the report was untrue.

Monday (May 28). Riot day today. Some time in the morning one of the members of a black gang had a fracas with a few guards. At evening chow all hell broke loose with module 4800 in the chow hall. Over a hundred black inmates were involved in a battle with deputies armed with riot guns. Many on both sides were hurt. The complete jail went into lock-down. At about 8 p.m. myself and another trusty were called out to roll a stretcher with another inmate on it to the hospital on the first floor. It looked like a battle station with injured inmates and deputies lying around. It is hot in here. The summer will be a nightmare.

June 17. Had another altercation today. I was standing with my check-in board in my hand when an inmate came by me on his way to his cell. As he passed me he whirled and thrust something at me. Instinctively I put up my left hand and got stuck in the web of my palm, near my thumb, with a sharpened pencil. I dropped the board and hit him on the left side of the temple. After he fell another inmate and I dragged him by his feet and left him outside his cell.

It was then I noticed that I had blood all over me (mine). I hope I got all the lead out. I cleaned out the cut as best I could but it is still sore. I'm getting too old for this.

June 18. My hand is killing me today and the nurse refused to let me go to the doctor although you can see the infection spreading up my arm... Deputy Reedy asked me how I was and I told him I'd been accidentally poked with a pencil... At 9 p.m. the deputy personally took me over to the clinic. A nurse bled the cut and then cleaned it. I didn't even cry. She didn't believe how brave I was until I told her I was a Canadian...

June 22. I received the Father's Day card today with the picture of you and the kids. You all look so good that I want to come home today. I have showed the photos to all the inmates. Since all 500 of them have to go past me at least once a day they have no choice. I have had quite a lot of marriage offers for Jeannie, Joey, and yourself. I also had a dozen for Johnny, six for Jimmy and one for Hanna (their dog)...

Finally, after a frustrating summer of delays, Meier appeared in Los Angeles Municipal Court on August 27 for the commencement of his preliminary hearing. He went in a great state of expectation. The district attorney's office couldn't hide Robertson any more. Robertson's varied and conflicting stories had been presented without question to the grand jury and to the Canadian courts. Now, Meier's lawyers would be all over him.

Meier's defense was left largely in the hands of an ex-policeman, Earl Durham, as Regis Possino was facing disbarment for possession of drugs. Meier had been warned all summer that Possino's ability to defend him was compromised as the judges were aware of his problems. Fortunately, Durham, a San Diego lawyer, agreed to represent him. Brenner was recovering from surgery so Deputy District Attorneys, Robert Schirn and Michael Tranbarger handled the prosecution. The presiding judge was Marion L. Obera.

For the preliminary hearing, Durham selected two main targets: Robertson, naturally, and the police's handling of the murder scene, which he believed was mismanaged.

The murder investigation had been conducted by Detective Bruce Campbell who had since retired. Campbell testified that he was at home on November 30 when alerted to the murder. It took him an hour and a half to drive to the hotel and he arrived to find a small crowd of officers in Netter's room surrounding the corpse. Found near a small desk was a torn piece of paper with the number of the Four Seasons Hotel in Calgary written on it.

Campbell was the head of the homicide team. When Durham began questioning his experience, Judge Obera called him to the bench and asked what he was doing.

"It's the theory of the defense that this crime was not investigated," Durham answered. "That is the very reason for the indictment in this case."

Durham asked Campbell if he had found any bloody footprints on the carpeting.

"It occurs to me there were some bloody footprints."

Looking at the photographs, Durham said that Netter was barefooted.

"Were any of those footprints photographed?"

"I don't recall... specific photographs of footprints although I believe there are indications in these photographs of possible footprints although on the carpeting it is a little hard to tell." Did the police technicians who checked the apartment for fingerprints examine the bathroom floor for footprints? Campbell said he didn't know.

"Officer Campbell, prior to being assigned to homicide were you given any special training relative to homicide investigation?"

"Well, I attended many seminars and schools given by police departments, part of which was homicide investigation... but not a specific school or specific training for that."

After having Campbell admit he could not name any manual he had read concerning the techniques of murder investigation, Durham asked: "This had all the earmarks of a homosexual murder, did it not?"

"Yes."

He asked if the police had conducted an investigation of the massage parlors that were circled on the newspaper found in the bathroom. Campbell said he contacted the massage parlors but they were uncooperative.

Did he discover if any of the massage parlors employed males? The operators would not tell him, he said.

Was Netter's body checked for signs of sexual activity? Was an anal swab taken? Oral or penile swabs?

"No," said Campbell.

"Why not?"

"Because I had no reason to."

"Did you believe this was a sex related killing?"

"That was one aspect of the investigation I was pursuing."

As there was evidence of a fight, did Campbell take a file and clean Netter's nails to see if any material could be retrieved? Campbell didn't recall that being done.

"That would be standard operating procedure in an investigation of this type would it not?"

"Well, not necessarily. No."

"And (knowing there had been) a struggle with an unknown assailant, you wouldn't take a steel file and clean the fingernails of the decedent?"

"I wouldn't."

"Is that your testimony?" asked an astonished Durham.

Campbell said nothing.

Turning to the clothes and bed linen, Durham said it "would be standard operating procedure in a scene such as this... to check the shorts and bed linen for semen, would it not?"

"Not necessarily."

Well then, he would have asked the coroner's office to check if there was any semen reposing in the body would he not?

Campbell again said no, he hadn't done this.

With regard to the amount of blood spilled and the likelihood that some had spurted onto Netter's murderer, was the bathroom checked for signs of blood?

"I checked it visually. I looked around."

"Are you familiar with the benzene test?"

"No."

Durham's mouth fell open: "You don't know what benzene is used for in homicide investigations?"

"No, I don't." (Benzene is used to discover traces of blood.)

If the police's first impression of the killing was that it had sexual overtones, there was absolutely no excuse for Campbell not to have checked for signs of sexual activity in the hotel room or determined from a medical examination of the body if Netter had been engaged in sexual acts prior to his death. The results either would have given weight to the police theory or refuted it. Had they found someone else's semen in the room, or on the body, they could have determined blood type. Because the investigators did not take more interest in the bloody footprints, chances to determine the size and weight of the murderer were missed. It was Durham's contention that it all added up to a sloppy, botched investigation, which left it wide open for the prosecution to concoct any theory it liked for the crime.

On the third day of the preliminary hearing Robertson arrived, this time without the bodyguards. He was no longer under the witness protection program and claimed to have taken himself out of protective custody because he felt safer. Robertson repeated the version of events which had been contained in the affidavit used at Meier's extradition, with his references to incriminating phone calls and McCrory's tossing around knives for the amusement of Meier's children. When shown TCV documents signed by Ivor Robertson, Robertson insisted that Meier had signed them, despite expert evidence to the contrary.

Durham's cross-examination began sedately enough and he asked Robertson to describe what had happened when he first saw Bill, the hitman, in Las Vegas. Robertson said that it was immediately after Bill left them that Meier announced he was an assassin.

"You sure of that?"

"Yes, I am sure of it."

"It's a fabrication on your part."

"No it's not. I'm here to tell the truth and you are getting it."

Durham returned to the counsel table and picked up a sheaf of papers.

During his preparation for trial, Durham discovered that a transcript had been made of a meeting between Robertson, Brenner and Westphal in October 1980. From this transcript yet another version of Robertson's story emerged, which Durham found most interesting of all.

In it, Robertson said that it might have been hours later, or even the next morning, when Meier said Bill was a hitman. Then even this detail changed and he said that it might have been mentioned a lot later, maybe in 1975, after the knife throwing incident in Meier's backyard. Durham wanted to know why there were so many different stories.

"Easily explainable. I arrived at the meeting (with Brenner) totally unprepared. Brought no notes. I had the good sense later to go back, study my notes, think it over and what I said today and in front of the grand jury is accurate." Asked where he had been staying prior to his journey to Calgary, Robertson said he was living at the Beverly Wilshire Hotel. Asked what he was doing in Beverly Hills, he said Meier had sent him down on an errand. He was to deliver a package to one of Meier's friends. While there, he said he saw the Wyshak family and took them out to dinner. He left Los Angeles on the 28th and travelled to Vancouver and then on to Calgary where he stayed for two days.

Durham delved back into the transcript of the October 7 meeting in which Robertson told Brenner another story — that he arrived in Calgary on the 29th and stayed there only one day.

Referring to the two crucial phone calls Robertson claimed Meier received in Calgary, Durham asked: "Didn't you tell Michael Brenner there was only one phone call?"

"I don't recall."

"Did you also tell Michael Brenner and Patrick Westphal there was no mention made of Netter by Meier?"

"No, I don't recall that."

"Didn't you in fact tell Brenner that the only person that was discussed was Liebich?"

"He wasn't the only one discussed," protested Robertson.

With that Durham began reading Robertson's statement from the transcript.

"On Saturday there was a phone call for Meier," he quoted. "He was told it was his wife, and he said his wife had just heard on the news that a man, head of a video corporation on Burrard Street, had been found murdered in Los Angeles. Then he laughed and said 'Could that be Liebich? Liebich, ha, ha. It could be anybody.'" Robertson said he didn't recall this.

"Did you tell Brenner that Meier and you just speculated on who had been murdered in Los Angeles at the Beverly Hilton Hotel?"

"Not that I recall."

In this version of events Meier, not knowing the identity of the murdered man, speculated that it was Liebich. Netter never came into it. There was nothing incriminating in that conversation whatsoever and had it been presented in that manner to the extradition judge, instead of the damning "I know... I know... Netter's dead ha, ha," Meier could never have been delivered up for extradition. This was not the version that Brenner, Westphal and Halprin presented to the courts. Meier was not shown puzzling over the identity of the murdered man. On the contrary, evidence given under oath has him knowing it is Netter, which gave rise to the theory of guilty foreknowledge and its argument that Meier must have been involved in Netter's murder.

Durham then read further details of Robertson's account in which Meier continues to speculate that the dead man must be Liebich. The transcript is confusing, as Robertson stumbles around trying to explain himself, but the fact emerges that Meier received only one phone call in the hotel room, from his wife. It led to a conversation about Liebich. This transcript records Westphal's confusion. He directly asks Robertson: "Are you talking about Liebich or Netter?"

Robertson replies: "Liebich, because he was saying to me that Liebich see, when he came off the phone he laughed and joked. 'That will be Liebich. That will be Liebich.' Whether he thought that was because Liebich was going down — practically living in Los Angeles..."

Asked for an explanation by Durham, Robertson said it was just "off the top-of-the-head conversation."

"What's true," demanded Durham, "the testimony you have given here today or what you told Michael Brenner four years ago?"

"The testimony is what's true. That isn't testimony."

"Were you lying on October 7, 1980?"

"No... I had no notes with me. I didn't know why we were meeting. There was no particular need for great accuracy."

Next Durham wanted to know of Robertson's relationship with Netter.

Weren't they friends who had travelled together to New York just shortly before he was murdered? No, said Robertson.[4]

Had he admitted to Hazelwood that Netter had put up a fight and he had killed him?

"Never."

"Didn't you tell Gordon Hazelwood that you were there and that you couldn't sleep at nights?"

"I sleep very well."

Durham asked him if he visited Netter on the evening of his death.

"No."

"You killed Al Netter, didn't you?"

"No."

The defense theory was that Robertson committed the murder on the 29th, then fled from Los Angeles without checking out of the Beverly Wilshire Hotel. On November 30, he flew from Los Angeles to Seattle and then to Calgary where he was met by Meier at the airport that afternoon. The pair travelled to Edmonton, where Robertson made a phone call that night from Meier's room in the Edmonton Caravan. It was Durham's theory that Robertson called the Beverly Wilshire Hotel to check out. Robertson denied making any calls.

Bringing a copy of the phone calls made from Meier's room in the Edmonton Caravan, Durham asked Robertson to look at an entry made indicating that a Mr. Robertson made a phone call to 213-275-4282 — the Beverly Wilshire hotel.

"Would that refresh your recollection?"

"No sir. I never made any calls. I also stated earlier I wasn't in the room most of that evening. They could have been made by anyone else. It could have been Ivor Robertson which wouldn't be me."

When pressed to explain the call Robertson continued his denials. "Anybody can make a call in another's name... I don't see R. Robertson. It says Robertson, Mister..."

Robertson was on the stand for a day and a half. Following his testimony Durham was ready to abandon the whole proceedings and let Meier be remanded for trial provided he could get reasonable bail. Confident that no jury would ever convict Meier once Robertson testified, Durham was impatient to move to trial. Robertson's performance put so different a complexion on the affair that Durham received a commitment from the prosecutors that they would not object to Meier's bail being reduced from $1 million to $100,000.

Durham and Tranbarger went to see Judge Obera. Tranbarger even proposed that Meier sign an extradition waiver — so he couldn't bolt back to Canada and force the authorities to repeat the extradition process — and therefore bail could be reduced to $100,000, or maybe $75,000.

Tranbarger argued eloquently on Meier's behalf that the defense had not had a chance to get at Robertson before and that now "both parties are in a better position to realize their positions and what they have to gain or lose at trial..." Durham piped up that Meier had nothing to fear by going to trail. He wasn't guilty and couldn't possibly be convicted.

But Obera said she didn't think $100,000 bail was enough. Meier could waive the preliminary hearing but she was making no deal on bail. Perhaps she would reduce the amount to $250,000, but she wouldn't commit herself. Faced with this, Durham said the defense would rather continue with trial. As they left Obera's chambers he muttered his thanks to Tranbarger.

Despite Hazelwood's testimony in Canada that Robertson had confessed to the murder, the lawyer was produced as the state's final witness, although his testimony would do nothing to help the prosecution. He testified that Brenner had tried to bully him into giving evidence against Meier at the grand jury proceedings.

"In fact, Michael Brenner offered you immunity (from prosecution) if you would change your story?" Durham asked in cross-examination.

"He did not say that in so many words... The import of it was that if I would give evidence against Mr. Meier that would implicate Mr. Meier that I would be given immunity... and otherwise the extradition proceedings would go against me. I would be extradited and held without bail until I gave such evidence." Hazelwood then repeated Robertson's murder confession complete with his vow to revenge himself on Meier by entangling him in the murder using his falsified notes.

Durham opened the defense by calling Wyshak who placed Robertson in Beverly Hills on the night of the murder.

"I met him on the 26th, 28th and 29th," said Wyshak.

On the 26th he had gone to the Beverly Wilshire and met Robertson in his room. On the 28th — Thanksgiving Day — Robertson came to Wyshak's Beverly Hills home and was introduced to the family. Then on

November 29 he was again at the Wyshak's and was there while the family had dinner in the evening. Under cross-examination Wyshak admitted that Robertson's name wasn't recorded in his diary as being with him on the 29th. He said Robertson spent most of the time entertaining his twelve-year-old daughter Robin with stories of his Scottish background.

Durham wanted Deputy District Attorney Brenner to take the stand. While such things happen on TV, in life it is rare for prosecuting attorneys to be asked to testify. Utterly convinced that Meier was being persecuted, Durham was about to challenge Brenner's prosecution. It was a risky maneuver as courts have a natural reluctance to let their officers be manhandled and if it results in nothing more than gratuitous harassment, it will almost certainly rebound against the defendant. But Durham didn't care; by now he was in a fury and was about to vent it on Brenner, whom he wanted removed from the prosecution.

During Brenner's October 1980 meeting with Robertson, asked Durham, had not Robertson denied that Netter's name arose in connection with the phone call from Jennie Meier? Brenner said he didn't have any independent recollection of that but glancing at the transcripts which Durham handed him, he said they were accurate.

"Well, basically that telephone call was a very important part of your case and your prosecution of John Meier, was it not?"

"I couldn't say that at the time. It was evidence."

"Basically you sought to prove by way of Robertson that there was foreknowledge... on the part of Mrs. Meier or Mr. Meier of the demise of Alfred Netter... You were aware, were you not, before the grand jury proceedings, that Robert Robertson had told at least three versions of the phone call incident?"

"I don't think I was aware of that."

"You questioned him relative to a conversation between he and Meier where Netter was not the supposed victim of a homicide but one Ehrenfried Liebich?"

"Counsel, I've got to tell you," replied Brenner. "I'm really at a loss to answer your questions. I don't know what you are referring to. I don't have an independent recollection of what I talked to Robertson about. Every time I talked to him it was tape recorded... you got those tape recordings. There can't be any dispute as to what was said."

"Mr. Brenner, as early as October 9, 1980, you knew that Robert Robertson was not a credible witness, did you not?"

"No, I did not know that."

"You knew he had given at least three versions of the very same incident that allegedly occurred on November 29, 1974?"

Brenner stubbornly refused to admit this point.

Durham then took his questions to the subject of Westphal, who was by then no longer an RCMP officer.

"Where is Corporal Westphal now?"

"I imagine he's in Canada."

"He is no longer with the Royal Canadian Mounted Police?"

"I am not certain. I think he has retired."

"Does the name Ayerok Petroleum mean anything to you?"

"Yes."

Schirn objected but Durham said that he wanted to continue asking about Ayerok to show bias on the part of Brenner. "Ayerok is a company, a Canadian company, Corporal Westphal was involved with the company. So is another investigating officer in this case by the name of Hirst[5] and Mr. Michael Brenner."

Obera asked how all this was material to the preliminary hearing.

"Westphal did not retire. He was suspended as far as we know and asked to leave the force because of stock manipulation... Mr. Westphal's partner Hirst" and Rudi Martin, who was a witness at the grand jury proceedings, are directors.

"In addition Mr. Brenner is a stockholder in that company. We are showing that the relationship between Mr. Brenner, as the prosecuting attorney, and the investigating officers in Canada, as well as witnesses, are so incestuous as to create bias in terms of prosecution of this case."

However, the judge had heard enough of Ayerok and told him to drop it. She said it didn't matter if Brenner hated Meier. If the evidence showed there was sufficient reason to hold Meier, that was all that mattered.

Durham ended his examination with a taunt: "Robertson made a fool out of you, didn't he?" Schirn jumped up and prevented Brenner from answering.

Finally, Durham produced a handwriting expert to testify that a number of papers Robertson had accused Meier of signing were in fact signed by him. The expert could find no trace of Meier's signature on any of the exhibits. Despite Robertson's testimony that he was not a forger, his penmanship was all over them, including the Ivor Robertson signature on the false passport application.

In summation, Schirn argued that the case was circumstantial but that Meier had the motive, the means and the opportunity to have Netter killed. Meier was the hidden lender of funds, the source to which the insurance proceeds eventually flowed.

"I think the evidence was clear that Mr. Meier was the only person who benefitted from the life insurance policy... it is rather obvious Mr. Meier was the lender."

Durham argued that there was not a piece of evidence linking Meier to Netter's murderer. "A reasonable jury properly instructed could never find John Meier guilty of anything. The prosecution has spent the last nine days trying a security fraud case... it is all conjecture, all speculation..."

He charged Brenner with bad faith — he had introduced the Ivor Robertson passport even though he knew it to be a forgery committed by his main witness. Once Durham found himself speaking on the subject of Robertson, he became almost apoplectic.

"I would like to talk about a paid government informant, Robert Robertson, a liar, a forger, and I believe to anyone present in the court, that man is a murderer... It was the prosecution who called him as their star witness — the only witness to point a finger at John Meier and say this man is guilty of murder."

"The prosecution vouched for his credibility. They have blinded themselves to the truth... I observed his demeanor on the stand when he lied, your honor. His jaw tightened, the seat got too hot and he moved. Other times, to buy himself time, he coughed before he answered a question. We have seen pathological liars before. This is the worst perjurer I've seen in a court of law. It was obvious to everyone. It was obvious to the prosecution."

"You will recall that right after Robertson left the stand we asked this court for bail in the amount of one tenth of the bail previously ordered in Mr. Meier's case. One hundred thousand dollars was agreed to by all four counsel because this man is a perjurer, he is a liar..."

Durham described the police investigation as tainted. It displayed an unconscionable disregard for standard investigatory practices. Schirn rose and said that other witnesses had established that Meier received the insurance money along with Robertson and that the matter of witness credibility should be left to a jury. Obera agreed. She ordered Meier to stand trial and, despite an earlier tendency to set bail at $250,000, ordered it to remain at $1 million. Perhaps she hadn't appreciated Brenner being ambushed. Durham nevertheless convinced her to lower it to $100,000 and she scheduled a bail hearing to take place a few days later. Inside his cell Meier wrote to his wife:

> I miss you and the children and want to get out and see you all again. I just don't want to get my hopes up too much on getting out next week. If I get too optimistic and can't get free it would have too much of an adverse effect on me psychologically. So I have to be prepared for either event: I get out or I stay in here and fight on.
>
> Monday (September 10). Two days away and I'm a wreck. I don't want to believe it because I know in my heart they don't want me out...
>
> Tuesday. One more day to go and I can't hold back the excitement. I feel that at last I will be free again. I've already heard that you have flown down here to be with me. Some secret.
>
> Wednesday (September 12). It's 9 a.m. and I am ready. I have said goodbye to everyone and am just waiting for 10 a.m. to call Earl's office...

But the anticipation was short-lived:

> It's now noon and Earl just left here. I feel devastated. Judge George whom I went before in December turned me down. He refused to hear my case. I feel so sorry for Earl, yourself, Lisa Hargan, who took it so bad in court... and all my friends who expected me to be out. As for me I'm just numb...
>
> Monday (September 17). Earl came to see me today after filing my petition for *habeas corpus* and a writ of prohibition. It is 15 pages long and the best summation that could be done on my legal situation. Someday the truth will come out as to who, why, and how I was framed during the past seven years.
>
> Tuesday. Brenner called Earl this morning — for the first time — and I know that Brenner must be worried about his case. The transcript of the preliminary hearing is ready and Brenner must also have read the appeal Earl put in. Their frame-up can't work now. I hope the Canadian government will step in and help me.
>
> Monday (September 24). Went to Superior Court today, made my not

guilty plea and asked for a quick trial date and was given November 13. Earl asked the judge for bail and he agreed to $200,000. After this I was taken back to the holding tank to await transfer back to jail. It was then I made my big mistake of the day. I decided to lay back on a bench and take a nap. My ears were hurting and I wanted to see if I could forget the pain by sleeping. I must have been down 15 minutes when I jumped up to find 30 cockroaches crawling all over me. Ears still hurting. I just hope my friends can get me out on bail. I need proper medical treatment.

Thursday (September 27). I have a dozen people trying to put everything together so I can get out tomorrow. I won't believe it until I walk out the door. I keep thinking all day how it will be to see you all again. Every day is becoming sheer torture between being ill and the growing anticipation of getting out.

Friday (September 28). My 51st birthday. What a way to spend it. Earl came all the way up from San Diego to see me. He is so depressed at my still being here.

Tuesday (October 2). It's 2 a.m. I am sitting here in a holding tank writing this. I was woken at 1 a.m. and told to get my things because I am being released on bail. I quickly packed and came down. There are 50 inmates sitting here. I'm a nervous wreck.

It's 3:30 a.m. I was put in a cell all by myself. I was given a suit and shirt both of which were brought in by Pat Hargan. The problem is that Pat is shorter and lighter than I am. The pants are 12 inches off the ground and the waist is 7 inches less than I normally wear and the shirt doesn't button. The suit jacket doesn't get past my arms. I still can't believe I'm getting out.

It's 4:15 a.m. At 4 a.m. I was given some papers, had my fingerprints taken and given the 50 cents I had on me when I came in here. I was then taken to a door and the next thing I knew I was standing outside the jail with 50 cents and looking like a goof in these clothes. I can't believe that I am free. I know the tears are running down my cheeks but I don't care. No matter what I look like and feel like I am coming home again. Thank God!

THE ELUSIVE JOHN ROSS

M eier's release from the concrete and steel labyrinth of Los Angeles County Jail was a setback for the prosecution. While in jail he was unable to mount a defense. Meier could not afford to hire a private investigator to collect evidence his lawyers needed. Once he was out, Meier went home to British Columbia and began assembling witnesses in preparation for trial.

It didn't take the prosecution long to regain the initiative. They began whispering to Meier's friends, who had risked their homes to raise his bail, that their pledges would be forfeit as Meier would desert and not return for trial. The first inkling of this came from Possino who called on January 28, 1985 and said pressure was being exerted on one of Meier's sureties to withdraw his share of the bail. Brenner would have Meier tossed back into jail.

When Meier appeared in court February 4, one of his friends had panicked into withdrawing his surety. Meier reentered Los Angeles County Jail to the disbelief of some of his old prison friends and the surprise of many of the guards. The other prisoners regarded Meier with a mixture of pity and amusement. He had received bail on a murder charge, had even been allowed to leave the country and then returned knowing his bail would be revoked and he would be thrown back into jail. He felt like the biggest fool in the prison. However, the guards took pity and had him placed in the hospital and gave him a trusty's badge to make his stay as comfortable as possible.

He remained there for three months. On May 1, he was released when Schrade and other friends came forward and raised $200,000. By now, another crisis was upon him. Durham and he were at loggerheads over his trial strategy.

Durham had financial difficulties and Meier could no longer pay him. Confident that he could win the case after seeing Robertson's performance, he wanted to rush to trial. Meier had been made cautious by his experience in Salt Lake City, where Barber had been equally confident he could win by destroying Robertson's story. Meier's preferred strategy was to assemble a large contingent of witnesses and attack the case on a broad front. He was against the strategy of concentrating all their resources on a limited strike against Robertson.

That kind of defense failed to allow for the prosecution's mystery witness which his lawyers had now caught wind of from Brenner. This witness caused Meier sleepless nights trying to imagine who this person could be. It had to be someone close to the events of 1974 and yet sufficiently hostile to give damning evidence. From what little Meier had been able to discover, the witness appeared to be somehow connected to the police.

When he appeared in court May 13, Meier asked Judge McKee to remove Durham and appoint a public defender. He told McKee he had no money to pay a lawyer. Durham exited gracefully, telling reporters Meier was innocent and wished him well. McKee asked for a financial statement to establish Meier's eligibility for public legal aid and adjourned the hearing for five weeks.

After assuring himself Meier did not have resources, McKee spotted attorney Albert DeBlanc waiting in the courtroom on another matter and called him forward and asked him to take the case. DeBlanc clearly was not interested. He was very busy, he said, and asked the judge to find someone else — but McKee interrupted and asked him, before turning the case down, to read the letter he had in his hand. He handed him Crossin's complaints about Brenner.

DeBlanc began reading with no great enthusiasm, but stopped when he reached Brenner's "twelve niggers" remark.

DeBlanc was African-American.

"I'll take it." Then he leaned close to Meier and said quietly "I don't know what this is all about Mr. Meier, but I'll tell you what, we're going to whip these miserable sons-of-bitches."

DeBlanc, a cautious lawyer, wanted no surprises but it soon became apparent that the prosecution was even more deliberate. All summer, as DeBlanc attempted to assemble evidence, he met resistance from Brenner's office. DeBlanc needed documents from Brenner which were promised but not produced. He concluded that the prosecution was worried about its case, although not enough to abandon it. DeBlanc wasn't about to underestimate the importance of the mystery witness; his strategy was to pressure the prosecution either to drop the whole thing or get it into court.

The year ended without bringing Meier any nearer to trial. A court-appointed investigator arrived in Canada in early 1986 to begin interviewing witnesses. When DeBlanc told the court the defense was planning to bring in fifty witnesses from all over the world, Brenner looked glum.

Meier, entering his sixth year of fighting Robertson's accusations, spent his time between home and Los Angeles, where he lived with the Schrades.[1] By now even Brenner had become friendly and sometimes would bring Meier a coffee as they sat outside the court. They were now on a first name basis and would sit and chat more like acquaintances than adversaries.

On May 6, Meier was sitting outside the court waiting for DeBlanc on what promised to be another of those interminable days when nothing much would be done. He was reading a newspaper when he heard Brenner's voice in the hall. Looking up he saw two men walking with the prosecutor. Brenner seemed in finer spirits than he had been for some time; he smiled and waved in Meier's direction. Although Meier didn't know it, today was the day Brenner was ready to spring the mystery man who was expected to salvage the prosecution's case.

The men with Brenner were strangers to Meier. He wondered who they could be and what part they were here to play. The trio stood a little way off and out of earshot — Brenner with his back to Meier, the others facing him. They were obviously in conversation and Meier watched uncomprehendingly as one of the men nodded, as if responding to a question, then deliberately pointed a finger at him. Brenner half turned to follow the finger and stared directly at Meier. He turned back but the finger didn't waver. Brenner slowly turned his head again and stood staring open-mouthed at Meier. Even from a distance Meier could read the shock on the prosecutor's face. Then Brenner swung around grabbed the finger-pointer and dragged him down the corridor towards his office.

Presently, DeBlanc arrived and asked if he had seen Brenner. Meier described the pantomime in the hall and asked what it might mean.

"I've no idea. I guess we'll soon find out," said DeBlanc.

When Brenner arrived in court, he seemed in a trance. He walked by Meier and went straight to DeBlanc and motioned him to step outside. They were gone about five minutes. DeBlanc returned, his eyes wide. "The case is over," he whispered.

"What?"

"You won't believe this, but I've just found out who the government's secret witness is."

"Who is it?"

"You."

"Me?"

"You're John Ross, aren't you?"

"John Ross?... Yes, but where did you hear that name?"

"Brenner just told me that they had brought some guy down from Ottawa to give them information on John Ross and the guy said that was you."

Deblanc relayed what he had heard about the conversation in the hall to Meier. The two men in the hall with Brenner were Canadian Security and Intelligence agents. Brenner reportedly said to them: "Well it's about time I got to meet John Ross. When do you think I can meet him?"

One of the agents replied: "Michael, that's not too difficult. There he is," and he pointed over Brenner's shoulder.

Brenner half turned and saw only Meier behind him. The finger hadn't wavered so Brenner turned again and could see only Meier.

"You don't mean him?" he gasped. "That's the accused."

"Michael — John Ross is John Meier."

Ross existed in Meier's CLEU file but there was not much information about him. From the file it appeared as if Ross had watched Meier and had been reporting on his activities. Ross had tipped off the police to Meier's meeting with McCrory, which lead to pictures being taken of Meier and McCrory together in Vancouver. There were no personal details of Ross on file and he remained a mystery to the prosecution. Brenner went to Ottawa for information about John Ross and Ottawa had responded by sending two security service agents to California. These were the men who had been standing with Brenner.

At once Meier realized what had happened. John Ross was the name the Security Service had given him as a cover. Any information he provided them was listed as coming from John Ross. Meier's file in CLEU headquarters would be covered with "John Ross" as he had been providing information on his dealings with everything from crooked politicians to judges suspected of corruption. It was standard practice to give an agent an alias, but it had fooled the RCMP officers investigating the murder. They did not have access to Meier's file held by the Security and Intelligence Branch.

Meier cast his mind back to his relationship with McCrory, which had been twisted into the basis for a murder charge. It began when Meier received a call from a union official, a mutual friend of his and Schrade's. He called to say that a friend of his, Bill McCrory, would be travelling to Vancouver and asked if Meier would meet him for lunch. Meier naturally agreed.

This friend described McCrory as being a union man but mentioned, almost as an afterthought, that McCrory also worked for the CIA. Meier, ever nervous of the CIA, became alarmed and asked what it was he did. He was a military advisor[2] of some sort, said his friend, but he was coming to British Columbia on union business.

At the time Meier didn't know what to make of this. He reported the conversation to the Canadian Security Service who were intrigued by what McCrory might be doing in Canada. They said they would check his background to see if the information were accurate. The following day two security officers arrived at Meier's home. They confirmed that McCrory was a union executive and had been working with the CIA for a number of years. Canadian Intelligence was determined to keep him under surveillance. They wanted to know whom he met and what he was up to. Meier was meeting McCrory in the Hotel Vancouver for lunch and the agents promised to be close by.

McCrory was charming company. At lunch Meier was struck not only by his politeness but by his military bearing and inspection-ready turnout. McCrory's pants were creased razor sharp and his toecaps were mirrors.

At the end of lunch Meier, as he had been instructed by the security officers, walked out the main doors of the hotel and directed McCrory towards Burrard Street. As the pair were leaving the hotel and turning towards Burrard, security officers took the photographs which ended up in Meier's file.

Meier saw McCrory on two more occasions in Vancouver and both were reported to the Security Service. At no time was McCrory at Meier's house or in the backyard throwing knives at targets. Nor did Meier ever see him in the United States. Just how he came to be named as the murderer is known only to Robertson and the people Robertson dealt with. For Brenner, that moment of realization must have been stupefying. In an instant, all hope of convicting Meier had vanished. DeBlanc said Brenner wanted to cut a deal.

On September 23, Meier stood before Judge William Pounder in the final act of a drama begun years before with Robertson pouring stories into the expectant ears of Westphal and Halprin, Leffler and Brenner.

When he was first told the prosecution was prepared to make a deal, Meier had asked why he should. Why didn't Brenner simply drop the charge? DeBlanc explained that the district attorney's office was in too deep to just cut and run. Reputations were on the line, an enormous amount of money had been spent — Brenner and the rest had to have something to show for it. Rather than drop the charges, they were prepared to go to trial in a desperate and vengeful gambit.

"Let them," Meier said — but DeBlanc talked him out of it.

"Forgetting for the moment that a miracle happens and they get a conviction, do you really want to put yourself and your family through a trial even though you know you can win it? Look at it from their side. They are afraid that if they simply drop the charges you'll sue for all that has happened. That's why you either make a deal or have this thing drag on."

On the night before he appeared in front of Pounder, DeBlanc told Meier that Brenner was offering to drop the murder charge if Meier would plead no contest to a charge of harboring a fugitive.

"What fugitive?" asked Meier. DeBlanc said there wasn't one. The charge was designed to cover the time he had already spent in jail. Had Meier not been so weary or worn down by his long fight, he might have resisted.

The charge was read and Meier pleaded no contest.

Pounder asked if he had anything to say.

"Yes. I want to make it clear that I am not, and never was, guilty of murder. I'm pleading no contest to this charge so I can end this fiasco and go home to my family in Canada."

The judge paused for a second, then said: "I accept the plea and in consideration of the time you have spent in custody I am ordering you to be released. You are free to go home."

Both Meier and Deblanc were in tears.

———

Continue reading the Afterword written by John Meier and excerpts from his diary on the Robert F. Kennedy Assassination

AFTERWORD

When I walked out of the courtroom in Los Angeles the tears that I shed were not of joy but of exhausted and frustrated relief. I went home to my family and together we started to build new lives.

Over the years, I have become convinced that telling my story is crucial. It is important for me personally because of what the U.S. and Canadian governments did to me and to those closest to me. My main motivation for wanting this story told is not for retribution, however, but because people must know the capricious power governments have over us.

I first met Gerald Bellett in 1974. He was one of the many reporters who covered my story. His continued interest eventually encouraged me to ask him if he would write about what really happened during those years. Then I turned over thirty years of diaries and thousands of documents. Gerry spent hundreds of hours interviewing me and dozens of others named in Age of Secrets. I am grateful to him for his years of dedication to this project which has allowed my story to be told.

Once I incurred the wrath of the AEC, the CIA and Richard Nixon's White House, I almost immediately found myself targeted by other agencies including the IRS and the Secret Service. Understandably, their power is awesome and their resources unlimited.

Their formula was simple. First they charged me with something since most people think that indictment is synonymous with guilt. Once they had ruined my reputation, they broke me financially. They persecuted me in the press and the courtroom.

Two things allowed me to survive. First, I knew that what I was doing was ethically and legally right. More essential was my family's support and love. I regret that my saga made their lives difficult and tentative for so many years. While standing on principle would normally generate pride, my principles cost my family dearly. I will always feel badly for what they went through for me. I also feel relief that my children have become such fine individuals.

My eldest son Johnny, who was forced into being the patriarch during my absence, works with helping the elderly.

My daughter Jeannie had a career in international marketing.

My daughter Joanne, who has always kept everyone laughing, was a dental assistant.

My youngest son Jim has a very successful career in the film industry.

Last and most important is my loving wife, Jennie. She took the brunt of the pressure and persevered. My love and respect for her are beyond words.

My grandchildren Jenny-Lyn, Jordan, Jessica, Julia, and my soon-to-be first great-grandchild James, inspire the hope that we will one day make our nations live up to the promises that they make. Today, the United States is being divided along political and racial lines, creating open hostility among people. Issues of right and wrong are being blurred in a skewed judicial and political system. We must look beyond our own propaganda that praises our society as being just and free. Government agencies frequently act, not in the interest of the individual or the society, but as self-perpetuating powers.

We dismiss too many of our problems as the work of extremists without considering why people are being drawn to such extremes. If we continue to ignore the dissatisfaction and the protests of concerned and frightened citizens, the violent acts of these fringe groups will become palatable to a growing number of desperate people.

My story is one of a man devastated by a corrupt system. Our governments are increasingly disrespectful of basic human rights such that we can no longer legitimately call our nations democracies. I hope that this story will contribute to changing this course.

John H. Meier

NOTES

3. The Atomic Energy Commission

1. See Donald L. Bartlett and James B. Steele, *Empire: The Life, Legend and Madness of Howard Hughes* (New York: W.W. Norton and Company, 1979)

4. The CIA Takes Notice

1. In 2019 *The Washington Post* stated that it is widely believed the television show, and therefore the film franchise, "Mission: Impossible" was based on the Robert A. Maheu and Associates private investigative agency.
2. In 1976 *Time* quoted a Pentagon official as saying that the Hughes Aircraft Corporation, which was totally owned by the Medical Institute, was a captive company of the CIA.
3. Ironically, 22 years later it would be Smith's son, William Kennedy Smith, who would be involved in a huge scandal. After a night on the town with his uncle, Ted Kennedy, Smith was embroiled in a controversial and highly sensationalized date rape case. He was acquitted.
4. See Gonzales Affidavit Chapter 14.

5. Hughes Cleans House

1. See Harvey Wasserman and Norman Solomon with Robert Alvarez and Eleanor Walters, *Killing Our Own: The Disaster of America's Experience With Atomic Radiation* (New York: Delacorte, 1982).
2. *Killing Our Own.*

9. Hoax

1. See Gonzales Affidavit, Chapter 14.
2. Author's parentheses.

10. The Plumbers

1. But nothing could be found. O'Brien had not even tried to hide any of his income from the IRS and had accounted for every penny, as Nixon — who was not above avoiding income tax himself — discovered, to his consternation.
2. Not to be confused with Virgilio Gonzalez, the Watergate burglar.
3. This project so perturbed the CIA that Richard Helms, the CIA's director, had lunch with Anderson in March to try and dissuade him from publishing classified material.
4. This was a New York publication which is now defunct.
5. See John Ehrlichman, *Witness To Power: The Nixon Years* (New York: Simon and Schuster, 1982).

11. Hear No Evil

1. He was a leg-man for a number of media personalities in Vancouver during the 1970s, digging up dirt for talk-show hosts and newspaper gossip columnists. He was also a part-time driving instructor and by a great coincidence one of his students was John Meier Jr. Intertel discovered Meier's whereabouts through this unlikely meeting.
2. See Jim Hougan, *Secret Agenda* (New York: Ballantine Books, 1984).
3. See H.R. Haldeman and Joseph Di Mona, *The Ends Of Power* (New York: Times Books, 1978).

12. Damage Control

1. This was contained in a letter Rebozo wrote to Danner which was entered as an exhibit.
2. It appears that the IRS supplied some details of its investigatory work to the committee in the form of digests but did not submit the actual case reports which the committee was seeking. These edited versions did not seem to be of vital use to the committee.
3. The question of Don Nixon receiving part of the $100,000 arose during testimony by Richard Nixon's lawyer Herbert Kalmbach, who said Rebozo told him Don (and Ed Nixon) had received some of it. Nixon's brothers and Rebozo denied it.
4. Eisenhower was married to Richard Nixon's daughter, Julie.
5. Walters would also say that it wasn't until February 1973, 14 months after Rebozo's warning, that an IRS memorandum was drawn up indicating Don Nixon was suspected of being involved in the mining business.

13. International Intrigue

1. *Witness To Power.*
2. See memoirs of Peter Wright, British Intelligence officer who incidentally adds MI5 chief Sir Roger Hollis to the list of traitors: Peter Wright, *Spycatcher* (Toronto: Stoddart Publishing, 1987).
3. To be fair to the CIA officer, Meier didn't say why he wanted the documents.
4. This remark was made by Hughes in his last news conference, January 7, 1972, when he condemned Irving's manuscript as a fake.
5. See Jim Hougan, *Spooks the Haunting of America: The Private Use of Secret Agents* (New York: William Morrow and Company, 1978).
6. Incidentally there were other burglaries against Hughes targets at approximately the same time. In March a Hughes office in Las Vegas was entered. Then Chester Davis' office was burglarized, as was the Mullen Company's in Washington. If one were looking for suspects, the British would have had a motive considering their concern about the North Sea oil reserves and their desire to find out what Hughes was doing for the CIA. There is an interesting note contained in *Empire* on page 533 which says that police investigators checked on the activities of two men who lived in Los Angeles at the time of the Romaine job but who sold up and moved to Canada where their trail was lost in Vancouver. One of the men was thought to belong to a club whose members were British Intelligence officers during the Second World War. This is intriguing, as one of the theories advanced by the CIA for the Romaine burglary was that it had been carried out by a "foreign government, not necessarily the USSR."
7. He never saw Hall again but Hall did call afterwards and at one time told him that he knew a writer — Michael Drosnin — who might be of some help to him. Considering all these

interconnections it is fair to assume Hall is Drosnin's Pro.

8. For a full account of Hall's murder, see *Spooks.*
9. An identical count had been thrown out of court by the Chief Federal Judge in Utah for being unconstitutionally vague and indefinite.
10. Lindsay admitted to spying on Meier during his stay in the hotel and of entering his room uninvited with a pass key. He provided copies of Meier's long distance phone calls to Kish and agreed to testify against Meier in the United States.

14. The Gonzales Affidavit

1. There is confusion over the spelling of this name. It appears as Gonzales on the top of the affidavit, but the signature clearly shows it was signed Gonzalez.
2. *Spooks.*
3. *Spooks.*
4. Chief of Station.
5. Marjel De Lauer, *The Mystery of the Phantom Millionaire* (New York: Ashley Books, 1972). The break-in was noted on the jacket.
6. Gonzales is asking here for information he clearly already possessed.
7. *Vancouver Sun,* January 18, 1975.
8. The Gonzales persona normally spoke with a discernable Latin-American accent; Gorman did not.
9. McInnes was questioned by the committee's staff members about his meetings with Gonzales and Abbott.
10. Not only the Church committee but members of the Watergate Special Prosecutors office read the affidavit and called Meier on August 19. Like the Ervin Committee they wanted all Meier's papers and interestingly, they asked Meier to call D. K. Ludwig and try to get answers to some questions but Meier refused. (Ludwig had given money to Nixon's brothers Don and Edward when they were supposedly between jobs.) However, he did call Ludwig and told him of the prosecutor's interest and Ludwig thanked him for the tip.

15. The Secret of Cay Sal

1. Papa Doc had once presented him with an autographed copy of a book he'd written.
2. See *Empire.*
3. Part of the Hughes legend is that he invented a brassiere that lifted the actress' breasts at the pull of a string.
4. This bank no longer exists.
5. Melvin Dummar was the gas station attendant who said he found Howard Hughes lying out in the desert near Tonopah in December 1967. He drove Hughes to Las Vegas, gave him some coins so he could make a phone call and for this Hughes left him one sixteenth of his fortune, about $150 million. The will in which Hughes displayed such generosity mysteriously arrived at the headquarters of the Mormon Church in Salt Lake City and was designated the Mormon Will since the church too was a beneficiary. It was declared a forgery by a jury in July 1978.
6. Mexico is obviously eliminated. Meier saw his body in the first week of January, at a time when the Hughes organization says he was alive and living in the Bahamas. According to Summa, Hughes left the Bahamas and arrived in Mexico February 10.
7. This would have been on December 24, 1975, at which time Hughes was dead and had been for a while.

8. There were a number of occasions when Meier was offered a deal. Once Wyshak had an agreement with Summa that it would call off the civil suit in return for getting access to Meier's Swiss bank account. Summa pulled out at the last minute. On March 13, 1974, Summa security chief Jack Cromar came to Vancouver to offer Meier a deal to stop the civil case and help get the IRS off his back. In exchange, Meier was to give no further interviews with the press about Hughes, the CIA and the White House and was to turn over all his files and diaries. He would be given a consulting contract with Summa after signing the usual declaration that he would never disclose company business. Meier agreed to consider the offer but turned it down on March 25 saying things had gone too far. If Howard Hughes would call him with the offer he might consider it. Cromar called him again on March 28 and tried to persuade him to change his mind.

9. The authors *Empire* give another example of Hughes' signature being forged, interestingly enough in connection with Chester Davis, page 271. They also conclude that if this was the first time someone at Romaine Street had forged Hughes' signature, it wasn't the last.

16. The Canada Files

1. Perez is once again in charge of Venezuela, having returned to office in February 1989. It was during the second month of his term that Venezuela suffered the worst rioting and social unrest in decades. Hundreds of people were killed after government austerity measures undertaken to please the International Monetary Fund brought a sharp increase in prices.

17. Trouble in Tonga

1. This was Hughes' H-1 aircraft which he designed to set speed records and offered to modify for use as a fighter. It was rejected by the military in 1937.

2. Quite some time later, on February 7, 1979, Meier was phoned by Brian Gray of the U.S. Labor Party. He said that his organization had picked up stories in the U.S. that some Peace Corps members were allegedly involved in the drug business and that Meier's name had come up. He wanted to know if Meier was working with Canadian Security to investigate the Peace Corps. Not knowing who he was, Meier did not respond.

3. See page 217 for Golden's opinion of Meier.

18. Canada Sells Out

1. His real name was Alan Cooper, but he had been given a new identity and when Meier knew him was going under the name of Copeland.

2. Wyshak was called by Taylor as an expert witness in U.S. federal law.

3. Reynolds launched a libel suit against the CBC but it eventually lapsed. He complained that he had been set up by CLEU. Incidentally it was CLEU who promoted the operation into Vancouver's organized crime network and Hameluck was one of the prime movers.

19. Presumed Guilty

1. It is ironic that Meier was extradited by Judge Paris on the basis that if a jury believed Robertson, it could find Meier guilty.

2. During sentencing Jenkins offered his own novel explanation to the mystery of how the documents were forged — Trevillion must have salted the forgeries into the documents

when she was in Mexico. As Barber would remark: "This late blooming fiction — which is entirely contrary to the theory of the case argued to the jury by the prosecution — is based upon inferences far too tenuous to be supported by any realistic view of the evidence presented."

3. He was speaking here of the Romaine Street documents stolen by Hall and his accomplices during the burglary. In fact, the CIA was mistaken in this. Meier had only kept the Glomar Explorer document from the ones Hall had shown him.

4. A more complete description of the Gemstone material can be found in Hougan's *Secret Agenda*.

20. Framed For Murder

1. In April 1978, Meier launched criminal libel proceedings against Robertson.
2. Siddle signed the affidavit in 1982 after he had retired from the force.
3. Froese's affidavit was dated September 17, 1982.
4. This trio were investors who lived in Gull Lake, Saskatchewan. Because of the troubles with the company they wanted to speak to Meier, who was planning to fly to London. He agreed to meet them in Calgary as a halfway point between Vancouver and Gull Lake, before he travelled on to Edmonton to catch his plane to London.
5. Details of this meeting are contained in an affidavit Hameluck signed in September 1982.
6. Unfair as it may seem, it is a peculiarity of extradition proceedings that such evidence can be allowed.
7. Siddon gave Meier unstinting support and tried his best to convince his government to stop the extradition.

21. In Search of Justice

1. The strain of the past few years had caused Meier to develop heart problems. He suffered a heart attack in 1981.
2. Nitroglycerin pills used to control heart problems.
3. Ayerok Petroleum Ltd.
4. Later Liebich would testify that Netter had in fact gone to New York with Robertson.
5. Hirst was one of the original officers who investigated Netter's death. He was formerly a sergeant in the RCMP's market manipulation squad. He left the force and became a director of Ayerok. In March 1982 the RCMP Commercial Crime Squad launched an investigation into the company after the disappearance of proceeds from a $1.5 million financing program and the company president was jailed. During the investigation the RCMP discovered Westphal and another Commercial Crime Squad officer were shareholders in Ayerok and had been active in promoting the sale of shares. Westphal was removed from the squad and put on traffic duty. He took early retirement.

22. The Elusive John Ross

1. Jerry Brown, the former Governor of California, lived across the street and was sympathetic to Meier's position. The extradition papers were not signed by him. Aides waited until he went out of town and then signed on his behalf.
2. Meier was later told by McCrory's lawyer that his client was used during the invasion of Grenada by U.S. troops.

GLOSSARY - INDEX

Toy, Samuel. *B.C. Supreme Court judge who ordered Meier extradited on a murder charge.*
311–313, 318–319
Tranbarger, Michael. *Los Angeles deputy district attorney.*
331, 337
Transcontinental Video (TCV). *A company in which Meier, Robertson and Netter all had interests.*
151, 299–304, 306–308, 312, 317, 319, 333
Trias, Olga Chamero. *Member of the Cuban embassy staff in Sydney, Australia.*
251–253
Trudeau, Pierre E. *Prime Minister of Canada 1968-79 and 1980-84.*
223–224, 266–267, 281–282
Truman, Preston. *Anti-AEC organizer and researcher from Utah.*
58, 266, 275, 289
Turner, William. *Attorney for the Securities Exchange Commission who investigated Hughes' takeover of Air West.*
117, 159, 162
Vesco, Robert. *Financier who fled the U.S. after looting an off-shore mutual funds company.*
44, 49, 127, 148, 243, 287
Walker, Jay. *U.S. businessman with State Department credentials.*
243-244, 249, 251, 257–258, 270
Wallace, Doug. *A writer who published a pro-Meier article during the Summa suit.*
234
Walters, Johnnie M. *IRS Commissioner.*
141–142, 213
Watergate. *The scandal caused by Meier and the Democrats' plot to panic Nixon into an irrational act as a result of hearing a tip from his brother that the Democrats were going to expose details of his illegal activities using documents located at the Watergate complex.*
80, 83–85, 90, 98, 100–101, 105–107, 109–110, 112, 114–115, 120–121, 124, 127–129, 131, 133–134, 136, 138–139, 142, 147, 154, 165, 209, 212–213, 219, 243, 270, 294
Waterhouse, William. *Tongan consul in Australia.*
230, 243, 246–249
Wentworth, Dean. *Lester's partner who helped Meier get out of Australia.*
254–255
Westphal, Patrick. *RCMP officer responsible for twice compiling evidence against Meier.*
258, 266, 296, 299–300, 302–304, 306–308, 311–316, 318, 334–335, 339, 348
Wright, Ken. *The head of Howard Hughes Medical Institute.*
38–41
Wyshak, Robert. *John Meier's Beverly Hills attorney.*
93–94, 112, 124, 126, 128–129, 143, 152, 161–162, 165–167, 169, 171, 211–212, 226, 228, 233, 235, 281, 334, 337–338
Wyss, Susi. *French clothing designer with contacts in European intelligence organizations.*
120, 160
Yakuza. *The Japanese mafia who had a contract on Meier from the U.S. government.*
244–245
Yee, John. *A TCV Investor.*
303-304

ABOUT THE AUTHOR

Gerald Bellett is a reporter with the Vancouver Sun in British Columbia. Since 1974, he has written about John Meier and his monumental struggle with the White House, the CIA and the Howard Hughes organization.

The story took him across North America from the deserts of Nevada, where he found the hidden gold mines of Howard Hughes, to the dangerous streets of Harlem in search of a CIA agent on the run.

Bellett exposed the CIA's infiltration of the Hughes organization and the agency's use of Howard Hughes to supply its favored politicians with campaign contributions.

He has won a number of awards including a National Newspaper Award for being part of the Sun's reporting team that wrote a series concerning a notorious serial killer.

He was born in Liverpool, England, and has lived in Canada since 1966. He now resides near Vancouver.

EXCERPTS FROM JOHN MEIER'S DIARY ON THE RFK ASSASSINATION

John Meier at his home meeting with United States Presidential Candidate Robert F. Kennedy Jr. to discuss Meier's diary notes on the Robert F. Kennedy Assassination.

courtesy Jim Meier

Editor's note: The following notes are exactly verbatim from the diary of John Meier which gives an accurate insight into the inner workings of the Hughes empire and the details of activity surrounding the assassination of United States Presidential Candidate Robert F. Kennedy. The notes go back to 1947, which is important to what occurred in 1968.

1947

Senator Owen Brewster of Maine, Chairman of a special Senate Committee investigating defense procurement during World War II, claimed that Hughes had received $40 million from the Defense Department without actually delivering the aircraft (Spruce Goose) he had been contracted to provide. Hughes was embarrassed at the hearing in 1947 so he destroyed the Senator in 1952 by putting unlimited campaign funds behind defeating Brewster in the Republic primary by Frederick Payne.

Hughes remained bitter until he died. Hughes made a decision after the Brewster problem to put a President in the White House and control him. On January 20, 1953, Richard Nixon became the 36th Vice President of the United States.

December 10, 1956

Don Nixon got a loan from Hughes Tool Company's Canadian subsidiary for $205,000. Don opened a restaurant in the Nixon home town of Whittier for the Nixon-burger. Richard Nixon was Vice President at the time, and asked Howard Hughes for this favor and to keep it a secret. In return V.P. Nixon would have the IRS reverse its original decision and the Howard Hughes Medical Institution was classified as a tax exempt charitable organization in 1957.

Hughes felt that it caused Nixon's defeat. The loan was handled by Noah Dietrich who was always against it. After Kennedy had been elected, his brother Robert said that the Hughes Loan was one of the three events that swung the narrow victory. I spoke to Don Nixon, Noah Dietrich and RFK on this subject.

1962

RFK knew that Maheu was CIA.

Attorney General Robert Kennedy complained to the press that one multi-millionaire had paid only $500 in income tax the previous year. He meant Hughes.

June 1, 1968
Saturday

I completed the speech and the supporting background documentation I had prepared for Robert Kennedy on the A.E.C. underground testing programs in Nevada. Spent the morning with George Roth, my research editor on additional background information. At noon, Bob Maheu called and told me to cancel my trip scheduled for Monday, and wait until after the fifth. I was upset and advised him a schedule had already been arranged and I was to meet with Harry Evans and Paul Schrade of the UAW who were assisting Kennedy in his campaign in California. They were also assisting Howard Hughes and myself in stopping the underground testing in Nevada.

Maheu said he needed me in Vegas but could not discuss it with me at that time. He said he would talk to me on Monday. I called Hughes and advised him of my concern about the change of plan and Hughes said he thought Maheu had something important for me about the testing project. Hughes felt I should work it out with Maheu. I knew Hughes was adamant about stopping the A.E.C. That was his first overriding priority.

I called Harry Evans at 2 p.m., (213) 381-6561 at his office, and advised him of the change and would try to get out on Monday and I would call him then. He sounded miffed. He said that he had made arrangements for me to meet with a few of RFK's supporters, including movie director Martin Ritt and L.A. County AFL-CIO president Sigmund Arywitz. Evans said he would pass my message on to Schrade (whom he believes will be upset by the change) and will make apologies for me to Ritt and Arywitz.

That night I took my wife, Jeannie, and Joanne, to see the movie "The Party" with Peter Sellers. I called my son Johnny who was in California for the weekend staying with Bob Maheu's family, and told him I would not be out for the weekend.

June 2, 1968
Sunday

I was with George Roth all day working on the A.E.C. program and organizing our publicity against the testing. On May 23, Hughes made the decision to take on the A.E.C. and stop the underground testing at all costs and told me I had the authority to spend whatever it took and do whatever it takes.

I completed my memorandum to Hughes outlining the fact that I had organized the National Evaluative Committee on Megaton Atomic Energy Tests and had brought on board Bill Haddad and Paul Schrade and his organization to help on the project.

On May 27, 28, and 29, I had been in New York along with George Roth. We met with Bill Haddad who has been a long-term friend and political associate of the Kennedy family. We flew on to Boston to meet with Dr. Frank Press and Dr. James Killan of MIT. On May 29 we had breakfast with Dr. Jerome Wiesner and then went to meet with Dr. George Kistiakowsky of Harvard. We had lunch with Dr. Lester Van Lester.

I had informed all of the above of the committee I had organized and they agreed to add their input to the committee. They felt that I should not be involved but they would continue working and give their report directly to President Johnson. They would also take all the research my staff and I collected, evaluate it, and present it as well to the President.

At 2 p.m. I called Preston Truman in Utah and he agreed to also actively join in the fight against underground nuclear testing. The rest of the day was spent with Roth working on the reports and the Hughes memorandum.

June 3, 1968
Monday

Maheu called in the morning and said he wanted me to call Don Nixon urgently and ask him to fly to Las Vegas to meet with Maheu on Wednesday the 5th. He wanted me to introduce him, as they had never met. That was the reason Maheu wanted me to stay in Vegas and not fly on to L.A. I left a message for Don Nixon at (213) 723-8847 and also at his home (714) 646-2572. He called me at 11 a.m. and advised me that he was very busy and was not able to make the meeting on the 5th. I called Maheu and when he heard

Don was not coming out, he told me to call Don back and have him call his brother again. At 3 p.m. Don called me back and I gave him the message to call his brother Richard Nixon. Don was upset that this Maheu would try and run his life!

At 4 p.m. I went to the Frontier Hotel to check on the telephone system, because on June 8th we were going to move our operations from the Desert Inn to the Frontier Hotel as Hughes had purchased the Frontier Hotel as well.

That evening I was at home when our new bedroom furniture was delivered.

June 4, 1968
Tuesday

Bob Maheu asked if certain Hughes key people could be at a staff meeting he was holding at 10 a.m., since he felt as the person running Hughes Nevada Operations he would be responsible for Hughes's offices at the Frontier Hotel. He felt that all communications to and from Hughes's suite should go through him. He said he had informed Hughes's companies, Hughes Tool Co. in Texas, Hughes Aircraft Co. in California, and Hughes's private offices at the Romaine Street address in LA, that this was to be done for security reasons.

2 p.m. I had a message to call Robert Kennedy at John Frankenheimer's beach house at Malibu. I called and Bob said he was with his wife and children resting and swimming. I told him I would come to LA on Wednesday and bring everything pertaining to the A.E.C. with me.

4:30 p.m. Don Nixon left a message to call him and I called him at the 732-8847 number and he said he had spoken to his brother Richard and that he (Don) would come on June 5th but he was not about to pay for his plane trip or his hotel. I told him I was going to LA on June 5th and I would try to get on the same flight back with him to Vegas. I was booked on Western, flight 64 leaving at 3:45 p.m. and arriving in Vegas at 4:30 p.m. I then called Maheu and his response was that the next time all you people should listen to me.

June 5, 1968
Wednesday

I got up at 4 a.m., went to shower and shave and put on the morning news about the primary. The newscaster was talking about the sadness of the shooting of Kennedy and I assumed he was talking about the JFK assassination in relation to the Robert Kennedy primary results. He then said that Robert Kennedy was shot at 12:15a.m. I was so totally shocked at this news that I cut myself deeply while shaving. I began frantically trying to reach either Paul Schrade or Harry Evans on the telephone when the newscaster reported that Evans and Schrade had also been shot. He listed some others as well.

2:30 p.m. I reached Harry Evans at the Kaiser Hospital in Hollywood (213/667-4011) where Paul Schrade was taken after the shooting at the Ambassador Hotel. Evans said that he was trailing a bit behind Schrade and was entering the doorway into the Ambassador's serving pantry when gunfire broke out. Because of the crush of people he was unable to get much closer. He knew that the Senator, Schrade, and several others had been shot. Evans said that an enormous number of shots were fired and that Schrade took a bullet in the head. Evans said that Frank Mackiewicz, RFK's press secretary, had called and said that although the Senator is still alive, it does not look promising for him. Evans said that Elizabeth Evans, who was hit by a ricocheting bullet, was no relation to him.

5:00 p.m. Don Nixon called from the Vegas airport, demanding to know where I was and why nobody was there to pick him up. When I explained the reason, he became even more agitated and said words to the effect of, "Who cares, what about my hotel room?"

His concern over Kennedy was nonexistent and placed well behind who was going to pay for the taxi and the room.

He checked into the Frontier Hotel and made several calls to me, which I did not return, and went to bed totally exhausted, shocked, and sick about the events of the day.

June 6, 1968
Thursday

5 a.m. Bob Maheu called to ask about the Don Nixon meeting and suggested 8:30 for breakfast at the Desert Inn Country Club. I went to the club. Maheu was all smiles and Don Nixon walks in all smiles. What followed next had to be seen to be believed. They embraced each other and Don Nixon said, "Well that prick is dead", and Maheu said, "Well it looks like your brother is in now." At the time I did not even know what they were talking about.

Maheu joked that they should now be calling Don Nixon "Mr. Vice President". I still did not realize that Robert Kennedy had died and when they saw that I was unaware Maheu told me, "John, you are out of it. Why don't you go home and Don and I will carry on without you." The last thing I recall was Don worrying about who was going to take him to the airport to catch the Western 1:05 p.m. flight to L. A. Maheu said he would take him personally as they had much to talk about.

I reached Harry Evans at the Kaiser Hospital in Hollywood. He had temporarily moved his union offices there while Schrade was healing. Evans said that he saw Schrade very early this morning. Schrade, Evans said, is extremely saddened over Senator Kennedy's death.

Schrade told Evans that he did not realize at first that he had been shot. He said he believed electrical cords from the television cameras had frayed and shorted out. Schrade thought he was being electrocuted. We talked at length. Evans was unhappy at the prospect of the California delegation ending up backing McCarthy, but he is fairly certain that's what will happen. Humphrey is not popular among Kennedy delegates, mostly because of his support for LBJ's Vietnam actions. Evans gave me his private number of his office at the Kaiser (213) 668-6060.

12 noon. Called Bill Haddad in New York and he told me he was very depressed and said he was one of the individuals handling the New York situation for the Kennedy family and asked me if I was planning to come out there. I told him I would try to catch a flight later in the day to New York and would see him the next day, Friday, June 7th.

I then called Bob Humphrey who had left a message for me to call him. He said that his father would like to see if I could come to Washington the following week to meet with him. Bob then said he would call me back. One hour later he called and asked me to confirm Tuesday, the 18th of June for my Washington trip.

I left the Desert Inn and went home to pack.

Later that evening I caught a flight to New York and stayed with my parents in Astoria.

June 7, 1968
Friday

4 a.m. Arrived at St. Patrick's Cathedral in New York after taking the subway from Astoria. Security was extremely heavy around the church where Robert Kennedy was lying in state. The security guard refused me admission until I mentioned Haddad's name. Then he took me to the front of the church. At 5:30 the cathedral was opened and the public was admitted. By the end of the day over 150,000 people walked past the casket.

I remained there for most of the day and in the evening I returned to my parents in Astoria.

June 8, 1968
Saturday

I left early in the morning for the cathedral for Mass, which lasted about one and one- half hours. They removed the casket and took it to central Penn station where the train left at 1 p.m. for the burial services at Arlington Cemetery in Washington.

June 9, 1968
Sunday

Prior to leaving for the airport back to Vegas, I heard that James Earl Ray was arrested in England for the murder of Martin Luther King, which was one more shock to my system.

Upon arriving in Vegas I drove my car to the new offices set up at the Frontier Hotel. That evening, I was worn out and took my family to the movies to see Gone With The Wind. Billy Maheu and a friend of Jeannie's accompanied us.

June 10, 1968
Monday

Went to my office at the Frontier Hotel and tried to organize my files and catch up on the last few hectic days.

Received a message to call Bob Maheu and when we talked he advised me not to discuss the meeting with Don Nixon, or discuss anything pertaining to Robert Kennedy or Paul Schrade.

5 p.m. Harry Evans called. He complained that the Frontier phone system was not working well and that he had tried to call half a dozen times, beginning at noon. Evans said that Schrade had undergone surgery on June 7 to remove the bullet fragments from his head. Evans said that the surgeon, Caspar Fuchs, from Florida, is tops in his field and that Schrade's prognosis is much better than it was. Evans said that it is now fairly certain that Schrade will live which was not quite so certain until today. In passing, Evans said that his call had somehow been transferred to Maheu's office and when Maheu got on the line he was rude. I told him not to give it another thought, that Maheu was tired from the stress of moving our offices.

June 11, 1968
Tuesday

9 a.m. Governor Paul Laxalt called me and asked me if I could fly up to Reno and then drive to Carson City for a meeting concerning the state of Nevada gaming commission. I caught a 12:40 p.m. flight from Vegas to Reno and was picked up at the airport by Robert Mulligan. We drove to the meeting with Frank Johnson and Paul Laxalt to discuss my being appointed to the Nevada Gaming Task Force. I agreed.

Governor Laxalt spent over one hour talking to me about the RFK assassination. Even though Paul is a conservative Republican, his heart went out to the Kennedy family.

I caught the 9:10 a.m. flight from Reno back to Vegas.

At home I had a call from Harry Evans and we discussed Paul Schrade. He said he had a conversation with Dr. Fuchs, Schrade's surgeon, and Fuchs said that Schrade's wound was about as serious as any person can survive. Schrade, Evans said, will have to undergo an extended period of recuperation. Evans asked me if I could make arrangements for a suite at the

Frontier for a couple of weeks, for Paul and a guest or two. I told Evans to leave it to me, and that I would work something out. Just as I hung up Howard Hughes called. He wanted to make it clear to the UAW that he wants to do whatever is needed to help with Schrade's recovery. Hughes said for me to tell Evans that anything Schrade might need, including doctors, or anything else will be provided. I told Hughes that Schrade is recuperating nicely and that I believe it would be a nice gesture if he offered Schrade the use of Hughes's Spring Mountain Ranch. Hughes asked me to call immediately and say that the ranch is available to Schrade whenever he is able to travel.

June 12, 1968
Wednesday

9 a.m. I called Milt Polland and discussed the RFK assassination and my pending trip to Washington to meet with the VP. I then made arrangements to fly back east. Called Robert Humphrey and arranged to meet with him on June 17, one day before the meeting with his father.

Called Evans office and then his home. Could not reach him. Left messages.

June 13, 1968
Thursday

7 a.m. Called Milt Polland to wish him a Happy Birthday, and he told me he had spoken to Mayor Yorty in LA who told him there was something strange pertaining to the Kennedy assassination and that the police chief of LA, Reddin, had said that RFK refused to have a security guard from the police department that was offered him. The fact is that no security was ever offered by the LAPD.

8 a.m. Had breakfast at the Frontier Hotel with Frank Diluzio to discuss the A.E.C. underground testing program.

2 p.m. Harry Evans called and I relayed the offer to let Paul Schrade use Hughes's Spring Mountain Ranch. Evans was elated and said that he would make arrangements for Schrade to talk with me on the phone. Apparently there is no phone in Schrade's room so Evans had to make special arrangements.

I called Schrade at 3 p.m. and we spoke for at least an hour. He described what had happened at the Ambassador Hotel early in the morning of June 5. Schrade said that he believed a live electrical wire from a TV camera had made contact with the wet concrete floor. He didn't realize he had been shot until a doctor told him at Kaiser Hospital.

7 p.m. Listening to the radio where they were discussing the RFK assassination and who was shot etc. they mentioned Thane Cesar who was a security guard at the hotel working for ACE Guard Security and was also employed by Lockheed Aircraft. I remember Thane from his trips to Vegas where he was meeting with numerous gaming people and was introduced to me by Jack Hooper, an associate of Bob Maheu.

June 14, 1968
Friday

Bob Maheu called and told me to come over to his house at 8:30 p.m. that evening and I did. He was furious and wanted to know why I was checking up on Thane. I was stunned at his anger and he said to me that if I kept discussing this matter, he would see that I was no longer around the Hughes operation. He then told me that he was responsible for all security matters in Nevada and he would personally handle the Paul Schrade convalescence at the ranch. I was to call Bob's relative Doyle Vaughn who would oversee matters at the ranch.

June 15, 1968
Saturday

8 a.m. Received a call from Jack Hooper who told me that he was speaking with Bob Maheu and I was never to mention his name or Bel Air Patrol! He told me Maheu wanted to speak to me after we spoke and I called Maheu 15 minutes later. Bob wanted to impress upon me that he was in charge of the Nevada operations and everything that I did in Nevada involving Hughes, he was to be informed about.

6 p.m. Took Jennie to the Desert Inn anniversary party.

June 16, 1968
Sunday

Father's Day. My children brought me breakfast in bed and gave me presents. I spent the rest of the day packing for my Washington trip.

2 p.m. Called Harry Evans and asked him if he knew Thanc Cesar. He said he did not although he recognized the name from press accounts. Evans asked if I would be in Vegas during the next week since he was going to be there to make arrangements to hold a union conference. I told him I should be in Washington all week. Evans said that Schrade would be leaving for Spring Mountain Ranch soon. I told him we would make sure that a Hughes private plane would pick him up at the Imperial Highway terminal at the LA airport and take him to Nevada.

3:50 p.m. Flew United 686 to Chicago where I connected with the TWA 9 p.m. flight to Baltimore.

12:25 p.m. Arrived and took a taxi to the Mayflower Hotel in Washington
DC.

June 17, 1968
Monday

11 a.m. Had brunch with Bob Humphrey, his brother Skip, and Mel Klein.

12 noon. Dr. Kistiakowsky called to tell me that he would meet George Roth and I for dinner at 5 p.m.

1 p.m. Met Bob Humphrey to discuss Mid-West Associates Co. that Bob had set up to market our Radiarc equipment in the mid-west.

2 p.m. Met with George Roth and Frank Huddle at the Library of Congress.

4 p.m. Called Robert Miller of the A.E.C. at (702) 734-1212

5 p.m. George Roth and I had dinner with Dr. Kistiakowsky

June 18, 1968
Tuesday

9 a.m. Called Milt Polland

10:30 Went to the Executive Office building to meet with Bill Welsh and

Colonel Hunt. They advised me that the VP would meet me in his office at 1 p.m.

1 p.m. Met with VP Humphrey at his office. We discussed the RFK assassination. Hubert was still shocked by the events in LA. He sat with tears in his eyes and told me how much he respected RFK and the Kennedy family. He had assumed that the nomination for the democratic candidate would have boiled down to Kennedy and himself. He said that if he had received the nomination, RFK would have been his first choice for VP on the ticket.

We then discussed Ted Kennedy and Hubert mentioned the fact that numerous people had come forward to ask him to consider Ted as his running mate. We then discussed Richard Nixon and Hubert said that Nixon would be a catastrophe for the country and should never be elected president. Humphrey phoned LBJ in front of me.

2 p.m. Dwayne Andreas a friend of the VP came to the office and was introduced to me by the VP.

3 p.m. Went to my hotel room where the telephone was ringing. It was Don Nixon who said he was calling from Toledo, Ohio, 243-9101. He asked me what I was doing at the VP's office. I was shocked that he knew where to find me and that I was having such a meeting. He said that Richard had called him and told him that Bebe Rebozo had called him, and then Richard called Don. Don asked me if I was going to New York on this trip. I told him that I was. He asked me if I would be able to meet with his brother Ed at the Nixon campaign headquarters. I said yes.

June 19, 1968
Wednesday

7 a.m. I caught TWA 262 from Baltimore to Newark, NJ. When I arrived at the terminal, someone was holding a sign with my name on it. The driver said he represented the Nixon campaign and said he was to be at my disposal while I was in New York. How did he know I was on this flight? He said he received a call to go meet me and that's all he knew. He drove me to the New York Hilton where I checked in. I then called Ed Nixon at Nixon HQ at 57 and Park, 758-6418, and went over to meet him. Ed was in an upbeat mood and said his brother Dick was exuberant about the events of the last few

weeks and no one could now stop him from becoming president of the United States.

10 a.m. Called Bill Haddad at 682-0284, and arranged to meet him Thursday for breakfast.

12 noon. Took the limo courtesy of Nixon and drove to see my mother and father in Astoria.

1:30 Called my Vegas office and had a message that Milt Polland was staying at the Regency in New York and wanted to meet with me. I called Milton and told him I was totally swamped and tired and unable to see him while I was in New York.

2 p.m. When I walked out of my parent's place the limo was surrounded by approximately 50 people, most of who knew me. When I asked one of them what was happening he said the driver informed someone that Richard Nixon was there. After I got into the limo I asked the driver why he said that. He smiled and said that when he got bored he always did. That way it gave him something to do.

June 20, 1968
Thursday

8:30 a.m. Breakfast with Bill Haddad, Bob Clampett, George Roth and Jack Cleveland. Bill looked drained and could hardly talk. He was downcast for the entire time. After breakfast Bill and I left to go to his office where we arrived at 10 a.m. Stayed until 2 p.m.

3 p.m. Checked out of the hotel and took the limo to visit my parents in Astoria once more. I only stayed 15 minutes so the driver didn't get bored again. Drove to the airport.

6:25 p.m. I caught TWA 57 at JFK to fly back to Vegas where I arrived at 8:30 p.m.

June 21, 1968
Friday

9 a.m. Returned a call to Bob Maheu (714) 642-9691. He asked me why he had not heard from me on the details of my trip back east. I advised him I sent a memo to Howard Hughes on the subject. He told me he was to be copied in on anything that was sent to the penthouse as he was running the

Nevada operations. If he reminds me of that once more I'm going to scream. He also wanted me to put on every memo that went to the penthouse that it came from him. Mr. Hughes had determined that in order to cover up any possible embarrassments or jeopardize any government contracts with the Hughes Corporation, through my activities, I was on paper accountable to the Hughes Nevada operations.

12 noon. Stayed at Spring Mountain Ranch until 5 p.m. Took my family with me and spent the day with Paul Schrade and some of his friends. We discussed details of the RFK assassination. Paul then told me how he leaned against a wall at the ranch and found a secret room where apparently Mrs. Krupp, the former owner's wife, had used for her lovers while she stayed there.

June 22, 1968
Saturday

Richard Nixon called my house to thank me for working along with Don and Edward and wanted me to say hello to Howard Hughes for him and thank him for all his help in the past. I laughed afterwards as I recalled the famous Nixon-burger venture where the Nixon family received money from Hughes to promote the Nixon-burger all over the U.S. Don always believed that they could have made millions on this project if it was not for the press embarrassing them at the time.

June 23, 1968
Sunday

Sunday FBI agents arrive at my house to interview me.

June 24, 1968
Monday

1 p.m. Received a call from Mr. Novick of Washington University (314) 863-0100 ext.4959 concerning Howard Hughes A.E.C. project.

June 25, 1968
Tuesday

10 a.m. Returned Don Nixon's call at (213) 723-8847. Don said that his brother had spoken to me and wanted to know when I could set a meeting up to fly to New York and meet with Don, Ed and Bebe Rebozo, Richard's finance man. I told him I had planned to be in NY on July 7 and I would talk to him before that. When I approached him on the RFK assassination subject, Don got very upset and told me he could not discuss it with me and that Maheu had advised him during his last meeting not to discuss the matter with me and that if I did bring up the subject of RFK, Maheu was to be told right away.

12 noon. Lunched with Las Vegas mayor Oran Gragson.

2 p.m. Bill Haddad called me.

3:30 p.m. Attended to board meeting of the Las Vegas Chamber of Commerce.

5 p.m. Returned a call to Milt Polland.

June 26, 1968
Wednesday

9 a.m. Returned call to Roy Crawford, one of Hughes private nurses at 735-8478. I was told that Mr. Hughes would like a memo from me discussing my conversations with Richard Nixon or any of his family. He also wanted me to send him a memo regarding my conversations with Paul Schrade. Roy then asked me a few questions pertaining to comments that Maheu had made in a memo to Hughes a week ago. I told him those were my comments and I was asked by Bob to put his name on it. Roy seemed taken back by that but would pass the information on to Hughes who was not feeling well at the present time.

June 27, 1968
Thursday

8 a.m. Have a toothache and went to see my dentist, Dr. Peterson at 2040 East Charleston.

1 p.m. Harry Evans called me. He said he had lunch with Jess Unruh

yesterday in LA. He said that Unruh sends his regards to me. Evans says that Unruh is uneasy over LAPD, Chief Reddin's pronouncement that Sirhan acted all by himself. Unruh wonders how Reddin could possibly know, when the official LAPD investigation, which is being called SUS Kennedy for some reason, is barely started. Evans told me that he hears from knowledgeable sources that Reddin is tired of being a cop and is looking for a job.

June 28, 1968
Friday

9 a.m. Jack Hooper called and said he wanted to come over to my house to talk to me. He arrived at 10 a.m. to say he wanted to give me a gift of a pony that he thought I would like to give to my daughter Joanne on July 3rd. I asked him how much he wanted for the pony and he said to consider it a gift from himself and Bob Maheu for all the work I had been doing. He then got around to telling me that both he and Bob would appreciate it if l would stop making comments to other people about RFK or any discussions I was having with the Nixon family. I cannot help but think that this was the time honored good guy - bad guy routine, and this time the good guy was Jack Hooper.

12 noon. Returned Don Nixon's telephone call from Miami (305) 865-1500 room 1703. Don wanted to confirm with me my trip to NY

3 p.m. Sent package on A.E.C. to Bill Haddad in NY regarding his working with us on the A.E.C. project.

5 p.m. Called Robert Humphrey at (612) 890-6424

June 29, 1968
Saturday

9 a.m. Received a call from Carl Lens who wanted to confirm with me the moneys being sent in care of the Nixon family by Howard Hughes. I told him I did not understand what he was referring to but would call him back.

2 p.m. Milt Polland called.

June 30, 1968
Sunday

7:30 a.m. Arrived at Spring Mountain Ranch where I spent most of the day.

5 p.m. Moe Dalitz called me and wanted to meet with me privately as soon as possible, that it was urgent. I told him I would get back to him on Monday, July 1st.

January 30, 1969

I attended the Mayor's Prayer Breakfast at the Frontier Hotel.

I received a telephone call from the F.B.I. office saying that J. Edgar Hoover wanted me to know that he authorized two agents to see me in Las Vegas.

February 1, 1969

I went to the Nevada Mining Association Meeting.

While at the Hughes Nevada Operations offices at approximately 10pm, while I was writing up another memo to Howard Hughes concerning the A.E.C., I had a call from the Frontier Hotel that the two friends that I was expecting where on the way to my office. They arrived and looked all around the office to see if anyone was there. Next they took out equipment that they said would also tell if the area had bugging equipment. Then I was asked if Robert A. Maheu had an office there. I said yes he did and I told them that he had his private files in a file cabinet with his Secretary Ceil Nolan.

They went in and asked if I had a metal ruler. I said yes, and handed it to one of them. He then placed it in each of the two cabinets and opened the drawers. They both pulled out all the files and read each memo and documents in each. They didn't seem to mind if I looked over their shoulders at the files. A copy machine was adjacent to the file cabinets and they asked me to copy the ones that they handed to me. I copied the ones marked JFK, Castro, Martin L. King, Glomar, Political Contacts, Howard Hunt, checks, Hughes Medical Foundation, etc. After approx. 2 hrs. they returned the original files back and asked me to join them in the lobby in another hour. By then it was approx. 2am when I met them in the lobby. They were very cordial when one of them told me that I should forget what

I saw and he recommended I get away from the Hughes Organization. I told them I planned to set up Nevada Environmental Foundation and was just waiting for Howard Hughes to agree to fund the company.

March 7, 1969

I met with the Governor of Puerto Rico, Luis A. Ferns, and return a call from Ken Wright at the Howard Hughes Medical Institute 373-9041. He said that it was urgent that I call him at his home 271-5344.

March 8, 1969

I flew on Eastern Flight 950 from Puerto Rico to Miami. I arrived at 10:45 and stayed at the Airport Hotel. I had an urgent call from Don Nixon who called from the Sheridan Carlton 202-ME 8-2626. I went to dinner with Ken Wright and his wife. Ken introduced me to Gordon of the CIA and another agent.

March 9, 1969

I had a call from Bebe Rebozo. He said to call him at the bank 3615484 or FR93855 or EM15951. I left Miami on Flight 25 at 6:40 to Las Vegas. I arrived at 10:15.

March 25, 1969

I flew on United Flight 571 from Las Vegas to Los Angeles at 1:05pm. At 3:00pm I took TWA Flight 98 to Dallas. I arrived at 10:30 and stayed at Watergate.

March 26, 1969

Have lunch with Ted Kennedy. Meet until 2:30. We discussed the JFK and RFK assassinations. At 6:00pm I took from National, TWA Flight 423 to Chicago and went on to Las Vegas.

April 25, 1969

I flew from Washington to Las Vegas with Senator Mike Gravel of Alaska, and his wife.

At 3:30. I attended Senator Ted Kennedy's Cocktail Party. My wife Jennie and I attended Senator Cannon's Appreciation Dinner.

October 21, 1969

Took National Flight 60 from Los Angeles to Miami at 9AM. I arrived at 4:23PM. I stayed at the Miami Airport Hotel.

October 22, 1969

At 3PM Take DOM 301 from Miami to the Dominican Republic. Arrive at 4PM. I was met by the Secretary of Agriculture and the Director of Protocol and was taken to the Ambassador Hotel.

October 23, 1969

At 10:30 I met with the National Development Commission. It is John Meier Day in the Dominican Republic. At 5PM I received the Christopher Columbus Award for Merit in Scientific and Ecological Studies. Secretary of State for Foreign Affairs Fernando Amiama presented it to me. I gave a speech at the Ceremony. At 8PM President Joaquin Balaguer held a reception for me at the National Palace. U.S. Ambassador Francis Molloy also attended today. Senator Mike Gravel, Joe Napolitan, Martin Haley, Don Nixon and other friends came from the U.S.

October 24, 1969

At 1:00 I had lunch with the President and members of the Cabinet.

At 7PM I attended the Ophthalmology meeting and was given a diploma by the Sociedad Dominicana de Oftalmología.

October 25, 1969

My friends and I were taken on the President's yacht all day. We also visited the President's Beach House. On the yacht I sat stunned as Don Nixon, after many drinks started talking about the RFK assassination, his brother being in Texas when JFK was assassinated and Bob Maheu telling Don about Bob's conversation, with Don in Las Vegas. Maheu took credit for the RFK murder. The ones that sat around the table, with their mouths opened were shocked. Don is a nice man who regrets being the President's brother.

October 26, 1969

At 11 AM I took DOM 302 to Miami. I arrived at 2PM. I then took National 405 from Miami to Los Angeles.

February 8, 2005

Call Larry Teeter concerning my trip to Los Angeles.

February 11, 2005

Call Harry Evans 909-355-2402 regarding RFK, HRH, and Paul Schrade 656-5623.

February 13, 2005

Take a taxi to the airport where I have a donut and coffee at the airport. Take Alaska 7 am Flt 674 Vancouver to Los Angeles. Arrive 9:30 am. I take a taxi to the Best Western Beverly Pavilion Hotel - 9360 Wilshire Blvd, Beverly Hills. Tel: (310) 273-1400.

5 pm I attend the Grammy's at Staples Center. I get a chance to meet with Janet Reno and get a chance to say hello to Lisa Marie Presley, Eve, Usher, Janet Jackson, John Mayer, Loretta Lynn, Alicia Keys, and others.

February 14, 2005

I have dinner with Larry Teeter at my hotel regarding the RFK murder.

Teeter lets me look at what he thinks will get Sirhan a new trial. He shows me what he has after I sign a non-disclosure for him. He also has me listen to a recording of a person who he says is the 2nd shooter. I am impressed with Teeter's information. I was not at the hotel when RFK was shot, so can't comment on what Teeter has.

February 17, 2005

I have dinner with Paul and Monica Schrade at Da Pasquale in Beverly Hills.

February 18, 2005

4 pm call Terry Moore cell (310) 291-1514 home 576-2476

5 pm I go to Moore Cramer Productions at 427 North Canon Drive Suite 215 Beverly Hills Tel (310) 276-5433. I met with Terry and her son Grant Cramer Tel:(213) 804-2708.

At 7 pm I meet again with Larry Teeter at my hotel.

I bring my documents to Teeter. He then tapes me for 30 minutes. He tells me that he will return my information after a new trial for Sirhan. I then spot two men sitting near us staring. I get up and tell one of the persons that work at the hotel. He tells me that they asked if he knew who was sitting with the heavy set man. They were told that it was Mr. Meier, who was staying at the hotel.

When I went back to the table to tell Teeter, he got very nervous and put my information in his briefcase and left. I walked with him outside to his car and returned to the restaurant. The men who were watching us left.

August 4, 2005

I am informed that Larry Teeter died in Conchitas Mexico. He was 56 years old. I am shocked to hear that. How could it happen? He was a good and honest lawyer.

September 2, 2005

2 pm I call Paul Schrade. He gives me Teeter's mother Marian's telephone in order to get her cooperation. Her number is (323) 665-6602. Paul also gives me Munir Sirhan's number in Pasadena (626)798-1236, 696 East Howard 91104 in Pasadena.

September 4, 2005

12:30 I call Marian Teeter. Marian lives at 1872 Lucretia Avenue LA 90026

September 6, 2005

11 am I am introduced to Dale Pope at 2800 Park Place 666 Burrard Street by Bill Majcher, the former head of the RCMP integrated market enforcement team, to get him to contact the L.A. County Bar Association.

September 7, 2005

9:30 am I call Munir Sirhan at 626-798-2136 re Sirhan Sirhan.

September 16, 2005

Dale Pope, my lawyer, sent a letter to the State Bar of California to request that all information relating to myself be returned to me.

September 26, 2005

Dale Pope tells me that a John Fulton advised him that they had Larry Teeter's files (approximately 280 of them) and John Fulton would get back to Dale.

October 17, 2005

Dale Pope writes back to John Fulton after I informed him that a burglary took place at Larry Teeter's home and that records were stolen.

October 21, 2005

John Fulton called Dale Pope and told him that there was a theft of records at Larry Teeter's home. John Fulton also said that the records that he has are in poor shape. Whatever that means. And that it may be difficult to find anything specific. Are they kidding me?